IGNITION & ELECTRICAL SYSTEMS NO. 5

INTRODUCTION

IGNITION AND ELECTRICAL SYSTEMS No. 5

Edited by Spencer Murray and the technical editors of Specialty Publications Division. Copyright © 1977 by Petersen Publishing Co., 8490 Sunset Blvd., Los Angeles, CA 90069. Phone: (213) 657-5100. All rights reserved. No part of this book may be reproduced without written permission. Printed in U.S.A.

1980 PRINTING

PETERSEN BOOK DIVISION

Erwin M. Rosen/Executive Editor
Spencer Murray/Senior Editor
Al Hall/Editor
Dick Fischer/Art Director
Jim Norris/Managing Editor
Chriss Ohliger Jay/Managing Editor
Eric Rickman/Photo Editor
George Fukuda/Assistant Art Director

"Space-age" electronic wizardry got its foot in the automotive electrical door via Chrysler Corp. in 1972, and it didn't take long for other domestic manufacturers to follow suit. Literally overnight, conventional points, condensers—indeed, conventional distributors themselves—went the way of the dinosaurs. Anyone who hasn't fiddled with a distributor in the last few years or who has tinkered only with "older" cars will find a few surprises when he uncaps a late-model distributor.

The intent of this book is to familiarize the at-home tune-up artist with Detroit's black-box magic and refresh the memories of those who still have occasion to delve into a conventional ignition system's innards. Though older cars with conventional systems are growing fewer as age and mileage take their toll, mechanics will still be faced with tuning them for a good many years to come. That's why, on the pages that follow, the latest state of the electronic art is detailed, together with close look-sees at many pre-'72 examples.

But ignitions as such aren't the only subject covered in this book. All the other links in the chain of electricity are discussed, all of them in layman's language so that anyone can understand them. Thus we include chapters on batteries, starters, generators and alternators, solenoids, switches, instruments, lights and accessories.

To echo a statement made in a previous edition of **Ignition and Electrical Systems,** "With the present worldwide fuel shortage, climbing labor prices and less money to spend, more car owners are doing their own car repairs and maintenance to lower operating expenses. Everything they need to know about automotive electrics is on the pages that follow."

SPENCE MURRAY

COVER: Some of the electrical wizardry of the modern car has been "exploded" to reveal inner workings. Our thanks to the following Los Angeles firms: Hollywood Generator Exchange for the Delco alternator; Vernon Parts Exchange for the Ford distributor; and Castle Ford, Inc., for the "old time" conventional points plate. Cover coordinated by Eric Rickman. Photography by Mike Levasheff of PPC Photographic Department. Cover design by Dick Fischer.

PETERSEN PUBLISHING COMPANY

R. E. Petersen/Chairman of the Board
F. R. Waingrow/President
Robert E. Brown/Sr. Vice President
Dick Day/Sr. Vice President
Jim P. Walsh/Sr. Vice President, National Advertising Director
Robert MacLeod/V.P., Publisher
Thomas J. Siatos/V.P., Group Publisher
Philip E. Trimbach/V.P. Finance
William Porter/V.P., Circulation Director

James J. Krenek/V.P. Manufacturing
Jack Thompson/Assistant Director, Circulation
Nigel P. Heaton/Director, Circulation Administration & Systems
Louis Abbott/Director, Production
Don McGlathery/Director, Research
Al Isaacs/Director, Graphics
Bob D'Olivo/Director, Photography
Carol Johnson/Director, Advertising Administration
Maria Cox/Director, Data Processing

Basic Series ISBN 0-8227-5014-7
Hot Rod Shop Series ISBN 0-8227-6004-5

Library of Congress Catalog Card No. 73-79968

IGNITION & ELECTRICAL SYSTEMS

CONTENTS

SPARK PLUGS...4

PLUG WIRES...18

   HOW-TO: PLUG WIRE REPLACEMENT.................................24

COILS...26

DISTRIBUTORS...34

IGNITION TUNING...68

   HOW-TO: IGNITION TUNE-UP.......................................80

AFTERMARKET IGNITION CONVERSIONS..82

   HOW-TO: INSTALLING A BREAKERLESS IGNITION.......................92

BATTERIES..94

STARTERS..106

   HOW-TO: STARTER REBUILD.......................................118

SOLENOIDS AND SWITCHES...122

GENERATORS AND ALTERNATORS...132

   HOW-TO: GENERATOR OVERHAUL....................................148

   HOW-TO: ALTERNATOR OVERHAUL...................................150

LIGHTS..152

REGULATORS..158

INSTRUMENTS...168

WIRING..176

ACCESSORIES...184

WIRING GUIDE AND FUSIBLE LINKS...192

Spark Plugs

THESE IMPORTANT ITEMS ARE OFTEN A BAROMETER OF YOUR ENGINE'S HEALTH AND ALTHOUGH THEY SELDOM CAUSE PROBLEMS, THEY CAN HELP SOLVE QUITE A FEW

To most people, spark plugs are the most "typical" electrical parts on their car. Despite the fact that spark plugs are low-dollar items that unselfishly spend their working life in an inferno of heat and dirt—only to be chucked, ultimately, into the nearest trash can—they are, nevertheless, not without an interesting past and a certain romantic appeal. After inventors spent several decades pushing lighted candles into holes bored in gas engine cylinders, or designing camshafts that would snap movable electrical contacts together inside automobile combustion chambers, the spark plug finally arose as the hero destined to save the internal combustion engine from a predicted early demise.

At first, spark plugs had their iron or mild steel center electrodes set into porcelain insulators. Neither of these materials worked very well, since the steel quickly eroded in the high temperatures of the combustion chamber and porcelain was easily broken by accidental bumping, vibration, and thermal shock. Modern spark plugs have electrodes of special heat-resistant steels, high-nickel steel, platinum, tungsten, iridium, or gold palladium, and while we still call the plug insulator a "porcelain," it is now molded from a special sintered alumina ceramic. Natural stones have also been used for plug insulators in recent times, but these have not proven compatible with modern fuels or with the latest developments in spark plug design.

In grandpa's day, spark plugs had to be made so that it was possible to take them apart for cleaning, but in the late 1920's "one-piece" plugs were developed for use in certain supercharged racing engines which had the annoying habit of blowing the insulators right out of the plug shells! By the 1930's, one-piece spark plugs had found their way into production cars. In the first few years following World War II, everyone thought that all major automotive spark plug problems had been solved, but with the introduction of high-compression engines in standard production cars many additional challenges arose which have spurred revolutionary changes during the past decade.

PATH OF THE SPARK

The spark plug is the last station of

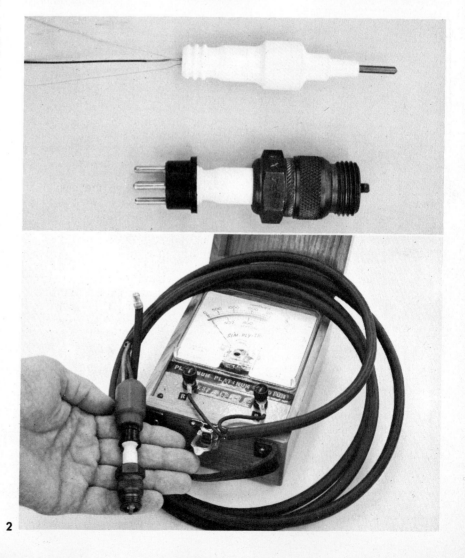

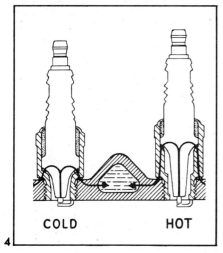

COLD   HOT

1. A study in insulator designs. Ribs added to plug insulator discourage flashover of spark from terminal to plug shell. Wet or dirty insulators can still cause trouble.

2. Special thermocouple plugs are used to determine the proper spark plug heat range for every car. Wires are threaded through insulator (shown at top), and joined to pronged thermocouple junction. Thermocouple is then joined to Pyrometer to obtain plug temperature reading during engine operation.

3. Allen's Surveyor, attached to its Analog 70 tester, makes a quick sniff of the quality of your spark plugs without any wires attached to the car. Surveyor picks up ignition signals through its "funnel," and translates them into a pattern on the screen.

4. The longer the insulator, the hotter the plug, because the heat has a longer path to travel.

a somewhat involved journey that the spark takes after it leaves the ignition coil. The spark itself is high-voltage direct current, and it is called "secondary" current to distinguish it from the primary (low-voltage) current. This primary current goes from the battery to the ignition switch through the primary (thin) wiring of the coil and then on to the ignition points and condenser. You may hear mechanics refer to the secondary part of the ignition system. The secondary circuit is the high-voltage circuit and consists of anything that conducts or insulates the spark on its trip from the coil to the plug. It includes the secondary winding of the coil, the large diameter high tension wire going from the coil tower to the distributor cap, the cap, the rotor, the spark plug wires and finally, the plugs. Secondary wiring usually has heavy insulation, whereas primary wire is made with a thin covering.

From the coil, the spark goes through a short secondary lead to the distributor cap. Directly under the cap is the rotor, and as it turns it conducts a spark to each of the cap electrodes. The electrodes connect to the individual towers on the cap where the spark plugs wires are plugged in. From that point the spark goes down the plug wire, into the plug, jumps the gap inside the combustion chamber to fire the mixture, and is absorbed by the metal of the engine. The current then returns through the engine to the chassis and up the ground cable to the ground terminal of the battery, thus making a

complete electrical circuit. Such a simple act as causing a spark to jump across a gap and fire a gasoline and air mixture ought to be the least troublesome part of an internal combustion engine, but it isn't. There are lots of problems in designing spark plugs so they will work in your engine, and there are reasons why you should select certain plugs for your purposes and avoid others like the plague. Let's look at those reasons.

HEAT RANGE

The efficiency and life expectancy of spark plugs is strongly influenced by the conditions that exist inside the engine's combustion chambers. Fuel/air ratios, compression ratios, emissions equipment, super-charger boost, exhaust system back-pressure, and a great many other things all have a definite bearing on combustion chamber *and* spark plug temperatures. Controlling the operating temperature of the plug's firing tip *is the single most important factor in spark plug design.*

When an engine is operated at low speeds or with light loads, the temperatures inside the combustion chambers fall to their lowest point. The spark plug must be designed so that it picks up and retains enough heat under these conditions to maintain the temperature of its firing tip *above* 750°. If it falls below this point, deposits will begin to accumulate on the plug tips which cannot be burned off. This condition is called spark plug *fouling* and, if allowed to progress, will prevent the plug from firing at all resulting in engine misfire.

If the same engine is operated at high speeds or with heavy loads, the combustion chamber temperatures start to climb. Should the plugs be designed to retain too much of this heat, they may begin to cause *pre-ignition*. Pre-ignition becomes a danger at about 1750°, the temperature where plug tips start to become incandescent. At low speeds with heavy loads, pre-ignition causes the engine to "ping" or "knock" very much like that caused by over-advanced spark timing or using a fuel too low in octane. The difference is that pre-ignition is *not as easily controlled,* since the fuel/air mixture is being touched-off by the red-hot plug *before* the spark actually fires. With the pistons still on their compression stroke, the burning mass is squeezed rather than being allowed to expand. At this point temperatures really begin to soar, and on successive compression strokes the heat may become sufficient to start the fuel/air charge burning everywhere at once rather than normally proceeding in a smooth flame-front from the spark plug electrodes.

At this time, the piston is once again rising in the cylinder making its compression stroke. The burning mass is compressed, and an explosion (called detonation) results forcing the piston and rod down in the cylinder while it is still traveling upward. Plugs are often destroyed by overheating and, if the detonation is severe enough, pistons and rods can be broken and blown apart. Detonation is a highly destructive force that can be avoided by installing those spark plugs designed for your particular engine and type of driving.

Obviously, spark plugs must be selected for an engine which will operate in the heat range between these two limits—fouling and pre-ignition—*regardless* of engine speed or load. As the old saying goes, *hot* engines need *cold* plugs. It might also be added that Aunt Tillie's old, oil-guzzling Packard had better use *hot* plugs to keep it firing on all eight when it makes its weekly 15-mph cruise to the supermarket. Therefore, the type of driving done or the engine condition may require a change in spark plug heat range from that specified for the particular engine. Slow city driving is hard on plugs. The long periods of idle in traffic creates an overly rich gas mixture. At idle, combustion chamber temperature isn't high enough, and the engine isn't running fast enough to completely

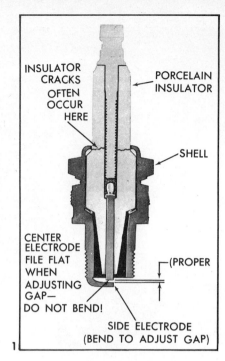

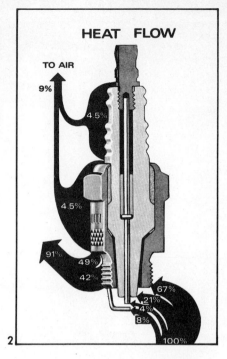

burn the gas; consequently, the plugs are fouled with unburned gas and idle becomes rough. If the majority of driving is done in slow city traffic rather than at turnpike speeds, or the engine uses oil as Aunt Tillie's, then plug deposits can be burned off by changing to only *slightly* hotter plugs. The hotter plug would be ideal for just city driving, but occasional jaunts down the freeway might produce some dangerous pre-ignition. A great solution to this problem would be to change to a projected-nose plug having the same heat range as the standard plug specified for your engine. The projected-nose plug has a longer insulator nose which extends further into the combustion chamber. This type of plug runs hotter in slow traffic and cooler at highway speeds, thereby reducing the chances of plug fouling in the city and pre-ignition at higher speeds. Important details of the projected-nose plug are discussed later and should be read before making a change. On the other hand, if the car is used almost exclusively for high speed turnpike driving or the engine has been modified, then the specified plugs might be too hot resulting in rapid electrode wear and dangerous pre-ignition. In this case, it's always safer to change to a slightly colder plug or the projected-nose plug.

The speed at which a plug can transfer combustion chamber heat to the cylinder head determines its *heat range.* Heat range is controlled by the length of the porcelain insulator nose and/or by the size and shape of the area between the nose and the outer metal shell—the threaded portion. The porcelain (actually ceramic) insulator nose of the plug extends into the

combustion chamber and absorbs its heat and passes it on to the plug's outer metal shell. The heat then moves along the shell to the cylinder head where it escapes into the air. A hot plug is made with a long insulator nose (and/or more space between the nose and the outer metal shell) than a cold plug. For this reason, the hot plug has more area to hold heat and is slow to dissipate heat. It, therefore, remains hot enough even at low speeds to burn off fouling deposits. *Cold* plugs have a short insulator nose and more contact between the insulator nose and the outer shell which enables it to transfer combustion chamber heat faster. At high speeds and under heavy loads, the cold plug will keep its cool well enough to avoid sending the engine into pre-ignition—and from there into the junk heap.

SPARKING

Contrary to what many non-car enthusiasts think, spark plugs do not *make* the spark; they merely provide a gap for the spark current from the coil to arc across. The shape and material of the electrodes, the gap width, and the existing pressures and temperatures determine the amount of voltage that's necessary to produce a spark. This amount of voltage is called the plug's voltage *requirement.* We will get into the coil end of the ignition system later on, but for now you should know that a coil only produces enough voltage to jump any gaps in the secondary. Suppose a coil is capable of producing a spark of 25,000 volts, but only 10,000 volts are required to jump the plug gap. In that case, the coil will only produce 10,000 volts. It's just

3

4

1. Center electrode rounds with use, should be filed flat after sandblasting and before adjusting gap.

2. Heat generally reaches the plug through its shell nose and insulator tip and is dissipated through the plug shell threads and seat. Smaller amounts of heat enter through the electrodes and exit into the surrounding air.

3. No spark plug manufacturer approves of plug firing cups, but they can make an old clunker run. Using the cup makes the plug run hot, and prevents fouling in an engine that uses oil.

4. The old and the new. From left to right: retracted-gap racing plug as used at Indy; standard-gap design used in Daytona stockers; multi-electrode plug from 1915 Mercedes; plug used in 1911 road racing Model T.

5. Resistor-type plug has an electrical resistance built into its center that helps to suppress radio and TV interference, and cut down current flow, which reduces electrode erosion. Note the spring that holds the black carbon resistor in place. Heat can cause the spring to relax, creating an unwanted gap. If spring is good, an ohmmeter will read 5000-10,000 ohms with one lead on the center electrode and the other on the plug terminal. The amount of the reading is not important, because the ohmmeter check is only for continuity. If the reading is infinity or varying as you shake the plug, then the plug is bad.

like an athlete doing the high-jump. He may be capable of jumping six feet, but if the bar is at five feet, it would be extra work for him to jump any higher. Move the bar up close to six feet, and he might miss. The voltage requirement works the same way. If the spark plugs require high voltage, the coil may not be able to produce that much voltage. The result would be no spark at the plug, and an engine that either misses or won't run at all.

Since air is usually thought of as a good electrical insulator, it may seem hard to understand how an electric spark can leap across the spark plug gap. Air, however, is a "something" and not a "nothing." The space between the plug electrodes is actually filled with millions of air molecules. When a sufficient voltage is delivered to the electrodes, these molecules become *ions*—molecules with an electrical charge. When placed in an electrical field—as between the electrodes of a spark plug—ions are capable of movement. This movement is what allows the spark to jump the plug gap. From this it can be seen that the spark plug's voltage requirement is simply the electrical pressure needed to produce ionization of the air or air/fuel mixture within the spark plug's gap.

Sharp edges on the electrodes tend to concentrate ionization and lower the voltage requirement, but spark plug electrodes begin to erode away with use, rounding the electrodes and widening the gap at the average rate of .001-inch in every 1000-2000 miles. Both of these changes increase the plug's voltage require-

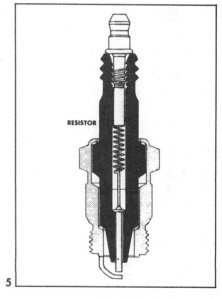

RESISTOR

5

ment, and when the voltage required to produce a spark finally exceeds the output of the ignition system, the plug will no longer fire.

Old worn plugs are most noticeable while accelerating. At this time, a plug requires much more voltage to be fired than during idle speeds—three times as much. However, as engine rpm increases, the coil has less time to produce voltage; therefore, its output drops as engine speed rises. Consequently, during acceleration, a plug with an enlarged gap (larger than specified) may require more voltage than the coil is able to provide. As a result, the engine will misfire and sputter until you let up on the gas pedal. Reducing acceleration will have the effect of reducing the plug's voltage require-

Spark Plugs

ment causing the engine to run smoother. Spark plug voltage requirements are also raised by deposits on the plug, high cylinder pressures, low temperatures (which separate the air molecules), lean mixtures, and overheated electrodes. Add it all up and that electrode gap seems like the Grand Canyon when the spark tries to jump it.

CONSTRUCTION

The spark plug's steel shell is its main structural part. It not only grips the insulator in a gas-proof seal but absorbs the stresses of being threaded into the engine's cylinder head and being gripped by the mechanic's wrench. At least we hope that's the way the mechanic does it. If he gets careless with a plug wrench he will find out very quickly that spark plug procelains are not made to be leaned on. The threaded part of the shell is made in a number of different sizes: 18mm, 14mm, 12mm, and 10mm. Fourteen millimeter is the most widely used thread, although most U.S. Ford products employ the 18mm size, with a tapered seat. The 12mm and 10mm sizes are at present found only in motorcycles, some foreign models and some older cars.

The length of the threaded portion

1. This AC resistor plug does away with the spring by using seals that will conduct electricity. Since 1969, this new ACniter plug has been standard equipment on General Motors cars and trucks. Resistor plug wire is standard also.

2. Look alike, don't they? One is an "R" prefix, with a 5000-ohm resistor. The "U" prefix plug has a booster gap.

3. Champion plugs with booster gaps have a hole in the top to vent ozone caused by arcing across the gap.

4. Huge 1910 spark plug contrasts oddly with modern 10mm plug from Honda bike. The large size was important in the old days to avoid fouling problems.

5. Four plugs shown are identical in electrode design, but have different reaches. Longer reach exposes more of plug shell to cooling from cylinder head—but if reach is too long, piston may collide with plug. Be safe and choose only the specified reach.

6. The surface-gap plug has no air gap but fires across the face of the insulator. They are standard in some 2-cycle applications, but offer no advantage in automotive engines.

7. Projected-nose plugs were made possible by advances in ceramics and a general change to overhead valve engines. High-compression, high-output engines made such a design necessary to permit their practical use in everyday traffic situations.

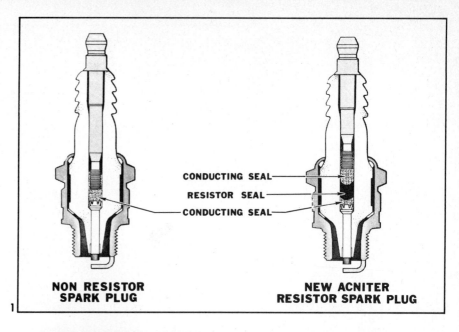

1

NON RESISTOR SPARK PLUG

CONDUCTING SEAL
RESISTOR SEAL
CONDUCTING SEAL

NEW ACNITER RESISTOR SPARK PLUG

2

3

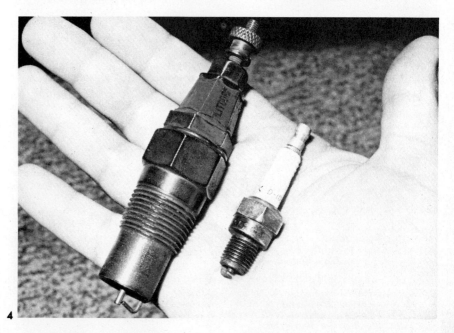

4

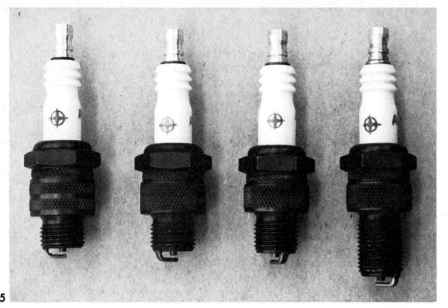

5

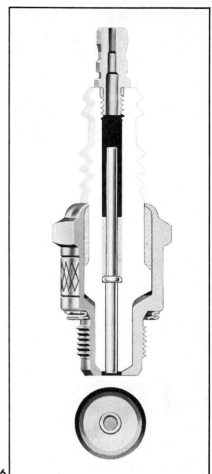

6

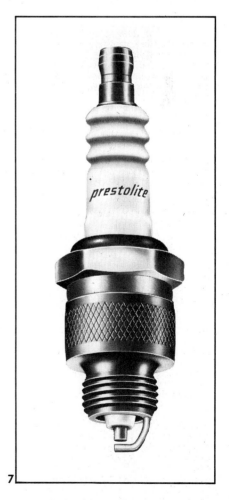

7

of the plug is called its *reach*. Common reaches are ⅜-inch, ½-inch and .472-inch (more about this later), 7/16-inch (some U.S. cars and a few older French engines), .460-inch (used today in many GM and Ford cars), and 3/4-inch (427 Chevys, Chrysler Hemi, and many imports). Long-reach plugs offer the advantage of being stronger and allowing better water jacket design around the plug boss; however, they are more expensive to manufacture than the shorter sizes. Of special significance to Volkswagen engine enthusiasts is the slight variation in thread tolerances between the .472-inch reach plugs used in cars built in common market countries, and the 1/2-inch reach plugs used elsewhere. In practice those two 14mm sizes have been used interchangeably, but with many complications, because the two plugs are definitely not interchangeable. Using the 1/2-inch reach plug may ruin the head threads which *is* a complication.

Each spark plug manufacturer has patented design features incorporated into its plugs which they claim make their product a little better than the rest. It would take too much space to discuss all of these in detail, but the two or three basic types that are made by *most* manufacturers deserve special description.

Resistance plugs with an electrical resistor located inside the insulator have been around for many years and were first made famous by the Electric Autolite Co. for use in Chrysler products. Electric Autolite quit making plugs when they sold the name Autolite to Ford several years ago. Now the old Electric Autolite Co. is known as the Prestolite Co. and they are making spark plugs once again. So if you see a Prestolite plug, the name is new, but the plug is made by the same people who turned out over one billion of the original Autolite plugs.

The resistor's original purpose was to get a better idle. An engine idles smoother with the wide plug gaps, but wide plug gaps are not possible when there is no resistance in the secondary circuit. Without resistance, current flow burns metal off the plug electrodes at a rapid rate. If you start off with wide plug gaps you soon have a gap so wide the car won't run.

Nowadays the secondary resistance is still there to control electrode erosion, but it also is necessary to cut down on radio and TV interference. For many years the secondary resistance has been in the spark plug wires, and most mechanics thought that if resistor plugs were used with resistor wires, the result would be too much resistance. But there is really nothing wrong with using resistor plugs with resistor wires. If additional secondary resistance will cure a radio interference problem, or if resistor plugs happen to be the only plugs available, then they should be installed without a moment's hesitation. The reason that very few tune-up men used resistor plugs and wires together was that new cars never came equipped that way from the factory.

In 1969 this was changed, and all General Motors cars used resistor plugs with resistor wires. However, instead of 10,000 ohms, these new AC plugs had a value of only 5000 ohms. Champion and Autolite quickly came out with 5000-ohm replacement plugs for the '69 and later cars. It appears that all the spark plug companies except Champion have allowed their 10,000-ohm plug to slowly fade away, replacing it with the 5000-ohm plug.

Spark Plugs

But Champion engineers, being sticklers for precision, put an "R" prefix on their 5000-ohm plug and continued to make their 10,000-ohm plug, which has always had an "X" prefix. Which should you use? Whichever is specified in the literature of the auto manufacturer or in the spark plug chart.

If you have an ohmmeter and want to measure the resistance values of your plugs, have at it. But don't expect every plug to measure exactly 5000 or 10,000 ohms. Precision resistors are completely unnecessary in suppression work. A "5000-ohm" resistor may actually measure anywhere from 3000-7000 ohms at room temperature. When the plug gets hot, the resistance will change drastically too. The resistance also changes as the plug is used. An ohmmeter should be used on new resistor plugs only as a continuity check, not as a means to make life difficult for the auto parts counterman.

Series-gap plugs are available from several major plug producers. The series-gap plug (or booster gap, as it is called by Champion) has an additional air gap in the center electrode located *inside* the ceramic insulator. Booster-gap plugs are able to keep firing in spite of semiconductive deposits on the plug's firing tip.

It takes time for spark voltage to build up in the conventional ignition system, and much of the useful spark energy can leak away through plug deposits before the voltage peak is reached. Thus the voltage may never attain a level sufficient to fire the plug. By incorporating an additional gap inside the plug, the voltage does not reach the plug electrodes until it has built up sufficient energy to jump across both the booster gap and the firing gap.

Although booster-gap plugs cost a few pennies more than standard plugs, many quality foreign car manufacturers provide them as standard equipment. If you have a problem with plug fouling, the booster gaps may be just the thing.

Copper-core plugs are currently being imported by the Japanese NGK company. Since copper has better heat conductivity than nickel-steel, it is able to carry heat away from the plug tip more effectively. This extends the plug's useful heat range by keeping its firing tip cooler at high speeds and under heavy loads.

PLUG SPECIFICATIONS

You've probably wondered what the numbers and letters used to designate a particular spark plug mean, and how it was decided that a certain plug was best for your particular car. The number/letter designation indicates the *heat range* of the plug as well its *thread size, reach* and *gap configuration*. All plug makers use numbers to indicate the relative heat range of their spark plugs, but American companies such as Champion, Autolite and AC use lower numbers to indicate colder plugs and higher numbers to indicate hotter plugs, while foreign manfufacturers like Bosch, Lodge, NGK and KLG use higher numbers to designate colder plugs and lower numbers for hotter heat ranges. An Autolite AG 2, for example, is a step colder than an Autolite AG 3, but an NGK B-6E is a step hotter than an NGK B-7E. Letters are used to indicate the thread size and reach, with the exception of Bosch plugs, which use numbers instead. Additional letters and/or numbers found in spark plug designations indicate such special features as internal resistors and booster gaps.

When a car maker brings out a new engine or makes important modifications to an older one, the design is referred to the engineering department of the auto manufacturer's spark plug supplier for proper "plugging." Champion handles this chore for Chrysler, American Motors and a large number of overseas manufacturers. Ford has its own company, Motorcraft, and GM has its AC division. (It's interesting to note that the letters "AC" stand for Albert Champion, a Scotsman who founded both the AC *and* the Champion spark plug companies.)

1. Platinum-electrode plugs usually have fine wire electrodes to give them heat range characteristics similar to projected-nose plugs. They offer better piston clearance, as well as longer life with lower voltage requirements in some applications. They are quite expensive, often costing over $5 each.

2. Gas volume—the space between the plug shell and the insulator—also affects heat range. These two plugs have nearly the same insulator nose length, but the one on the right is hotter since its greater gas volume allows more access to combustion chamber heat.

3. The ½-in. reach plug (left) and .472-inch reach plug (right) are often listed as interchangeable in plug charts, but differences exist. Use of the larger ½-in. plug may result in thread damage to the head. VW owners often confuse the two plugs.

4. This projected-nose racing plug features J-style, cut-back electrode. Electrode material is also heavier to limit heat build-up that might cause preignition. Racing plugs should be installed with a torque wrench after referring to car builder's and plug maker's specification charts.

5. J-gap plugs can be bought in heat ranges suitable for racing or (for certain cars) street use. Some hot rodders modify standard plugs to this configuration.

6. End view of projected-nose, J-gap racing plug illustrates how poor a target the spark gap is for flying carbon particles that might lodge within a conventional gap. Another advantage of J-gap plugs is their lower voltage requirement for starting, because of the sharp edge on the side electrode.

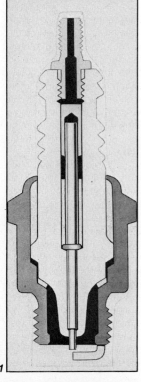

In addition, all plug makers list replacement sizes for cars which do not carry their brand as original equipment. The spark plug companies go to great lengths to compete in this replacement market and do a great deal of research to ensure that the plugs listed in their charts are the best possible choice for the cars for which they are recommended.

The most important concern is to find a plug of the proper heat range. For this purpose special thermocouple spark plugs are installed in the car being tested which record the plug's true firing tip temperature on instruments in the dynamometer room. Ultimately, plugs are selected which have the widest possible safety margin to prevent preignition.

SPARK PLUG APPLICATIONS

There are a great many different spark plug gap and electrode designs, including two or three special racing types. Since the average motorist usually does not understand the special rewards made possible by these various design features, he sim-

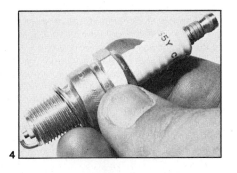

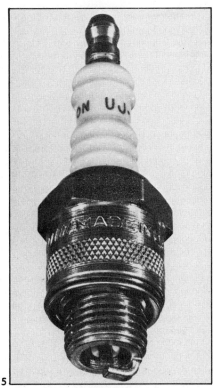

4

5

ply replaces the plugs in his car with the same type installed at the factory. If his driving is average, with no excessive high-speed travel or prolonged idling, he is right to stick with the original equipment. But under extreme conditions, such as racing or a lot of low-speed running, there are better choices. Also, special conditions in the engine, such as excess oil in the combustion chamber, require a special plug. Let's take a look at some of the various gap styles and find out exactly what they are able to accomplish.

Most people would recognize a standard-gap plug faster than they would their local congressman. It lights the fire in millions of lawnmowers, die-hard flatheads and quite a few production cars. In its colder heat ranges it can be used for racing, but in most cases there is a better type available for the job.

J-gap plugs are sometimes called cut-back-gap plugs. Autolite uses the letter "X" after the plugs's number to indicate this modification, Champion uses the letter "J" and AC uses the prefix "M." A Champion J-6 plug is a regular-gap ⅜-in.-reach plug, while a J-6J indicates the same plug with a side electrode that's been cut back. In reality these are standard-gap plugs, but the side electrode on them extends only midway out over the center electrode.

The chief advantage of the J-gap design is that it requires less voltage to fire. The reason is that the sharp edge of the cut-back side electrode aids ionization of the air gap. The J-gap plugs are therefore more suitable to high rpm and are also less likely to be shorted out by carbon particles that might be bounding around inside the combustion chamber. This makes them ideal for a street/strip car, competition sports car or any racing car short of an all-out, fuel-burning blown dragster or Indy car.

The projected-nose spark plug was

6

a development of the late '50's made necessary by the introduction of high compression, high-output V-8 engines. Modern engines, which in some cases before smog control put out as much horsepower per cubic inch as an all-out racing engine did just a few years back, need cold plugs to prevent preignition. The trouble is that in American traffic they spend most of their time idling or rolling along at low speeds. Under these conditions a cold, racing-type plug quickly fouls. Thanks to modern ceramics, the projected-nose plug has become a practical solution to the problem and is now installed in a great many production cars.

The firing tip of the projected-nose plug is exposed directly to the explosions in the combustion chamber. At low speeds, this extreme heat keeps the plug insulator clear of fouling deposits. At high speeds, the insulator is cooled by the incoming fuel charge, which prevents preignition. In fact, at high speeds a projected-nose plug actually runs cooler than a regular-gap plug would under the same conditions! Champion identifies their projected-nose plugs by adding the letter "Y" to their number, Autolite tacks on the number "2," AC adds the suffix "S" and NGK inserts the letter "P."

Platinum-gap plugs sound like something that you should shop for at the jewelry counter, but there are definite practical reasons for making spark plugs with precious-metal electrodes. In the U.S., Champion is the only company that uses platinum, but the British Lodge and German Bosch companies both devote a large part of their production to the manufacture of platinum-gap plugs.

Platinum plugs were first developed in England during World War II for use in aircraft engines. Before ceramic engineers had found a way to make projected-nose plugs, platinum electrodes were the only means of extending spark plug heat ranges. The fine-wire platinum electrodes retain their shape even when heated to incandescence, and they burn away fouling deposits. On the intake stroke they are cooled by the incoming air/fuel mixture. Platinum plugs first became popular in this country with Porsche owners, who imported Lodge H-NP's by the carton to solve their fouling problem.

Since projected-nose plugs are much less expensive and do a better job in wedge-type combustion chambers than platinum-gap plugs, they should be given the nod over the platinum types. However, if there are clearance problems that won't permit the use of a projected-nose plug in your engine and you need an extended heat range plug to prevent low-

Spark Plugs

speed fouling, platinum-gap plugs might be for you. Champion HO-3, UJ-64P and UL-60P platinum plugs have been widely used in racing 327 Corvettes for this reason.

When combustion chamber space is as limited as elbow room for six Olympic weightlifters crammed into a Volkswagen, the basic plug design may have to be modified to prevent its gap from being pounded shut by a flying piston. This is usually accomplished by means of a cut-back side electrode mounted *beside* rather than *over* the center electrode. Platinum-gap plugs of the type made by Lodge also provide excellent minimum clearance characteristics, as do retracted-gap racing plugs.

Multiple electrodes had their heyday when metals had not yet been developed which would resist rapid gap growth in high-performance engines. Although several types are be-

ing made overseas by reputable companies, those found in the U.S. are usually in the "gimmick" plug category. However, there are exceptions, notably in aircraft engines, where multiple-ground-electrode plugs are used almost exclusively. Aircraft engines operate at constant rpm, with little or no idling.

The automobile engine is a different animal, used for lots of low-rpm chores, and multiple-ground-electrode plugs have a tendency to foul, because the insulator tip is covered and doesn't get hot enough to burn off deposits. Plugs with more than one ground electrode do have excellent resistance to gap growth, but their fouling tendencies and the difficulty of cleaning the tip of the insulator mean they require special treatment. We advise against them.

The surface-gap plug is a development which has not yet seen wide use. It seems to offer some advantages in high-performance two-stroke engines, but any practical value in

conventional automobile engines has yet to be shown. The most outstanding feature of the surface-gap plug is its very stable voltage requirement. High cylinder pressures (as from supercharging)·do not increase its voltage requirement nearly as much as they do with conventional plugs.

Several manufacturers offer a projected-nose racing plug, but in most cases these are simply extra-cold versions of their street projected-nose designs. Champion's projected-nose racing plug is a distinct line from their regular projected-nose plugs and is distinguishable by numbers in the 60's. Its most noticeable feature is the use of the J-gap side electrode, which makes firing better at high rpm. This Champion plug also has a stronger shell, slightly larger insulator and a removable gasket to set it apart from the "production" numbers. Don't consider these plugs unless you're a serious racer.

And finally, we have retracted-gap plugs, which are just the thing for your supercharged fuel-burner. These spark plugs are also known as the push-wire type, because the side electrode is located in a hole bored into the plug shell. A special tool is used to push this wire back and forth in its hole for gap adjustments, although in some plugs no adjustment is possible.

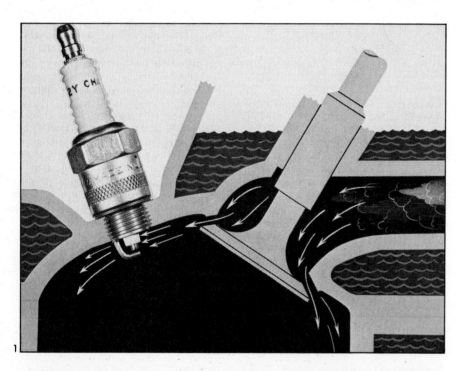

1. Projected-nose plugs have a greater heat range than conventional plugs. While their long insulator makes them hotter at low speeds (for better fouling resistance), insulator is cooled by incoming air/fuel mixture at high speeds to make it colder than a standard-gap plug.

2. Special clearance gaps place the side electrode beside the center one. This sometimes allows a projected-nose plug to be used in engines where clearance is limited.

3. A special tool like this is used to change the gap of retracted-gap plugs. These are available from speed shops and plug manufacturers.

4. Firing tip of push-wire, retracted-gap racing plug. Note the location of the side electrode in its hole. Some of these side electrodes are tapered and can't be regapped, but this one can.

5. Vixen plug sandblasters have been made for years. They are probably the least expensive cleaner around. Any sandblaster must be used with an air compressor.

6. Retracted-gap plug is the classic racing plug. It is a must for supercharged fuel burners, but a dud on the street since it quickly fouls in low-speed situations. The push-wire side electrode is adjustable in some designs.

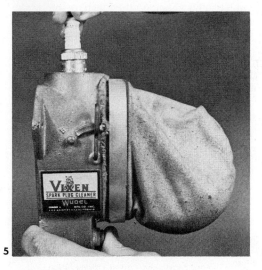

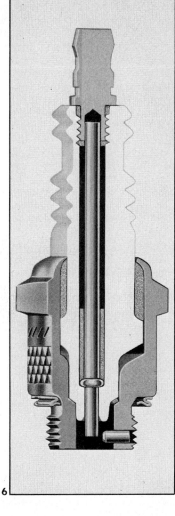

mally be of the same heat range may have different preignition levels because of electrode design. A thin, overheated electrode is much more likely to go into preignition than a heavier, cooler one—unless, of course, it is made from some metal like platinum. Keep this in mind the next time you see a bargain-store cheapie which claims to be an exact replacement for a name brand and heat range.

PLUG CARE AND MAINTENANCE

Spark plug replacement and maintenance is one job that even the most unskilled home mechanic can do. Unfortunately, it's probably easier to get a date with Raquel Welch than to get at the spark plugs on some of our American V-8's. If you have one of these irons, you might as well just put in a brand-new set every 8000 or 12,000 miles and forget about maintenance. Owners of other cars, however, can increase their plugs' useful life while keeping their transportation razor-sharp just by a periodic session with spark plug tools. The work isn't complicated, but there are a couple of tricks concerning it that are very useful.

Most engines need new plugs every 10,000 to 12,000 miles, although auto manufacturers claim that some new ones can go for 22,000 miles because of leaner mixtures and the new high-energy electronic ignition systems. It takes about twice as much voltage to fire a plug at high speeds as it does at an idle, and *three times* the voltage under hard acceleration. If the engine cuts out when you're bombing away from a stoplight, it's probably a sign that the plug gaps have eroded.

When replacing plugs, remove and install only one plug wire and plug at a time before moving on to the next. This prevents mixing plug wires and gives you an opportunity to read each plug.

Spark plugs should always be installed carefully and in clean surroundings. A stuck plug can sometimes be loosened by tightening it a bit before trying to unscrew it or by applying penetrating oil or Liquid Wrench. Tapered-seat plugs must be installed according to torque specs—about 15 ft.-lbs. for 14mm plugs and 20 ft.-lbs. for 18mm plugs. If a torque wrench is unavailable, tighten the plugs finger-tight and then an additional ½-turn. If you go any tighter, you'll have to blast them out when removal time comes around.

After seized plugs are out, check the threads in the cylinder heads for dirt and damage and clean them with

Retracted-gap plugs have the least fouling resistance of any type of plug and are therefore not suitable for street use. They are intended for all-out racing engines or highly modified, supercharged fuel-burners which are never operated at low rpm and which demand very cold plugs.

EFFECT OF GAP DESIGN

In general, any electrode design which features sharp edges has a lower voltage requirement than one with flat or rounded surfaces. However, the sharper the edge, the sooner it erodes away. If inspected under a magnifying glass, a new spark plug electrode can be seen to have many sharp little irregularities. Each time a spark jumps from one of these, it is burned smooth, until in an old, worn plug the electrodes merely have a smoothly pitted appearance. This is why plugs designated for street use do not have cut-back or J-gaps. The concentrated area of "sharpness" found in these plugs erodes away first, widening the plug's gap. Cut-back or J-gap plugs have to be reset every 1500 miles or so, which is unimportant in a race car but intolerable in a street car. Remember, a

wide gap also increases a plug's voltage requirement, and as hard as plugs are to get at in many modern cars, it's very important to have as little gap growth as possible. In normal operation, street plugs suffer a gap increase of only about .001-in. every 1000-2000 miles.

Since projected-nose plugs place the spark gap deeper in the combustion chamber, a change to these from standard-gap plugs can have two immediate effects on engine operation. The first is more efficient burning of the air/fuel mixture; the other is that the spark plug timing is effectively advanced. The spark does not fire sooner, but its new location in the combustion chamber causes the mixture to "light up" sooner. For this reason, it may be necessary to retard the ignition from 1 to 4° when projected-nose plugs are installed in place of standard-gap plugs. This timing change does not apply, of course, to engines whose timing specs were made up with projected-nose plugs in mind.

The electrodes of racing plugs are somewhat heavier than those of standard plugs. Thinner electrodes do not carry away heat as well as heavier ones. Spark plugs which may nor-

Spark Plugs

a spark plug thread chaser, a tool available at most auto supply stores. In well-cared-for engines, a quick wipe with a clean cloth is all that's needed.

The new plugs should be checked with a gapping tool to make sure that the electrode gap is the same as factory specs. Use the bending bar on the gap gauge to bend the side electrode. Never close the gap by banging the plug against a hard surface, because you can crack the porcelain insulator. Spark plugs should be gapped with a round wire gauge for complete accuracy. Don't use flat feeler gauges. The wire gauge should pass through the gap with a solid snap, but don't force it.

Carelessly installed spark plugs can wreck a cylinder head—especially an aluminum one. Lubricate the plug threads with a thin film of oil before screwing them in. (You can get a few drops from the oil dipstick if nothing else is available.) If your engine has an aluminum head, it's a good idea to coat the threads with an antiseize compund. Cadmium-plated plugs, such as Champions, also go a long way toward preventing plug-seizing problems.

When tightening the spark plugs, be careful not to overtighten them. Overtightening can crush the gasket and make it useless. Crimped-on gaskets such as those found on Champion plugs need only be tightened about ½-turn with the wrench after the plug has been seated by hand. Most car makers, however, specify a torque wrench reading for spark plug installation. Also, many gaskets work best when a torque wrench is used to guide the mechanic. Check your car's specs, and if a certain spark plug torque is listed, stick to it.

. Keeping your plugs clean is important, since a heavy accumulation of deposits can eventually ruin a plug. Your engine makes a pretty good plug cleaner. You've got to be careful, though, because if the plugs are loaded with deposits from lots of slow driving, you can ruin them by simply floor-boarding the accelerator. Such an approach can fuse soft deposits into a permanent conductive glaze. The right way to remove deposits by using the engine is to accelerate to the speed where the engine begins to miss. Then back off the gas until the engine smooths out. You've got to keep the cylinders firing if you're going to do any good. Hold this speed for a few miles; then repeat the whole process several times. If the miss occurs at a higher speed each time, you're getting the cleaning job done.

Sandblast cleaning can restore plugs almost to like-new condition. However, many mechanics simply sandblast the plug, stick it into the tester on the cleaning machine, find that the voltage requirement is too

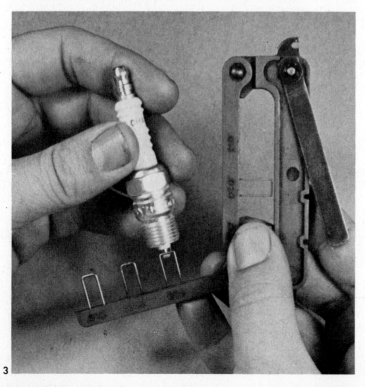

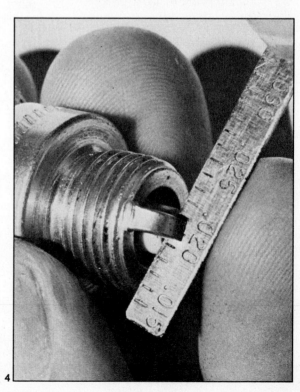

high and tell you that you need a new set of plugs. This is because sandblast cleaning increases a plug's voltage requirement rather than lowering it. Why? Because sandblasting not only removes the conductive deposits from the electrodes—which may actually be helping the spark to jump—but it rounds off the electrodes by its abrasive action. Spark plugs should always have their electrodes filed to a sharp, square shape after sandblasting. First sandblast, then

file. You'll return the plug almost to its original voltage requirement.

After cleaning and filing, always regap used plugs to their original specifications. A gap that's too close makes a rough idle, and one that's too wide increases the voltage requirement and produces missing during acceleration and at high speeds.

PLUG MYTHS

Many myths and misconceptions

have grown up about spark plugs. Take, for example, the "spark plug intensifiers" that have been demonstrated at county fairs for decades. These devices prey on the popular assumption that a hotter spark will improve a car's fuel economy and power. Actually, it doesn't matter if the spark is hot, cold or lukewarm, as long as it manages to ignite the air/fuel mixture in the combustion chamber. It is true that in slightly sick engines such devices can help, but only because they are nothing more than electrical resistances or auxiliary gaps. Their effect is identical to that of ordinary booster-gap plugs. The crime is that the intensifier is sold at a price that far exceeds the cost of a set of resistor or booster gap plugs.

Another misconception is that hot plugs produce a hotter spark than cold plugs do. As we have seen, hot and cold plugs have nothing to do with the power of the spark itself, but only refer to the relative ability of the plug to conduct heat away from the firing tip. When you remember that racing engines require colder, not hotter plugs, this idea seems even more ludicrous.

"Gimmick" plugs can be spotted by their advertisements, which are elaborate and exaggerated. Often the gimmick makers will offer "scientific proof" of benefits, such as increased rpm with a closed throttle, but they neglect to point out that the design of their plugs changes the effective spark advance at low speeds. This may very well speed up the idle, but it will probably result in a power *loss* at higher speeds!

For most of us, the factory-supplied spark plugs or equivalent are probably the best choice. However, for special cars or special driving situations, one of the specialized kinds of plugs can be a real boon to drivability and performance. ♙

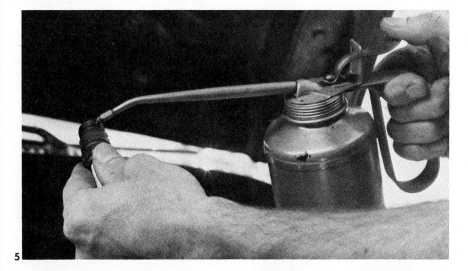

5

1. This plug is in great shape after sandblasting, but the electrodes are still rounded by corrosion and the abrasive. This may raise voltage requirement, but don't throw that plug away. File the center electrode square and sharp to make it good again.

2. Bend the side electrode back out of the way, then file the center electrode. It's a lot easier if done with a small bench vise.

3. Plug gappers come in many styles. This model includes a small file, a built-in reminder that plug cleaning is not complete until the center electrode is filed sharp.

4. A taper gauge is handy for gapping J-gap and minimum-clearance racing plugs. Wire loop gauges slip through these gaps too easily.

5. Any plug should have its threads oiled when installed in any engine; however, antiseize compound must be applied to plugs being fitted to aluminum cylinder heads.

6. Special pivoted ratchet wrench is needed to get at some plugs. On certain cars, plugs have to be taken out from under the fender after front wheels are removed.

7. You've got to keep things clean when you're switching plugs. This "blowout" was caused by a small piece of dirt that lodged between the gasket and the cylinder head as the plug was installed.

6

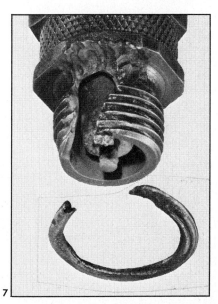

7

Plug size and type don't tell the whole story. You must "read" the plug.

One of the most valuable skills which you can acquire is the ability to determine engine operating conditions from the appearance of its spark plugs. An inspection of the firing tips of the old plugs at each spark plug change can often be a tip-off that there is something in need of attention that has not yet become a serious problem. Also, when a serious problem does suddenly turn up, a look at the spark plugs will often pinpoint the trouble. By carefully studying the following photos you can familiarize yourself with the most common abnormal plug conditions and their causes. Remember that most of these conditions are caused by engine trouble, not plug trouble. The idea is not to change — for example — to a hotter plug when the type that has served the engine previously begins to oil foul, but to replace the piston rings, valve guides, or whatever, to correct the trouble that's making your plugs look like a petroleum-based fudgesicle.

NORMAL PLUG / Description: Insulator light tan or gray. Few deposits. Indicates proper type and heat range for engine and use. Recommendation: Replace plug at regular intervals with same type and heat range. Plugs showing this reading indicate good longevity and will give acceptable performance.

DETONATION CLUE/ Description: Side electrode snapped off. Plug appears more carbon coated than overheated. Cause: Overheated carbon deposits have begun to cause detonation. Treatment: Remove cylinder head, clean away carbon deposits and check closely for hot spots in the combustion chamber.

CORE BRIDGING/ Description: Combustion chamber deposits build up between the insulator and plug shell. Cause: Excessive carbon build-up, poor oil, bad oil control, long idling — then rapid acceleration. Treatment: Use good oil, check rings, valve guides, avoid extended idling in traffic if possible.

SILICA DEPOSITS/ Description: Hard conductive deposits of fused sand, lead and fuel additives. Cause: Dirt, dust and sand entering with the air/fuel mixture. Treatment: Repair or replace air cleaner on carburetor. Check for any loose bolts, leaks and bad intake gaskets or poorly fitting air cleaners.

SPLASHED DEPOSITS/ Description: Dark spots flecking insulator nose. Cause: Recent tune-up is clearing up old combustion chamber deposits which are splashing onto insulator. Treatment: Condition will soon disappear; however, rapid acceleration could prove harmful by loosening up deposits in the chamber.

BENT ELECTRODE/ Description: Side electrode has peculiar "question mark" shape. Cause: Using pliers-type gapping tool — especially on filed plugs or worn center electrode. Treatment: Regap plugs or replace those that can't be brought up to specs without deforming the electrode or bending it excessively.

GAP BRIDGING/ Description: Combustion chamber deposits lodged between electrode. Cause: Too much carbon build-up in cylinders, poor oil control or long idling — then all-out acceleration. Treatment: Check your engine for the above trouble then clean and reinstall your plugs with proper gapping.

TOO WIDE GAP/ *Description: Excessive gap width between insulator nose and electrode. Cause: The action of intense heat, combustion chamber pressures, corrosive gases and spark discharge cause gap to widen. Treatment: Regap plug and then check for adequate secondary resistance in circuit.*

INITIAL PRE-IGNITION/ *Description: Electrodes burned away, insulator tip blistered or deformed. Cause: Excessive spark advance, plug too hot, inferior fuel being used. Treatment: Bring timing up to specs, check advance, switch to better gas and try using a colder plug, with a booster gap if available.*

SCAVENGE DEPOSITS/ *Description: Yellow, white or brownish crust-like deposits over electrodes and insulator. Cause: Typical of chemical make-up of some gasolines, but usually a result of "old fogey" driving. Treatment: Clean and file electrodes, go out and "stand-on-it" to clean out combustion chamber.*

ALUMINUM THROW-OFF/ *Description: Molten chunks of aluminum imbedded between electrode and insulator. Cause: Pre-ignition causes hot spots on aluminum piston heads. Treatment: Check timing, ignition advance, change to a top grade of gasoline and install colder plugs. Be sure plug is right reach.*

OIL FOULED PLUG/ *Description: Soft, wet, oily deposits covering insulator and nose of plug. Cause: Excess oil reaching combustion chamber. Treatment: Check or repair worn oil control rings, valve guides, crankcase vent, oil level, oil bath air cleaners. Use hotter plugs. Booster gap plugs will fire longer.*

GLAZING/ *Description: Hard, glassy, brown coating on insulator tip and electrode. Cause: Fast acceleration after low-speed driving. Treatment: Accelerate slowly after long periods of in-town driving. Glaze is conductive and can ruin plugs, so don't squirrel around the pits. Don't idle engine for long periods.*

CARBON FOULED PLUG/ *Description. Dry, fluffy black carbon deposits over the entire firing end. Cause: Plug too cold, choke not open, over-rich mixture, low voltage, weak condenser, sticking valves. Treatment: End richness, free the valves, raise voltage, use hotter plug. Check carb float level.*

WORN PLUG/ *Description: Electrodes are obviously rounded and thinned, insulator pitted and encrusted with old deposits. Cause: Plug has been in service for an extremely long time. Treatment: Be sure to replace your old plugs with a set of new ones after driving approximately 8000 to 12,000 miles.*

MECHANICAL DAMAGE/ *Description: Insultor nose broken, electrode bent. Cause: Loose object or inadequate piston/valve-to-plug clearance. Treatment: Look for loose parts, check for engine damage, see proper clearance between plugs and engine's moving parts is maintained. Use correct reach plug.*

Plug Wires

THIS HIGH-VOLTAGE PIPELINE IS OFTEN TAKEN FOR GRANTED, BUT IT CAN BE AN UNEXPECTED TROUBLE SOURCE—OR A WELLSPRING OF HIDDEN PERFORMANCE POTENTIAL.

The best spark plugs money can buy aren't worth the price of a used toothbrush if the high-tension cables can't deliver voltage to them. High-tension ignition cables are probably the most overlooked part of the entire ignition package. Anyone who's had to sit out a rainstorm along the freeway or has been late to work on a cold, damp morning has already found out the importance of a weatherproof and efficient set of high-tension cables. Yet the most reliable system can sometimes be improved by incorporating better components or by devoting more care to its construction.

RESISTANCE CABLES

A great many people would be surprised to find out that what they call their spark plug wires aren't *wires* at all. If you cut through the insulation of most cables used on production cars, you'll find that there is actually no metallic wire inside them. Instead, there is some form of semiconductive synthetic core that transmits the spark from the distributor to the plugs. If you connect one of these cables to a battery, it won't carry the current needed to light a flashlight bulb, but it is conductive enough to provide a path for the high-voltage spark impulse to race along. The idea behind these so-called resistance cables is to eliminate radio and TV interference. Without them, your car radio is affected and your favorite song will be accompanied by the sound of jumping sparks.

Resistance-type wires have been loudly condemned as sources of ignition trouble and poor gas mileage. Even many regular automotive service centers routinely swap them for metallic-core cables at the first sign

of trouble. If your car is regularly driven on the street, you *should* be using resistance cables to comply with federal communications laws, but that's not the only reason. Those resistor wires were not tossed into the picture at the last minute to satisfy the bureaucrats.

Resistance wires were designed into the car's system, and the resistance they provide is there because the coil, condenser and plugs all work best with that amount of secondary resistance in the system. An engineer might be able to design an ignition system that would put out a more reliable spark if he didn't have to use resistor wires, but in that case he would change other parts so that the system would work well without the secondary resistance provided by the wires.

Some kinds of resistance wire certainly are troublesome, but there are also types available which are not only as efficient as metallic-core cables, but can also take rough use. Resistance cables that cause trouble are those that have broken or burned-out conductors. This is nearly always the result of the cable having been bent sharply, stretched or poorly connected to its terminal.

One way to locate faulty wiring, a cracked distributor cap and any bad connections is to observe engine operation at night. The absence of any light makes it easy to see any stray

sparks. If everything is tight and in proper condition, then no sparks should be visible.

One early type of resistance cable was nothing more than a hollow plastic tube filled with carbon grains. It worked—until the grains settled, due to engine vibration, leaving great gaps in the spark path.

There are also resistance cables which use a solid piece of graphite-impregnated nylon. These work fine until the first time they are bent or pulled upon, particularly in cold weather. Like nylon-cord tires that tend to get a flat spot after being parked overnight, the core of these cables takes a rigid set. When bent, as in removing the leads for a plug change, the nylon core cracks. Thereafter, every time the plug fires, the spark has to jump this crack. The burning-out process has started. After only a few hundred miles the interior of the cable is so eaten away that a chronic engine miss develops.

Another type of resistance cable uses many very fine strands of

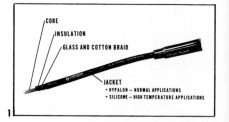

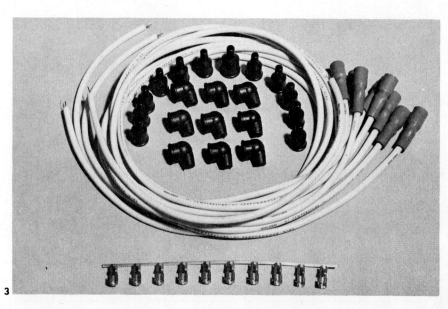

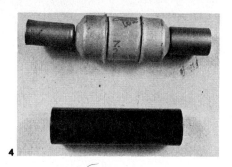

4

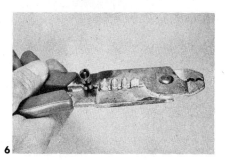

6

5

graphite-impregnated nylon or plastic, and a second type has a core of braided textile material that is saturated with carbon. These types resist damage due to rough handling, but since the core is so flimsy it is difficult to guarantee solid contact be-

1. Chrysler's glass-filament suppressor spark plug cable is flexible and dependable. Wire consists of approximately 10,000 glass strands covered with carbon crystals. Insulation for normal applications is hypalon, with silicone used for high-temperature applications.

2. Packard 535 is a silicone-insulated, 19-strand copper wire cable with silver plating on the individual wires. Autolite 7SH is also silicone, but it is a 7-strand stainless steel conductor. The hypalon wire is an example of how non-brand-name merchandise is frequently inferior. It has 16 strands of plated copper, but the strands are so fine that they break very easily.

3. Belden makes this high-temperature, high-performance silicone wire in a kit to fit almost any 8-cylinder engine. This example is typical of quality kits on the market today.

4. If you don't have resistor wires but you want to cut down on radio interference, either one of these resistors could be used. The black one screws into lead between coil and distributor; other is type which fits on top of each spark plug. These resistors were most popular during '50's and '60's, before widespread use of suppressor wires. Their main use was to reduce interference on aftermarket radios.

5. Plug wire terminals come in many different shapes and sizes. The screw-on ones with the plastic outer part are made by Rajah, which also makes a soldering type that is all metal.

6. Some wire pliers have a large hole near the handle that can be used for applying stock spark plug terminals to the wire.

tween it and the terminal attachments. Eventually a spark begins to arc between the cable core and its terminal, and the connection is soon burned away. The heat of the spark usually destroys the cable's insulation as well, and in some cases it goes so far as to ruin the distributor cap.

The most successful type of resistance cable has a tube-shaped core that is both flexible and elastic. This type of conductor not only resists breakage even when stretched moderately or tied in a knot, but provides the best possible contact between the semiconductor and its terminal attachments. If the terminals are carefully and properly installed on this type of cable, it is just as reliable as the metallic conductor types.

A fairly recent development in the resistance wire field is a metallic resistance wire made by Essex. It has a monel conductor wound in a spiral over a magnetic layer. The spiraled conductor and the magnetic layer work together to set up a magnetic field that suppresses radiation. Resistance values are only 450-700 ohms per foot, compared with 3000-7000 ohms per foot for ordinary resistance cable. The low resistance allows more current to flow, giving a hotter spark. Essex calls their new wire Magwire. It is also marketed by Holley as TP (Track Proven) wire, and by Triple-A Specialty Company as MSW (Magnetic Suppression Wire).

Magnetic suppression looks like an excellent idea, because the metallic conductor will not increase in resistance value as it gets older. Even the best carbon-impregnated resistance wire increases in resistance value as it gets old or is handled. Sometimes it builds up so much resistance that the car won't even run. Magwire should last the life of the car.

No matter what kind of resistance wire you have, it must be treated gently. Any time you disconnect spark plug wires, pull on the terminal or boot, not the wire.

WIRE RESISTANCE VALUES

Resistance in the spark plug wires, or in any part of the ignition system

that conducts the spark, is called secondary resistance. It is there primarily to cut down on the current flow as an aid to prolonging plug life. Without the resistance, the spark creates radio and TV interference and can even make an airplane have trouble getting through to the local airport tower.

We know that secondary resistance is a good thing—if it is designed into the ignition system. The trouble is that the secondary resistance can grow as the ignition system ages until one cold morning there is not enough fire to light up the car's engine.

An ohmmeter is used to check for the proper resistance values in plug wires. Usually a wire runs about 20,000 ohms. The total resistance of any spark plug wire, no matter how old or handled, should not exceed the amount of resistance in a brand-new wire of the same length, at least not by much. Total resistance for most wires will run about 20,000 ohms. If you have one that is 40,000 ohms, test a new wire of the same type and length for comparison.

A bad wire usually tests very high for its length. Long wires can go 150,000 ohms or more when they are bad. If you get an infinity reading with the ohmmeter set on the high scale, it means that there must be a break in the wire. It's also a good idea to wiggle the wire while you are testing it. If the ohmmeter varies at all, get rid of the wire.

A word of caution about checking with an ohmmeter. Any carbon-impregnated wire increases in resistance as it is handled. Flexing the wire separates the carbon particles slightly and increases the resistance. It's something you just have to learn to live with.

METALLIC CABLES

The number of strands of wire used in metallic-core ignition cable has little to do with its electrical efficiency. However, cables which feature many fine strands have a somewhat more limp feel than those with a few heavy ones. The "softies" are a bit easier to push through tubular wire looms,

Plug Wires

while the stiff ones hold their shape better when unsupported, which helps keep them from dangling against the exhaust headers and hot cylinder heads.

Three wire materials are commonly used in metallic-core ignition cables: steel (stiff and durable), copper and copper alloys (soft, low resistance), and silver-plated copper (maximum conductivity). Your best guide in buying a high-quality cable is to stick with the well-known, reliable brand names like Motorcraft, Belden, Delco and Packard.

Packard 440, which has a silver-plated copper core, has long been a favorite with hot rodders, sports car racers and top racing engine builders. Another Packard wire, 430, is identical to it in construction but has a steel wire core.

For top reliability, metallic cables are the best. Metallic cables can be soldered to their end terminals, and then you know they are going to stay put. Incidentally, acid-core solder is taboo; use rosin-core only.

If you use metallic-core wires on a combination street/strip job, keep a piece of resistance wire for substitution between the coil and distributor when you go back on the street, again to prevent any possible radio and TV interference.

INSULATION

Insulation quality is one thing that really sets the top-notch cables apart from the also-rans. In the early days of the automobile, ignition cables were nothing more than ordinary wires with an extra-heavy rubber insulation. Heat, gasoline, oil and ozone quickly destroyed the rubber, making for extreme unreliability. Later the rubber was covered with a cotton sheath and given a heavy coat of lacquer. This delayed the oil and ozone attacks, but the lacquer developed cracks. This kind of wire is still available from several makers (such as Belden) for use by people who restore antique cars.

The next advance was to encase the rubber insulation with a thick layer of neoprene, which is fuel, oil and ozone-proof. This method is still used and is highly satisfactory. Its only shortcomings are that it remains somewhat susceptible to heat and the inner insulation core of rubber can become spongy and water-absorbent with old age.

The latest development in insulation is the use of silicone rubber, which is extremely resistant to heat. Autolite 7SH has this kind of insulation, and so does Packard 535. One word of warning: *Buy only name brands.*

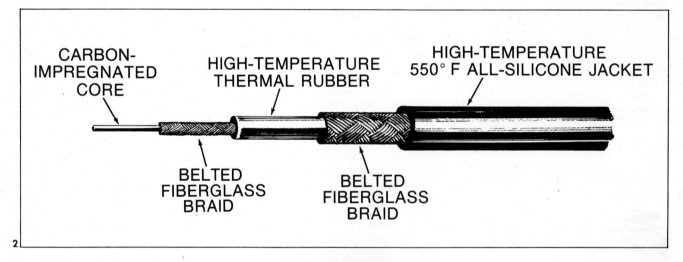

CARBON-IMPREGNATED CORE — HIGH-TEMPERATURE THERMAL RUBBER — HIGH-TEMPERATURE 550° F ALL-SILICONE JACKET — BELTED FIBERGLASS BRAID — BELTED FIBERGLASS BRAID

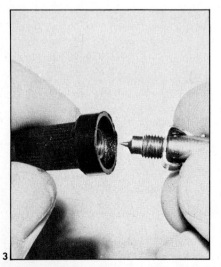

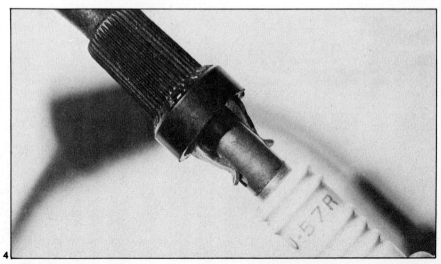

There are a lot of bargain-store specials on the market with cheap plastic insulations that are about as durable as an ice cream cone in Death Valley. Check the outside. If it's not stamped with a reputable brand name and type designation, pass it by:

BOOTS AND NIPPLES

The rubber-like shields that cover the spark plug terminals are commonly referred to as plug boots. Those that slip over the wires to cover the distributor cap towers are called nipples. This is another area where unbranded wire sets usually fall on their faces. Some cheap plug boots are nothing more than synthetic rubber, which melts and cracks after just a few hours on a sizzling plug insulator.

1. Solder-type Rajah terminals can be put on in several different ways. In this method you first melt some solder into the empty terminal, then strip the wire and fold back a piece of it along the insulation for full contact with the terminal. If the terminal is kept hot with the soldering iron, the melted solder will flow into the wire as it is pushed in.

2. The very highest quality ignition cable, such as this by Jack Cotten of Pasadena, Tex., has two layers of fabric, a layer of neoprene and an outer sheath of silicone rubber. Cable like this can last indefinitely.

3. Installing screw-on Rajah terminal is easy. You just flare the wire out inside the plastic cap and screw the metal part into it.

4. Rubber covers fit easily over solder-type terminals, either straight or angled. Screw-on Rajah terminal (shown here) would really look best if left exposed.

5. Rajah terminals come both straight and angled. Disadvantage of screw-on type is that it is difficult to get a rubber covering to fit over them.

6. A common type of terminal is this simple wire clip. It has only a small contact area, and it works better with metal-core wires than resistance wires.

The best plug boots are molded from silicone material, but most of those supplied by reputable ignition cable makers are all right.

Distributor cap nipples face a different set of conditions entirely. Conditions are usually comparatively cool around the distributor, but sometimes there is a good bit of gasoline and oil vapor. For this reason, neoprene makes the best nipple material. Take your distributor cap along for a trial fitting so that you can be sure that the nipples you buy will fit tightly and stay waterproof when installed.

TERMINAL ATTACHMENTS

Ignition cables are no better than the terminals attached to them. Many production cars simply have a wire clip that presses into the end and side of their resistance-type cables. Poor contact between the terminal attachments and the cable's resistance core is one of the main causes of burnouts.

Two methods of attaching terminals to resistance cables provide relatively trouble-free service. One system employs a small screw on the terminal itself, a screw which threads directly into the core of the cable; Volkswagen plug connectors are of this type.

Another type of terminal which works particularly well is a simple U-shaped prong, one side of which inserts into the center of the cable while the other lies flat along its outside. A brass outer terminal can be inserted into the metal sockets inside the distributor cap towers. As a general rule, terminal attachments which pierce a resistance cable's insulation should be avoided. In a great many instances these have caused resistance cables to burn off at the point where the insulation has been punctured.

Magnetic suppression wire cannot be terminated in the field. The terminal connections are a weak point of

this wire, and the manufacturer feels that he can't take the chance of having it done outside the factory. For that reason, magnetic suppression wire is not yet available in bulk, only in terminated wire sets.

The terminals used with metallic-core cables come in a much greater variety and range in quality from good to excellent. There are many patented spark plug connectors available for metallic-core cables which provide good insulator shielding and will not vibrate off. The British Lucas plug connectors are very popular with sports car racers, while many of the hot rod set choose the famous Rajah connectors, available in several different styles.

Metallic cable terminal attachments that fit into the distributor cap come in two basic styles. The most common is the familiar brass clip which squeezes together to grip the wire as it is pressed into the distributor cap. British cars with Lucas distributors have screw-in type distributor cap terminals which require that a washer-like fitting be attached to the wire core. Even if you are only wiring up the old family sedan, you can pick up some welcome gains—particularly in starting reliability—by soldering the terminal attachments in place.

When the high-tension cables of your car begin to show signs of wear and tear, there's always the temptation to just dash down to the local parts shop and pick up a prepackaged set. A little additional time spent making up your own wiring set usually pays off in the long run by making it as permanent, durable and reliable as any other part of the car.

The drawback to buying a ready-made system is that if it's a real top-quality affair, it'll cost you about twice as much as one you can assemble yourself. On the other hand, if it's a relatively inexpensive setup, you're probably going to find that some

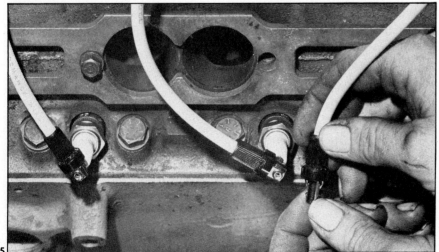

Plug Wires

parts of it are not all they should be in the way of quality.

One of our gripes about most cheap wire sets is that the cables have the nipples molded right onto them. If the nipple goes bad, you've got to throw away the whole wire.

But even the best sets are only built to ''stock'' specifications. The terminals are not soldered on, and the plug connectors are a type that may vibrate off. Obviously, if you want the very best in high-tension wiring, the most satisfactory approach is to select the individual components yourself and put them together in the best way possible.

If it's a street job, you'd better narrow your choice to a resistance-type cable. This in turn dictates the type of terminals you'll have to use. If the cable manufacturer also makes terminals, it's a good bet that these will best match the cable's design.

With wire-core cable the best material for the terminals is brass. This is not only because brass resists corro-

sion better than most other materials, but it is also easier to solder.

Whether you are using resistance or metallic cable, your plug connectors must be selected to fit the spark plug being used and to suit the spark plug location of your engine. Some Volkswagen plug connectors require that the spark plug terminal nut be removed. If you select these but the plug you intend to use comes only with a solid terminal, you've neatly painted yourself into a corner.

ROUTING

The first step is to cut the wires to the proper length. On inline engines this isn't usually much of a problem, since wire routing is simple and there aren't many heated or moving parts for the cables to rub against. On V-8's, things can be a bit more complicated. One way to score on the first attempt is to fit each wire into the distributor first, route it over the engine, then lop it off at the individual plug locations. Another procedure that works well—particularly on some Fords and Chevys where the cables are routed *under* the exhaust

headers—is to cut the plug terminal off the old cable, butt the end of the new one against it and bind them together with electrical tape. Then all you have to do is start pulling the old wire from the distributor end and it will snake the new cable right into place.

In all cases, keep your cool, take your time and do not forcibly pull on the wires. Always make sure that the cables are *as short as possible* without causing them to make any sharp bends or to come in contact with heated, vibrating or moving parts.

After the cables have been cut to length, including the high-tension lead that fits between the coil and distributor, it's time to install the boots and nipples. Boots and nipples that do not slip easily onto the cables can be lubricated lightly with glycerine, brake fluid, a small amount of soapy water or silicone. *Never use grease or oil.*

If you're going to solder on the terminals, here's how to do it. Install the distributor terminals first. Strip about 3/16-in. of insulation from the end of the cables and tin (lightly coat with

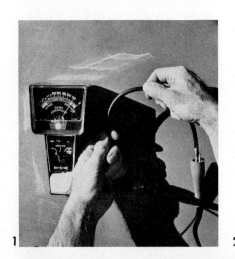

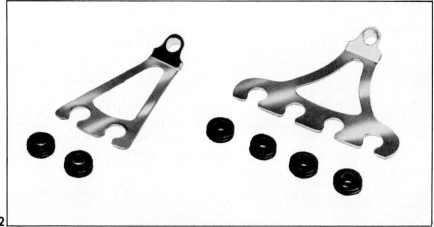

solder) the end of each terminal attachment with a soldering iron before installing it on the wire: The projecting end of the metallic wire can then be passed through the hole in the center of the terminal attachments. Individual strands of wire should be bent over so that they radiate across the end of the terminal. After doing this, the wire can be bonded to the terminal with just a quick touch of the soldering iron. Never use a torch or try to make the solder joint without first having tinned the terminal. This would apply far too much heat to the cable itself, damaging the insulation.

Some patented plug connectors, like the Rajah, require no soldering since they have a built-in screw which firmly grips the wire core of the ignition cable. The simpler sleeve-type connectors that are commonly sold in parts stores may require a slight modification to make them suitable for soldered connections. One way is to drill a small hole in the side of the terminal so that the metallic wire can be slipped through it and soldered to the outside of the connector. Always use rosin-core solder.

LOOMS

Chromed tubular wire looms look jazzy but can be a headache. The problems occur when they are able to pick up a lot of heat and are solidly grounded to the engine block. They not only overheat the cable's insulation but can cause electrical interference and induction firing. The best wire looms and supports are the type that carry the wires in neoprene insulating rings.

Induction firing is a phenomenon which occurs when long ignition cables are allowed to lie closely against one another. Spark energy passing through one cable can induce a current in the other, which sometimes causes two cylinders to fire at once. The result may be mechanical damage or a carburetor fire. When routing your wires, allow as much space between them as is practical and avoid having them run parallel for long distances.

Needless to say, ignition cables must be connected between the distributor and the spark plugs according to the firing order of the engine. The No. 1 terminal of the distributor is usually marked in some way. The cable leading from this terminal must connect to the spark plug of the No. 1 cylinder. Your car's manual will list the firing order of the engine, or it may be cast in raised numbers on the intake manifold or the engine block. The remaining cables are connected in succession around the cap from the No. 1 terminal in the direction of distributor rotation, and run to each cylinder in turn according to the firing order.

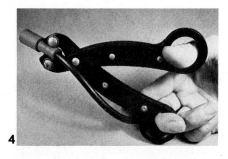

1. Any wire, whether resistance type or otherwise, can be checked for continuity with an ohmmeter. Measurement of this resistance wire produces a reading of about 900 ohms on the hand-held Allen ohmmeter.

2. Wire dividers with vinyl grommets, such as this set from Eelco, are recommended for keeping your wires away from hot manifolds and preventing crossfiring.

3. There's going to be trouble here. The owner who carelessly routed his plug wire in this fashion is inviting a short and an engine miss. An angled terminal would have solved the problem.

4. These insulated ignition pliers made by Sun Electric and other equipment companies will keep you from getting shocked. Note that they are being used to pull on the boot, not on the wire.

5. Switching wires one at a time will help prevent mistakes. Here the man is changing caps. The old cap is kept alongside, and he is moving the wires one at a time to the new cap.

6. Pictured are angled-type Rajah screw-on terminals. It's a good idea to use a loom with neoprene insulating rings to keep plug wires away from hot headers.

HOW-TO: PLUG WIRE REPLACEMENT

1. Nobu's Auto Lab in Hollywood, Calif. swears by Delco suppression wire, so we decided to use a reel of it for this car.

2. Lubricate the tip of the cable with a silicone spray first so that the boot can slide on easily. Don't use motor oil.

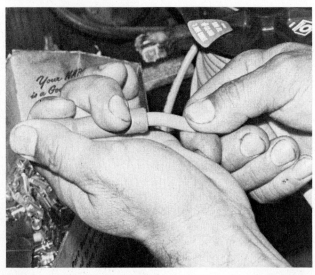

3. Now the spark plug rubber boot slips on. It's amazing how many mechanics forget to put on the boot before the terminal.

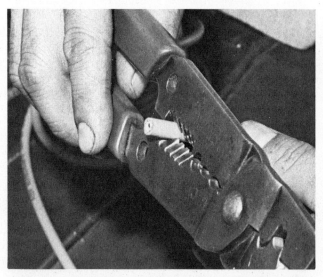

4. Using these special, extremely handy automotive wiring pliers, a little more than ¼-in. of insulation is stripped off.

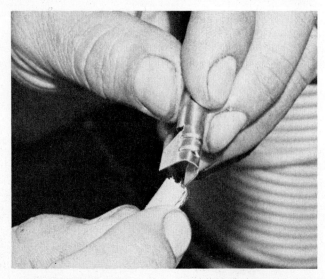

5. The end of the wire is then bent back up and over the insulation to provide a good contact with the metal terminal.

6. The special pliers are used again to crimp the terminal. Pliers like these can be purchased at most auto parts stores.

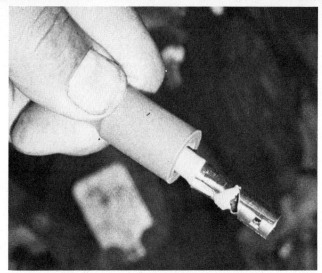

7. Note how the tabs of the terminal are folded inward to grasp the cable. It's difficult to do this with plain pliers.

8. With one terminal attached, next measure for proper length by using the old wire as a guide. Do only one wire at a time.

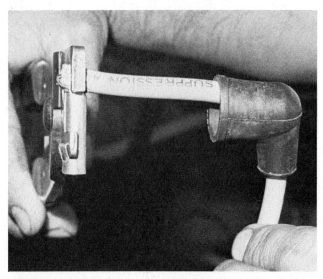

9. The distributor on this car required 90° terminals, so the auto pliers are used again to attach the special terminal.

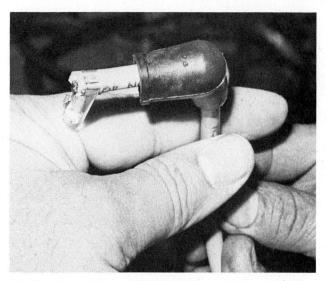

10. This type of terminal is one of the two kinds commonly used for 90° installations. Note the type of boot it requires.

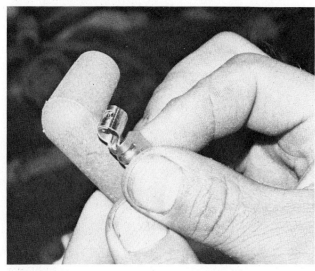

11. The other kind of 90° terminal is just as satisfactory, but it takes a different boot, which is usually red in color.

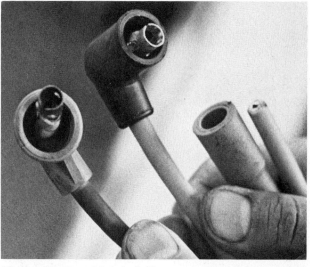

12. Use the correct terminal. The one on the left is a straight terminal that's been bent to 90°; you'll break wires that way.

Coils

A BIG BUILD-UP AND A
QUICK LETDOWN ARE WHAT IT TAKES TO FIRE SPARK PLUGS,
AND THIS IMPORTANT COMPONENT PROVIDES BOTH.

The ignition coil is probably one of the most trouble-free parts of the modern automobile, but when it does start to weaken, your car can become as unreliable as a jewel thief in a room full of diamonds. The coil has just one job, but it's an important one: to produce the high-voltage current needed to fire the spark plugs.

An automobile battery alone can produce a dandy spark, as you've probably noticed when connecting booster cables or if you've accidentally shorted one of your car's "hot" wires against the chassis. Unfortunately, 6 volts or even 12 volts just isn't enough pressure to ionize the plug gaps and push an electrical current across them. Through the wizardry of electricity and magnetism, the coil transforms the battery's low "primary" voltage into a super-high "secondary" voltage for firing the spark plugs.

HOW IT WORKS

There are two ways in which electricity is measured: amperage for amount and voltage for pressure.

When electricity comes from a controlled source, such as a car generator, or from a non-variable source, such as a battery, it's just like getting water out of a garden hose. We can adjust the nozzle for great pressure, but then we lose on the amount of water coming out. If we turn the nozzle so that a lot of water comes out, then the pressure falls off to almost nothing. The pressure produced by the battery is small (only 6 or 12 volts) but very high (comparably) in its rate of flow—amperage. The battery's voltage is our starting point.

A negative-ground system, which is almost universally used today, is one in which the negative (−) battery cable is grounded to the chassis and the positive (+) battery pole is wired to the starter motor solenoid and the car's switches, of which the most important is the ignition switch. The path of the electrical current is circular; it exits from the positive battery terminal, travels through the car to operate its components and returns through the chassis to the negative (grounded) side of the battery. This circuit is a continuous cycle until a wire is cut or shorted, a battery cable

is disconnected or the battery goes completely dead.

In a negative-ground system, the positive battery cable is connected directly to a terminal on the starter motor solenoid. The ignition switch usually picks up its voltage from this same terminal by a "hot" wire running from the terminal to the switch, though in some older cars the hot wire was attached directly to the battery cable. At the ignition switch the car's electrical components are sorted out according to their sequence of operation. Many components—the heater blower motor and often the radio, for example—are wired so that they will operate no matter what the position of the ignition switch is; these tap power from the switch's "hot" terminal. For all the others, the position of the switch determines

which components receive battery voltage.

It is important to remember that this hot wire to the ignition switch *always* has voltage, regardless of the position of the switch. For this reason it is wise to disconnect either this wire or the battery cable itself while working around dashboard wiring, unless you really know what you're doing.

The operation of the ignition switch or any other simple switch can be understood by visualizing it as a drawbridge and the current from the battery as a vehicle waiting to cross that bridge. When the switch is in the "off" position, an electrical conductor (the bridge) within the switch is raised and makes no contact with the rest of the switch's conductors; in electrical terminology, this is an open circuit. In this position, the current

(the vehicle) from the battery can't cross or go any further. Turning the ignition switch "on" physically moves the conductor (lowers the bridge) to contact another conductor within the switch, thus allowing the current to cross over and continue on until an accessory switch is encountered. If a particular accessory switch is "on," then the current may enter the switch and the accessory to operate it. After passing through all the "on" accessories, the current returns through the chassis and. up the ground cable to complete the circuit.

Let's take a quick look at the starting solenoid and the ignition switch, because they are involved with the coil in the operation of the starting system of your car.

In order for your car to start, battery voltage from the ignition switch is needed at only two places: at the "hot" side of the coil and at the starter solenoid. Your ignition switch and wiring system are designed so that they can supply coil voltage only, or coil plus solenoid, but not solenoid only. Remember that one terminal of your ignition switch always has voltage, even when your ignition key is in the "off" position.

When you turn your ignition key to "on," current is sent through a special resistor wire from the ignition switch to the coil; we'll explain why resistor wire is used later. In the usual negative-ground electrical system, this wire is attached to the coil terminal marked with a "+"; on some coils, this same terminal is marked with a "SW" (for switch) or "BATT" (for battery). However it is labeled, this is the coil terminal in the primary (low-voltage) system which receives battery voltage. There is one other coil primary terminal, which is marked with a "−" or "CB" (for contact breakers) or "DIST" (distributor); the wire from this terminal leads to the distributor's breaker points or their modern electronic equivalent and from there to ground. With voltage

now supplied to the coil, the engine will run if something, namely the starter motor, spins it over.

When you turn your ignition key to "start," the ignition switch momentarily interrupts the current that's going directly to the coil and instead diverts it into another primary wire that runs to the starter solenoid. There are three other wires attached to this solenoid. One of them is another primary wire running to the coil—to the same coil terminal as the hot wire coming from the ignition switch. This solenoid-to-coil wire is called the bypass wire; it picks up battery voltage from the solenoid and delivers it to the coil. Its purpose is to bypass the ignition switch-to-coil resistance wire, so that during starting and *only* during starting, the coil receives the full 12 volts of current from the battery.

The other two wires attached to the solenoid are really two parts of the same wire: the heavy battery cable. One part runs up to the positive post on the battery, so it is always hot; the other runs down to the starter motor. The solenoid is really nothing more than an electromagnetic switch that connects these two parts of the battery cable.

When current flows from the ignition switch to the solenoid, the many turns of fine wire in the solenoid's case create a magnetic field, which pulls forward an iron plunger inside the solenoid. This plunger connects the two cable terminals on the sole-

noid's case, completing the battery-to-starter-motor circuit. Heavy current then flows from the battery, the starter motor goes into operation and the engine turns over.

As soon as the engine starts running, you release the ignition key and it returns to the "on" position. Current to the starter solenoid is then cut off, the solenoid's magnetic field collapses and a spring inside the solenoid pushes back the plunger so that it breaks the battery cable circuit. This cuts off power to the starter motor, which promptly disengages from the flywheel. The bypass wire current to the coil is also cut off, but this does not matter, because the ignition switch is now supplying current to the coil through the normal resistance wire (see illustration).

The purpose of the resistance wire is to cut down coil voltage once the engine has started. Cranking an engine, especially when cold, can quickly discharge a battery. During the starting process, the bypass wire allows a full 12 volts to the coil. However, once the engine has started, 12 volts would quickly burn the points, so the voltage must be reduced before reaching the points. The resistance wire cuts the 12 volts to approximately 6 volts before it enters the coil. During cranking, point damage is minimal, because the points are exposed to 12 volts for only a very short time and the engine is turning over very slowly. Once the engine has started, the points move

1. When fitting a replacement coil, it is imperative that you buy either an exact duplicate or one which will function perfectly as a substitute. If in doubt, bring along your old one.

2. All coils look pretty much the same. You have to read the specs or test it in use to know if a particular coil is right for your car. Major-brand coils are good, but beware of any coil that is not identified by name.

3. During manufacture, the windings of this coil are inserted into the coil case and surrounded with oil; then the unit is sealed. The oil acts as an insulator in preventing high-voltage arcing in the coil. Others makes may use an insulating pitch, but either works well if precision-made.

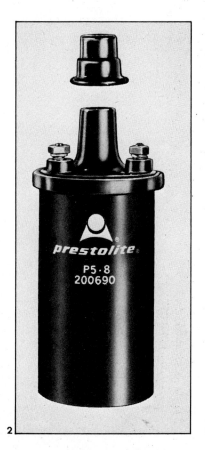

2

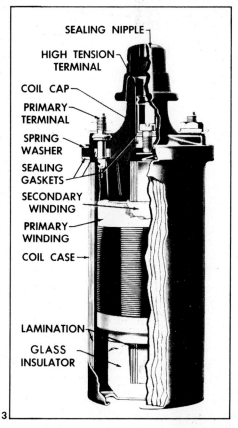

3

SEALING NIPPLE

HIGH TENSION TERMINAL

COIL CAP

PRIMARY TERMINAL

SPRING WASHER

SEALING GASKETS

SECONDARY WINDING

PRIMARY WINDING

COIL CASE

LAMINATION

GLASS INSULATOR

faster, and wear increases with engine speed. Even at an idle speed of only 800 rpm in a V-8, the points open and close 3200 times in one minute; at 5000 rpm they open and close 20,000 times per minute. It's obvious that point wear takes place at higher engine speeds and not during cranking, thereby necessitating resistance.

Now let's look at the coil itself. It is basically a transformer designed to convert a low voltage (6 or 12 volts) into a voltage high enough to jump the spark plug gap and ignite the air/fuel mixture in the combustion chamber. The guts of a coil consist of a primary and a secondary winding of wire coiled (hence the name coil) around a vertically mounted soft iron core. Looking at a cutaway of the coil, you can see that the primary (low-voltage) winding is a fairly heavy wire connected to the inside bottom half of the incoming primary terminal. On a negative-ground system, this terminal is often marked with a "+" (with a "−" in a positive-ground system). The sign indicates which terminal receives battery voltage.

The wire is then vertically coiled a few hundred times and its other end attached to the outgoing primary terminal at the other side of the coil. In a negative-ground system, this terminal is signified by a "−" sign or one of the other markings mentioned previously. The current exits the coil from this terminal and goes to the distributor points.

Placed within the primary winding is the secondary (high-voltage) winding, which consists of about 200 ft. of extremely fine wire wrapped in several insulated layers around the soft iron core. The end of the secondary winding connects internally to the coil's secondary terminal. This is the protruding tower situated between the primary terminals. Connected to it is the large-diameter, high-voltage cable that carries approximately 25,000 volts to the distributor cap for distribution by the rotor to the plugs.

Now you are familiar with the basic structure of the coil and know where the current enters and exits, but what actually goes on inside that cylinder? How does it work? Though it is deceptively simple in construction and contains no moving parts, the operation of the coil depends upon a complex interaction of *induction, magnetism* and *electrical transformation*. This last principle is perhaps the easiest to understand, so let's discuss it first.

Like the coil, any transformer has primary and secondary windings which are not physically connected to each other. When current flows in the primary winding, the electromagnetic phenomenon of induction causes another current to flow in the secondary winding; the voltage of this secondary current depends upon the ratio of the number of wiring turns in the secondary winding compared to the number of turns in the primary winding. In the coil, this ratio is very large, so the secondary voltage is around 25,000 volts even though the primary voltage is only 6 to 12 volts.

What happens next depends upon interacting laws of electricity and magnetism first postulated by Heinrich F. Lenz, a German physicist of the 19th Century. Lenz found that when a current flowed in a wire, a magnetic field was set up around the wire; a very strong magnetic field could be established by wrapping many turns of wire around an iron core and passing a current through the wire.

This is exactly what is done with the primary windings in the coil. Whenever the ignition switch is on and the distributor points are closed, the primary circuit is complete. Current then flows through the coil, setting up a strong magnetic field. The magnetic field envelops the thousands of turns of fine wire in the secondary windings as well as the soft iron core.

When the points open, however, the primary current is interrupted, and the magnetic field instantly collapses. Lenz found that whenever there was relative movement between a magnetic field and an electrical conductor, a voltage was induced in the conductor. The strength of that

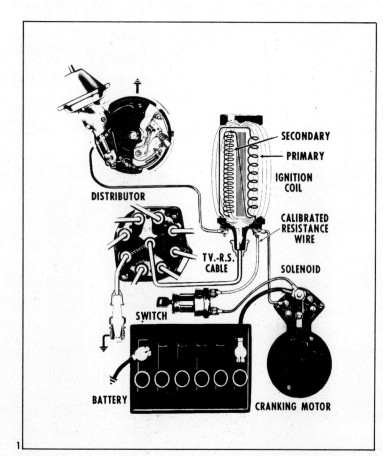

voltage depended upon the strength of the magnetic field and the speed of the relative movement. In the coil, the collapse of its magnetic field provides the relative movement, and immediately a very powerful voltage is induced into the secondary windings. This secondary voltage is very high because there are so many secondary windings and because the collapse of the magnetic field is so fast. A thick, heavily insulated wire carries the secondary voltage from the coil to the distributor, which distributes it to the spark plugs.

When the distributor points open and the high voltage is induced in the secondary windings, a self-induced voltage also appears in the primary windings, amounting to about 250 volts. The self-induced voltage has no place to go except to the condenser. The condenser is connected into the primary system, usually mounted in the distributor next to the points. After the 250 volts of electrical pressure has rammed into the insulated side of the condenser, filling it to capacity, there is an unbalanced condition in the primary. The result is that the pressure from the condenser fires back through the primary in the opposite direction, charging up the grounded side of the condenser and creating another unbalanced condition. The condenser continues to oscillate back and forth through the primary, and these oscillations help ''pump'' the secondary current across the spark gap at the plug.

Attached to the top of the distributor shaft (and rotating with it) is the rotor. The rotor is a plastic cap with a metal pointer extending from it. Inside each of the other cap towers is a metal insert that extends into the cap's interior and forms a contact at the bottom. The contacts are evenly spaced from each other and form a circle within the cap The plug wires fit tightly into these towers and con-

tact the inserts. Just as the points in the distributor open, the distributor rotor lines up with a cap contact connected to one of the spark plug wires. The pressure (voltage) behind the secondary current is conducted from the rotor to this contact. From the contact it goes up the spark plug wire to energize the plug, ionize the gap and project the current across the spark plug gap to ground.

The amazing thing is that all of this is happening thousands of times a minute (about 18,000 times per minute at 4500 rpm in an 8-cylinder engine) with perfect timing. To cope with these extreme demands, the ig-

nition coil has to be of a very highly specialized design.

CONSTRUCTION

One of the most important things that an ignition coil must be able to do is to magnetize and demagnetize itself almost instantaneously. This is why soft iron is used for solenoids, electric motor armatures, relays and ignition coils. Soft iron not only has the ability to accept magnetism, but the property of losing it quickly as well. Hard steels and nickel, on the other hand, will retain magnetism for years and are therefore used to make permanent magnets.

3

4

1. This ignition circuit is typical of those on most domestic cars.

2. On this coil, the wire connected to the terminal marked "SW" would run to the ignition switch, while the wire from the "CB" terminal would connect to the distributor. On coils marked simply by "+" and "−" signs, the wire from the coil to the distributor must be of the same polarity as that of the battery's ground cable.

3. Most modern cars mount the coil on the firewall or inner fender structure, where it is cooler and not subjected to extreme engine vibration.

4. Though coil location varies from engine to engine, it's never far from the distributor. Older cars usually had the coil mounted directly on the engine block, where it was certainly handy.

Coils

Coil windings are generally of copper to keep internal resistance as low as possible. The copper wire is insulated by a coating of lacquer, which keeps the windings from shorting out against one another and weakening the coil's output. Each layer of windings in the secondary coil is insulated from the next by a sheet of specially impregnated paper. After the windings and their core are assembled, they are slipped into a metal "can." Most good-quality stock ignition coils are further sealed and strengthened by filling the can with oil. The coil's "tower" or "nose" is then fitted to seal the container and provide a terminal for the high-tension cable and the two smaller primary wires.

BALLAST RESISTORS

From what we know about coils, forcing more current through the primary windings of a coil should result in the production of more secondary voltage when the distributor points open. That is exactly what happens. The way to get more current through the coil windings is to increase the electrical pressure (the voltage).

Putting a resistor in the primary wire between the battery and the coil may seem like the wrong thing to do, because resistance results in a voltage drop, which cuts down on the amount of current going through the coil windings. But that is exactly what most American car makers have done. The resistance is bypassed during starting so that the coil will receive full voltage, but at other times the resistance is in the circuit so that the coil in a 12-volt system actually runs on 6 volts.

At low engine speeds, the distributor shaft rotates slowly, causing the points to open and close slowly and to remain closed for a relatively long period of time. This action allows current to flow in the primary circuit for a relatively long time. But with these long current flows, the ballast resistor gets hotter. The hotter a resistor gets, the more resistance it produces, thus lowering the current to the coil.

At high engine speeds, the points open and close very quickly, giving the coil less time to become saturated with current. The reduction of current through the resistor allows it to cool off and permit more current flow to the coil. Thus the ballast resistor is really a means of controlling the spark and lengthening the life of the coil by cutting down on current flow when it is not needed.

Some ballast resistors are built into the coil, while others are outside,

mounted on the firewall. The ones you can't see are the tricky ones. They are built into the primary wire itself, between the ignition switch and coil. To replace them, either replace the wire or put in a nonresistor wire with a firewall-mounted resistor.

COIL FAILURES AND TROUBLESHOOTING

Most coil troubles are the result of defects in the secondary windings. Either the insulation between the windings breaks down, reducing the spark voltage, or the insulation from ground breaks down, allowing the current to escape internally. Coils subjected to a great deal of vibration are particularly vulnerable, since shaking the windings against one another can wear away their thin lacquer insulation.

Broken windings and internal connections are nearly always the cause of complete and sudden coil failures, but such trouble is actually quite rare. The most common coil defects result from a gradual deterioration of internal insulation. Complete failure is usually preceded by many signs of an impending breakdown.

One of the most common tip-offs that the coil needs a check is hard or unreliable starting. Another symptom of "coil-itis" is chronic high-speed missing and cutting out during acceleration. If the car's battery is up to par, the distributor tuned and the plugs in good shape yet the trouble persists, your suspicions should definitely be focused on the coil. You can perform preliminary coil checks without special equipment, and if these indicate that a coil defect does indeed exist, you can replace the coil

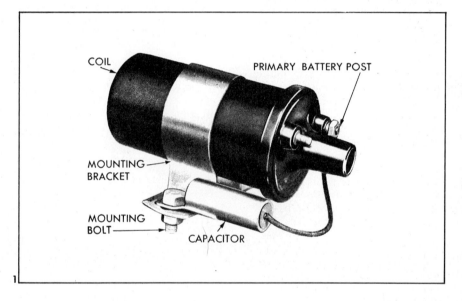

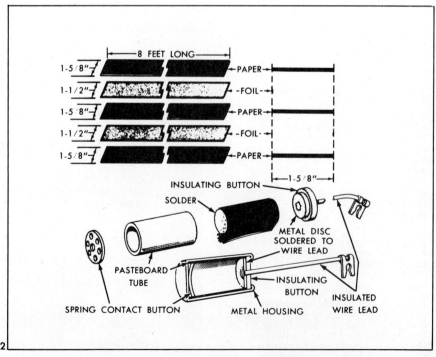

and that's that. But if your home tests are not conclusive, don't declare the coil blameless yet. It's time for more elaborate test procedures.

The first test is to remove the high-tension cable that passes between the coil and distributor from the distributor cap. Hold the end of the cable about 3/16-in. away from some grounded part of the engine and operate the starter with the ignition turned on. A *bright blue* spark should jump the gap. A weak, yellowish or red spark indicates insufficient spark voltage. This last condition definitely points to a weak coil—providing the points, condenser and battery are all in good shape.

To back up your on-the-car test, take the coil to a garage for a thor-

1. Not too long ago, automakers added a capacitor to the coil's primary terminal and grounded it to the engine block to suppress radio interference from the ignition system. In recent years, radio suppression plug wires have for the most part replaced this type of capacitor.

2. A condenser is just a lot of tinfoil, but it must be precision-made or it may cause a lot of trouble.

3. Dynastart is one of the most fascinating tools we have ever used. It takes the place of the points and condenser, causing a continuous stream of sparks to flow from the end of the rotor. Cars stranded with bad points or condenser are quickly started if the battery will turn the engine over. You can drive the car too. But speed and throttle opening must be kept very low, because timing is over-advanced with Dynastart.

4. If spark voltage is too low, an electrical shop should test the internal resistance of the primary circuit. Primary voltage which is too low can reduce coil output by thousands of volts.

ough test. They will have some kind of a tester that will check the coil output. Be careful about rejecting any coil before checking it against a new coil of the same make and specifications. If the coil tests weak when compared with a new coil of the same specifications, replace the coil.

If your preliminary test with the high-tension cable produces no spark at all, attempt to pinpoint the trouble before replacing the coil with a new one. A 6- or 12-volt bulb—depending on your car's electrical system—with two test leads attached to it is all that's needed. Start by taking off the distributor cap. Then either turn the engine until the points are open or separate the points with a small piece of cardboard. Turn on the ignition switch. One test light lead can now be connected to ground somewhere on the engine. Touch the other test lead to first one of the coil's primary terminals and then the other.

If the bulb lights when touched to the primary terminal that leads to the distributor, it indicates that the coil is getting current and that the primary windings are all right. If the bulb lights when touched to the other primary terminal but not when attached to the one leading to the distributor, the primary windings are faulty and the coil is no good. If the light does not go on when connected to *either* primary connection, the trouble is somewhere else—possibly in the ignition switch. More than one car owner has installed a new coil only to discover that the ignition switch or starter relay was the culprit.

If your tests show that the coil is receiving current at both primary terminals, remove the high-tension cable from the center distributor cap tower and try shorting across the open dis-

tributor points with the non-oily tip of a screwdriver. If a spark jumps from the coil's high-tension secondary wire to a grounded point on the engine as the screwdriver is removed, the trouble is probably oil, dirt or water on the points—or simply *burned* points. The screwdriver, if clean and dry, will conduct a spark that wet, dirty or burned points cannot.

If this last test also fails to produce a spark at the high-tension wire, disconnect the small, thin primary wire that passes between the coil and the distributor and attach a test wire to the coil in its place. Ground the other end of the wire against the engine block and then pull it away. In this case, the test wire is duplicating the job of the points. Grounding the wire

3

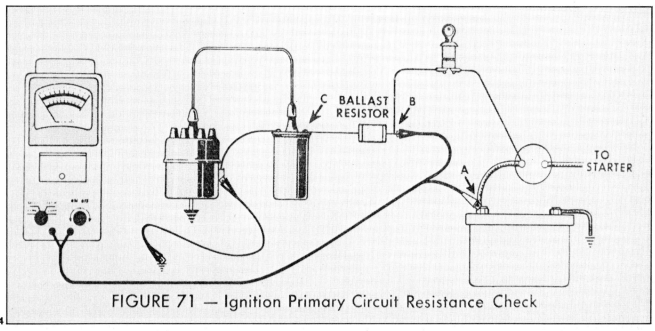

FIGURE 71 — Ignition Primary Circuit Resistance Check

Coils

does the same thing as closing the points. Pulling the wire away should create the same effect as opening the points, namely producing a spark from the coil's high-tension wire.

If a spark jumps from the high-tension cable when the test wire is removed from the ground, the coil is okay and the trouble is in the points (which are probably grounded) or condenser (which may be shorted). If a spark does not jump during this test, the secondary windings of the coil are probably faulty.

There is one other thing that could be causing the trouble, and that's poor contact between the engine and the ground pole of the battery. Whenever there is a "mysterious" electrical problem in your car that seems impossible to trace, the ground strap between the battery and the engine is one of the first things to check.

While you are doing all this testing, we must emphasize the need for maintaining a healthy respect for the power of the coil's secondary voltage. With a clean, dry rag, carefully wipe off any part of the secondary wiring that you are going to touch while testing. If you suspect that the wiring insulation is not up to snuff, wear a rubber glove or grasp the wire with a piece of rubber. The best bet would be to use a pair of special insulated pliers, such as the ones illustrated in the previous "Plug Wires" chapter. And please don't stand on a damp surface. If you are careless you'll get a jolt you'll remember.

In some cases a coil tests out perfectly, yet the car remains hard to start and misses at higher speeds, suggesting that there is inadequate spark voltage. If the engine has recently been tuned up, repaired or newly installed in the car, it's a hint as to what the real problem is. Nine times out of 10 the trouble is *reversed coil polarity* This occurs when the two primary wires leading to the coil have been reversed by incorrect reconnection. When this happens, the spark voltage has positive polarity. It should always be negative, regardless of the way the battery is installed in the vehicle. If it isn't, the sparking current has a low "pressure" in relation to the spark plug ground electrode that it must jump to. The end result is a weak spark, even though every part of the ignition system is in perfect condition. Another indication of reversed coil polarity is "dishing" of the spark plugs' side electrodes.

You can test for reversed coil polarity with a common lead pencil. Simply remove one of the spark plug leads and hold it about ¼-in. from the spark plug terminal or any ground

point. Then insert the point of the pencil between the ignition lead and the plug while the engine is running. If the spark flares on the ground or spark plug side of the pencil, the polarity is correct. If it flares between the ignition lead and the pencil, however, the polarity is wrong, and the primary wires should be exchanged at the coil.

If the plug connector terminals are deeply recessed in a boot or insulating shield, the test can still be carried out by straightening all but one bend from a paper clip and inserting the looped end into the plug connector. The polarity test can then be performed between the tip of the paper clip wire and a grounded place on the engine.

Stock coils are most susceptible to damage from high temperatures and vibration. For this reason weak coils are most likely to fail completely on a long summer trip. If you're getting your car ready for its annual vacation blast down the turnpike, it's a good idea to have the coil tested as part of your pre-trip tune-up. Cars whose coils are mounted in especially hot locations that are subject to a great deal of vibration often show a remarkable tendency toward coil failure. If it's possible to do so without making the high-tension cable to the distributor too long (more than about 12 ins.), relocate the car's coil in a cooler, steadier spot.

When replacing a defective coil, it is very important to make sure that the new one is the correct voltage (6- or 12-volt) for the car. Also, it must be of the correct polarity. If you happen to have a car with positive ground, remember that the coil primary terminal marked positive (+) must be connected to the distributor, while on cars with negative ground it's the other way around. If the original coil is being discarded due to evidence of arcing at the tower, always replace the nipple or boot on the coil end of the high-tension lead. Any arcing at the tower carbonizes the nipple, so placing it on a new coil will invariably cause another coil failure.

HIGH-PERFORMANCE COILS

If anything, the number of special high-performance coils on the market has decreased in recent years. There are two reasons for this. First, production coils are more reliable than they were in years past, and secondly, many car makers offer factory-installed high-performance ignition systems as an option.

In most cases, you don't need a high-performance coil. If a plug re-

quires only 10,000 volts to jump its gap, then a "super coil" advertised to produce 40,000 volts will produce just 10,000 volts for that same plug under the same conditions. As the plugs wear, their gaps increase and they require more voltage to fire them. In this case, or in the case of oil-fouled plugs, a high-performance coil will produce the necessary additional voltage.

A stock coil is also designed to produce enough voltage to keep an engine firing up to a certain rpm. At high engine speeds the points are closed for only a very short time. This gives the coil less time to become saturated with current, resulting in lower voltage to the plugs. If an engine has been modified to increase its maximum rpm output, then a stock coil may be insufficient at these higher engine speeds, so a high-performance coil would be needed.

If your old coil is weak, you might want to buy a high-performance coil. If you do, be sure it is made for your car and that you hook it up exactly according to instructions. A non-stock coil can be designed to operate with or without primary resistance. The instructions with the coil should be specific on that point. If hooked up wrong, the coil will either put out a very weak spark or overheat and possibly fail.

Before you buy a new coil of any kind, go over the rest of the ignition system pretty thoroughly. Unless you do, you may never obtain any benefit from the replacement. Remember, no hop-up part can cure an engine that's in need of a complete tune-up, valve job or overhaul.

ELECTRONIC IGNITION SYSTEMS

The biggest automotive advance in recent years has been the development of electronic ignitions. There are several different types. In the most common factory installations, the biggest advantage is that the troublesome distributor points are deleted and the primary current is switched on and off by electronic components. As far as the coil is concerned, however, its function if not always its shape has remained unchanged.

In Ford electronic systems, the coil has retained its traditional shape and is still mounted in the engine compartment separately from the distributor. However, in several GM inline engines, though the coil is also mounted separately, its shape is new. It looks like a little transformer. And in GM's HEI (High-Energy Ignition) for V-8's, the coil is mounted right in the distributor cap. In HEI, the wire from the ignition switch to the coil is *not* a resistance wire, since the amplifier module automatically controls the dwell period, limiting it at low rpm and extending it at high rpm.

Factory-installed electronic ignitions tend to be of the inductive-discharge type. That is, they operate like normal ignitions except for the substitution of electronic components for the points. Many aftermarket systems, though, are of the capacitative-discharge (CD) type. In these, the discharge of a capacitor is what surges through the coil's primary; its rapid rise and collapse trigger the secondary discharge to the spark plugs.

The advantages of a CD system are that the capacitor's discharge is of considerably higher voltage than the battery voltage, so the coil's secondary voltage is correspondingly higher. Since the primary voltage is high, the coil does not need a lengthy dwell period in order to establish the magnetic field, so it can operate effectively at very high engine rpm.

However, aftermarket CD systems are usually designed to operate in conjunction with the points. They are "bolt-ons," in other words, so you will still have some problems with the points, including the need for periodic replacement. A plus is that point life is greatly extended, since CD systems cut down on the current across the points, preventing point arcing and burning.

Because the primary current is less, the increased primary voltage does not harm stock ignition components, so your original coil can still be used. If your car is an older model not equipped with factory electronic ignition, it could greatly benefit from the installation of a CD system. 🐛

3

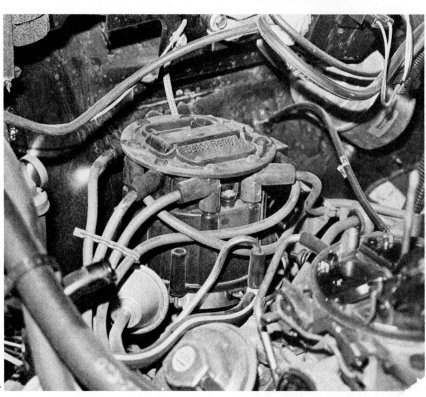

1. A favorite replacement coil among performance enthusiasts for many years was Mallory's Flash Fire. Its molded, one-piece construction made it durable, and its terminal locations prevented any flashover during wet weather.

2. If the coil seems to be the culprit that's causing ignition troubles, it should be thoroughly tested by an automotive electrical shop. Luckily, most replacement coils are not expensive.

3. The Mallory Voltmaster Mark II is a popular replacement coil of great performance and extreme reliability.

4. GM's High-Energy Ignition system for V-8 engines has the coil mounted integrally with the distributor cap. A breakerless electronic ignition system of the inductive-discharge type, the HEI distributor cap needs only one wire from the ignition switch; all other connections are internal.

4

Distributors

TRANSMITTING THE SPARK IS ELECTRICALLY EASY, BUT MECHANICALLY COMPLICATED. THOSE WHO UNDERSTAND THE INS AND OUTS WILL BE REWARDED—WITH SMOOTHNESS AND POWER

The distributor is nothing more than an engine-operated switching device that is completely uncomplicated electrically, although somewhat involved mechanically. Its function in the ignition system is to switch the current supplying the coil's primary windings on and off, and to distribute the coil's high-voltage secondary output to the individual spark plugs according to the firing order of the engine. The distributor is customarily driven off the camshaft on four-stroke engines and, in the case of all American production cars, this is accomplished by a pair of helical spiral gears—one on the distributor shaft and one on the cam. The ratio of these gears is 1:1 so that, like the camshaft, the distributor shaft turns at one-half engine crankshaft speed.

The switching of the primary circuit is accomplished by the breaker points—often simply called "points." These are operated by a multi-lobed cam on the distributor shaft. In 8-cylinder engines this cam usually has eight lobes (ridges) and eight flat spots. There are ordinarily six lobes and six flat spots in the distributor of a 6-cylinder engine, four in a 4-cylinder distributor, etc. The points have a nylon or phenolic block attached to them which rides against this cam. As each lobe of the cam passes under and contacts this rubbing block the points are opened. A lobe is immediately followed by a flat spot which allows the points to close by not contacting the rubbing block. At this time, the points are kept closed by a spring, the tension of which is very important to proper ignition operation. If the point spring is weak, the points will begin to "bounce" at high rpm, causing the timing to become very erratic. A spring that's too heavy will promote rapid wear of the rubbing block and the point gap will decrease with operation. This can soon bring about a marked fall-off in performance as well as harder starting and a rough idle.

The distributor's high-tension, or secondary circuit consists solely of the *rotor* and the *cap* into which the coil's high-tension cable and the plug leads insert. The rotor is mounted on the end of the distributor shaft and conducts a spark to every cylinder of the engine with each complete rotation. The rotor is in permanent electri-

cal contact with the center terminal of the distributor cap, which in turn is connected to the high-tension lead from the coil. Along the top of the rotor lies a strap of metal that is long enough to reach close to the circle of contacts inside the cap that serve the individual spark plug leads. The amount of cam rotation necessary to put the points through one complete closing and opening cycle is just adequate to move the rotor tip from one plug-lead contact to the next. Thus, a different plug is fired each time the points open.

THE SPARK ADVANCE

It is not enough merely to direct a spark to each cylinder; it has to get there at precisely the right time. At low engine speeds the spark plug fires at approximately 3 to 10 degrees of crankshaft rotation before the piston reaches the top of its compression stroke. This gives the fuel/air mixture an instant to "light up" before it starts to expand and drive the piston down on its power stroke. The fuel/air mixture takes just about the same time to get "lit" at high engine speeds, but since the engine is turn-

ing faster, the piston would have already started down before the expanding gases could develop their "push." An engine operating under these circumstances would definitely have a steady loss of power as engine speed increased. For this reason the spark has to be fired *earlier* at high rpm than at an idle. Doing this is the job of the distributor's centrifugal spark advance mechanism.

Before 1930 all cars had manual spark advances. This usually took the form of a lever mounted "turnsignal style" on the steering column. When the driver moved out onto the highway, he advanced the spark timing by pulling the lever downward on its notched quadrant. For starting, driving at low speeds, or ascending steep hills, the spark lever was raised a few notches to retard the timing slightly. When cranking the engine, its spark control had to be placed all the way up in the full-retarded position.

Although some all-out competition sports cars and grand prix racers retained their manual spark controls until the 1940's, such units have subsequently been replaced by "automatic" advance mechanisms in all mod-

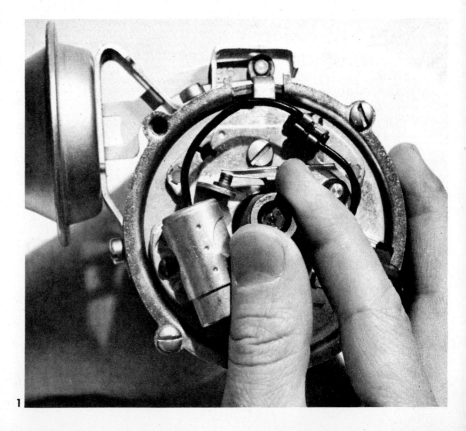

1

ern automotive applications. A number of worthwhile reasons forced this general change'over. Probably most important for the average driver was that "broken arm" type accidents—which frequently occurred when hand-cranking an engine without fully retarding the manual spark control—were all but eliminated by automatic advance devices. Crank starting, you may recall, was a feature retained on many cars for over 20 years after introduction of the electric starter.

Another reason for abandoning manual spark controls was the greatly increased compression ratios and higher rpm of later-model engines. 35 years ago a real idiot could knock the tops of all four pistons out of a Model A Ford by lugging the engine on a steep grade without retarding the spark. Think of what his grandson could do to a 454 Corvette without the safeguards built into the automatic advance unit of its distributor!

There are currently three spark advances in common use. The first is the pure centrifugal type, found most-ly in special high-performance hot rod distributors, Ford high-performance cars, '68 and '69 L88 427 'Vettes, VW transporters, early VW Beetles, Porsches and the Formula Vee race cars. This unit operates quite simply by just advancing the spark as engine revs increase, and retarding it as rpm approaches an idle. Its chief disadvantages are relatively poor low-speed economy and the possibility of excessive advance under certain full-throttle conditions.

The pure vacuum-advance distributor has had wide use both in the U.S. and abroad, but in recent years its only significant application has been on Ford's economy 6's with Loadomatic distributors, and late VW passenger cars. Vacuum advances on VW's function well enough under most everyday driving conditions, but tend to limit top speed and full-throttle acceleration. This is the reason they are usually replaced with centrifugal advance distributors when VW engines are installed in race cars or dune buggies.

For many years the only distributor used on Ford passenger cars was the Loadomatic. It was made by the Holley Carburetor Co., the same people who make the famous 4-barrel carburetors.

The third type of distributor uses both centrifugal *and* vacuum advances. This "dual advance" type is found on the vast majority of both domestic and foreign cars. The vacuum advance unit receives its vacuum supply from one of two sources—from either *below* the throttle valves (intake manifold vacuum) or from a location *above* the carburetor throttle valves (spark-ported vacuum). *Manifold vacuum is highest* at idle and *decreases* as the throttle valves open but *spark-ported vacuum* functions differently for it is *lowest* at idle but *increases* with throttle opening. During idle and part throttle running, manifold vacuum advances the spark for more economical operation but, when the throttle is opened, vacuum advance is not provided, thereby reducing the chances of engine "ping" or damag-

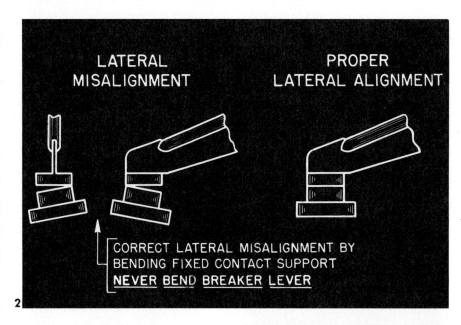

LATERAL MISALIGNMENT

PROPER LATERAL ALIGNMENT

CORRECT LATERAL MISALIGNMENT BY BENDING FIXED CONTACT SUPPORT
NEVER BEND BREAKER LEVER

2

1. The condition of the centrifugal advance mechanism can be checked quickly by wiggling the cam while holding the distributor shaft stationary. Excessive free-play means that the unit needs attention. Cam should move only against obvious spring pressure.

2. Bad alignment shortens point life considerably, and the result is a poor spark because of insufficient point contact.

3. Points should be aligned by bending the stationary contact only. Don't worry about it breaking off; it is made of a metal that can take quite a bit of flexing.

4. With a wide gap, the dwell is small. But as the rubbing block begins to wear, the gap closes and the dwell becomes larger.

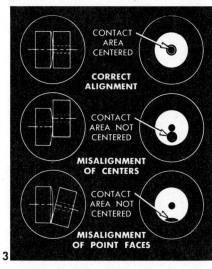

CONTACT AREA CENTERED

CORRECT ALIGNMENT

CONTACT AREA NOT CENTERED

MISALIGNMENT OF CENTERS

CONTACT AREA NOT CENTERED

MISALIGNMENT OF POINT FACES

3

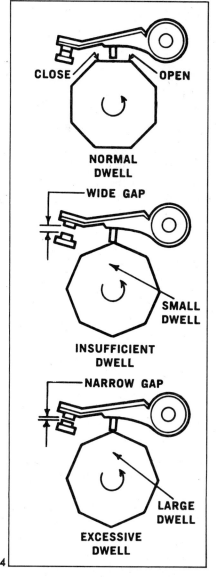

CLOSE   OPEN

NORMAL DWELL

WIDE GAP

SMALL DWELL

INSUFFICIENT DWELL

NARROW GAP

LARGE DWELL

EXCESSIVE DWELL

4

Distributors

ing detonation. Since 1966, most manufacturers have switched over to spark-ported vacuum for emissions reasons. Spark-ported vacuum is more tailored to the performance and economy demands of the engine. It is not available at idle or any other time the throttle closes, so the spark is not advanced. As the throttle opens, vacuum increases and timing advances to increase performance and economy when you need it most—that is, as the throttle opens. The centrifugal advance ensures the best settings for maximum acceleration rates and top speed. The two advance methods work independently of each other, according to the demands of the engine at the time.

All vacuum advance units on dual-advance distributors are controlled by either intake manifold vacuum or spark-ported vacuum. Regardless of vacuum source, all single-diaphragm and single-action diaphragm units operate in the same manner. A tube running from a special vacuum port above or below the throttle valves is connected to a vacuum chamber on the distributor. Inside the vacuum chamber is a thin diaphragm that separates the chamber into two halves. One side is exposed to vacuum and the other to the ambient pressure of the outside air. When there is vacuum in the chamber, air pressure deflects the diaphragm against its spring loading so that a rod attached to it can advance the timing of the spark by rotating the breaker plate. This changes the relative position of the breaker point rubbing block and the distributor cam. When vacuum drops, the diaphragm in the vacuum chamber is not so greatly deflected, retarding the spark timing slightly. The only significant departure from this system is the distributor used on older Chevrolet 6-cylinder engines. On these cars the vacuum unit moved the entire distributor body, not just the breaker plate.

The centrifugal advance works by changing the position of the cam in relation to the distributor shaft. This is accomplished by means of two governor weights held close to the distributor shaft by small springs. As the shaft's speed of rotation builds up, the weights tend to fly apart, stretching the springs. Pins on the weights act against a plate fitted to the base of the distributor cam. The further the springs allow the weights to fly out, the further the cam's position—and the spark timing—is advanced. The precisely calibrated tension of the springs is therefore the prime controlling factor in the operation of a centrifugal advance.

Automakers provide accurate data on advance curves, etc. in the shop manual for your particular make and model car. Applying this information, however, requires special testing equipment that is not generally available to the home mechanic. The important thing to remember is that any defects that thorough machine testing might uncover are usually the direct result of dirt, lack of lubrication, wear or faulty parts in the distributor. We'll talk about shop tests in the ignition tuning chapter, including a rundown on some of the machines and test devices used, but right now let's stick to things you can do yourself with a minimum of reliance on professional methods. Most repairs are just a matter of cleaning, lubing or replacing.

TROUBLESHOOTING

You can, in most instances, detect improper distributor operation by the way the car behaves. Slow cranking when the engine is warm, backfiring, noticeable losses in performance, ragged idling or "breaking up" at high speeds are some of the usual symptoms. If the compression is

1

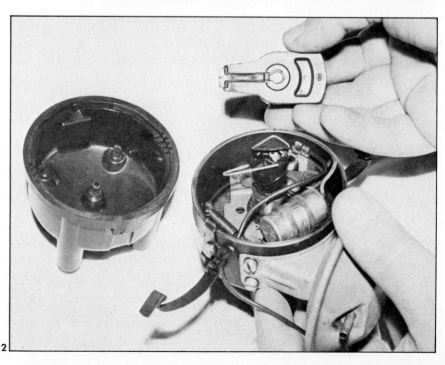

2

good, the carburetor properly adjusted and not leaking and the ignition system in otherwise perfect shape, the distributor and its advance mechanism deserve a close inspection. In fact, just by checking, cleaning and lubricating the distributor each time it is removed to install new points, you can usually prevent most trouble before it ever has a chance to affect the engine's operation.

On many cars, you can check the condition of the diaphragm in the vacuum advance mechanism quite easily without even removing the distributor from the car. Just disconnect the vacuum line from the distributor to the carburetor and take the cap off the distributor. Move the breaker plate by hand until the full-advanced position is attained, being careful not to bend the points. Then place your finger over the vacuum port and release the breaker plate. It should move only very slightly and then stop. After a few seconds, remove your finger from the vacuum port. The advance mechanism should snap smartly to the full-retarded position.

If placing your finger over the vac-

1. Serial number of this distributor is on breaker plate. On some, number is located on metal band fastened around distributor housing.

2. Ever had somebody toss your distributor rotor·into a cornfield? You can make a rotor by insulating the shaft with some high-dielectric plastic electrical tape, then taping a bent wire on top of it, as shown.

3. Late-model GM distributors use slip-in leads instead of a screw. However, the slip-in lead must be used in conjunction with a radio interference shield over points.

4. Loosen the point screw slightly before trying to change the gap setting. Always check dwell on this GM 6-cylinder distributor with the engine running, because point gap may change from what it was with the engine off.

uum port will not hold the plate in the advanced position, the diaphragm is leaking and the vacuum chamber unit will have to be replaced. If the plate does not snap back to the retard position when the vacuum port is uncovered, the advance parts are binding or the spring is broken. Distributor vacuum chambers are serviced as a complete unit only, so if you find yourself with a diaphragm that leaks like a cheesecloth canoe, you'll have to buy a whole new vacuum unit. If the advance plate is binding or sticking, it can usually be put back in serviceable condition by taking it out, cleaning it and lubricating it—according to the manufacturer's recommendations, of course.

The efficiency of centrifugal advance mechanisms can be impaired by three things. The most common is plain old dirt and lack of lubrication. After a year's service the average centrifugal advance should be removed, cleaned, checked for wear and properly lubricated. This is absolutely necessary if precise action is to be obtained. The weights and linkage of the centrifugal advance must be completely clean and *lightly* lubricated with engine oil. Most distributors have a felt wick in the center of the distributor cam which needs to be regularly given a few drops of oil to keep the centrifugal advance properly oiled. The weights should be checked to see that they are free from rust or burrs which would tend to hinder their smooth movement.

Secondly, wear in the distributor shaft, its bearings, thrust washers or cam can seriously disrupt the timing and functioning of the centrifugal advance. If the distributor shaft can be shaken noticeably from side to side (with the hold-down clamp removed), the shaft or its bearings are worn. Shaft end play should be no more than .012- to .015-in. Removing the clamp permits the distributor to

move, so timing should be checked after this end-play test is made.

Most distributors have replaceable bushings in the distributor housing, but some do not, such as those used on many Chevrolets. If replaceable, the bushings or bearings can be removed with a bushing driver or an arbor press. If you don't have these tools, you can take the distributor body and the new bushings to an automotive machine shop and have the work done there.

Excessive end play can usually be corrected by installing new thrust washers on the shaft. The repair is made by driving out the pin holding the drive gear and removing it from the shaft. The shaft can then be withdrawn and checked for straightness by rolling it on a flat surface or in a V block. If all's well, the shaft can be reinserted, the washers slipped on and the gear pressed back on and pinned.

If the distributor cam shows any visible wear at all, you can bet your next month's salary that it is seriously affecting the engine's timing. In most cases this is a very inexpensive part which can be installed in a few minutes. Proper cam lubrication usually prevents such trouble, and as everybody knows, an ounce of prevention is worth a pound of replacement parts. A badly lubed cam can also affect the operation of both the centrifugal and vacuum advances by slowing the motion of the cam and breaker plate. To function perfectly, a distributor must be kept as friction-free as possible.

One final factor which can spoil the accuracy of centrifugal advance units is incorrect point spring tension. Like a poorly lubricated cam, this may also affect the operation of the vacuum advance system to some degree. The point spring tension should be adjusted if possible, but in many cases excessive or inadequate point spring tension is the result of instal-

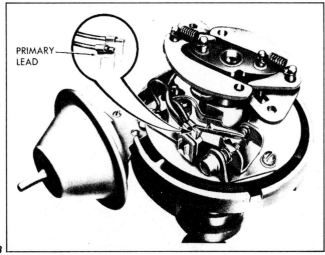

PRIMARY LEAD

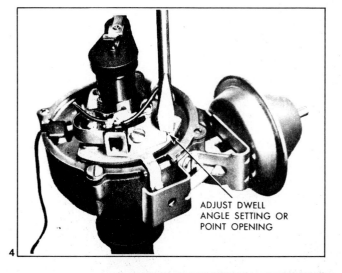

ADJUST DWELL ANGLE SETTING OR POINT OPENING

3

4

Distributors

ling the wrong points in the car. Incorrect springs installed in the centrifugal advance can also ruin its precision. When any distributor parts are replaced, make certain they are the correct ones for your particular engine, since the same distributor with different advance rates is probably used in many different makes and models. Each time you change points, mark the exact location of the distributor to ensure correct reinstallation and then remove it. Clean it thoroughly, inspect it for wear and lubricate it properly. You'll not only save yourself the cost of many repairs, your car will run better.

POINTS

The breaker points are the key electrical part of the distributor. They control not only the primary current flow in the ignition system, but ultimately the engine's spark timing. The length of time for which the points stay closed has a very important relationship to coil "saturation." That is, the longer the points feed battery current into the coil's primary windings, the stronger the magnetic field becomes. As a result, greater spark voltages are produced.

However, there is a limit to how long the points can remain closed effectively, due to the design of the distributor cam. The time during which the points remain together is called *cam angle* or *dwell*. Both terms refer to the number of degrees of distributor rotation during which the points remain closed. The initial gap to which the points are adjusted determines dwell. Although there is a specific tolerance for these settings, efficiency is lost beyond a certain point. If points are set too wide, they open gradually. This can cause excessive arcing and burning of the contacts and shorten the coil saturation time as well. If points are set too close, dwell time is increased, but "point

bounce" often occurs at higher speeds, the idle becomes rough and starting is more difficult.

There are several ways by which engineers have tried to get around the problem of coil saturation vs. efficient point operation. One notable method has been to employ two sets of points rather than one. This technique was originated on hot rods in the 1940's and later found its way into production cars. Dual points were standard in the distributors of some older Chrysler products as well as in most high-performance Fords.

The dual points accomplish their purpose by being wired into the primary circuit in such a way that battery current flows to the coil when either set is closed. Their position in relation to the cam is staggered, so that one set opens before the other. The spark isn't fired, however, until the *second* set opens to finally break the primary connection. But the *first* set is already starting to close when the second set fires the spark. The first set will therefore have been closed for many degrees before the set of points that actually initiated the spark. The result is a greatly increased total dwell time over that of a single-point unit, which in turn increases the coil saturation time to produce a hotter spark.

Many different breaker point designs are in use today. Traditionally the point set has been in two parts: the *stationary contact assembly,* which is grounded to the breaker plate of the distributor and includes the breaker point pivot post, and the *movable contact assembly,* which is insulated from ground and connected to both the condenser lead and the primary wire from the coil. The movable contact assembly includes the rubbing block that bears against the cam, as well as the spring that closes the contacts.

There has been a trend toward unifying the stationary and movable contact assemblies into a single contact set assembly. This had long been the

practice in some hot-rod distributors, but was introduced in passenger cars when GM brought out its window-type Delco-Remy distributor. In 1968 Ford Motor Co. joined the club with a *pivotless* point assembly which utilized the spring itself as the sole mounting for the movable contact.

INSTALLATION AND CARE

A lot of the troubles experienced with ignition points can be avoided by proper installation and maintenance. In granddaddy's day no one ever bothered to remove the distributor from the engine just to put in a set of points. When you raised the hood on a Model A, the engine was completely exposed—sides, front and top. The distributor was located right on top of the cylinder head, and you wouldn't have been able to work on it any better if it were sitting on your kitchen table.

But today things are different. Not only are the distributors of most cars hard to reach when installed on the engine, but even the most accessible ones are set at an angle inclined to produce eyestrain and discourage the precautionary attention that should be given to point alignment and advance

1. The felt oil wick found in the center of the cam in most distributors is for lubricating the centrifugal advance. It needs a few drops of oil at every tune-up.

2. The distributor shaft of the centrifugal advance or dual-advance distributor is separate from the distributor cam. As engine speed increases, the centrifugal advance moves the cam on the shaft, thereby opening the points sooner and advancing the ignition timing.

3. One light spring and one heavy are characteristic of most centrifugal advances. Delco V-8 distributor has weights topside where they can easily be checked.

4. Visual inspection of the distributor cap, rotor and coil can reveal numerous trouble spots. Early detection and repair will prevent more serious problems later.

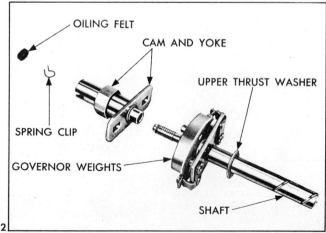

OILING FELT

CAM AND YOKE

UPPER THRUST WASHER

SPRING CLIP

GOVERNOR WEIGHTS

SHAFT

mechanism lubrication. Therefore, you should pull the distributor out of the car if you are going to do a first-class job.

Undoubtedly the thing that keeps many tinkerers from taking out the distributor for point installation is the fear that they won't be able to reinstall the thing correctly once the job's done. Yes, sometimes it does take a little coaxing to get the oil pump drive to engage and the gears to mesh properly, but you'll find that with proper techniques you can make the job a "no sweat" affair. After you've done it once or twice on your own car, you could probably repeat it blindfolded.

3

First, always aim the rotor in the same direction before pulling the distributor. Aiming it at the No. 1 cylinder is all right if it's your own car that you're working on, but if you work on many makes it's a better idea to simply pick a definite location for the rotor in relation to the car, regardless of whether it points to a timing mark or not. This saves the time it takes to locate marks and try to remember from one make to another where the darn thing should be headed. Probably the best way is to simply turn the engine until the rotor is pointed directly at the front of the car. You also have to remember the position of the distributor body, so that lines and

wires will hook up easily when you put it back.

After you've marked the rotor and body positions—at least mentally—you can remove the distributor hold-down clamp and pull the distributor out. As the distributor is withdrawn, one of two things will happen. First, the rotor may not move at all. Second, it may rotate just a small amount as the helical gears disengage.

If the distributor is the type that is driven by the oil pump gear, the rotor will not turn. Also, you will see no gear on the end of the distributor shaft after it's out of the car. If it does turn, remember (or mark) the rotor's final position in relation to its original location. When reinstalling the distributor, all you'll have to do is place the rotor in the final position and insert the unit into the engine. The gears should engage and turn the rotor back to its intitial place.

On a few cars, the oil pump drive may not align with the tang on the distributor shaft end. If this happens, don't panic. Just reach down into the distributor hole with a long screwdriver and turn the oil pump drive until it is in the right position.

The professional mechanic doesn't bother with the screwdriver technique. Once he has the gears engaged, he holds the distributor down with one hand and hits his remote start button with the other. As the engine rotates, the oil pump drive eventually lines up and the distributor will drop that final quarter inch into cor-

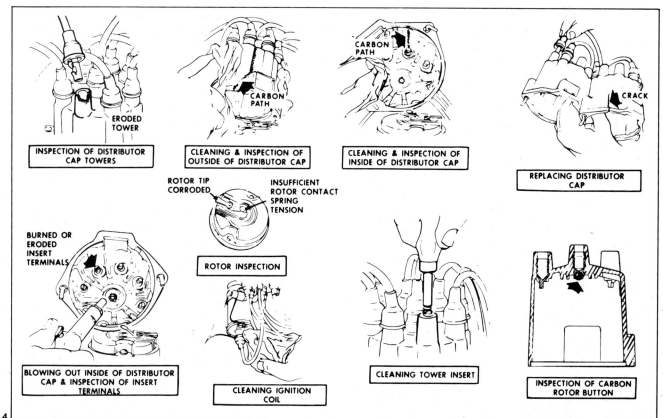

INSPECTION OF DISTRIBUTOR CAP TOWERS

CLEANING & INSPECTION OF OUTSIDE OF DISTRIBUTOR CAP

CLEANING & INSPECTION OF INSIDE OF DISTRIBUTOR CAP

REPLACING DISTRIBUTOR CAP

BLOWING OUT INSIDE OF DISTRIBUTOR CAP & INSPECTION OF INSERT TERMINALS

ROTOR INSPECTION

CLEANING IGNITION COIL

CLEANING TOWER INSERT

INSPECTION OF CARBON ROTOR BUTTON

4

rect position. Don't try this method yourself unless you are sure you have the gears meshed right.

TIMING THE ENGINE

If the engine is accidentally rotated while the distributor is out—go shoot yourself. No, it's not really that bad. All you have to do is remove the spark plug from the No. 1 cylinder and hold your thumb over the plug hole while an assistant turns the engine over. Stop when the piston is at top dead center (TDC) on the compression stroke, as evidenced by the compressed air pushing your thumb away from the hole. Practice it several times until you are sure that the piston is on top dead center of the compression stroke. If it is, then the slash or mark on the crankshaft pulley or flywheel should align with the stationary mark on the engine. If the stationary mark is calibrated in degrees, then the slash should align with 0°—this is TDC. If you can see the piston through the hole or feel it with a broom straw, then the TDC positioning is completely verified.

Once you have the piston at TDC in the No. 1 cylinder, find out which wire goes to that cylinder. It will be easy if the wires and cap are still in position on the engine. Once you have found the right wire, all you have to do is insert the distributor so that the rotor points directly to the No. 1 cylinder wire tower in the cap (with the cap in an installed position) and position the distributor body so that the points are just ready to open. You can determine exactly when the points open by placing a piece of tissue or thin paper between them. The instant the points open, the paper will come loose.

If you keep the rotor pointing to the correct wire tower and are sure the points are just about to open, then you can insert the distributor in any position relative to the engine block. It makes no difference to the timing of the engine. However, only the original, stock position will allow you to put the cap on the distributor without twisting the plug wires into a pretzel. Also, any vacuum lines or wires will hook up more easily if you put the distributor body back in the original position.

Snug down the distributor hold-down bolt and connect all the wires and the cap. The engine should fire up. If it won't, you probably made one of two common mistakes: (1) You thought the points were positioned about to open when they were actually about to close. Double-check the rotation of the cam. (2) The piston was on the exhaust stroke instead of the compression stroke.

Suppose somebody not only turned the engine over with the distributor out, but also pulled all the wires out of the cap and threw them away. What then? Don't panic. The only problem here is that you must know the firing order and cylinder numbering sequence of the engine. The firing order is usually stamped on the intake manifold or other visible engine location. Also, many distributor caps have the No. 1 cylinder wire tower marked with a "1." If the cap is not so marked, then time any one cap tower to the No. 1 cylinder. Then connect the next segment in the distributor cap to the next cylinder in the firing order, until you have worked your way all around the cap in the direction of rotation. When starting from scratch this way, be sure to position the distributor body so that any vacuum lines, tach drives, etc. will hook up easily.

POINT ALIGNMENT

For maximum efficiency and minimum deterioration, the contacts must meet accurately, both horizontally and vertically as well as at 0° angle. If the mismatching is severe, you should probably return the points to the dealer and demand a better-made set. In most cases, however, a little judicious bending of the stationary contact mount will correct minor alignment problems. Any major bending is of questionable merit when weighed against the possibility of irreparable damage.

The points supplied on many foreign cars, including some VW's, have a fiber washer installed on the breaker point pivot post between the stationary and movable point assemblies. This washer can be filed to correct vertical alignment errors, since the construction of the movable point arm is such that bending it is impossible.

There is one exception to this business of point alignment, and that's the pivotless points used by Ford. According to a Ford service bulletin, you can expect a slight irregularity in their wear pattern; it's normal. So stop condemning these points or the man who installed them.

1. The distributor cap is an important part of the ignition's secondary circuit. Unless it is kept clean and free of moisture, serious trouble can develop. This cap has a carbon track between two of its plug-lead terminals which cuts off spark to one of the cylinders.

2. By laying this rotor inside the cap, it's obvious that rotor selection is important. Installing a rotor that's too short means that the spark has to jump a greater distance before getting to the plugs. This error increases secondary voltage requirement in the same way that increasing plug gap does.

3. Correct rotor has proper clearance with distributor cap terminal for minimum voltage loss.

4. Rotor gap in this distributor is very close. Late-model cars have an increased rotor gap to help shorten spark duration, thereby reducing radio and TV interference.

After the points are checked for alignment and any discrepancies corrected, they can be installed in the distributor and adjusted to specs. This calls for a set of flat feeler gauges or an electronic dwell meter. Although most service manuals give specifications in *degrees of dwell* or *cam angle* as measured with a dwell meter, setting gap with a feeler gauge can be just about as accurate. But don't ever attempt to employ a feeler gauge on used points. The slightest pitting of the points results in an inaccurate measurement.

When new points are installed, some mechanics like to adjust the gap .002- to .003-in. wider than specified to compensate for initial rubbing block wear. It's probably better practice to simply recheck the gap after a hundred miles or so, particularly if you want top performance from the new set of points right away.

Rubbing block wear can be a real problem unless the cam is properly lubricated. Vaseline and other greases with a low melting point should not be used. They are rapidly broken down by engine heat and thrown off the moving parts to short out the points. Never use brake shoe grease. It dries hard, then grinds the rubbing block down to a nub quicker than sandpaper. Wheel bearing, chassis, lube, rear-end, goose and bear grease should also be avoided. There might have been some excuse for using the wrong grease years ago, when distributor cam grease was hard to find, but now it can be purchased in almost any large auto parts store. A small tube lasts long enough to lube every distributor cam you will ever see. We have been saving the little pellet of grease that comes with some new point sets and have found that one pellet supplies enough grease for several distributors.

We should say a word here about those circular files that are sold for the purpose of "seating" the rubbing block. We have used them, and in every instance the point gap closed up in just a few thousand miles. The file removes the burnish put on the block at the factory and leaves a rough surface that in our experience wears out much faster.

Some distributors, such as the Delco-Remy, have an oil-saturated wick that distributes lubrication to the cam. This wick should be reversed in its retainer at 12,000 miles and replaced every 20,000 miles. It should never be oiled. A new wick is included as part of some replacement point sets. For points without a lubricating wick, a light smear of rubbing block grease works very well for limiting rubbing block friction and wear.

This is one occasion when it's very handy to have the distributor out of the car. By rotating the shaft by hand, you can work in the lubricant and ensure that it is spread evenly on the cam and thoroughly fills the pores of the rubbing block. Nothing else can do quite so much damage and cause so much trouble as oil on the point contacts, so go easy.

The practice of merely smoothing used points with a point file is of dubious value. While badly pitted points can quickly be made reusable by filing them, the surfaces are left rougher than they should be. This only reduces the effective contact area and speeds further pitting on the faces. Another thing to remember is that the tungsten contacts must not be filed so much that they will burn through into the softer metal underneath. The tungsten facing on the contacts of many stock point sets is so thin that even one filing will sometimes seriously weaken the facings.

Filing should only be the first step in reconditioning points. After filing, they should be honed mirror-smooth with either a fine stone or crocus cloth. Points dressed by this method will have the appearance and efficiency of a brand-new set. However, one must be very careful to hone the surfaces absolutely flat—not to a bulging, rounded contour which would severely reduce the effective contact area and result in excessive localized burning.

After filing (only if absolutely necessary), honing and polishing, the points may require slight realignment as described above. It should be remembered that points which show signs of severe burning and discoloration or which have developed deep pits indicate an imbalance in the ignition system which must be corrected or the trouble will soon recur. This correction can usually be taken care of by checking and replacing the condenser.

Contact point burning may also result from an abnormally high primary voltage or the presence of oil or other foreign matter on the point surfaces. Oil or crankcase vapors that work up around the distributor shaft are a frequent cause of point burning, but one that is easy to detect since the oil produces a smudgy line on the distributor's breaker plate directly under the contacts. Over-oiled parts, clogged engine breather pipes or plugged PCV valves are the usual cause of this. Anything other than a lightly frosted appearance of the contacts should be considered abnormal.

THE CONDENSER

If you ask an electrical engineer what the condenser does in the ignition system, you will get several answers, because the condenser does several things. Its primary purpose is to create a clean cutoff of current flow when the points open. Current that might arc across the space between the points finds the condenser a greater attraction and rushes into it to create an unbalanced condition. Without the condenser, induced cur-

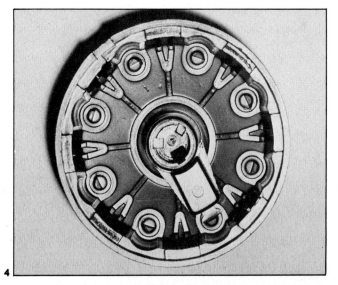

3   4

rent in the primary would flow across the point gap, bleeding off the energy in the coil and resulting in no spark at the plug.

Because the condenser creates a clean break as the points open, some people think its only purpose is to reduce arcing at the points. That's like saying that the purpose of a horse is to create horse manure. It's a useful by-product, but not the primary purpose of a horse. The condenser is there to help the coil do its job. Reduction of arcing and longer point life are merely a bonus.

The condenser is a very rugged and reliable part of the ignition system. There is absolutely no reason to replace it unless actual testing proves it to be weak. Nor is there any need to replace the condenser with each change of points, although this is routinely done at many garages. It takes less time to put in a new condenser than it does to test the old one. These days, when a mechanic's time is so costly, condenser testing is almost a lost art.

If an engine misfires at high speed or if the breaker points become burned and pitted after only a short time in service, the condenser is often suspected of being at fault. However, simply changing the condenser may be money down the drain. The misfiring could be caused by spark plugs or high-tension cables that have an excessive voltage requirement, while oil on the points is probably responsible for the burning and pitting of the contacts.

In many cases, apparent condenser trouble is due not to a bad condenser but to a poor ground contact. A very large percentage of condenser trouble can be eliminated by simply making sure that all external connections are clean and tight. This applies par-ticularly to the condenser mounting strap, which must be in good electrical contact with the distributor. When a new condenser is installed or the old one replaced after testing, the mounting strap and the part of the distributor it attaches to should be brightened with emery paper if necessary to ensure a perfect ground for the case.

The construction of the condenser has a definite bearing on its efficiency and resistance to failures. Inside the condenser's sealed case are two rolled strips of foil which are separated from one another, sandwich fashion, by strips of thin paper impregnated with an insulating compound. One strip of foil is pressed into contact with the condenser's case, while the other presses against a metal disc soldered to the condenser's lead wire. Poor contact of the foil with either the condenser case or the lead-in wire is a frequent source of condenser failure. Often vibration causes interrupted contact and results in erratic ignition.

The other major cause of condenser breakdowns is the use of a low-quality dielectric (insulation) which absorbs moisture or allows rapid current leakage. These problems are typical of cheap replacement condensers. A high-quality condenser combined with a clean, tight installation job should allow you to forget about condenser troubles completely.

TESTS AND CHECKS

Most contact point pitting results from an out-of-balance condition in the ignition system, causing transfer of tungsten from one contact point to the other. The result is a "mountain" on one contact and a "valley" in the other. The direction in which the material transfer takes place can be used as a basis for analysis and correction of the pitting. For example, if the material transfers from the nega-tive contact to the positive (the movable point on negative-ground cars), either the condenser capacity needs to be increased within the specifications given by the car maker or else the condenser has become weak and must be replaced. If the material transfer takes place in the opposite direction—from positive to negative—the condenser is *over* the proper capacity and must be replaced by one with a lower rating.

When testing for capacity (which is highly important in determining the automotive condenser's worth), the condenser should be tapped lightly to show up poor internal contact and hidden weaknesses. Most service garages now have condenser testers and can check the unit in your car if it is suspected of malfunctioning, but if this equipment is not available, a test condenser is a handy substitute.

A test condenser is simply a standard ignition condenser with two leads equipped with test clips soldered onto it. One clip can be placed on a good ground somewhere on the distributor housing and the other snapped onto the distributor's primary terminal. This hookup replaces or augments the condenser in the car. If the original condenser is the cause of the trouble, attaching the test condenser will immediately clear things up, unless the old condenser is grounded. In that case you will have to disconnect it to allow the test condenser to do its job. Before throwing out the old condenser, make certain that the real trouble is not merely a loose or high-resistance connection. As mentioned earlier, poor ground connections are responsible for many apparent condenser troubles.

Delco introduced a new unitary points/condenser unit for use on some '72 GM cars. Mounted on the points, the condenser is connected to the insulated point arm by two thin ribbons of metal that flex each time

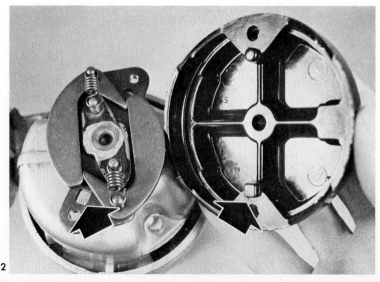

the points open and close. With no wire lead connecting the points and condenser, there's much less radio interference and therefore no need to use a metal shield over the points. But as this design is somewhat more complex to make than the older separate points/condenser, the manufacturer believed he was justified in asking a higher price for replacement units.

When the price commission took exception to the replacement unit price and insisted that it be reduced, Delco simply removed the unit from the market, so what started out as an improvement in the ignition system turned into just one more example of govermental interference in automotive design, with the customer coming out on the short end as usual.

Unfortunately, those distributors designed for the unitary points had no mounting hole for a separate condenser. Consequently, to install separate points and condenser, it became necessary to drill the proper holes or install a GM conversion kit. However, the kit and its installation added another $15-$20 to the price of a tune-up. Those people were trapped; reluctantly, they paid their $20—just in time to see the government permit the return of Delco's Uni-set. The unit returned in late '74 and appeared to be identical to the original product. Designed for GM's V-8 distributor, the Uni-set cost approximately $1.75 more than the individual condenser and point set, but installation was faster and those annoying distributor shields could be discarded. The new point sets weren't on the market for very long, though, since all Detroit vehicles were converted to pointless electronic ignitions as standard equipment by 1975.

ELECTRONIC IGNITIONS

Before Detroit arrived at breakerless electronic ignitions across the board in 1975, the auto companies had tried a variety of other transistorized and breakerless systems. Chrys-

1. Cap latch on GM V-8 distributor should seat in a little depression cast into body. A good tune-up man feels the latch with his finger to be sure it's seated, because it's almost impossible to see it.

2. GM V-8 distributor cap has round and square projections to locate it. Even so, it can be installed wrong.

3. Cam lubricator on Delco-Remy 6-cylinder distributors is a wheel-like felt device. It is prelubricated and does not need to be dipped in oil. Note quick-disconnect terminal that is used on many Delco breaker-point assemblies.

4. Some late Delco distributors used antistatic shields to cut the radio interference caused by condenser wire.

ler was first. They introduced their magnetic-pulse units on some '72 models and made them standard equipment starting on the '73's. Now every company has a magnetic system similar to Chrysler's. Conventional breaker points burn easily, because they are capable of handling only a limited amount of primary voltage. If the primary voltage could be increased, then secondary voltage would also be much higher, resulting in cleaner, longer-lasting plugs, higher voltage at higher rpm, less engine misfiring and therefore lower emissions. Transistors were the answer. GM and Chrysler eliminated the mechanical breaker points and used transistors instead to make and break the primary current. However, Ford

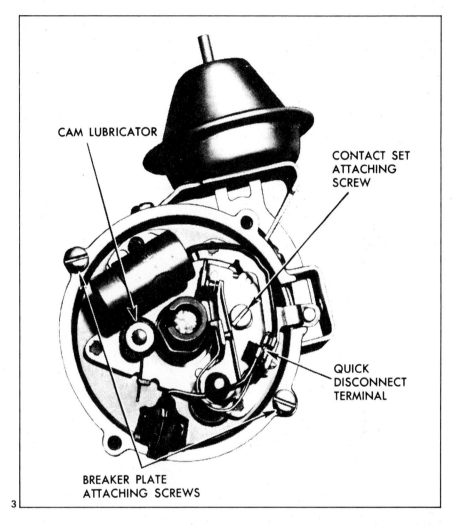

CAM LUBRICATOR

CONTACT SET ATTACHING SCREW

QUICK DISCONNECT TERMINAL

BREAKER PLATE ATTACHING SCREWS

3

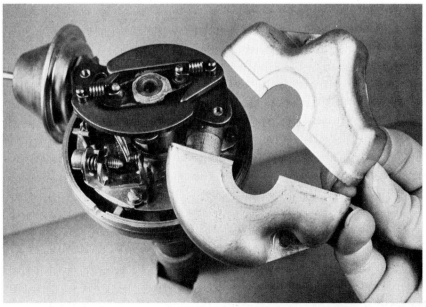

4

Distributors

used the transistors but kept the points by inserting a resistor into the wiring harness so that only a very small voltage (3.9) passed through the points. This resulted in minimal point wear.

Transistors are a great replacement, because they don't wear out, they can handle much higher voltage and they operate much faster than points. However, the transistorized control boxes (amplifiers) are much more expensive to produce than the simple points. Making them as a limited option was not very profitable, so GM (except for Pontiac) and Ford discontinued their production.

Chrysler, however, used breakerless ignition as standard equipment for '73. Producing nothing but electronic systems is much less costly than producing just a few, resulting in a relatively economical way for Chrysler to reduce emissions. The Ford and GM systems (except Pontiac) were available at a time when emissions weren't as important as they are today.

Oldsmobile and Pontiac initiated GM's Capacitor Discharge Ignition system in 1967. Pontiac soon dropped it, but Oldsmobile 4-4-2's offered it on their 1969 models. The CDI system consisted of a magnetic-pulse distributor, a transistorized ignition pulse amplifier and a special coil design. It should be remembered that this coil cannot be tested on a conventional tester.

Aside from a red coil and distributor cap, the distributor appeared to be conventional from the outside, but removing the cap exposed a quite unconventional unit. Like standard Delco distributors, the rotor and centrifugal advance weights were situated at the top, but the conventional contact cam was no longer present beneath them. In its place was an iron timer core. The timer core was mounted on the shaft and, like the conventional cam, rotated with it. On its outside rim were equally spaced projections or teeth, one for each engine cylinder.

Filling the spot usually occupied by the breaker plate, points and condenser was a round magnetic pickup assembly. This assembly consisted of a round ceramic permanent magnet, a metal pole piece and a pickup coil. The magnet was sandwiched between a mounting plate at its base and the pole piece on top, while the coil was situated between the two. The pole piece also had the same number of equally spaced teeth as the timer core. The pickup assembly, like the conventional breaker plate, was actuated by the vacuum control unit to provide vacuum advance. The centrifugal advance weights operated in their usual manner and moved the timer core for mechanical advance in the same way a contact cam is moved. The pickup coil was connected by two wires to the pulse amplifier. Within the amplifier was a circuit board decorated with transistors, resistors, capacitors, a thyristor and a transformer, but with no moving parts.

In GM's CDI system, the battery is connected to the pulse amplifier by way of the ignition switch. When the ignition is turned on, 12 volts of DC battery current travel through a primary wire to the amplifier, where the current is converted to AC for use by an AC transformer within the amplifier. The transformer raises the 12 volts to 300 and sends them on to a capacitor (condenser), where the power is momentarily stored. A zener diode in the amplifier circuit prevents overloading by limiting capacitor voltage to 300.

When the teeth on the pole piece align with the teeth on the timer core, a current pulse resulting from magnetic attraction is picked up by the pickup coil and sent through the wires to the pulse amplifier. When the amplifier is signaled by the pickup coil, the thyristor in the amplifier is triggered by a series of transistors. The 300 volts are released through a primary wire to the primary side of

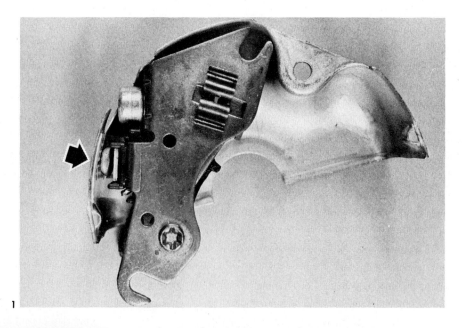

1

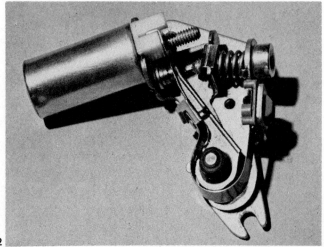

2

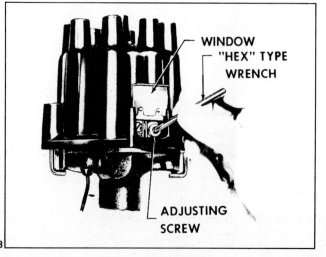

3

WINDOW

"HEX" TYPE WRENCH

ADJUSTING SCREW

the ignition coil. The voltage travels through the primary winding and out the negative terminal to ground. The capacitor is part of the primary circuit, so when all 300 volts have drained from it, the circuit is broken. Breaking the circuit in this manner has the same effect as breaking the circuit by opening conventional contact points. The result in both cases is the collapse of the magnetic field within the primary winding, causing high voltage to be induced into the secondary winding, which goes on to fire the spark plugs.

The transformer within the capacitor discharge system is responsible for providing the coil's primary winding with a much greater voltage than the 12 volts provided by the breaker point system. In the conventional system, the 12 volts in the coil are multiplied to approximately 20,000 volts by the secondary winding. The coil used in the CDI system is constructed to handle higher voltage; when 300 volts enter the primary, a voltage much

higher than 20,000 leaves the secondary. Fouled spark plugs are a common problem in high-performance cars subjected to city traffic, but the high voltage produced by the CDI system solves this problem by burning off deposits. Other transistor systems don't contain a transformer, so a greater strain is imposed upon the battery. The CDI system makes only a minimum draw on the battery, because the transformer multiplies voltage to the necessary amount. This is a great advantage in cold-weather starting, when a battery is often unable to operate at full capacity. Extended spark plug life and efficient ignition at higher engine speeds (rpm) were obtained easily by the CDI system. As with the Chrysler system or any transistor ignition system, emissions from engine misfire and point wear were minimized.

The Delco-Remy Magnetic Pulse system was first made available in '67 on the big L-88 and the 435-hp 427 Corvettes. It continued in use on the 427 until 1970, when it was adopted by the LT-1 (370-hp 350) 'Vettes and the rare 460-hp 454. The system made its last appearance in '71 on the LT-1 and the 425-hp 454.

The Magnetic Pulse ignition system consisted of a special distributor, an ignition pulse amplifier and a coil with a special primary winding. A second resistance wire was also added. It went from the coil's negative terminal to ground. The Magnetic Pulse distributor contained the same parts as the Capacitor Discharge Ignition system and operated in the same way.

Both systems included an amplifier unit, but only the CDI unit contained a transformer and a capacitor. This was the major difference between the

two systems. The CDI setup transformed 12 volts into 300 and stored it in the capacitor, which gave it an advantage over the Magnetic Pulse system by demanding less from the battery. As with CDI, the Magnetic Pulse amplifier was connected to the battery through the ignition switch. When the switch was turned on, 12 volts passed through the switch and into the amplifier. Once the car was started, this 12 volts was reduced by a resistance wire, as on conventional systems, in order to reduce the demand on the battery. Battery voltage flowed through the amplifier, into the primary winding of the coil and back to the amplifier housing to be grounded externally.

As explained above, in the CDI system battery current flowed into the amplifier, where it was transformed into 300 volts and stored in the capacitor. Unlike the Magnetic Pulse system, battery current did *not* enter the coil until signaled by the distributor. Battery current *did* enter the primary winding in the Magnetic Pulse unit before the distributor had signaled the amplifier.

As with the CDI system, when the teeth on the timer pole aligned with the teeth on the stationary pole piece, the pickup coil picked up the pulse and sent it through the wires to the amplifier. This triggered a transistor, which functioned as contact points by opening the circuit. As with conventional ignition, the magnetic field within the coil's primary winding then collapsed, so a high secondary voltage was induced into the secondary windings and went on to fire the plugs.

The Magnetic Pulse arrangement also eliminated the standard contact

1. When replacing points in a Delco distributor that has static shield, make sure the points you get have the slip-fit wire bracket. Regular screw-in type may short out on shield.

2. Delco came out with their Uniset combined points and condenser in '72, but were forced to take them off the market for a while. They came back with them in '74, just before points were eliminated entirely! With the Uniset, you don't need static shields.

3. Delco distributors have a "window" through which you can adjust point dwell with a hex-type wrench.

4. Typical Autolite-Ford dual-advance distributor combines a single-diaphragm advance unit with centrifugal advance weights located below breaker plate.

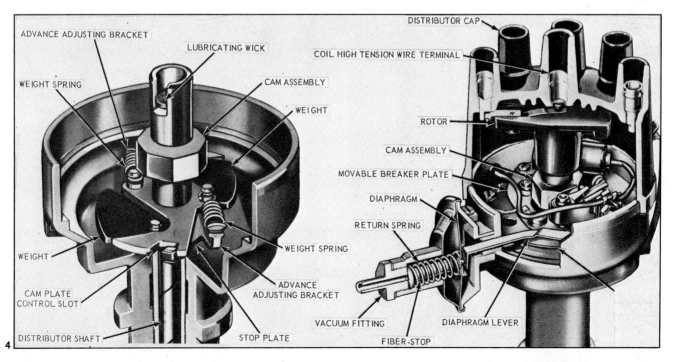

Distributors

points, so primary voltage too high for contact points could be handled and transformed into higher (but not as high as CDI) secondary voltage. This resulted in cleaner-burning, longer-lasting plugs and more efficient ignition throughout the speed range without the expense and hassle of frequent tune-ups and dwell adjustments. Tachometer readings could be taken in the conventional manner, but to avoid inaccuracy or damage to the system, it's a good idea to check with the instrument supplier first.

The Delco-Remy Unit Ignition system was optional on late '71 and all '72-'73 Pontiac Grand Prix SJ, Grand Ville and Grand Safari models equipped with the 455-cu.-in. 4-bbl. engine. This system had the same components as the Magnetic Pulse system and operated in the same way, but as the name implies, the Unitized system combined the coil and the electronic module (a new space-age name for the amplifier) into a one-piece unit. The Delco-Remy unit can be easily recognized by its strange appearance.

Ford had its own transistor system from 1964 to '67. It was used on the 427. Unlike its competitors, Ford's setup used conventional breaker points but no condenser. The system differed from the conventional by the presence of a ballast resistor block, a tachometer connecting block, a cold-start relay and a transistor control box, referred to as an amplifier. If the breaker points were closed and the ignition switch was turned on, current flowed from the battery, through the ignition switch and through the resistor block to the amplifier. The amplifier was mounted under the dash away from engine heat. Contained within it was the main transistor (PNP transistor), a condenser, a zener diode and a toroid.

The PNP transistor consisted of three parts: the top part was called the collector, the middle part the base and the lower part the emitter. When the current passed through the PNP transistor, the transistor broke it down into two circuits, one high-voltage and the other low. The high-voltage circuit was the power circuit; it went through the primary winding of the ignition coil and was grounded, while the low-voltage or switching circuit went through the closed breaker points to ground.

The resistor block in Ford's 427 system was actually two separate resistors—the collector resistor and the emitter resistor. Both were connected in series to the collector/emitter circuit of the transistor. There was also a 7.9-ohm base resistor wire be-

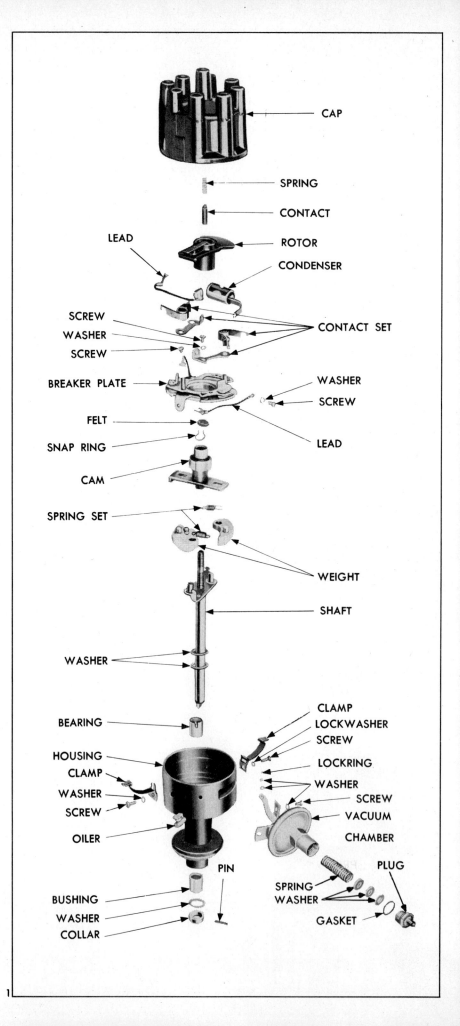

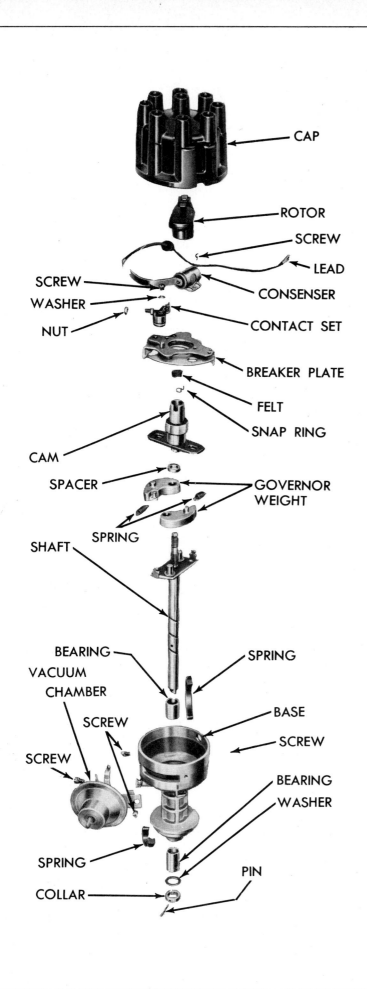

CAP

ROTOR

SCREW

LEAD

SCREW

CONSENSER

WASHER

NUT

CONTACT SET

BREAKER PLATE

FELT

SNAP RING

CAM

SPACER

GOVERNOR WEIGHT

SPRING

SHAFT

BEARING

SPRING

VACUUM CHAMBER

SCREW

SCREW

BASE

SCREW

BEARING

WASHER

SPRING

PIN

COLLAR

tween the base part of the transistor and the distributor. This wire limited the voltage across the points to 3.9 volts and resulted in long point life. Breaker point rubbing block wear was also minimal, because the contact cam was highly polished. This resulted in little change to the .020-in. point gap. It's important to realize that replacing the resistor wire with anything but a duplicate will destroy the transistor. The emitter resistor was also in series with the base resistor in the base/emitter circuit. Combining the resistances in each circuit produced a 1-amp base current, which was further reduced by the base wire to 0.5-amps at the points and a collector current to the coil of about 12 amps.

In Ford's '64-'67 system, current will not pass through the transistor if the points are open or if the primary winding is not grounded. That is, both the switching circuit and the power circuit must be completed before current will pass through the transistor. When the points are closed, current builds up in the primary winding of the coil. The instant the points open, the transistor circuit is broken and current flow stops. As with a conventional ignition, this causes the magnetic field within the primary winding to collapse. A high voltage is thereupon induced into the secondary winding and goes on to fire the plugs. However, unlike the conventional system, the primary voltage of the transistor system is much higher, because the resistance is lower and switching is much faster. The result is much greater secondary voltage at all engine speeds.

In a conventional ignition system, a tach/dwell meter is generally hooked up to the coil primary lead and ground, but to do this with the transistor system would cause inaccurate readings and probably burn out the transistor. Ford's solution to the problem was to install a tach block into the system solely to provide a place to attach tach and dwell leads. The red meter lead connects to the red tach block terminal, and the black lead connects to the black terminal on the block.

A cold-start relay is placed in the Ford circuit at the starter relay. It provides full battery current to the coil

1. Once available on many Chrysler high-performance engines was this dual-point distributor. Dual points give more coil saturation by increasing dwell time; while one point is breaking the circuit, the other is closing it. After '73 this unit was replaced by Chrysler's breakerless electronic ignition.

2. Typical Chrysler 8-cylinder distributor with centrifugal advance weights located below breaker plate. The "bearings" are actually bronze bushings.

Distributors

primary when the starter draw is high. While the engine is running, the relay contacts are closed. They open during cranking except when battery voltage drops below a certain level. At that time, the points close again and the ignition resistor is bypassed to permit full battery current for easier cold-weather starting.

Certain precautions must be observed with this Ford ignition system. As mentioned, a tach/dwell meter or a voltmeter must be connected to the tach block only and not in the conventional manner. If a tachometer is installed permanently inside the car, tach damage from the higher current is a possibility. As a precaution, a 10-in. piece of Ford resistor wire should be spliced into the tachometer leads

that go to the coil's ignition terminal and to the ignition switch.

EMISSIONS DISTRIBUTORS: CHRYSLER

In their struggle to conform to government smog regulations, the new-car makers have had to do some strange things to distributors. It all started with Chrysler Corporation's insistence that they could make an engine emission-free by modifications instead of by hanging an air pump on it. Everybody thought Chrysler was out in left field, and that eventually they would have to go to an air pump like everyone else. Up until 1972, though, Chrysler proved themselves 100% correct. However, beginning with 1972 models, tougher legislation and dirtier air finally forced Chrysler to install air pumps on certain engines sold in California.

The 1970 model year was the first in which Chrysler supplied an emissions distributor. This distributor, with one exception, was basically unchanged from the non-emissions distributors of previous years. The one exception was the addition of a retard solenoid incorporated into the vacuum advance unit of all 1970 and '71 383- and 440-cu.-in. (except the 440 with three 2-bbls.) engines.

The solenoid's function was to lower emissions during hot idle by retarding the ignition timing whenever the throttle closes. Attached to the distributor solenoid are two wires, a hot wire that receives battery voltage and a ground wire attached to the carburetor and grounded by the curb idle screw. When the engine is at normal operating temperatures and the throttle closes, the curb idle screw returns to its closed position

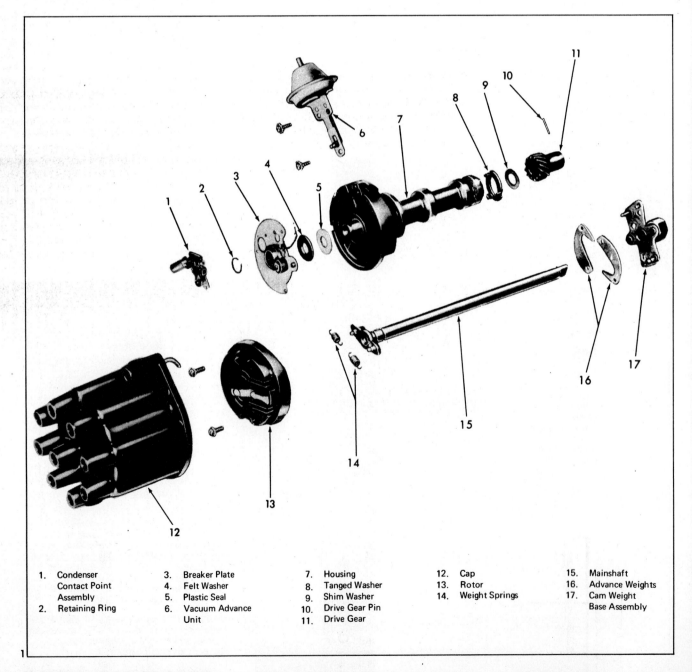

1.	Condenser Contact Point Assembly	3.	Breaker Plate	7.	Housing	12.	Cap	15.	Mainshaft
2.	Retaining Ring	4.	Felt Washer	8.	Tanged Washer	13.	Rotor	16.	Advance Weights
		5.	Plastic Seal	9.	Shim Washer	14.	Weight Springs	17.	Cam Weight
		6.	Vacuum Advance Unit	10.	Drive Gear Pin				Base Assembly
				11.	Drive Gear				

and contacts the ground wire terminal. This creates a ground for the retard solenoid on the distributor and completes the electrical circuit. This activates the solenoid, which retards the timing during hot idle (normal operating temperatures).

Whenever the engine is cold or the throttle is even partly opened, the idle screw does not contact the terminal. Therefore the solenoid is not activated, resulting in normal timing advance. Consequently, ignition timing on engines equipped with Chrysler's '70-'71 emissions distributor must be set with the engine fully warmed up, the curb idle correctly set, the throttle fully closed and the vacuum hose disconnected from the distributor and plugged. To check whether the solenoid is operating properly, first set the timing. Then, with the engine at hot idle, discon-nect the ground wire at the carburetor. The engine idle speed should increase noticeably; if not, either the solenoid is bad or the carburetor ground switch is not making contact. If the contact is good, replace the solenoid. The solenoid *must* be checked in this manner, never with meters or jumper wires. Remember, when checking dwell on these engines, inaccurate readings can be avoided by first disconnecting the solenoid.

All 1971 Chrysler Corp. cars sold in California had to be equipped with a NOx emissions control system, and all California 383's and 440's (except those with three 2-bbls.) had both the NOx system and the retard solenoid. The NOx equipment affects distributor operation, so it deserves some discussion here. To accept the emissions control system, certain engine modifications had to be made. One was the installation of a new camshaft designed to increase valve overlap, thus lowering combustion chamber temperatures. The other modification was changing to a 185° F thermostat. NOx emissions increase as combustion temperature increases, so this camshaft modification helped reduce NOx by reducing temperature. The hotter thermostat reduces HC and CO emissions by raising engine temperature.

On 1971 California Chrysler cars, the NOx control system was different and more complex on automatic transmission cars than on those with manual transmissions.

Manual transmission cars were equipped with a transmission switch, a thermal switch and a solenoid vacuum valve. These three components work to control ignition timing by controlling the vacuum supply to the distributor. If the temperature in the fresh-air cowl inlet is *above* 70° F, timing is retarded in the lower gears, but when you shift into high gear, it advances, because the engine runs cleaner at higher speeds. When the temperature is *below* 70° F, the solenoid vacuum valve is inoperative and normal vacuum advance is provided no matter what gear is selected. The thermal switch is located on the firewall and senses temperatures in the fresh-air cowl inlet. The transmission switch is mounted into the transmission housing and senses the driver's gear selection.

In these '71 Chrysler models, the solenoid vacuum valve is spliced into the vacuum line that runs from the carburetor to the distributor. It is electrically connected to the other two switches and is turned on or off by them. Running through the center of the solenoid is a vacuum passageway. Within the passageway is a spring-loaded plunger. Under certain conditions to be mentioned later, an electrical circuit to the solenoid is completed and the solenoid is energized. At this time, the magnetic field created within the solenoid windings pulls hard enough on the metal

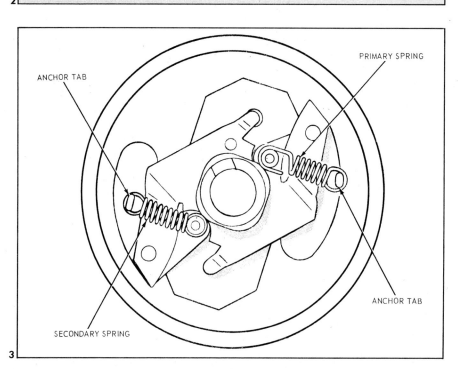

2

ROTOR
RETAINING
SCREWS — WEIGHT SPRING — WEIGHT — SHAFT — BASE — POLE PIECE — MAGNET

VACUUM ADVANCE — GEAR PIN — COIL SET

ROTOR

WEIGHT

DISTRIBUTOR CAP — BREAKER PLATE — BRASS WASHERS — FELT — HOUSING — DRIVE GEAR

3

ANCHOR TAB

PRIMARY SPRING

ANCHOR TAB

SECONDARY SPRING

1. Typical late-model Delco with the Uniset points, showing how the shaft goes through all major parts.

2. This is an exploded view of a Delco magnetic-pulse distributor. In conjunction with CD control box, unit was offered as optional equipment on '67-'69 GM performance cars.

3. The "curve" of the centrifugal advance mechanism can be adjusted on some distributors by bending the anchor tabs for the springs, as on this Pinto unit. There is usually a hole through the breaker plate to facilitate this, so that it can be done without disassembly of breaker plate.

Distributors

plunger to overcome its spring tension. The plunger is pulled tightly against the vacuum-inlet (carburetor) end of the solenoid. Pulling on the plunger also opens a vent at the other end for the purpose of bleeding off any vacuum that might be trapped within the unit. This operation shuts off the vacuum supply to the distributor and retards the timing.

At other times, the circuit to the solenoid isn't completed, so no pull is exerted on the plunger. An incomplete circuit permits the spring to pull the plunger away from the vacuum entrance, allowing carburetor vacuum to enter, pass on to the distributor and advance the timing.

The NOx emissions control system is activated by electrical switches. Knowing the path of the current is helpful in understanding the system. When the ignition switch is turned "on," battery current passes through a ballast resistor to the solenoid vacuum valve, then on through the ignition coil to the thermal switch.

The thermal switch is sensitive to heat. When the heat under the hood is *below* 70° F, the switch opens, thus breaking the circuit to the vacuum valve. An incomplete circuit to the valve prevents it from operating, so vacuum passes through to the distributor and advances the timing. If the temperature is *above* 70° F, the thermal switch stays closed, and current is permitted to pass through it and on to the transmission switch.

If the transmission is in any gear other than high, then the transmission switch will be closed and the current from the thermal switch will pass through it and be grounded. If closed, the transmission switch provides the only ground in the system; and once the current is grounded, the circuit is completed and the solenoid vacuum valve is energized. Remember—once energized, the solenoid vacuum valve shuts off the carburetor vacuum to the distributor and retards the timing. If not energized, vacuum continues as usual and the timing is advanced.

As soon as the transmission is shifted into high gear, the transmission switch is opened and the current is not grounded. If the current isn't grounded, then the solenoid is not energized and the vacuum is unaffected, resulting in normal advanced timing.

By now, you may be thoroughly confused by a jumble of details. If so, reread and look at the appropriate illustrations. The details of operation may seem to complicate what is really quite a simple system, but to form a complete, accurate picture, they must be presented.

To check out the emissions control system for proper operation, you can make a simple test. Run the engine until under-hood temperature is above 70° F. With the engine running and the transmission in neutral, disconnect the wire from the B+ connector on the ballast resistor. You should be able to feel the valve de-energize. By reconnecting the wire, you should feel it energizing and probably notice a decrease in engine speed. When high gear is selected, you should feel nothing, because the solenoid is not energized, but engine speed should increase in high gear. There may be times when the transmission switch will not function because it is not tight enough to contact its ground. Check the switch for tightness and torque to 15 ft.-lbs.

The NOx equipment is a bit more complex on Chrysler's '71 automatic transmission cars. To gain a full understanding, it's first necessary to be familiar with the stick-shift setup as explained above. The automatic transmission setup consists of the special cam, the 185° F thermostat, a speed switch, a control unit assembly and a solenoid vacuum valve. The solenoid vacuum valve is identical to the one used on the manual transmission cars and is therefore interchangeable. However, aside from the cam and thermostat, it is the *only*

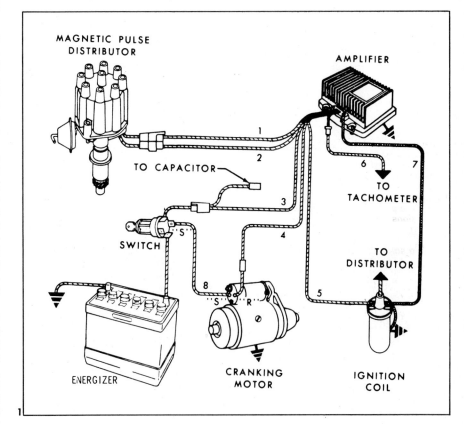

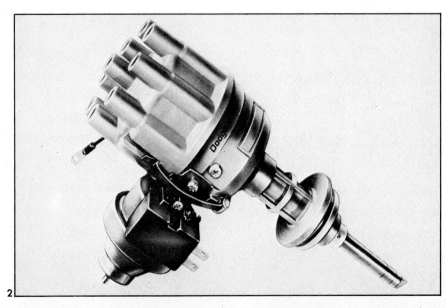

system component that can be interchanged between manual and automatic transmission cars.

The speed switch is mounted on the transmission housing and aligned with the speedometer cable or mounted in mid-cable, as on the Valiant and Dart. The switch senses vehicle speed through the speedometer cable. When the car drops below 30 mph, the switch closes and provides a ground. This energizes the solenoid and shuts off the vacuum, retarding the timing. The speed switch performs the same basic function as the transmission switch in the manual-trans setup.

The control unit assembly is located on the firewall. It contains a control module, a thermal switch and a vacuum switch. Like the thermal sensor, it senses fresh-air inlet temperature, but in addition, it senses manifold vacuum. In the automatic trans-

1. Most manufacturers came out with transistorized distributors before they all switched to breakerless magnetic units. This was the Ford unit with point-controlled transistor.

2. A retard solenoid was incorporated into the vacuum advance unit of all '70 and '71 Chrysler-product 383's and 440's. However, it was not to be found on the 6-pack 440. Its job was to lower emissions during hot idle by retarding timing.

3. The solenoid vacuum valve remained unchanged from '71 to '72. The valve is connected into the vacuum line that goes from the carburetor to the distributor. It is wired to the other two switches in the NOx system and is turned on or off by them, thereby either preventing or permitting vacuum advance.

4. The NOx wiring circuitry is quite simple on '71 manual-transmission Chrysler products; however, a bit of worn insulation could affect the whole system and increase emissions as well as decrease performance and economy.

mission version, the solenoid vacuum valve is energized to retard the timing when air temperature is *above* 70° F, when speeds are *below* 30 mph and during acceleration. During acceleration, manifold vacuum is low, so it doesn't reach the vacuum sensor. When all three of these conditions occur, vacuum is shut off to the distributor and the timing is retarded, thus reducing NOx emissions. At any other time—that is, when air temperature is *below* 70° F, at speeds *above* 30 mph or when the car is *not accelerating*—the solenoid is not energized; carburetor vacuum is permitted to reach the distributor for normal timing advance.

To make things even more confusing, there is a temperature-operated vacuum bypass valve on 1971 Chrysler Corp. California-sold 2-bbl. 383's that have automatic transmission but no air conditioning. The NOx emission control system retards timing during hot idle, and apparently this particular engine tends to overheat more easily during idle than others. The vacuum bypass valve is threaded into the water jacket and senses when the temperature reaches a dangerous level. The heat makes the valve open, allowing vacuum to reach the distributor and advance the timing. Advancing the timing increases engine speed and makes the water pump work harder to cool the engine. This valve bypasses the NOx system at this time and continues to do so until the engine temperature is back to normal. When the temperature decreases, the valve senses this and shuts, causing the NOx system to take over.

The 1972 Chrysler products retained the NOx system but discontinued one component each from the manual and automatic transmission versions. Manual transmission cars continued the transmission switch

and the solenoid vacuum valve, but no longer used the thermal switch. In '72 the under-hood temperature no longer controlled vacuum advance on stick-shift models. Dropping the thermal switch resulted in normal vacuum advance regardless of temperature. For '72, vacuum was controlled only by gear selection. The solenoid is energized to retard the timing only when lower gears are selected. It's de-energized to advance the timing when the car is shifted into high.

Automatic-transmission cars continued the speed switch, the control unit assembly and the solenoid vacuum valve. For '72, the control unit consisted of only two components instead of the three used in '71. The control module and the thermal switch were continued, but the vacuum switch of '71 was no longer used. As in '71, vacuum advance was prevented when the fresh-air inlet temperature was above 70° F and at speeds below 30 mph, but unlike '71 models, advance was not prevented during acceleration.

Chrysler's temperature-operated vacuum bypass valve was continued for '72. Its operation remained the same, although it was no longer used on the 383. The 383 was replaced in '72 by a new 400-cu.-in. engine, and the bypass valve had a new application. The valve is on some '72 California cars equipped with the 440 engine plus automatic transmission and air conditioning.

The retard solenoid of '70 and '71 was no longer used in '72. It was replaced with an advance solenoid. This solenoid is found on all Chrysler Corp. California cars equipped with the 400- and 440-cu.-in. engines and on non-California cars with the 400 engine or the manual-trans 440 with 4-bbl. The solenoid, wired to the starter relay, is energized only during starting to advance timing 7.5° for

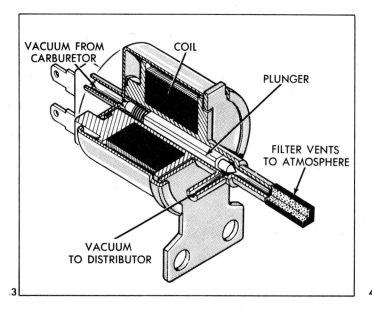

3

VACUUM FROM CARBURETOR

COIL

PLUNGER

FILTER VENTS TO ATMOSPHERE

VACUUM TO DISTRIBUTOR

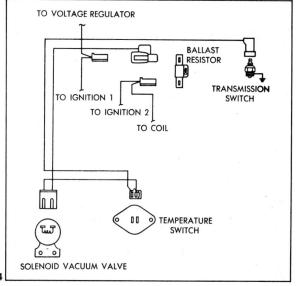

4

TO VOLTAGE REGULATOR

BALLAST RESISTOR

TO IGNITION 1

TO IGNITION 2

TO COIL

TRANSMISSION SWITCH

TEMPERATURE SWITCH

SOLENOID VACUUM VALVE

Distributors

easier starting. Once the car has started, the solenoid is de-energized and the timing returns to normal, which lowers emissions during idle. If starting the car becomes difficult, check for an inoperative solenoid.

An electronic ignition system was available on some 1972 Chrysler products and appeared as standard equipment on all Chrysler cars from 1973 on. The electronic ignition system eliminates conventional contact points and prolongs plug life. This reduces the need for frequent ignition maintenance. Regular checks of timing are not required, and dwell is not adjustable. The result is a more efficient engine and reduced emissions.

The Chrysler electronic ignition system can be identified by the presence of a double primary wire from the distributor, a dual ballast resistor on the firewall and a control unit located on the firewall or left fender shield. The primary circuit remains basically the same as the contact-point system with one significant exception: There are no contact points or condenser.

It was explained earlier that in a conventional system, the contact points perform as a switch by turning the primary current on or off. The electronic system replaces the points with a power switching transistor in the control unit. The transistor does the same job as the contact points, but faster, more efficiently and without the maintenance problems of the contact points. The secondary circuit remains the same as the conventional one, consisting of the secondary coil winding, the distributor cap and rotor, the spark plug wires and plugs and the car's frame.

Chrysler's magnetic-pulse distributor is quite conventional in appearance until you remove the cap. Then

everything but the rotor looks rather unusual. Located directly below the rotor and attached to the distributor shaft is the reluctor. The reluctor takes up the space occupied by the cam on the conventional distributor, and like the cam, it has six or eight ridges, depending on the number of engine cylinders.

Mounted directly below the reluctor is a plate almost identical to the conventional contact plate, but instead of the condenser and contact points there is a pickup coil assembly. This assembly consists of a rectangular permanent magnet sandwiched be-

tween two metal pieces. One metal piece is shaped so that it anchors the assembly to the contact plate, while the outer piece, or pole piece as it is called, is also part of the pickup coil. As the distributor shaft rotates, the reluctor rotates past the pickup unit in much the same way that the cam passes the conventional contact-point rubbing block.

During one distributor shaft revolution (equal to two crankshaft revolutions), all six or eight reluctor ridges pass close to the pickup unit. The reluctor ridges pass closer to the magnet than do its low areas, so

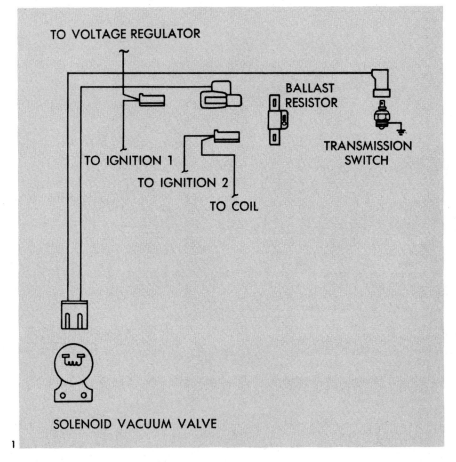

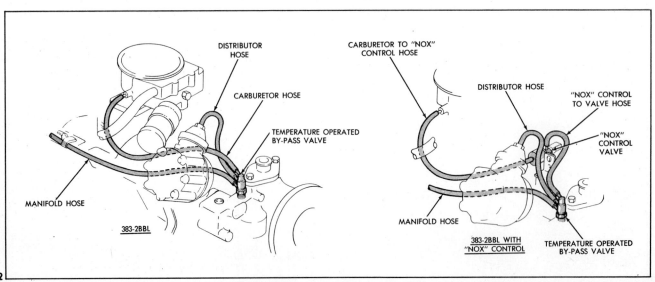

magnetic attraction is greatest at that time. Magnetic attraction is at its minimum when the space between the reluctor and the magnet increases. This occurs when the low areas of the reluctor pass the magnet. This is similar to the make and break action of the conventional breaker-point distributor.

Each time a reluctor ridge passes the magnet, the attraction is strong enough to be transferred through the pole piece to the pickup coil. This little coil is actually another magnet, but a stronger one due to the large amount of finely coiled wire contained within it. This coil produces an amplified voltage, which is then sent through the pickup coil leads to the control unit on the firewall or fender. To simplify things, one could say that a reluctor ridge signals the pickup unit each time a spark plug is to be fired. That is why there is one ridge for each plug. This signal is received

1. Wiring diagram for '72 NOx system as used on manual-transmission models. Note that temperature switch, used in '71, was dropped.

2. If your '71 or '72 Chrysler Corp. car is equipped with a bypass valve, it's wise to tag the hoses as to location before removing them.

3. The NOx wiring is a bit more complex on those '72 Chrysler products equipped with automatic transmission. As the illustration notes, the speed switch must be properly torqued to 150 in.-lbs.; any less might result in incomplete electrical contact.

4. Here's a schematic of Chrysler's electronic ignition system. The 8-cylinder is shown; however, circuitry for 6-cylinder is no different. Note the double primary wire from the distributor.

by the pickup coil and sent through the wire to the control unit.

Located within the control unit is a power switching transistor that does the job formerly done by the contact points. When the control unit receives the signal, the transistor opens the primary circuit. As with open contact points, this induces the high voltage into the ignition coil's secondary winding, which fires the spark plug.

As mentioned, dwell adjustment is not necessary. Therefore no provision was made for adjustment, although dwell readings can still be taken. The procedure for setting ignition timing remains the same as with the conventional distributor.

The last year for Chrysler's original NOx system was 1972. It was replaced by the OSAC (Orifice Spark Advance Control) system. Like the NOx system, this setup reduces NOx emissions by controlling the vacuum to the vacuum advance unit. The OSAC valve is mounted on the firewall. Contained within it is a tiny orifice which delays spark-ported vacuum (vacuum from above the carburetor throttle plates) to the distributor by approximately 17 secs. This delay occurs when going from idle to partial throttle and only when the outside temperature is 60° F or above. When the engine idles, the throttle valves are nearly closed, so spark-ported vacuum is low. At partial throttle, the valves begin to open, spark-ported vacuum increases and timing is advanced. This system is much simpler than the original NOx system but serves the same purpose. Maintenance of the OSAC system includes checking the hoses for leaks and tightness and preventing the entrance of any dirt that might clog the valve.

The temperature-operated vacuum bypass valve of '71 and '72 was still in use on some '73 engines and performed in the same way when coolant temperature at idle reached 225° F. Standard for '73 was a hotter 195° thermostat that helped reduce HC and NOx. Still available in '73 was the advance solenoid of '72. It was retained unchanged in '73, but its use was limited to the 400-cu.-in. engine with 4-bbl. carb and manual transmission.

At Chrysler Corp., emissions distributor changes were slight for '74 and '75. The '73 OSAC valve was retained for '74. Its operation was the same under identical conditions, with one exception: For '73 the valve delayed vacuum to the distributor when ambient temperature was 63° F or above. However, for '74 there was no temperature sensor, so temperature didn't affect delay. The OSAC valve was moved from the firewall to the air cleaner for '74. The temperature-operated vacuum bypass valve was renamed the Thermal Ignition Control valve (TIC) for '74, but it was the same device.

For '75 the solenoid advance was dropped from Chrysler distributors, but the distributor was the same breakerless unit introduced in '72. To protect the catalytic converter, the throttle is held open slightly to reduce unburned HC. A new speed switch receives ignition pulses from the ignition control module, and when engine speed is above 2000 rpm, a throttle position solenoid is energized to keep the throttle open. Below 2000 rpm, however, the throttle returns to normal curb idle.

In 1976, Chrysler again introduced something new that, like the electron-

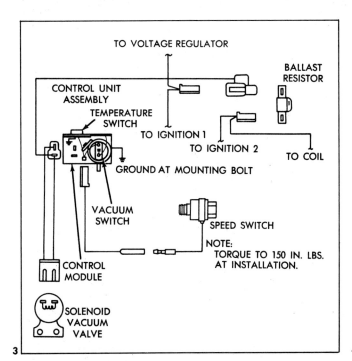

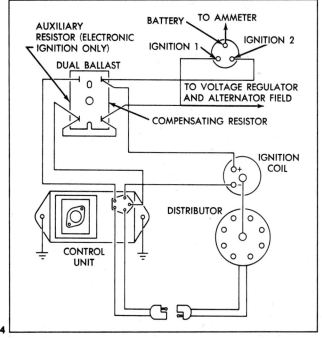

Distributors

ic ignition, may show up on all cars in the future. Called the Lean-Burn system, it was an option on some engines. It controls the timing through a small computer in an effort to reduce emissions and fuel consumption. Information from seven sensors on the engine is fed to a spark-control computer, which within milliseconds determines the exact amount of spark lead. The spark "curve" is infinitely variable for different engine operating conditions.

The "start" pickup tells the computer when the engine is cranking over so that proper timing can be supplied at that time, after which the "run" pickup takes over. The run pickup senses both engine speed and the moment when each piston comes up to TDC (Top Dead Center). Other sensors include the water temperature unit, air cleaner temperature sensor, throttle position transducer, carburetor switch sensor and a vacuum transducer. The computer puts in extra advance during the first minute of engine operation, which raises the idle for faster warm-up. Then gradually advance returns to normal. Subsequently advance is controlled by the vacuum transducer, temperature sensors and the carburetor switches. The vacuum transducer works like a normal vacuum advance that is hooked to manifold vacuum; that is, advance is greatest when vacuum is greatest. The coolant temperature sensor will not allow any extra advance below 150° F engine temperature, but when the engine is at 225° F or more, it signals the computer to allow more advance for faster idle and extra cooling.

Chrysler has even taken possible failure into consideration. If the computer malfunctions, the engine is switched into what is called the "limp-in" mode, in which the engine continues to run (although not efficiently) so that you can get to a repair facility.

The electronic Lean-Burn system so closely controls the engine's timing that leaner mixtures can be fired, thus meeting fuel economy and emission standards. The availability of this option was expanded for 1977 to other engines in the Chrysler/Dodge/Plymouth line, and we may see wider applications of the system in the future as government requirements become even stiffer.

EMISSIONS DISTRIBUTORS: GENERAL MOTORS

The following text discusses only those systems which directly affect distributor operation in regard to the reduction of harmful emissions. The majority of these systems utilize devices to control vacuum supply to the distributor. As a result, ignition timing is either retarded or advanced according to some predetermined condition, such as temperature, vehicle speed or gear selection.

The specific operation of the systems is presented below. By understanding operation of emission control systems, troubleshooting and tune-ups should become easier and more meaningful.

GM introduced its first emissions distributor by installing a thermostatic vacuum switch on some of its '66 and '67 Oldsmobiles. This switch was

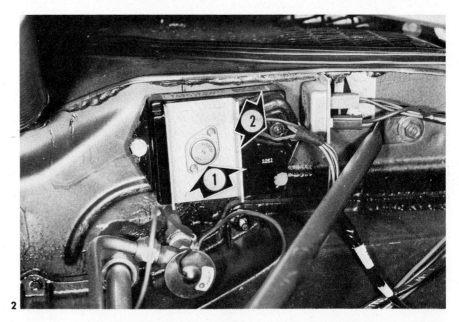

restricted to those 400- and 425-cu.-in. engines equipped with AIR (Air Injection Reactor) and air conditioning. The same switch was continued on certain engines up to and including 1970. Vacuum advance units on these AIR-equipped Oldsmobiles receive their vacuum from above the throttle valves (spark-ported), so there is no vacuum at idle or at any other time the throttle closes. The result is no advance during idle. This is to prevent detonation made possible by the leaner idle mixtures.

For those engines equipped with air-conditioning compressors, retarding the spark caused a coolant overheating problem during idle. To rem-

1. Chrysler beat everyone else to the punch when they introduced pointless electronic ignition in 1972. They made it standard in '73; others did so in '75. With all of these units, you must use a brass (nonmagnetic) feeler gauge if you have to set the reluctor-to-pickup air gap (.008-in.).

2. The control unit or "black box" is mounted on the firewall. You should periodically check the tightness of the retaining screw on the plug-in harness (2). Here you can see the switching transistor (1).

3. The rear of the EIS control unit is completely sealed with epoxy, so no repairs can be made. The whole unit must be replaced if there is a malfunction. Have your dealer check it out with his factory tester first before blaming the control unit.

4. The OSAC valve, mounted on the firewall, contains a tiny orifice which delays vacuum advance by 17 secs. A temperature-sensing device is also part of the unit. When the outside temperature is below 60° F, the orifice opens to allow vacuum flow. Hoses must be kept tight for proper operation.

5. The temperature-operated bypass valve of '71 and '72 was carried over to some engines for '73. Its operation is the same; during overheating, the OSAC system is bypassed and manifold vacuum is provided at idle to advance timing.

edy this problem, the thermostatic vacuum switch was installed. The switch connects into the water bypass hose, which runs from the water outlet to the top of the water pump. Extending from the side of the switch are three vacuum ports. One connects to the carburetor (ported vacuum), one to the intake manifold and the third to the distributor vacuum advance unit.

Contained within the switch is a sensor which functions when coolant temperature rises above 220° F. At that point, manifold vacuum (normally high at idle) is permitted to pass to the distributor for full vacuum advance. Full advance results in a faster idle, causing the water pump and fan to work harder. Since the spark fires earlier, less cylinder wall is exposed to heat, thereby lowering coolant temperature. At temperatures below 220° F, the switch is not activated and manifold vacuum is blocked, permitting only carburetor (spark-ported) vacuum to enter the distributor. The result is no vacuum advance at idle.

Pontiac soon followed Oldsmobile in 1967 with an emissions distributor of its own. A double-acting diaphragm vacuum advance appeared on some of Pontiac's California models. These Pontiacs were equipped with either AIR (smog pump) or CCS (Controlled Combustion System) in '67. The AIR system was new in '66 but found only on cars produced for California. The CCS was first used in '67 but was especially rare, because it was available only on the California-produced, low-compression (8.6:1) 400-cu.-in. Pontiac engine.

The CCS of '67 was similar in name only to the CCS of 1968 on. It consisted of a closed PCV system with a specially calibrated (leaned) carburetor and distributor in addition to the double-acting diaphragm vacuum advance unit.

All stick-shift Pontiacs ('67 and '68) equipped with AIR also included a

vacuum advance valve connected to both carburetor and manifold vacuum ports. The valve permitted vacuum advance during deceleration, when both HC and CO emissions are particularly high.

The GM double-acting diaphragm unit can be recognized by the presence of two hose connections instead of the usual single hose. The inner side of the diaphragm is the vacuum retard side and is connected by a hose to an intake manifold vacuum port. This port is located below the carburetor throttle valves, resulting in high vacuum at idle. At idle, this vacuum pulls on the retard side of the diaphragm to retard the timing 5° on 6-cylinders or 10° on the V-8's. The outer side of the diaphragm is the conventional advance side, which is connected by a hose to a port above the throttle valves.

As mentioned earlier, this spark-ported vacuum is just the opposite of manifold vacuum. Ported vacuum is very low at idle but increases with throttle opening. It reaches its peak at full throttle. Therefore, in this case of the double-acting diaphragm, normal vacuum advance is provided as the throttle opens.

How does this affect emissions output? Both HC and CO are products of the incomplete combustion that occurs mostly during idle, low speed and deceleration. At these times, the throttle valves are barely opened, so manifold vacuum is high. This manifold vacuum exerts a pull on the retard side of the diaphragm, retarding the timing. Retarded timing is necessary at idle to prevent detonation, because the AIR and CCS systems included a carburetor with a very lean fuel mixture setting. A lean mixture means less fuel in the combustion chamber and less HC and CO.

Ported vacuum was also used on some '66 and '67 Buicks and all '67 and later Cadillacs. This was Buick's only emissions-affected distributor until 1968. However, like Oldsmobile,

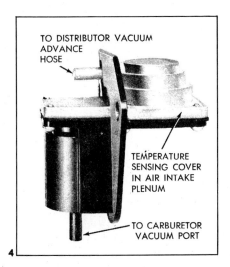

TO DISTRIBUTOR VACUUM ADVANCE HOSE

TEMPERATURE SENSING COVER IN AIR INTAKE PLENUM

TO CARBURETOR VACUUM PORT

4

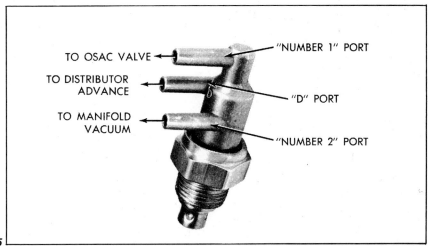

TO OSAC VALVE

TO DISTRIBUTOR ADVANCE

TO MANIFOLD VACUUM

"NUMBER 1" PORT

"D" PORT

"NUMBER 2" PORT

5

Distributors

Cadillac used a thermal vacuum switch.

The first year for GM's new Controlled Combustion System was 1968. Standard equipment for all Oldsmobiles, Pontiacs and Buicks of '68, it was retained by them and picked up by others later. The CCS uses leaner carburetors, ported vacuum for retarded initial timing, a 195° F thermostat (a hotter engine burns the fuel more completely) and a thermostatically controlled air cleaner designed to keep the incoming air at 100° F. The latter provided easier cold starts and faster warm-ups. The thermostatic vacuum switch which provided vacuum advance when high coolant temperatures occurred was retained by Oldsmobile and picked up by others for certain large engines and some air-conditioned models.

Stricter emission laws forced the introduction of GM's Transmission Controlled Spark system (TCS) in its 1970 models. The system is identical for Pontiac and Oldsmobile 6-cylinders, but differs somewhat in Olds V-8's, Buicks, Chevrolet Division cars and Cadillacs.

The TCS system reduces NOx emissions by preventing vacuum advance in the lower gears. This is accomplished through the interaction of three components: a temperature switch, a vacuum solenoid valve and a transmission switch. Vacuum for advance is permitted to reach the distributor only when the car is in high gear or reverse, or when engine temperature is below 85° F or above 220° F.

The solenoid connects into the vacuum line passing from the carburetor to the distributor. It has three vacuum ports—one inlet and two outlets. The inlet is for receiving spark-ported vacuum from the carburetor. One outlet goes to the distributor, while the other is a vent port to the carburetor air horn. Contained within the solenoid is a vertically mounted metal plunger with tapered ends. The plunger is enveloped in a coil of fine wire. When energized, its tapered end is pulled into the inlet. This prevents the entrance of ported vacuum. At the same time, any vacuum trapped within is vented to the carburetor's air horn.

The transmission switch, mounted at the transmission, is wired to the temperature switch and the solenoid valve. On stick-shift models, the switch is operated mechanically by the shift lever. The shift lever contacts the end of the switch and provides an electrical ground for it until shifted into high gear. When high gear is engaged, the switch is no longer grounded and the circuit to the solenoid is broken. The result is a de-energized solenoid. The automatic transmission switch performs the same function, but relies on fluid pressure in the direct clutch circuit to tell it when high gear or reverse is engaged. Pressure is present in this clutch circuit only when high or reverse is engaged.

When de-energized, the solenoid plunger is no longer held against the inlet port. Therefore vacuum from the carburetor is no longer blocked but is instead allowed to pass to the distributor to advance the timing. When the temperature is below 85° F or above 220° F, the temperature switch breaks its ground contact and the solenoid is de-energized, resulting in vacuum advance. The '70 Buicks and Oldsmobile V-8's use the same system but without the temperature switch. Advance is only provided in high gear or, if equipped with automatic transmission, in both high and reverse gears.

The thermal vacuum switch described earlier was used on some of these Buicks and Olds. All 1970 Cadillacs also had the switch, along with the vacuum solenoid and the transmission switch. When coolant temperature in these Cadillacs rises above 220° F, full manifold vacuum is provided at idle to advance the timing and lower the temperature. Once the temperature drops below 220° F, the outlet is shut off and spark-ported vacuum returns in high and reverse.

The TCS for '70 Chevrolet products was the same as Pontiac and Oldsmobile sixes, with three exceptions. First, the temperature switch is calibrated for temperatures below 63° F or above 232° F instead of 85° F and 220° F. Second, a time delay relay was added. This relay is a switch that stays closed for 15 secs. after the ignition is turned on. Full manifold vacuum advances the spark during this time to prevent stalling. The third exception is that all Chevys other than the 6-cylinders with synchromesh transmission used manifold vacuum instead of spark-ported. Some engines also were equipped

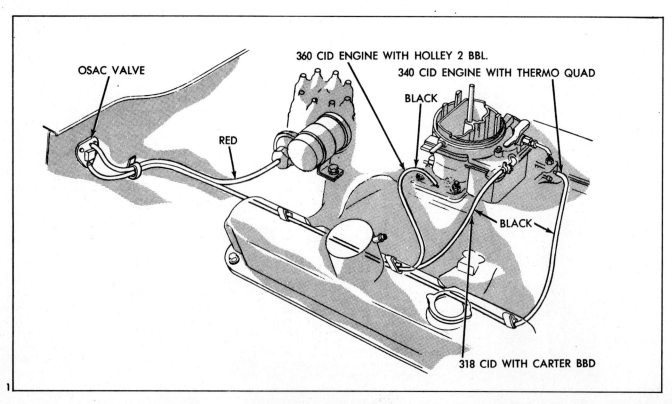

OSAC VALVE

RED

360 CID ENGINE WITH HOLLEY 2 BBL.

340 CID ENGINE WITH THERMO QUAD

BLACK

BLACK

318 CID WITH CARTER BBD

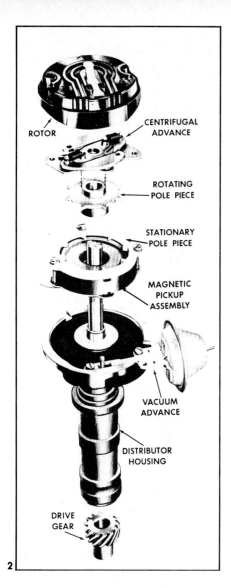

with a thermostatic vacuum switch to improve engine cooling.

Some 1971 Oldsmobiles (mostly air-conditioned models) combined the thermostatic vacuum switch (TVS) with the TCS solenoid vacuum valve into one unit. This was called the distributor vacuum control switch. However, many Oldsmobiles, particularly non-air-conditioned models, retained the TCS solenoid in its 1970 form. When coolant temperatures reached 218-224° F, expansion within the intake manifold caused an expansion pin in the vacuum control switch to move upward and unseat a ball check valve. The ball check valve opened the manifold vacuum port. At that time, full manifold vacuum advanced the timing to cool the engine, regardless of gear position. Oldsmobile 6-cylinder models used a new CEC valve to control emissions during deceleration, as explained further below.

The 1971 Buick retained the same system it used in '70, but the Cadillac system was modified slightly for 1971. For that year, an override was used to bypass the TCS solenoid when the car was in park or neutral. A new component, a neutral switch, was added to the system.

Whenever park or neutral is selected, the switch is activated. A vacuum passage within the switch opens, allowing carburetor vacuum to pass through to the distributor for advance during fast idle. At this time, the TCS solenoid is bypassed and vacuum is controlled by the thermal vacuum switch (TVS). In any other transmission positions, the passage through the neutral switch is closed and the TCS solenoid regains control of vacuum advance. The neutral switch prevents overheating in traffic by providing advance in neutral or park. The thermal vacuum switch is unaffected in its operation by the neutral switch. It continues to provide full manifold vacuum advance even at high coolant temperatures.

1. The NOx system of '72 was replaced in '73 by the OSAC system. OSAC valve is mounted on the firewall and controls NOx by delaying vacuum to the distributor for approximately 17 secs. as the throttle opens.

2. Exploded view of GM magnetic-pulse distributor used on Corvettes and Oldsmobiles before the current HEI systems were introduced across the board at GM in 1975.

3. The High-Energy Ignition now standard on all GM cars was first introduced on Pontiacs. A magnetic breakerless unit more like the Chrysler system than their former unit, the HEI can fire today's lean mixtures with high voltage from the special coil mounted in the cap, and wiring is a lot simpler than before.

For 1971, 6-cylinder Pontiacs and Oldsmobiles and all Chevrolets used a new Combination Emission Control system (CEC). Some Pontiac V-8's used the '70 TCS system, while others combined the TCS with TVS, as did some Oldsmobiles. The CEC system retained the TCS switch and other TCS components and operated in a similar way. However, the TCS solenoid was replaced by a CEC solenoid valve.

Like the TCS valve, the solenoid shuts off vacuum advance in the low forward gears. That's where the similarity ends. The CEC valve performs an additional function.

Both HC and CO emissions are high during deceleration. If the throttle is allowed to close down to the curb idle position during deceleration, a high vacuum results. This pulls huge amounts of fuel in through the carburetor idle system. Engineers found that by keeping the throttle at a slightly greater opening, vacuum is reduced and fewer emissions are created, because the mixture is not so rich. The CEC valve performs this throttle-opening function.

Like the TCS solenoid, the CEC solenoid also contains a metal plunger with a tapered end. This plunger is also enveloped in a coil of fine wire which, when energized, pulls the plunger away from the vacuum port and permits vacuum to pass to the distributor for timing advance. However, the plunger in the CEC solenoid is longer than the TCS plunger and has a screwhead on its end which contacts the throttle lever. When the solenoid is energized, the tapered end of the plunger moves away from the vacuum port, allowing vacuum advance. At the same time, the screwhead end moves toward the throttle lever and rests against it to prevent it from closing completely. As mentioned earlier, opening the throttle allows more airflow. Extra air leans the mixture and reduces HC and CO emissions during deceleration. The CEC valve does both jobs at once, so that anytime there is vacuum advance, there is also greater throttle opening.

The TCS solenoid is normally energized, so vacuum to the distributor is blocked until high gear is selected. At that time, the circuit is broken, the solenoid is de-energized and the plunger moves away from the vacuum port, permitting vacuum to pass to the distributor. The operation of the CEC solenoid is just the opposite. Normally the CEC solenoid is de-energized and vacuum is blocked. When high gear is selected, current passes through the solenoid to energize it, the plunger is moved away from the vacuum port and vacuum goes to the distributor.

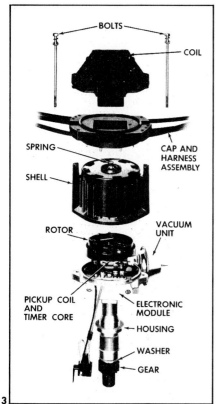

Distributors

Situated at the screwhead end of the CEC solenoid are a vent and a clean air filter. When the solenoid is de-energized, vacuum to the distributor is blocked. Any vacuum trapped within the solenoid or vacuum advance is bled off to the atmosphere through this filter and vent. When the solenoid is energized, the plunger moves to the other end, which opens up the vacuum port and blocks the air vent.

The solenoid is controlled by a transmission switch, a temperature switch, a 15-sec. time delay relay and a reversing relay. The latter provides a ground for the transmission switch. The transmission switch operates the same as on the '70 models. It is actuated by the shifter shaft on manual transmissions and by fluid pressure (in high and reverse) in the direct clutch circuit of cars with automatic transmissions.

GM used the same transmission switch in '71 as they did in '70. This switch is grounded until high gear is selected. This works fine with the TCS solenoid, but not with CEC. With the TCS system, selecting high gear breaks the circuit at the transmission switch, which de-energizes the solenoid and permits vacuum advance. As mentioned earlier, the CEC solenoid operates in the opposite way. It provides vacuum when energized rather than when de-energized. Using the same transmission switch breaks the circuit in high gear, de-energizing the solenoid and blocking vacuum.

For this reason, a reversing relay was wired onto the transmission switch of every CEC system. Whenever high gear is selected with the CEC system, the transmission switch is not grounded, but the reversing relay closes. This provides the ground

necessary to complete the circuit to the solenoid and energize it for vacuum advance. The reversing relay always operates opposite to the transmission switch. In any gear but high (high and reverse on automatics), the transmission switch is closed and the relay is open. When high gear is selected, the switch opens and the relay closes.

When the engine is cold, the GM CEC solenoid is energized as soon as the ignition is turned on. That way it provides full vacuum to the distributor. The solenoid remains energized as long as engine temperature is below 82° F.

The cold override temperature switch is a three-way switch—cold override, neutral, or "hot" light activation. The switch is threaded into the cylinder head. It doubles as the temperature sending switch which activates the "hot" light on the dash when engine operating temperature is too high. At temperatures below 82° F, the switch contacts are closed, the circuit to the CEC solenoid is complete and vacuum is provided. When 82° F is reached, the contacts separate and the circuit is broken. The switch remains in this neutral position as long as engine temperature is above 82° F and below 232° F. If the temperature rises above 232° F, the switch moves to its third position and the "hot" light goes on.

On some air-conditioned, automatic-transmission Corvettes and Camaros (big-blocks only), activation of the "hot" light also completes a hot override circuit to the solenoid for vacuum advance. Advancing the timing lowers the coolant temperature to the point where the circuit is broken and vacuum is shut off. As soon as engine temperature reaches 82° F, the temperature switch contacts open and the delay relay points close for 15 secs. The point closure completes

a circuit to the solenoid, permitting vacuum advance for 15 secs. This helps eliminate stalling when the engine is cold. The relay is always closed for 15 secs. after the ignition key is turned on, regardless of engine temperature. Once the 15 secs. are up, the relay points separate and the circuit is broken, thereby de-energizing the solenoid and shutting off the vacuum.

Models equipped with air conditioning and automatic transmission require a higher curb idle speed than other cars. This faster idle leads to dieseling (run-on) after the key is turned off. Chevrolet solved this by including a solid-state device on air-conditioned cars that turns the compressor on for 3 secs. after the engine is turned off. The added load of the compressor slows the engine down enough to keep it from dieseling when shut off.

The CEC valve looks very much like an antidieseling solenoid. The solenoid is recognizable because it has no vacuum hose. Unfortunately, the CEC valve occupies the same space on the carburetor as a solenoid. As a result, many people have mistaken the CEC valve for an anti-dieseling solenoid and used it to set curb idle. Curb idle should be set with the normal throttle-cracking

1. The first year for GM's TCS system was 1970. TCS reduces NOX by preventing vacuum advance in the lower gears. System consists of a temperature switch, a vacuum solenoid valve, a transmission switch and, on some models, a time-delay relay. Illustration shows TCS used on a 1970 Chevrolet.

2. Illustration shows operation of GM TCS solenoid. When energized, the plunger is lifted upward to block manifold vacuum. When de-energized, the plunger drops downward, allowing vacuum to pass to distributor for timing advance.

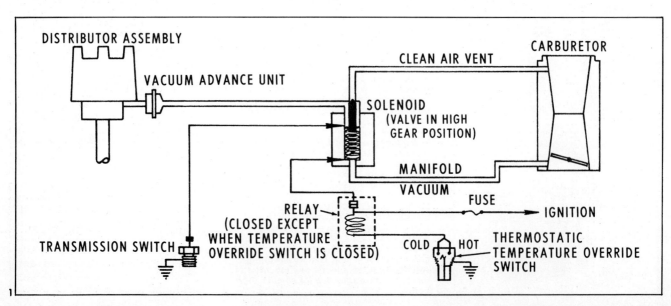

screw and *never* with the CEC valve. In the shop manuals, Chevrolet states in bold print: "Do not adjust CEC valve." It is to be adjusted only after CEC valve replacement, after a major carburetor overhaul or after the throttle body has been replaced.

The manuals also make it clear that if the CEC valve is used to set engine idle or adjusted out to the specified limits, a decrease in engine braking may result. The valve plunger is designed to extend only a specified amount during deceleration in order to contact the throttle lever. Contacting the lever increases throttle opening and engine speed. If curb idle is set with the plunger, the throttle will be held open too far on deceleration. The result? When you take your foot off the gas, the car keeps going.

Because the throttle is automatically held open on deceleration, idle speeds for '71 cars with CEC are about 50 rpm less than earlier models. Earlier models used higher idle speeds to increase throttle opening and reduce emissions, but this made antidieseling solenoids necessary to eliminate engine run-on. The CEC valve achieves the same effect during deceleration. Thus idle speeds can be lowered, so antidieseling solenoids were unnecessary for those '71 models with CEC.

For 1972, Chevrolet Division dropped the CEC system on V-8 engines. It reappeared only on the 6-cylinders. Continuing run-on problems prompted a return to antidieseling solenoids on both the sixes and V-8's. On air-conditioned models with automatic transmissions, the solenoid was used in addition to the '71 solid-state device that turned the compressor on after the key was turned off.

The CEC operated the same as it did in '71, but the delay relay delayed vacuum for 20 secs. after high gear was engaged.

The '72 V-8's use a vacuum solenoid similar to the TCS solenoid of '70. As with the CEC system, the solenoid is normally de-energized to block vacuum. When energized, it permits vacuum advance. Unlike CEC, there is no throttle-opening function.

Pontiac for '72 used CEC on their 6-cylinders and 307 V-8's; however, the deceleration feature is limited to the sixes. All 4-speed V-8's retain TCS; all other V-8's use Speed Control Spark Advance (SCS). The CEC system is the same as the Chevy CEC for 1972. Vacuum advance is provided 20 secs. after the transmission shifts into high, or whenever engine temperature is below 82° F.

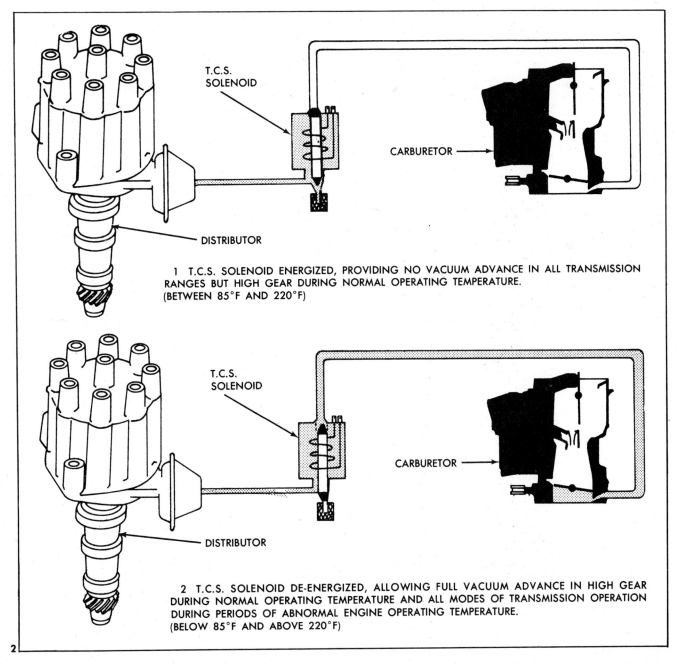

1 T.C.S. SOLENOID ENERGIZED, PROVIDING NO VACUUM ADVANCE IN ALL TRANSMISSION RANGES BUT HIGH GEAR DURING NORMAL OPERATING TEMPERATURE. (BETWEEN 85°F AND 220°F)

2 T.C.S. SOLENOID DE-ENERGIZED, ALLOWING FULL VACUUM ADVANCE IN HIGH GEAR DURING NORMAL OPERATING TEMPERATURE AND ALL MODES OF TRANSMISSION OPERATION DURING PERIODS OF ABNORMAL ENGINE OPERATING TEMPERATURE. (BELOW 85°F AND ABOVE 220°F)

Distributors

The TCS or SCS systems consist of a temperature switch, a vacuum solenoid valve and (depending upon the system) either a TCS transmission switch or a SCS speed-control spark switch. When de-energized, the TCS solenoid provides vacuum advance only in 4th gear and when engine temperature is below 95° F or above 230° F. When de-energized, the SCS solenoid permits vacuum advance only when vehicle speed is over 38 mph in any gear or if the engine temperature drops below 95° F or rises above 230° F.

Oldsmobiles for 1972 used the same TCS system as in '71. It combines TCS with TVS into one unit called a distributor vacuum control switch. In '71, some engines used the control switch while others used just the TCS solenoid. For '72, the control switch was used by all except those Cutlass models with 2-bbl. 350 engines and no air conditioning. These Cutlass models used straight TCS.

Like other GM lines, Buick began using EGR (Exhaust Gas Recirculation) in '72 to help reduce NOx emissions. It worked by burning exhaust gases in the intake manifold. Since EGR does not directly affect distributor operation, we won't discuss it here. Buick retained the TCS system in its 1970-'71 form.

Cadillac for '72 used the SCS system. A speed sensor, located at the transmission, works off the speedometer gear. When vehicle speed is over 33 mph, the electrical contacts within the sensor open and the circuit to the vacuum solenoid is broken. This de-energizes the solenoid. Internal spring pressure then forces the valve away from the vacuum port, permitting vacuum to the distributor for timing advance. When the speed drops to 25 mph, the contacts within the sensor close. This completes the circuit to the solenoid, thereby energizing it. Working against spring pressure, the valve then closes the vacuum port and blocks vacuum to the distributor.

The thermal vacuum switch (TVS) was still present on all '72 Cadillacs to provide full manifold vacuum whenever coolant temperature rises above 220° F. The SCS regulates only carburetor (spark-ported) vacuum and not manifold vacuum. Therefore, it has no effect on TVS operation. For '73, Cadillac dropped the SCS and began using EGR.

The '73 Buick retained the TCS adopted in '70. The solenoid blocks vacuum when energized; when de-energized, it permits vacuum to pass to the distributor.

In 1973 Pontiac combined TCS

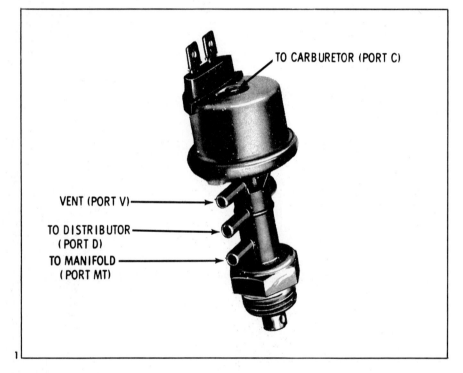

1. Some '71 Oldsmobiles combined the TVS with the TCS solenoid vacuum valve into one unit and called it the distributor vacuum control switch. Switch senses coolant overheating and opens up manifold vacuum to the distributor regardless of gear position. Manifold vacuum advances timing and cools the engine.

2. The 1971 Chevys used a CEC system, as did some Pontiacs and Oldsmobiles. Many TCS components were retained, but the TCS solenoid was replaced by a CEC solenoid, which holds the throttle open during deceleration for reduced emissions. Picture on left shows system when car is in low gear (note that transmission switch is closed), while picture on right shows high-gear operation.

3. The ultimate in complexity, '73 Pontiacs combined the TCS/EGR emission control systems.

TO CARBURETOR (PORT C)

VENT (PORT V)

TO DISTRIBUTOR (PORT D)

TO MANIFOLD (PORT MT)

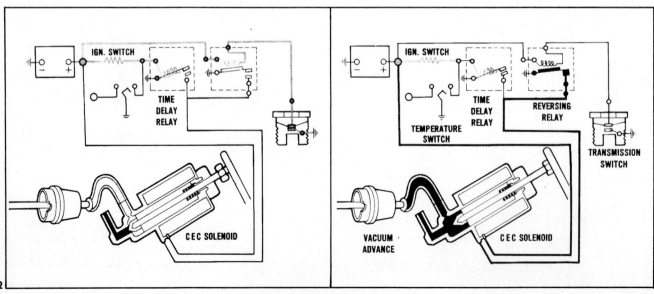

IGN. SWITCH

TIME DELAY RELAY

CEC SOLENOID

IGN. SWITCH

TIME DELAY RELAY

REVERSING RELAY

TEMPERATURE SWITCH

TRANSMISSION SWITCH

VACUUM ADVANCE

CEC SOLENOID

with EGR into one big mess of an electrical system. The EGR system reduces NOx emissions by mixing metered amounts of exhaust gas with the incoming air/fuel mixture. The NOx emissions are minimal at idle and increase with acceleration, so at idle the EGR valve is closed. It opens as the throttle opens.

The TCS/EGR system consists of the following five components: a distributor vacuum solenoid which, when energized, permits vacuum to pass to the distributor; an EGR vacuum solenoid which, when energized, closes and blocks vacuum to the EGR valve; a time delay relay that receives its signal from the transmission switch and then waits from 33 to 55 secs. before completing a circuit to ground, thereby energizing the distributor solenoid; and a thermal feed switch located at the rear of the left-hand cylinder head that shuts off TCS and permits EGR until cylinder temperature is between 125° and 155° F.

During cold starts, this thermal feed

switch is bypassed by the thermal override switch. The thermal override switch is located in the right-hand head; its contacts close below 71° and above 235° F. This grounds the circuit and provides vacuum advance.

The fifth component is a transmission-controlled spark switch, which opens in 1st gear and provides a ground for the thermal feed switch and the time delay. When coolant temperature is below 71° F and cylinder-head temperature is below 125° F, the contacts in the thermal override switch close. This provides a ground for both solenoids, which energizes the TCS solenoid, providing vacuum advance. It also makes the EGR solenoid close, blocking vacuum to the EGR valve. When coolant temperature reaches 71° F, the thermal override switch opens and the circuit is broken, thereby shutting off both solenoids.

The solenoids remain de-energized until cylinder-head temperature reaches 125° F. When outside air

temperature is 70° F, this takes about 6 mins.; 12 mins. at 0° F. When a head temperature of 125° F is reached, the thermal feed switch closes, completing the circuit between the transmission switch and the time delay. When 2nd gear is engaged, after 33-55 secs. both solenoids are energized—EGR off, TCS on. When coolant temperature reaches 235° F, the thermal override switch closes and vacuum advance cools the engine by energizing both solenoids—EGR off, TCS on.

Six-cylinder 1973 Pontiacs combine CEC with EGR. The solenoid valve is the same CEC solenoid used on the '72 models. The system also contains the same transmission switch that energizes the solenoid in high gear (and in reverse as well on automatics). A thermostatic coolant temperature switch provides thermal override below 93° F. The time relay energizes the solenoid for 20 secs. after the ignition key is turned on, permitting vacuum advance for better cold en-

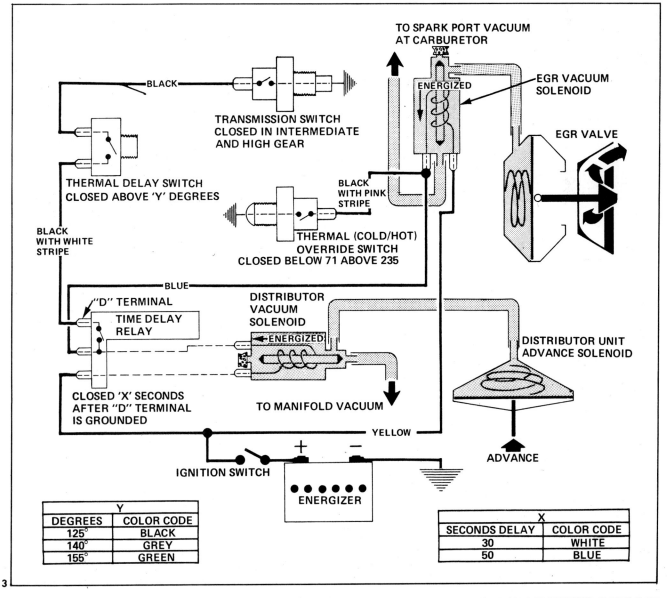

Y	
DEGREES	COLOR CODE
125°	BLACK
140°	GREY
155°	GREEN

X	
SECONDS DELAY	COLOR CODE
30	WHITE
50	BLUE

gine starting and driveaway. If coolant temperature is below 93° F after the 20 secs. have passed, the solenoid remains energized until the temperature rises above 93° F.

The EGR vacuum-actuated valve controls the exhaust gas flow to the intake manifold, where the exhaust gas is burned. The valve is controlled by spark-ported vacuum, so at idle, there is no EGR. As the throttle opens, vacuum increases along with the EGR.

Since NOx emissions increase with throttle opening, on automatic 6-cylinder '73 Pontiacs the vacuum advance is controlled by spark-ported vacuum rather than manifold. At idle, no advance is provided, but as the throttle opens, vacuum increases and timing advances. As explained much earlier, this helps to reduce NOx emissions.

Chevrolet carried the TCS system in '73 with only a few changes from the '72 system. The 20-sec. high-gear vacuum delay was replaced with a 20-sec. starting relay. This relay closes and completes the circuit for 20 secs. after the key is turned to the "on" position. This energizes the solenoid and provides vacuum advance for that duration. However, if the key is turned on and the car doesn't start within 20 secs., too bad—you won't get any vacuum advance until the relay cools enough to reactivate itself.

A temperature override switch provides vacuum advance whenever coolant temperature is below 93° F. The solenoid remains energized until 93° F is reached, even if the 20 secs.

have elapsed. The 6-cylinder Chevys retained the CEC solenoid, while the V-8's, as in '72, had only the vacuum advance solenoid. Larger throttle openings were required to compensate for the retarded timing. As a result, an electric idle stop solenoid was installed on each car to prevent run-on. The switch that engaged the air-conditioning compressor after the key was turned off was eliminated. All Corvettes had a dual temperature override switch which provided vacuum advance when coolant temperatures exceeded 232° F.

All '73 Olds V-8's were equipped with a Thermal Vacuum Switch (TVS). If the engine overheats, this switch allows manifold vacuum to reach the distributor and advance the timing. The 350 2-bbl. models contain a vacuum reducing valve within the hose that connects the manifold to the

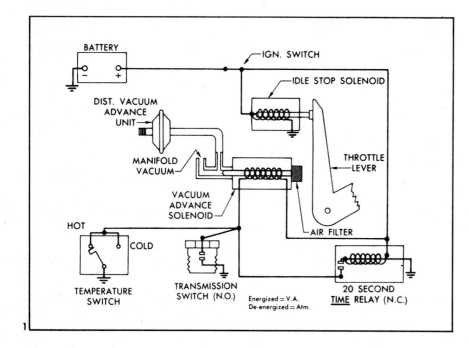

1. The TCS for the '73 Corvette included a dual temperature override switch to provide vacuum advance during overheating.

2. Just tracing the vacuum lines on a new car takes the equivalent of a wiring diagram today. Check the differences between the federal and California models of '77 Oldsmobiles.

3. Ford's dual-diaphragm vacuum advance unit can be recognized by its two hoses instead of usual one. The inner or retard diaphragm is connected to the manifold vacuum, while the outer or advance diaphragm receives spark-ported vacuum. At idle, manifold vacuum pulls on the retard diaphragm to retard the timing and lower emissions.

4. The Ford Motorcraft electronic ignition was introduced in 1974 and is shown here in complete form. Basic reluctor/magnetic pickup arrangement is similar to Chrysler and other manufacturers' systems.

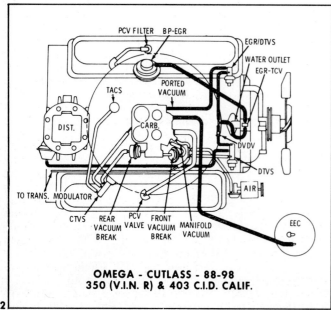

OMEGA - CUTLASS - 88-98 350 (V.I.N. R) & 403 C.I.D. CALIF.

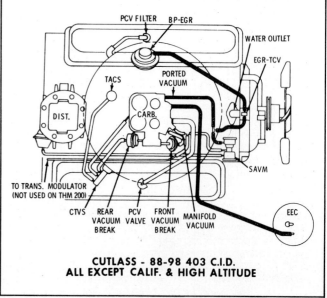

CUTLASS - 88-98 403 C.I.D. ALL EXCEPT CALIF. & HIGH ALTITUDE

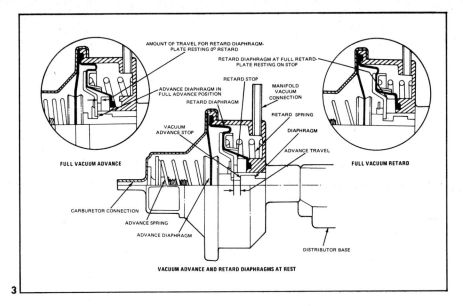

AMOUNT OF TRAVEL FOR RETARD DIAPHRAGM-
PLATE RESTING 0° RETARD
RETARD DIAPHRAGM AT FULL RETARD-
PLATE RESTING ON STOP
RETARD STOP
MANIFOLD
VACUUM
CONNECTION
ADVANCE DIAPHRAGM IN
FULL ADVANCE POSITION
RETARD DIAPHRAGM
RETARD SPRING
VACUUM
ADVANCE STOP
DIAPHRAGM
ADVANCE TRAVEL
FULL VACUUM ADVANCE
FULL VACUUM RETARD
CARBURETOR CONNECTION
ADVANCE SPRING
ADVANCE DIAPHRAGM
DISTRIBUTOR BASE
VACUUM ADVANCE AND RETARD DIAPHRAGMS AT REST

3

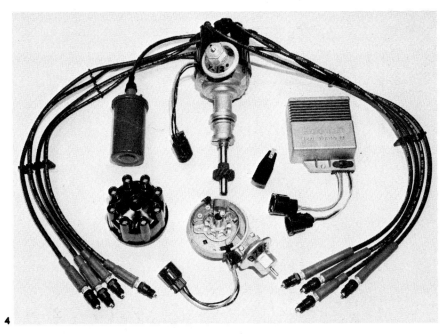

4

TVS. When coolant temperature exceeds 226° F, the TVS switch then provides full manifold vacuum to the distributor.

Engineers felt that this vacuum was too high and might result in detonation. As a safeguard, a reducer valve was installed to reduce manifold vacuum by 3 ins. All 350 4-bbl. engines and all 455's had a yellow spark delay valve installed in the vacuum hose from the carburetor to the TVS. It blocks vacuum to the distributor for 35 secs. during acceleration. After that time, the valve opens and vacuum passes to the distributor.

At GM, distributor controls for '74 changed very little. On the 6-cylinder engines the CEC solenoid was replaced with a vacuum advance solenoid. The new solenoid, mounted on the coil rather than the carburetor, looks the same as the CEC, and in controlling vacuum, it is identical. As in '73, the solenoid passes ported

vacuum from the carburetor to the distributor when it is energized; when de-energized, it blocks vacuum, vents the distributor through the solenoid and retards timing. Furthermore, the solenoid is energized and de-energized under the same conditions as in '73—right down to the same 20-sec. delay relay.

However, there is one major difference between the CEC solenoid and the '74 vacuum advance solenoid. When energized, the CEC plunger extends and contacts the throttle lever while providing vacuum for advance. When it contacts the lever, the throttle opens slightly, permitting more air to enter and help burn unburned HC during deceleration. For '74 the plunger does not extend—but the idle stop solenoid takes over that function instead.

The only other change in the TCS system for '74 was the new location of the coolant temperature switch: It

was moved from the cylinder head to the thermostat housing.

For Chevy V-8's, the changes were even fewer. In '73, TCS was included on manual-transmission cars, station wagons with automatic and the small V-8, and all automatic 307's. For '74 it was found on manual-transmission cars only. Additionally, Corvettes had a Thermo-Override system which provides full manifold vacuum when coolant temperatures are below 93° F or above 232° F.

The year 1975 brought big changes in emissions equipment. It was the year of the catalytic converter and also the first year that all U.S. cars had a breakerless ignition. GM retained the same TCS, but timing was retarded slightly to compensate for the increased throttle opening.

GM's HEI, or High-Energy Ignition, consists of a magnetic-pulse distributor. Unlike its competitors, the control module is quite small, because it's located beneath the distributor cap. The coil too is unconventional, because it is much smaller—but it generates higher voltage than the conventional item because it contains more windings. The coil is similar to a true transformer, because the iron core surrounds the windings rather than the inverse, which is the case with cylindrical coils. The coil is inserted into the top of the distributor cap on V-8 engines and protected by a cover.

On GM inlines, the coil is mounted externally on the engine. The magnetic pickup assembly includes: a rotating timer core with eight external teeth, a stationary pole piece with eight internal teeth and a pickup coil and magnet. The pickup coil is wired to the module and the module is wired to the primary of the ignition coil. When the teeth of the timer and pole piece align, voltage is sent to the pickup coil, which signals the module to shut off the ignition coil's primary circuit. This causes the magnetic field within the coil to collapse. A high-voltage spark then goes to the spark plug. There is no primary resistance wire in the HEI system, so the ignition coil receives full battery voltage. The capacitor within the distributor is for radio suppression; there is no condenser.

HEI, like all of Detroit's breakerless ignitions, is designed for reducing emissions. Plugs last longer, and without any points to burn, unburned HC from misfiring is eliminated. Without points, ignition timing doesn't fluctuate. Catalytic converters are expensive; a misfire situation could flood a converter with raw gas and quickly destroy it. HEI is there to prevent that from happening.

For 1977, some of the GM V-8's were equipped with a DVDV, or Dis-

Distributors

tributor Vacuum Delay Valve. Inserted in the hose between the TVS and the carburetor port, this device meters ported vacuum to the distributor through a .005-in. orifice, delaying full vacuum advance for up to 30 secs. When the vacuum signal at the carburetor increases, the valve moves to restrict and delay the vacuum to the ignition. Also, when ported vacuum *drops,* a pressure differential is created within the valve. This momentarily equalizes the vacuum between the distributor and the source, which retards the spark.

Also in evidence on the GM '77's were the VRV, or Vacuum Reducer Valve, and the SAVM, or Spark Advance Vacuum Modulator. The former reduces the vacuum signal to the DTVS by 1.5 ins. if the engine temperature exceeds 220° F. The SAVM is like the '67 Pontiac dual-diaphragm advance unit (except that it is remote from the distributor), with hoses to the distributor, manifold vacuum and ported vacuum. The valve responds to engine load by supplying ported vacuum to the distributor when both ported and manifold vacuum are above 7 ins., and it supplies manifold vacuum when both sources are below 7 ins. The EST-CTS (Electronic Spark Timing-Coolant Temperature Sensor) changes resistance when the engine temperature changes to give more timing advance when the engine is cold and needs it.

To improve cold driveaway and engine warm-up, the '77 GM 4-cylinder engines were equipped with a trapped vacuum spark advance. This supplies the distributor with full vacuum below 115° F; above that the thermal vacuum switch opens and full vacuum will then bypass the delay valve through the TVS switch.

EMISSIONS DISTRIBUTORS: FORD

Ford Motor Co. uses many of the same emissions controls that other manufacturers do. The controls operate in basically the same way, but they are called by different names. The systems discussed here are only those that directly affect distributor operation or control of vacuum advance.

Prior to 1968, Ford used only the PCV system. On California cars and Lincoln Continentals, this was combined with the Thermactor system, which is Ford's name for air injection.

In '68 and '69, Ford used their Improved Combustion (IMCO) emission control system. IMCO, similar to GM's Controlled Combustion System, helps reduce HC and CO. The system works by a special thermostatically

controlled air cleaner, which is connected by a duct to the exhaust manifold. The intake air is heated before it goes into the carburetor. The result is faster warm-ups and the ability to use leaner mixtures, hence lower HC and CO emissions.

Ford's first year for using vacuum control devices as a means of reducing emissions was 1968. Included on some '68 and '69 models was a dual-diaphragm vacuum advance unit and a ported vacuum switch (PVS). The dual-diaphragm unit is situated on the distributor in the same place as a conventional single-diaphragm unit. It doesn't appear very different from the single diaphragm, although it is a bit larger and has two vacuum hoses instead of the usual one. Contained

within its outer shell are two diaphragms that operate independently of each other. The inner (retard) diaphragm is connected to manifold vacuum, while the outer (advance) diaphragm receives its vacuum from the carburetor (spark-ported).

During idle and deceleration, the throttle is nearly closed and HC and CO emissions are high, but manifold vacuum is also high. When pulled by manifold vacuum, the retard diaphragm moves inward toward the distributor to retard the timing and lower HC and CO emissions. As the throttle opens, spark-ported vacuum increases, pulling on the outer (advance) diaphragm. This makes the diaphragm move against the tension of the advance spring, which ad-

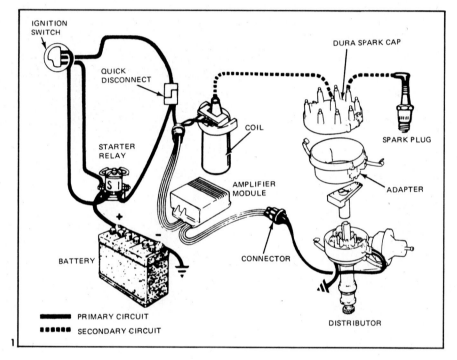

1

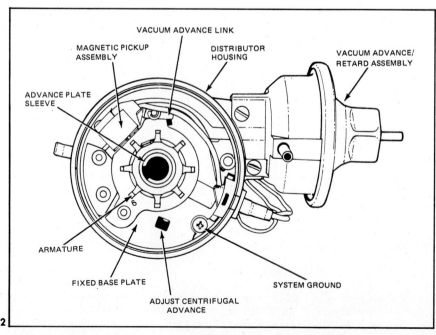

2

vances timing as the throttle opens for better gas economy and improved performance.

Ford's distributor vacuum control valve (PVS—Ported Vacuum Switch) looks and operates like GM's TVS described earlier. The valve is threaded into the coolant outlet, where it senses coolant temperature. It has three ports—one connected to spark-ported vacuum, one to manifold vacuum and one to the distributor. When the engine overheats at idle, the valve senses this and opens the port to manifold vacuum. The vacuum passes to the distributor to advance timing and cool the engine. When the engine cools, the manifold vacuum port opens again to prevent advance at idle.

On some models, a distributor vacuum advance control valve (deceleration valve) is used in conjunction with the dual-diaphragm unit. During deceleration, backfiring normally occurs in the exhaust. At this time, the decel valve permits the high intake manifold vacuum to travel to the advance diaphragm to advance timing and reduce afterburning (backfiring).

In '70 and '71, on all Ford products except Continentals, IMCO included four new devices and was renamed the Distributor Modulator (Dist-O-Vac) system. The smog pump, discarded by Lincoln for two years, made a comeback and was combined with IMCO on all Continentals. Dist-O-Vac was used only by other Ford cars.

On Dist-O-Vac cars, a speed sensor is spliced into the speedometer cable. A thermal switch, situated in the front door pillar, senses outside temperature and activates at 58° F or above. An electronic control amplifier combined in one unit with a solenoid valve is located on the dash panel inside the passenger area. The vacuum advance hose from the carburetor passes through the solenoid valve within the amplifier, then on to the PVS and the distributor. When outside temperature is below 58° F, the thermal switch contacts close, completing the circuit to the amplifier. The solenoid valve then permits carburetor (ported) vacuum to pass to the distributor for advance. When the outside temperature hits 58° F, the thermal switch contacts open, breaking the circuit to the amplifier. A plunger within the solenoid valve then blocks vacuum to the distributor. When vehicle speed reaches 30 mph, the speed sensor signals the amplifier, spark-ported vacuum goes to the distributor and timing is advanced.

For '72, Dist-O-Vac was replaced with two spark control systems, ESC (Electronic Spark Control) and TRS (Transmission-Regulated Spark). ESC was used on all '72 Pintos, Continentals and on some other models. TRS also had a wide application. ESC is the same as Dist-O-Vac except that the control modulator is finally separated into its two components, the amplifier and the modulator (solenoid) valve. The amplifier receives the signals from the speed and thermal sensors and either breaks or completes the circuit to the solenoid. The valve is normally open and de-energized. When energized, it closes to block ported vacuum to the distributor's primary vacuum advance, thereby preventing advance. The thermal switch in the door pillar closes at temperatures of 65° F or above, blocking vacuum, and opens at 48° F for vacuum advance. Vehicle speeds at which the speed sensor activates are now 23, 28, 33, 35 or 40 mph, depending upon the engine. On some cars, the PVS was retained to provide manifold vacuum for timing advance during engine overheating.

The TRS, like GM's TCS, consists of the distributor modulator valve, an ambient (outside air) temperature switch (in the door pillar) and a transmission switch activated by fluid pres-

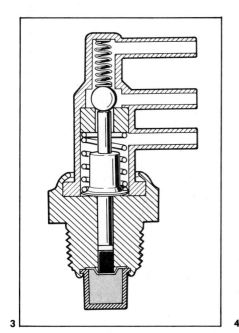

3

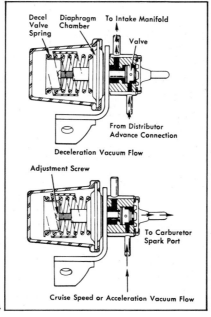

Deceleration Vacuum Flow

Cruise Speed or Acceleration Vacuum Flow

4

1. The 1976 Motorcraft system was called Dura-Spark. Now there is the Dura-Spark II version shown here with its unusual distributor cap. All of the current electronic units are used with silicone plug wires.

2. Under the cap, the Dura-Spark II isn't much different from conventional distributors. Ford has used its dual-diaphragm advance/retard unit for almost 10 years now.

3. Ever wonder what's inside one of the thermostatic vacuum valves used on so many cars now? Here's a cutaway of a Ford Distributor Vacuum Control valve, which adjusts flow of manifold or ported vacuum to the distributor according to temperature.

4. AMC began controlling vacuum advance for emissions control in 1970, when certain cars were equipped with a decel valve and dual-diaphragm vacuum advance units. During deceleration, manifold vacuum goes to the advance side of the dual diaphragm to advance timing, prevent backfiring and reduce emissions.

5. This illustration is of a typical CSSA (Cold-Start Spark Advance) setup used on many 1977 Fords. This allows extra advance during a cold start or when the engine is overheated.

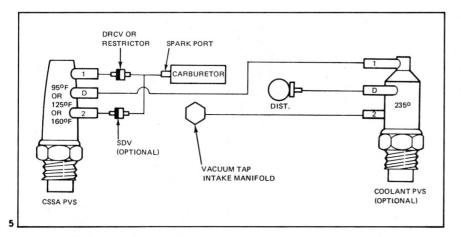

5

Distributors

sure in automatic transmissions or mechanically on the manuals. The modulator valve is normally open. When energized, it blocks vacuum and prevents vacuum advance.

The '73 Fords, like many other makes, were equipped with EGR to control NOx emissions. All Ford sixes with stick shift combined a spark-control system with EGR and called it TRS + 1. THE TRS portion of the system operates the same as the '72 TRS. A modulator (solenoid) is still used, but the '73 version has three ports. Two connect to the vacuum lines from both the EGR and distributor vacuum ports on the carburetor, while the third is an outlet to the EGR valve.

All sixes with automatic transmissions used a different spark control system. It consists of a three-way solenoid valve, a temperature switch (in the door) and a vacuum bleed line to the air cleaner. The solenoid is the same as the stick six, but the outlet goes to the distributor rather than the EGR valve. When the outside temperature is above 60° F, the switch closes to complete the circuit to the solenoid. The solenoid is energized, and the EGR port on the carburetor connects to the distributor. Below 49° F, the solenoid is de-energized and the advance unit operates normally.

Many '73 V-8 models used the Delay Vacuum Bypass (DVB) spark-control system. The system consists of a spark delay valve, a check valve, a solenoid vacuum valve and an ambient temperature switch. When the outside (ambient) temperature drops below 49° F, the contacts in the temperature switch are open and the circuit to the solenoid is incomplete, resulting in a de-energized solenoid. When de-energized, the valve in the solenoid is open, allowing carburetor (ported) vacuum to pass to the distributor. When the temperature rises above 60° F, the contacts in the switch close, which completes the circuit, energizes the solenoid and blocks one of the two vacuum paths. The vacuum goes to the spark delay valve; during hard acceleration, this vacuum is blocked by the valve for 5 to 30 secs. before being released to the distributor. A one-way check valve is installed in the hose between the solenoid and the distributor. When the solenoid is energized, the vacuum hose from the solenoid to the distributor is vented to the air. The check valve prevents the vacuum from the delay valve from escaping. In '73, EGR was also used. The ESC was retained on the '73 Pinto.

Ford offered an electronic breakerless type of ignition system on some 1974 models, and the same system has been standard since 1975. Operation is simple, and there are almost no differences between the '74 and later versions of the system. The am-

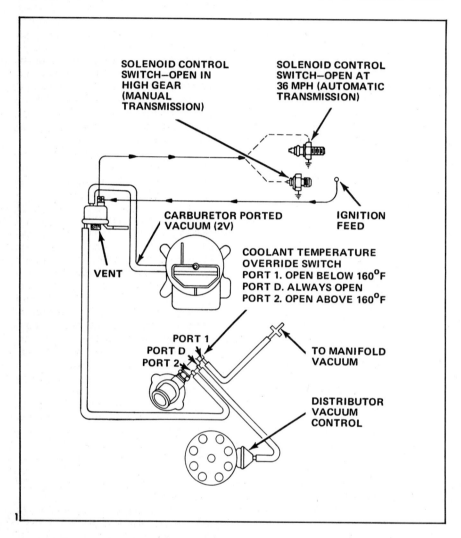

1. AMC's TCS system remained basically unchanged from '70 to '73. This illustration shows system on V-8 engine that uses a coolant temperature override switch.

2. The dual-diaphragm vacuum advance unit used only on some '70 models was supplied by Delco. Its operation is similar to that of Ford's unit.

3. Some AMC models have a coolant temperature override switch that's used in conjunction with TCS. Switch called by any other name is still the same switch as GM's TVS or Ford's PVS.

4. The AMC Prestolite electronic ignition system (BID) has an unusual vacuum advance unit and a "trigger" wheel with two sets of blades to make and break the magnetic field.

plifier modules are not interchangeable, however, because of minor internal differences.

In the breakerless system, when the ignition switch is turned to the "on" position, the primary circuit is on and the coil is energized. In place of the conventional points, a spoked armature is mounted on the distributor shaft, and a magnetic pickup coil is mounted inside the housing. When the spokes of the armature approach the magnetic pickup, they induce a voltage that tells the amplifier to turn off the primary current in the coil. A timing circuit in the amplifier turns the current back on again after the coil field has collapsed.

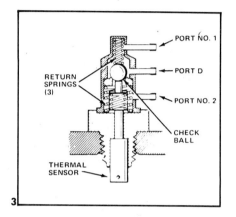

3

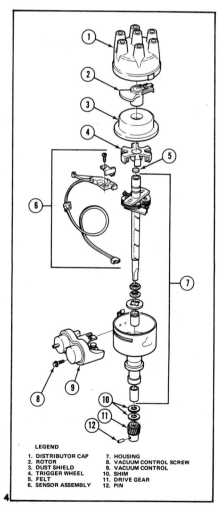

LEGEND

1. DISTRIBUTOR CAP
2. ROTOR
3. DUST SHIELD
4. TRIGGER WHEEL
5. FELT
6. SENSOR ASSEMBLY
7. HOUSING
8. VACUUM CONTROL SCREW
9. VACUUM CONTROL
10. SHIM
11. DRIVE GEAR
12. PIN

4

When the current is on, it flows from the battery through the ignition switch, the primary windings of the ignition coil and through the amplifier module circuits on its way to ground. When the current is off, the magnetic field built up in the coil is allowed to collapse, inducing a high voltage into the secondary windings of the coil. High voltage is produced each time the field builds up and collapses.

The high voltage flows through the coil high-tension lead to the distributor cap, where the rotor distributes it first to one of the spark plug terminals and then to the plug itself. The process repeats for each power stroke of the engine.

Aside from timing adjustment, the only adjustments that can be made to the breakerless type of ignition are in the vacuum advance and centrifugal advance areas. These are handled the same way as on older, point-type units. All the rest of the ignition system—the vacuum portions and the temperature-controlled portions—is the same as on earlier models.

Some of the 1977 models were equipped with a Cold Start Spark Advance (CSSA) that works in conjunction with the PVS (Ported Vacuum Switch) to allow ported-vacuum advance below 125° F and straight manifold vacuum advance to speed up the engine for more cooling above 235° F.

EMISSIONS DISTRIBUTORS: AMC

During 1966 and '67, AMC emission control equipment was confined to a PCV and a smog pump. In '68, the smog pump was dropped on all but V-8's with manual transmission. A thermostatically controlled air cleaner (TAC) was used on most V-8 models. The TAC does the same thing as GM's CCS and Ford's IMCO.

These modifications were carried over to 1970, when a few additional controls were added. A decel valve is present on the stick sixes and the 390 V-8 with manual transmission. It works exactly like Ford's decel valve described earlier. During deceleration, intake manifold vacuum goes to the advance side of the dual-diaphragm unit (also like Ford) and advances the timing to prevent backfiring within the exhaust system. The dual-diaphragm advance is used on all cars with decel valves and on all 304 and 360 V-8 engines.

All '70 California AMC models were equipped with the Evaporative Emission Control system. This was standard for all AMC cars in '71. The Delco dual-diaphragm advance unit appeared on some '70 models but did not reappear later.

All AMC's 1971 California cars and all 304 V-8's with automatic transmis-

sions were equipped with TCS to help reduce NOx emissions. The TCS consists of a transmission control switch, a solenoid vacuum valve and a temperature override switch. When energized, the solenoid blocks vacuum to the distributor. When de-energized, ported vacuum goes to the distributor and advances timing. The transmission switch opens at speeds above 30 mph on automatic transmissions and when high gear is selected on manual transmissions. This breaks the circuit to the solenoid, which de-energizes it and permits vacuum advance. In lower gears and below 30 mph, the switch closes to complete the circuit and energize the solenoid for no vacuum advance. When outside temperatures are above 63° F, the circuit is completed and there is no advance. For cooler temperatures, advance is provided. The smog pump was retained on all stick V-8's.

For '72, the TCS system was retained. The transmission switch on the automatic was operated by the speedometer gear rather than by governor pressure as in '71. New for '72 was the coolant temperature override switch, which is threaded into the thermostat housing on all V-8's with automatic transmission. If coolant temperature is below 160° F, intake manifold vacuum is allowed to reach the distributor for full vacuum advance. When 160° is reached, manifold vacuum is blocked and ported vacuum goes to the distributor. Providing advance at low temperatures eliminates stalling and makes starting easier. For '73, TCS was continued and EGR was added.

AMC switched to an all-electronically controlled ignition system for the 1975 model year. The system they chose was the BID system, manufactured by Prestolite. It is basically similar to the system used by Ford and Chrysler, in that the breaker points have been removed from the distributor and replaced with an electromagnetic device to trigger the coil.

Inside the distributor, a star-shaped armature turns on the shaft. As it turns, it generates a minute current in a magnetic sensor pickup. This current is sent to an amplifier module (located nearby under the hood) and transformed into signals to the coil. Points, condenser and breaker cam are eliminated from the system, thereby increasing its reliability. The rest of the ignition system operates as it did on earlier models.

The rest of the ignition controls, such as the TCS and CTO (Coolant Temperature Override), remained on the AMC models through 1977, though there were minor differences in controls between the federal (49-state) models and those sold in California only. ✦

Ignition Tuning

THERE'S A GOOD DEAL MORE TO TUNING THAN MERELY SWAPPING PARTS IN THE HOPE OF ACCIDENTALLY STUMBLING UPON THE SOLUTION TO YOUR ENGINE'S ILLS.

Every driver should know at least enough about the workings of his car to determine if the work his mechanic is doing is being properly carried out, even if the driver never expects to lift a screwdriver himself. But the man who does his own tune-ups should not make the same mistake that some service garages do, namely, putting in a lot of new parts and hoping everything will be all right. The right way to approach an ignition tune-up is to replace only what *needs* to be replaced but also to check *everything* to make sure that all weak spots have been weeded out.

Let's start by taking a grand tour of the ignitions used in different cars, with particular emphasis on some of the fine points that deserve special notice during a tune-up. Many of these things are basic points that you'll need to know to do a good tune-up. In each case we'll start with the spark plugs and work backward to the ignition switch, describing any special features which may be unique to that particular maker's automobiles. We'll deal with both the earlier breaker point ignitions and the later no-points distributors.

GENERAL MOTORS

All General Motors cars are equipped at the factory with 14mm AC spark plugs. Some GM cars use a special tapered-seat 14mm plug with a ⅝-in. hex rather than the usual 13/16-in. Naturally this requires a special wrench. Please don't try to put a gasket on any tapered-seat plugs; they don't use them. GM uses different plug reaches in different models, but torque specs for all (except tapered-seat plugs) are 20 to 25 ft.-lbs. in iron heads (35 ft.-lbs. for Olds V-8's and '67 Buick V-6, 300, 340) and about 25% less in aluminum heads. Tapered-seat plugs must be tightened to no more than 15 ft.-lbs. Any more than that makes it extremely difficult to remove the plugs at the next tune-up. If a torque wrench is not available, the plugs can be tightened about ½-turn with a plug wrench after they are finger-tight in the head.

It is recommended that spark plugs be changed each 5000 miles for best service, unless otherwise recommended in the owner's manual. Pack-

ard radio resistance cable is used for the plug and high-tension leads, and the location of the distributor cap terminal serving No. 1 cylinder is usually marked inside the cap.

All recent pre-electronic ignition GM V-8 distributors have screw-like distributor cap hold-downs that are released by inserting a screwdriver into the \slot, pushing down against spring pressure and turning them 180° in either direction. The rotor used in all 8-cylinder distributors is screwed into place atop the centrifugal advance mechanism. When replacing the rotor, the round and square lugs molded into its underside must engage the correspondingly shaped holes in the cam flange. The rotors on 6-cylinder distributors merely lift off.

The breaker points are a single assembly in late-model pre-electronic ignition GM cars. The Delco points are fitted with a quick-detachment terminal for the primary and condenser wires. This greatly speeds point changes. However, care must be taken to reinstall the wires in their original positions or else interference with the rotor, cap and spark advance may occur. GM Delco distributors have a sheetmetal radio interference shield over the points. If you buy replacement points that have a screw instead of friction-fit leads, the head of the screw may not clear the metal shield, thus grounding the points and killing the ignition. Stick with genuine Delco points and you won't have that trouble. They are made to fit under the shield.

1. Tuning specs vary from engine to engine in today's emission-controlled cars. To eliminate this confusion, manufacturers place a label in the engine compartment of each car. This label provides tuning information for that particular vehicle.

2. Point gap on Delco V-8 distributors is adjusted with a small Allen wrench or a special flexible point-adjusting tool for those hard-to-reach places. Window-type distributor permits dwell adjustments with engine running, thus eliminating need for cap removal as on non-Delco V-8 unit.

The correct point spring tension is 19 to 23 oz., measured with the hook of the point scale just back of the point surface. Tension is changed by bending the spring, but changes are hardly ever necessary. The point assembly has a pilot lug which must engage a matching hole in the breaker plate to prevent incorrect installation. GM shop manuals advise their shop mechanics to set all new points at .003-in. wider than the specified gap setting to allow for initial rubbing block wear.

When new points are fitted, the cam should be wiped clean of all old grease and a new cam-oiled wick installed. The felt wick that comes with the new point set is prelubricated and should not be dipped in oil. Six-cylinder distributors have a round, wheel-type lubricator, while the 8-cylinder window-type units have a straight felt strip. Remove the old wick by squeezing its base together with a pair of long-nose pliers and pulling it from its loop. The new wick must be positioned so that *only its tip* brushes against the cam; otherwise excessive lubrication will take place and eventually contaminate the point contacts.

If the distributor is checked with a dwell meter, dwell variation should not exceed 3°. If it does, it is an indication that the distributor has an excessively worn breaker plate bushing or shaft bearings. Since dwell meters are relatively inaccurate at high rpm, GM recommends that tests should not be made above 1750 rpm.

Condenser capacity for GM cars should be between .18 and .23 microfarads. If one point picks up material transferred from the other, condensers of slightly higher or lower capacity within the prescribed range can be substituted, according to the direction (See ''Tests & Checks'' in distributor chapter) of the build-up.

Distributor shaft end play should not be more than .002- to .007-in. Runout—which can be checked by rolling the distributor shaft on a sheet of plate glass or turning it in V blocks against a dial indicator—should not exceed .002-in.

The distributor shaft is lubricated at its lower end by crankcase vapors and at the top by a reservoir of permanent grease. If the distributor is disassembled or the body washed in solvent, be careful to replenish this grease supply before returning the distributor to service. When replacing the centrifugal advance on the distributor shaft, the top of the shaft should first be coated with Delco Cam & Ball Bearing Grease or its equivalent prior to assembly. The elimination of external oilers or grease cups has served to extend the service interval for GM automobiles.

The Delco coils found in GM autos have *two* wires connecting them to the ignition switch. One of these is a normal wire that supplies full battery voltage to the coil when the key is turned to the ''start'' position. The other wire is a resistance type of wire which is used instead of a separate ballast resistor in the primary circuit. The resistance wire supplies current to the coil only when the key is in the ''on'' position. When installing custom coils or ignition systems, it is often necessary to locate and remove the stock ''ballast.'' In the case of General Motors cars, this is done simply by replacing the resistance wire with a regular wire.

GM'S HIGH-ENERGY IGNITION

Since a High-Energy Ignition (HEI) system puts out about 10,000 volts more than a conventional GM system, a larger distributor cap and rotor are required to keep the high voltage from leaking. The new distributor cap is no thicker than the conventional one, however, so it's prone to trouble. Why the extra voltage? Well, when GM engines were set very lean at idle back in 1971 to help meet the emissions specifications, a phenomenon referred to as ''acceleration glazing'' (caused by excessive start/stop driving) reduced spark plug life by about 50% on the '71-'73 models. This occurred because there was insufficient voltage available to fire the glazed plugs. To extend plug life back to its original 10,000-12,000 miles, GM increased the system voltage, so we're right back where we started.

The HEI is really too new to pinpoint all the gremlins that can and will pop up, but you should be aware that each application uses a different cap-mounted coil. They all *look* alike and *hook up* alike, but system specifications and coil windings differ, not only from GM division to GM division, but from engine to engine within a division. Don't substitute a coil that does not carry the same part number as the one it replaces or you'll ruin it. You'll also destroy it if you hook up a tach/dwell test unit to the coil terminal marked ''tach'' if that test unit lacks the circuit capability required to test a transistorized ignition.

You may also have problems with the GM pickup coil. Occasionally one overheats and exceeds the stated ohm value. The engine will not start again until the pickup coil cools to less than that stated value. This is a tough one to test for, because the pickup coil is down in the distributor. By the time you clear a path to it, it's likely to have cooled sufficiently to test out okay. Then what do you do? If you suspect pickup coil malfunction, heat it up and cool it down quickly for test purposes with a hair drier and a can of refrigerant.

FORD MOTOR COMPANY

For many years Ford products were unique in this county in having a positive-ground electrical system. This was retained until 1956. In that year Ford passenger cars adopted the 12-volt negative-ground system that is now standard on all U.S. cars. The hot rodder who mixes parts from old and new Fords or uses older Ford parts in other machinery must be constantly aware of this difference.

Autolite or Motorcraft spark plugs are standard on Ford products. All are now of the 18mm tapered-seat variety. Since they have the same 13/16-in. hex as standard 14mm plugs, you need no special wrench. These plugs use no gaskets and are all of the same ⅜-in. reach. When installing them, it is highly important

2

that the tapered seat in the heads and on the plugs be absolutely clean. Tapered-seat plugs must be torqued to 15-20 ft.-lbs. Overtightening can make later removal very difficult.

Ford manuals make a point of cautioning mechanics that the excessive use of abrasive-type plug cleaners can be very damaging, since the ceramic insulators may be eroded away. This may be partially due to the fact that the larger gas volume of the 18mm plugs lets more of the cleaning abrasive into the plug's interior.

Autolite or Motorcraft radio-resistance cables with molded-on right-angle nipples are standard. The No. 1 terminal on the distributor cap is usually marked on the outside of the cap itself.

Distributor cap and rotor removal are conventional on most Ford automobiles, as is the removal of the breaker set. On certain Fords, a one-piece pivotless point assembly is used, which is somewhat quicker to replace. On the earlier types of points it is possible to adjust contact spring tension by loosening the spring mounting screw and sliding the spring back and forth to achieve the desired load. Dwell variations should not exceed 3° below 2000 rpm, and the distributor cam must be lubricated with a suitable grease during the point installation.

Ford has also marketed a breaker-controlled transistor system that uses the centrifugal-advance, high-performance distributor equipped with only one set of points and no condenser. When tuning one of these, do not connect a dwell meter or tach to any part of the system other than the ta-chometer block. This last item consists of a double ballast resistor, a relay to bypass the resistors for starting and the panel's terminals. Tests of the transistor system should be made as specified in individual Ford Motor Co. shop manuals to avoid ruining the transistors.

FoMoCo vacuum advances can be adjusted by adding or subtracting washers from the vacuum chamber assembly. The only exception to this is the Loadomatic all-vacuum distributor, which is controlled by two calibrated springs—one for high advance and one for low. Adjust the centrifugal advance of dual-advance distributors before checking the vacuum system. This is done by inserting a tool through a hole in the breaker plate and bending the spring mount to increase or decrease spring tension. The greater the tension, the less advance. Such adjustments, of course, must be performed on a distributor-testing machine.

The high-performance centrifugal advance distributor is controlled by calibrated springs only, and advance curve modifications require that the springs themselves be changed or modified. Factory specifications demand that the centrifugal advance curve of the high-performance unit be within ±1° of the exact figure at all engine rpm.

The standard dual-advance distributors are allowed a maximum of 6° of dwell variation at constant rpm going from 0 to maximum vacuum (not over 25 ins. Hg) on the testing machine. If dwell variation exceeds this, there are worn or bent parts in the vacuum advance mechanism. FoMoCo distributors have oil cups which must be attended to periodically for proper service life.

The coil in conventional Ford ignition systems is served by a resistance wire from the ignition switch and has no separate ballast resistor. The transistor system has a separate ballast resistor unit, as mentioned earlier. The coil of the transistorized system should not be tested on a coil tester because its construction makes such tests inconclusive. Cars equipped with overdrive have an extra wire on the "Dist." terminal of the coil. This wire serves the overdrive kick-down switch. The current for the ignition system is drawn from a terminal on the starter relay.

FORD'S SOLID-STATE IGNITION

The '74 Ford ignition system experienced considerable trouble in the form of poor signal transmission, caused by loose connections between the distributor and the electronic module. Packed in the ends of the connector plugs to keep moisture out is what GM refers to as "DEC" grease, for "Distributor Electronic Control." Whenever you disconnect these plugs, replace the DEC grease. Use enough so that it oozes out when the plugs are reinstalled.

Ford changed the harness wire pin connectors and the wire colors for '75, which is of no interest unless you find it necessary to test the pin connectors to troubleshoot the circuitry. And if you do, like most of us, you'd expect the '74 and '75 systems to be the same. So if you get a series of weird readings, let that jog your memory—you're testing the wrong circuits for the wrong thing.

For '77 Ford updated their ignition by changing to the Dura Spark II, a solid-state system that incorporates high-energy secondary components.

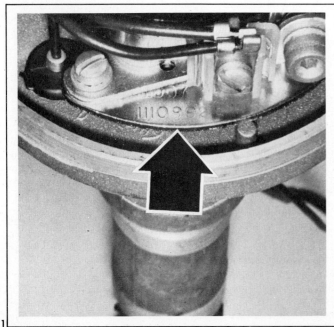

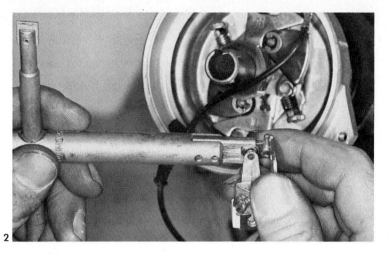

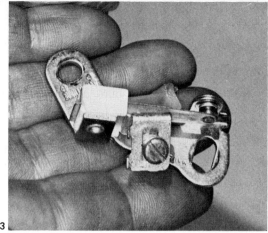

1. Somewhere on every distributor there is a part number. Look it up in a spec book and you will find the advance curves for that distributor.

2. This tool is especially made for aligning Ford distributor points so that their surfaces can meet squarely. Bend the stationary point only.

3. Pivotless points shown removed from Ford distributor (there is really nothing wrong with these points). This type has a higher rpm potential because the breaker "arm" is lighter.

The distributor, coil and module are essentially the same as the previously used SSI system except for calibration. The new system has an adapter on the distributor to accommodate the new, larger distributor terminal housing and the larger rotor used with the high voltage. The terminal housing features spark plug-type terminal towers. The high-tension spark plug wires were increased in size to 8mm and have silicone jacketing for improved capability. Spark plugs are the new carbon resistor type and have a wider electrode gap (.060-in. in California and .050-in. elsewhere).

The high voltage and wide spark plug gap increase spark plug life and overall engine performance. The system can be readily identified by the large blue distributor cap and high-tension wires.

The spark plug wires used with the Dura Spark II systems are *very* expensive (about $80 per V-8 set at this writing) and should be treated carefully. At approximately $10 per wire, you don't want to pull off wires willy-nilly while checking for spark. Also, the spark plug cables are of two types, both of which are blue in color and have silicone jacketing to withstand the tremendous heat given off by today's clean-burning engines. Both cable types may be used within the same engine compartment, so care must exercised when replacement is necessary. Type SE (identified by letters printed in black) is used where somewhat cooler temperatures are prevalent and Type SS (white printing) where very high engine temperatures are present.

When removing the cables, use Ford tool No. T74P-6666-A to avoid damage. Grasp the insulator and twist it back and forth on the spark plug to free the insulator. Do not pull directly on the wire or it may become separated from the connector inside the insulator.

CHRYSLER CORPORATION

Champion supplies the spark plugs used in all Chrysler Corp. cars. All are of the 14mm size, but various reaches are used in different engines. Chrysler's crimped-on type of plug gaskets do not require a torque wrench for proper seating. About ⅓- to ½-turn with a plug wrench after making them finger-tight is all that's required. Racing plugs and plugs with other types of gaskets should be torqued to 30 ft.-lbs. The cables used for Chrysler plug leads simply say "radio."

Until 1972, the construction and layout of the Mopar distributors was highly conventional, including the construction and placement of the points, condenser and advance units.

However, on some '72 models Chrysler introduced a new breakerless ignition system, which has been standard on all Chrysler products since '73. No maintenance is required on this distributor.

On the previous, conventional system, the cam must be greased regularly at each point servicing. There is also an oiler on the distributor body to lubricate the shaft and its bushings. Three drops of SAE 10W engine oil are administered according to the service interval for the particular model. In addition, there is a felt lubrication wick in the center of the cam which serves the centrifugal advance. This requires three to five drops of SAE 10W oil too.

Maximum shaft end play on either type of distributor should not be more than .006- to .007-in. If the drive gear is removed to correct excess end play by renewing the thrust washers, be sure the drive gear is properly aligned with the rotor when it is replaced. The bushings of these distributors are fully replaceable, so servicing can return the unit to like-new condition. The advance curve of the high-performance, dual-point distributors must fall within ±1° at all rpm.

Chrysler Corp. cars employ a separate ballast resistor unit in series with the coil's primary connection. Most models draw ignition current from a terminal on the alternator regulator, but some of the compacts supply the ignition from the starter relay.

The most common problem with the Chrysler electronic ignition system seems to be a bad coil that causes a stumble. Chrysler uses an oil-filled coil, and since primary build-up time is considerable, the coil tends to overheat consistently and eventually burns out. Chrysler originally used the same switching module for all applications, but in an effort to correct the coil burnout problem, the switching module transistor was changed to three different ones, identified by the sticker color on the module—gold, green and silver.

Because the switching module controls engine firing, you must be careful not to replace a defective module with a new one of the incorrect rating. If you install a 6-cylinder module on an 8-cylinder engine, it will fire too slowly and result in a sluggish car. But a 6-cylinder engine when incorrectly equipped with an 8-cylinder module will have too rapid a rate of firing; at high engine speeds the rpm will build up and the engine will blow. Incidentally, the switching module has a tendency to vibrate loose from its firewall mounting, so it should be tightened periodically.

If your Chrysler electronic ignition quits dead on the road, check the pickup coil tooth. The Chrysler distributor continues to use the single-pivot connection on the breaker plate, which is characteristic of the conventional Chrysler distributor. With sufficient wear, the breaker plate loosens; then when the vacuum advance kicks in, it pulls the pickup coil down. This causes the breaker plate to lean or tilt and eventually brings the coil's tooth into contact with the revolving reluctor teeth, breaking off the coil tooth and stopping the car. By the way, those reluctor teeth are very sharp. Would you believe that some people (including mechanics) actually think those teeth should be filed to get rid of the sharp edges? Don't do it! Keep them sharp.

A third potential problem area lies in the secondary circuitry. Chrysler didn't change it one bit, so all the secondary problems you'd encounter with a conventional ignition and distributor are still quite apparent.

AMERICAN MOTORS

Fourteen-millimeter plugs from Champion are used in all American Motors cars. Since 1965 all AMC engines have used ¾-in.-reach plugs, although in previous years 7/16-in. reaches predominated and were still being used in the 196-cu.-in. ohv American 6-cylinder engine in 1965. Since the 232-cu.-in. six was then using ¾-in.-reach plugs, a few mechanics have made the mistake of installing these in the "little" six, with disastrous results. Standard Champion plugs require only about ⅓- to ½-turn with a plug wrench after being seated finger-tight. Racing plugs should be torqued to 25-30 ft.-lbs. even in aluminum engines. Radio resistance high-tension cables are standard equipment.

The remainder of the American Motors ignition system is of either Autolite or Delco-Remy manufacture, with all recent models employing the Delco system. For this reason, servicing is identical to the procedures required for Ford products having Autolite systems and General Motors products with Delco components. Recent AMC V-8's use the Delco window-type distributor. American Motors differs from GM, however, in choosing to use a separate ballast resistor rather than resistance wire in the primary current source. Ignition current is always picked up at the starter solenoid.

AMC switched over to electronic ignition for cleaner-burning engines in 1975 and named its system BID. Built for AMC by Prestolite, it has proven quite dependable. The only major malfunction to date with the AMC BID system is a tendency toward sensor failure—and when the sensor fails, the engine quits, as in the case of a Chrysler electronic ignition with a broken pickup coil. It's a good idea to carry a replacement sensor unit with you, along with a copy of Petersen's *How to Tune Your Car*, 4th edition, which contains a step-by-step installation procedure. A few minutes spent with a screwdriver and pliers can save you a hefty tow bill.

FOREIGN MAKES

The following basic ignition systems are found in the majority of imports reaching these shores: Bosch and VW, Lucas, Marelli, Ducillier, S.E.V. and the licensed variations found on Japanese autos. VW owners and dune buggy enthusiasts will, of course, have the Bosch and VW systems to contend with, while the TR, Sprite and MG owners will want to know about he Lucas.

Most VW's come with Champion or Bosch plugs, although some are supplied with Beru or other brands of European manufacture. These are all 14mm, .472-in.-reach plugs. Some models have projected noses and others standard gaps. For years VW resistance ignition cable was infamous for its vulnerability to internal breakage and burning out. Finally VW did something about the problem by using plug connectors with built-in resistances rather than resistance cables. VW kept its 6-volt electrical system until the 1967 models, when the switch was finally made to a 12-volt battery. All VW's are negative ground.

A number of different distributors have been fitted to VW's. Often two or three different types have been used concurrently on the same model car. Some are Bosch units, while others are of VW manufacture. The earliest Volkswagens had pure centrifugal advance distributors by Bosch, and these have always been popular replacements for the VW distributors among the performance-minded. There followed a brief period when dual-advance distributors were fitted, but from 1966 to 1970 all VW passenger cars had vacuum advance only. In the 1971 models, a switch was made back to the dual system, using both vacuum and centrifugal advance. The VW types have different point and rotor designs from the Bosch, so make sure that you are getting the right parts for your own distributor.

Static timing was used on 1967 and earlier VW's. That is, the initial spark timing is done with the engine cold and not running. This requires only a simple test light that can be connected between the distributor's primary terminal and ground. The timing marks are located on the crankshaft pulley and are very easy to see. Some mechanics, however, have been confused about the location of the stationary mark. It's simple—the stationary mark is the "split" in the center of the crankcase.

1. Hook on point tension gauge must be used just back of point surface—anywhere else will give false reading.

2. Take a good look at the tip of the rotor and the contact spring; also look for carbon tracks. If in doubt about condition, replace the part.

3. Point resistance is read on the Allen cam angle meter. If the needle stays within the black bar (about 2/10 of a volt), the points are okay.

4. Cam angle is directly related to point gap. The more gap, the less cam angle. "Dwell" and "cam angle" are synonymous terms.

A strobe timing light must be used to set the timing on all 1968 and later VW's. These engines have emission control devices, so timing should be done at idle speed with the vacuum line disconnected and the engine at normal operating temperature.

Similarly, both Bosch and VW coils have been installed with the same production run, but both have the same terminal layout and output so that no troubles arise in replacing one with the other. As with all VW wire connections, the coils have spade-type terminals for quick disconnects. The electric heating element of the automatic choke is wired through the ignition, and the entire system receives its voltage from a terminal on the starter solenoid.

The British Lucas ignition system is used in practically all English cars, including Ford of England and BMH. But while a few machines are fitted with Lodge and KLG plugs, the big manufacturers use American names like Autolite and Champion. Ford of England uses the Autolites, naturally, while BMH and Rootes (Chrysler) fit Champions.

Japanese imports generally use their domestic NGK plugs. Spark plugs for the Toyota have special small hexes to fit between the push-rod bulges in the head.

The electrical systems of most English cars are positive ground, a perverse practice to which they adhere rather like they do driving on the left of the roadway. The same basic models of Lucas distributors are used in many makes of cars, and to know one is to know them all. The construction of these units is excellent and their precision of operation is quite up to the rigors of competition.

However, there are several small features that should be noted, especially by those more familiar with domestic products. First, there is a vernier adjustment on the spark advance that makes it possible to alter the initial advance without loosening the distributor. Normally this is adjusted to the fourth graduation, but changes of altitude and different grades of fuel can be quickly compensated for by giving the knurled adjusting knob a few twirls in either the advance (A) direction (for higher altitudes and better fuels) or retard (R) direction (for lower altitudes and inferior fuels).

Secondly, there is a ground wire connecting the breaker plate to the body of the distributor. Care must be exercised when installing this to route it in a way which will not foul the advance operation. It is also important to make a clean, tight connection on the ground wire.

The Lucas movable point assembly is a very strong, lightweight phenolic combination pivot and rubbing block to which are riveted the spring and the contact mount. Since the same distributor is used for so many different cars, it's usually easy to find a set of points for, say, a 1965 Singer—which probably isn't listed in the parts store catalog—by buying a set for the more widely known MG.

Most foreign cars are static timed, but a strobe timing light can be used. One car, the Peugeot, is timed in a way reminiscent of the old Model A Ford. A rod (actually the plug wrench handle) is inserted into a hole in the bellhousing and the engine turned by hand until the rod slips into a hole bored in the flywheel. This locates the firing point for No. 1 cylinder, and the distributor is set accurately.

TUNE-UP TOOLS

There are probably more different kinds of tools used for tune-ups than for brain surgery or watchmaking. They range from such simple aids as spark plug gappers and feeler gauges to the elaborate electronic analysis units found in shops. Our purpose here is not to describe the construction and operation of these tools, but simply to outline briefly what they do. We'll separate them into three classes: those that are suitable for the home mechanic and small shop, those found in the average service station and those used in large service centers and garages.

Every home mechanic should have an accurate plug gapping gauge. It should incorporate a file and bending bar as well as loop gauges and a taper gauge. This is a professional plug man's tool, and it can handle just about any spark plug job you can name. A spark plug wrench should also be in every car owner's toolbox. It should have a magnet or a rubber sleeve inside it to hold the plugs in place during removal. A set of flat feeler gauges for gapping breaker points and a timing light are also necessary for doing a good tune-up.

Whenever points are replaced or regapped, the engine's timing should be readjusted, since even minute changes in point gap can advance or retard the ignition timing by several degrees. However, a change in timing does not affect point gap.

Timing lights are of two types. The strobe type is indispensable for setting the timing of American cars. The more inexpensive units must be used in a darkened room or at night, how-

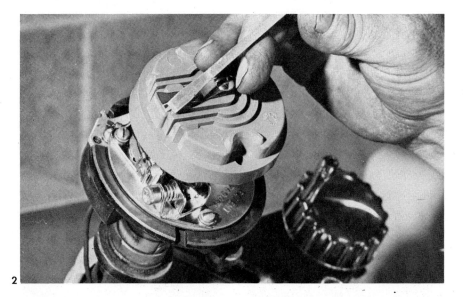

2

3

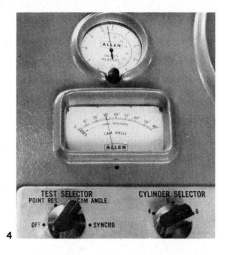

4

ever, which can have its disadvantages. Yet for the nonprofessional they represent a considerable savings over the $30 or higher cost of battery or AC-powered lights that can be used in daylight. Strobe timing lights have a cable which is connected to the plug lead of the No. 1 cylinder. A light of about 1/1200-sec. duration flashes every time the plug fires. This makes the moving mark on the engine's crankshaft pulley or flywheel appear to stand still, since there is light to see it with only when the No. 1 plug fires. By loosening the distributor and turning it in the engine, the mark on the pulley can be advanced or retarded until it aligns perfectly with the stationary mark on the engine.

Static timing lights are used to time most foreign cars. They can be used on any car, although they are definitely more time-consuming. A light for static tuning can be made quite cheaply or purchased for a few dollars. It consists of nothing more than a bulb with two test leads.

To use a static timing light, the engine is turned until the appropriate timing mark lines up with the pointer on the engine. One timing light lead is attached to ground and the other to the primary terminal of the distributor with the ignition switch on. The distributor is first turned in the engine until the light goes out, then moved slowly toward the No. 1 cylinder firing position in the direction opposite cam rotation. At the instant the points open, the light goes on. The hold-down bolt is tightened with the distributor in this final position.

When turning the crankshaft to the timing mark, do *not* reverse the engine if you accidentally go past the mark; continue for another two full crankshaft revolutions. Otherwise slack in the camshaft and distributor drives will prevent accurate timing.

Another handy tool which is not beyond the reach of the home mechanic is a VOM—Volt-Ohm-Milliammeter. The VOM is usually found in electronic stores, because it is considered more of a radio and TV repair tool than an auto repair instrument. However, there is no reason why an auto repairman can't take advantage of the excellent VOM's that are available. Besides, they are usually less expensive than an automotive instrument. The ohmmeter can be used to check the condition of ignition cables and resistors. The voltmeter is helpful for checking points, primary wiring, etc. The VOM can, of course, be used to test other parts of the automotive electrical system as well, which makes it more useful than

an ignition analyzer to the home mechanic who wishes to make a minimum investment in equipment.

Another tool that a non-professional tuner can afford is the combination dwell meter and dwell tachometer. Models with separate dwell and tach dials sell for upwards of $40, but those with a single combination dwell/tach dial may be had for less.

Service stations are usually equipped with all the above tuning devices, but theirs are often of heavy-duty construction which makes them a bit larger and able to stand up to years of hard service. In addition to timing lights, VOM's, dwell meters and ignition analyzers, service stations usually have one of the less expensive oscilloscopes. This last piece of equipment might also be in the tool kit of the nonprofessional.

The oscilloscopes in most service station tune-up bays are of relatively limited ability in comparison with really elaborate setups, but they are useful for pinpointing misses and faulty ignition components. We'll talk more about scopes later when we get to the really advanced tune-up aids.

Service stations sometimes have a spark plug cleaning machine. Most plug cleaning machines have a tester which allows the plug to be operated under different pressures to simulate engine compression. It is a common misconception that the spark plugs must be able to fire at a pressure equal to the engine's maximum compression pressure. Actually, the idea is to adjust the machine by moving

the pointer on the tester dial to indicate 100% sparking efficiency at the maximum level with a new and properly gapped plug. Used plugs are then checked and compared to this "norm." Plugs should be tested only after cleaning them, filing the electrodes square and gapping them to specifications.

The spark plug manufacturers themselves are the first to admit that the air pressure test is only an indication of how well the plug will spark in the test machine. It has about as much relation to an engine as bouncing two spark plugs on the floor and deciding that the plug that bounces higher is a "good" plug. The machine fires a plug in pure air, and the engine fires a plug in an air/fuel mixture. The machine fires a plug cold; an engine fires a plug under high temperatures. There is just no comparison. The machine is primarily a sales tool, a means to satisfy the car owner who might be irritated if he found out that there is no real way to "test" his spark plugs outside his car's engine.

We feel that the spark plug test machine has value, but only as a means of demonstrating what happens when a spark plug fires. Fouled plugs will show up beautifully as the spark travels the full length of the insulator along an oil path to ground. A new plug in the machine will show how the spark jumps from a different part of the electrode every time it fires. This "hunting" of the spark results in a slightly different required

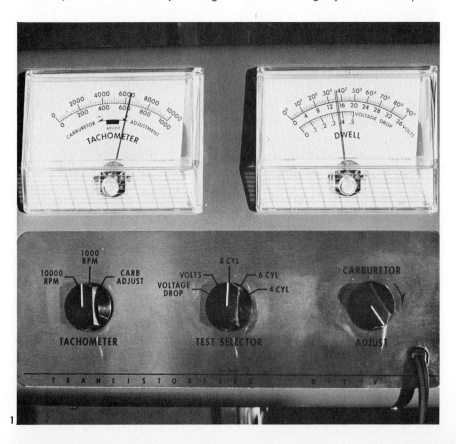

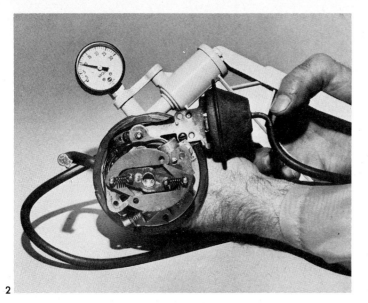

RIGHT ROTOR WRONG ROTOR

2

3

1. More expensive tach/dwell meters, such as this Allen model, read rpm and dwell at the same time. This also has a voltmeter and a very sensitive rpm scale for carburetor adjustments.

2. Mityvac suction tool is great for checking vacuum advance unit. It will test for leaks and check out the vacuum advance curve too.

3. Not all rotors are the same length. Look-alikes can cause trouble if they're accidentally installed in the wrong distributor.

voltage each time the plug fires, and this variation will show up on an oscilloscope.

Large diagnostic centers and service garages will definitely have at least one of the more versatile oscilloscopes and a distributor testing machine. The testing devices used in these big operations are usually integrated consoles that contain all types of analyzers, meters and scopes built into one cabinet. Some units contain two scopes, one of which is used solely for coil and condenser tests.

The oscilloscope is the heart of any of these systems, since it can be used to analyze most ignition ills quickly, without taking anything apart. Speed and efficiency are the only real advantages that these elaborate testing devices have over less sophisticated methods. For example, burned points and a weak condenser could be diagnosed by simply taking the points out for a visual inspection. But in so doing, the mechanic would spend more time than it would take to inspect the entire system with a good scope. Besides, if the trouble is not the points, he's wasted as much time making his inspection as he would have needed to replace them if they were faulty. In an age suffering from a shortage of trained mechanics and a superabundance of car owners de-

manding fast service, such analytical machines are practically worth their weight in gold.

Various controls on the scope make it possible to change the display to study the spark of each cylinder individually, all cylinders simultaneously for comparison or in rapid succession to pinpoint cylinder-to-cylinder differences in detail. A typical ignition test and diagnosis would be carried out as follows.

First, a test lead is connected between the coil's high-tension terminal and the high-tension wire to the distributor. Another lead is connected to the No. 1 plug and plug wire. These hookups monitor the ignition system's secondary circuit. The primary circuit is wired into the machine by making connections at the distributor's primary terminal and the coil's battery terminal. The readings achieved in the tests are compared and evaluated in relation to the car manufacturer's specifications for the particular vehicle being tested.

As the engine is started, the operator notes voltmeter. This tells him if the voltage being delivered to the coil is up to specifications. If not, the battery and cable, the ignition switch and the ballast resistance bypass are checked.

The scope display selector is then turned to the individual cylinder position for a check of the breaker points. It is possible to do this because the coil's primary current is being transmitted through the scope. The operator compares the scope pattern with the "typical" pattern illustrated. Dirty or burned points form a pattern that is not straight up and down at the point-open signal of the display. Weak point spring tension, misaligned points or poor contact show up as deviations from a normal point-closed signal, which is a short, straight downward line followed by a series of

closely grouped, rapidly diminishing oscillations.

Lastly, the secondary circuit is tested on the scope. By turning the display knob to show all cylinders, the height of the firing line for each cylinder can be compared with the others. If the voltages are uniform but too high, then late ignition timing, worn plugs or an excessively large rotor gap is indicated. If the height of the patterns varies from cylinder to cylinder, then breaks in the plug cables, irregularly worn or gapped plugs, a cocked or worn distributor cap or a bent shaft may be indicated.

The voltage available to the plugs can also be determined by disconnecting a plug lead so that no spark fires. The height of the pattern should exceed 20,000 volts. Other positions of the controls make it possible to check the insulation of the secondary circuit, its resistance and the condition of the spark plugs.

The important thing to remember is that a complete picture of the ignition system can be obtained without removing or visually inspecting a single part. Additional tests using the scope will show up any irregularities in the spark advance, which calls for complete testing on a distributor machine.

Synchrograph-type distributor testers (distributor machines) can not only determine the amount of advance at different speeds but can pinpoint the number of degrees of rotation between the firing of one cylinder and the next. In addition to a motor that drives the distributor at varying speeds, the testing machine has a vacuum hose. The hose can be connected to the distributor to simulate engine vacuum for checking the functioning of the vacuum advance. Most irregularities in timing occur as a result of wear or dirt in the distributor's moving parts. Since the unit can be observed and tested while in actual operation, the particular source of trouble is quickly discernible. On some distributors it is possible to adjust the advance mechanisms to get the desired curve, but on most it is necessary to replace or perhaps modify the calibrated springs that control the rates of advance.

Distributor testing machines use a strobe light similar to an ignition timing light. The flash of light illuminates an arrow on the machine that appears to be stationary. The arrow points to a number on the degree scale or protractor. As the advance mechanism operates, the arrow appears to move to other figures, indicating the number of degrees of advance at different rpm. The machine can be operated at various speeds to simulate the full rpm range of the engine.

Distributor defects also show up and can be diagnosed by the manner in which the tester records the distributor's operation. For example, point-bouncing due to a weak spring or binding pivot will show up as erratic or faint flashes of light preceding the regular flashes. A worn cam or distributor shaft or a bent shaft are indicated by variations in excess of 1° from the exact timing of the individual sparks or by wandering and erratic flashes.

Many manufacturers, such as Allen, Autoscan, Hanson, Heyer, Hoyt, KalEquip, Marquette, Neihoff, Proto, Simson and Sun make excellent tune-up equipment. Your local auto parts store probably handles several makes, including some we haven't mentioned. If you are undecided about which make to buy, compare the guarantees. And find out whether repairs on the equipment can be done locally. If you have to send the unit to the factory for repairs, it may be several weeks before it is returned to you.

Most of the major garage equipment is so expensive that it is not practical for home use. However, most of the makers of large garage equipment also make hand-held tune-up meters which are both accurate and dependable.

Inexpensive tune-up meters are marketed widely through department stores, discount stores and chain stores. Be very cautious about buying equipment that is really low-priced. Good tune-up equipment is expensive. When you find a unit that is unusually low in price, you have a right to question its quality.

TUNE-UP PROCEDURES

When doing your own tune-ups, it is very helpful to have at least a sensitive voltmeter or VOM and a tach/dwell meter. Below we outline a typical tune-up of an ignition with breaker points. We describe some of the tests that can be made with test equipment. These tests can pinpoint automotive troubles that might otherwise escape your notice or be almost impossible to detect.

The first step in a good home tune-up is to remove and inspect all the spark plugs. By comparing their appearance with the photos in the spark plug chapter, you can often identify engine troubles or ignition weaknesses. If you are using resistor plugs, they can be tested with an ohmmeter. If there is no reading or a resistance in excess of 20,000 ohms, replace the plug regardless of its apparent condition. Booster gap and regular plugs should not be given a resistance test, because it would be inconclusive. If the plugs have been in service for 10,000 miles or more, you'll save time, performance and fuel by replacing them now. Spark plugs that are fired by the new high-energy systems will last 20,000 miles or more, however. Plugs with less than maximum mileage should still be inspected to determine if cleaning is necessary. If there are no significant deposits, it's best not to sandblast the plugs. If the electrodes are eroded

slightly, they should be squared up with a file and regapped. If their condition is almost like new, a simple regapping is all that's required.

The ohmmeter can now be connected to the terminals at either end of each spark cable and the resistance noted. Despite what some car makers say, it's best to keep the resistance of resistor-type cables on the low side of 15,000 ohms. Metallic-core cables should be checked for continuity and high-resistance joints. This type of cable should show perfect conductivity (zero resistance) on the VOM.

The distributor cap should be washed clean with soapy water and air dried thoroughly. Inspect the interior contacts and terminals for wear and erosion. If the contacts show enough wear to widen the rotor gap, the cap needs replacing. Similarly, if the rotor tip is noticeably eroded or worn, it should be discarded in favor of a new one.

The points can be tested in the car with a voltmeter to determine if the contact faces are "making" adequately. A voltage drop of more than two-tenths of a volt on a sensitive meter indicates that there is poor contact between the points. To do the voltage drop test correctly, you need a voltmeter with a low-reading

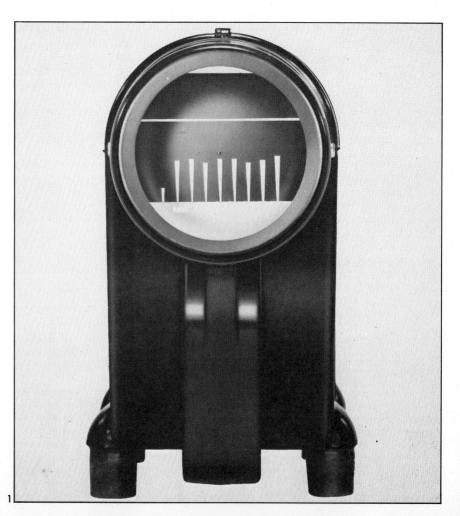

1

scale of about one to three volts. A higher scale can be used, but it won't be as accurate, because we want to read in tenths of a volt.

To test the points for voltage drop, remove the center wire from the distributor and ground it to the block so the engine won't accidentally start. Then bump the starter gently until the distributor points are closed. Be sure the points are closed—you should see daylight between the rubbing block and the cam.

Connect one voltmeter clip to the primary terminal on the side of the distributor, if it has one, or to the

1. This plug scope is one of the less expensive forms of scope testers. It measures the voltage being delivered to the plugs. Short line at left is a "minimum" mark for comparison. The eight tall marks show comparative voltages of cylinders.

2. Low-priced neon timing lights such as this can be had for less than $10, but they must be used in partial darkness. One cable slips into the distributor No. 1 terminal, the other clips to the No. 1 cable or spark plug.

3. Small analyzers are less expensive than buying a full set of individual instruments. But be sure you are going to use all the features of the analyzer or you may be buying more than you need.

primary terminal on the distributor side of the coil. Connect the other clip to a good ground on the engine. Turn the ignition switch on and read the voltage drop on the meter. It should be not more than two-tenths of a volt. A higher reading on the voltmeter means that there is excessive resistance somewhere in the circuit between the two voltmeter clips. That would include all connections and grounds. Usually the trouble is dirty or worn points that aren't making good contact.

If visual inspection reveals only normal frosting of the contact surfaces, the points can be smoothed with a point file and retested. Point filing is rarely satisfactory, however. It is usually best to replace them. If you have access to a condenser tester, test the condenser for capacity, breakdown, leakage and series resistance. Some electronic technicians use an ohmmeter to check condensers, which they call capacitors. The ohmmeter will give an indication of capacity, but it should not be used to test a condenser because it may not detect a bad condenser. A zero reading means the condenser is bad, but an infinity reading won't show high series resistance.

The series resistance test is not a simple resistance test. It is done on a

condenser tester by inserting the condenser into a high-frequency oscillator circuit. It determines whether there is any resistance between the pigtail and the foil or between the can and the foil.

Next, check the distributor cam for wear, and also all advance parts and their bushings. Wiggle the cam back and forth to detect any looseness, and check the condition of the "bumpers" on Delco centrifugal advances. If the distributor has been in service for a year or more, the advance parts should be washed clean with solvent and thoroughly relubricated.

When installing the points and advance parts, make sure that they are lubed to the manufacturer's specs. Also, be certain that the points and the condenser are in good ground contact with the breaker plate. The points should be gapped to specifications and the cam greased with distributor cam grease, not brake grease. Any point misalignment must be corrected. Also, a protective coating is applied to some new points, and this must be wiped away before they are put into service.

With the distributor back on the engine and everything hooked up, the dwell angle can be tested with a tach/dwell meter—if you have one. There is no need to check the dwell if the points were set to specs with a feeler gauge, unless you just want to double-check your work. If by chance the correct point gap results in a dwell reading that is many degrees off, it indicates that you have the wrong parts in the distributor or that something is bent out of line, such as the points or the breaker plate. There's a chance you might have the wrong distributor, too, or even the wrong specifications. *Remember* —changing the dwell (point gap) also changes the timing, but timing changes do not affect dwell. Therefore, always adjust the dwell and *then* the timing.

Adjust the engine idle at the carburetor until the manufacturer's prescribed idle speed is reached. In the last few years, American cars have come with a tune-up decal. This decal is located in a conspicuous spot in the engine compartment. It provides idle speed, dwell and timing specs for that car's engine and should be consulted during each tune-up.

Switch from the tachometer to the dwell scale and adjust the points until the specified angle is indicated. If the points were gapped to specs, dwell should be within the permissible zone. If not, the gap can be readjusted until dwell is exactly right.

Now it's time to hook up the timing light. Connect its cables to the No. 1

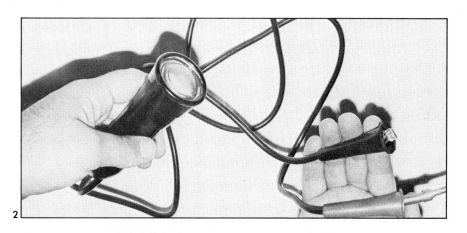

2

3

spark plug wire, either at the cap or the plug, and start the engine. Most engines require that the vacuum hose be disconnected from the distributor at this time. This will slow down the engine enough so that the timing mark can be seen. Aim the timing light at the engine's timing pointer and move the slightly loosened distributor back and forth until the correct mark aligns with the pointer. Then tighten the hold-down bolt. It's helpful at this time to brighten the timing mark with chalk or white paint so that it can be seen more easily. And that concludes your home tune-up. It wasn't so bad, was it?

A complete tune-up includes much more than spark plug and distributor work. You should also check the battery, starter and compression and adjust the belts and the carburetor idle. Additional items that should be checked or serviced are the air cleaner, crankcase breather, smog valve, fuel filter, heat riser valve, cooling system and engine valves, if adjustable. If you want to go all out, also tighten the intake manifold and check charging voltage, choke operation, fuel pump pressure, the air/fuel ratio and look underneath the car for possible oil leaks.

In a garage, many of these items are checked as a part of every tune-up. The idea is to catch the weak parts before they break down and cause trouble on the road. If the mechanic is talented, he can spot impending trouble.

Much of the foregoing can be ignored if your car is equipped with any of the four factory electronic ignition systems. All that need be done

with these ignitions is to gap and change the spark plugs at the indicated intervals, replace spark plug wires when needed and set the timing on the distributor. Much easier and cheaper tune-ups, better gas mileage and plugs that last two or three times longer than with ordinary ignitions are some of the advantages of pointless ignitions.

IGNITION EMERGENCIES

Every driver is likely to have an on-the-road ignition failure at least once in his life. It's like death and taxes. Usually you're all dressed up and in a hurry to get someplace when the spark disappears. There you are, left with a car that's deader than King Tut's mother-in-law—and not so much as a point file or a feeler gauge on hand, let alone an ignition analyzer! There's often a strong temptation to get out that ultimate tool kit, the dime, and phone the nearest garage that offers road service. But that won't impress your friends nearly as much as "bringing 'er back alive" yourself.

If the basic cause of the trouble appears to be a battery that just doesn't have the oomph to crank the engine and still provide a good spark, part of the problem is no doubt being caused by bad ignition wires, worn-out plugs or burned points. But these items can't be replaced when you lack sufficient tools, parts and time. What *can* be done is to take some of the load off the starter. The following method is brutal, but it works—assuming that you have a spark plug wrench in your car. Remove from two to four of the spark plugs from every other cylinder in the firing order and place their cables where they will not

be grounded or throw a spark. This will not only speed up the engine's cranking speed, but will increase coil saturation enough to noticeably improve the spark. Once the car is running, you can screw the other plugs back in and hook them up. Shades of Grandpa and his '31 Essex!

You can also get yourself started when voltage seems to be getting low by decreasing the plug gaps to lower the spark plugs' voltage requirement. In fact, wide gaps that haven't been checked for some time might be the cause of the trouble. A common paper clip can be used for a gap gauge. If the weather is damp, wipe all the plug insulators dry as well as the coil nose, wiring and the inside and outside of the distributor cap. If the plug terminals seem to fit loosely, squeeze the connectors together

1. This is GM's new high-voltage distributor and coil system. Both V-8's and 6-cylinders use the same system; only the number of wires is different.

2. This hand-held tach/dwell also has a high ohms scale and a 0-20 voltmeter. Disadvantage is the limited range of each scale, but it was necessary in order to get so many scales into such a small package. The rpm scale reads from 0-1000.

3. Autolite Ford points come in two styles. If you don't like the pivotless kind, the regular pivot type can be readily substituted.

4. The number of tune-up instruments on the market is unending. This instrument produced by RAC features dual-range tach. One scale measures from 0-8000 rpm, while other measures from 0-1200 rpm. Also included are a dual dwell-angle scale, a points resistance scale and a volt-amp meter.

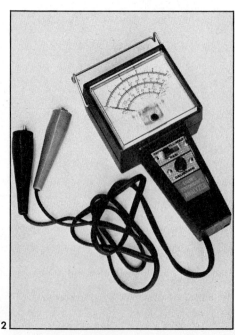

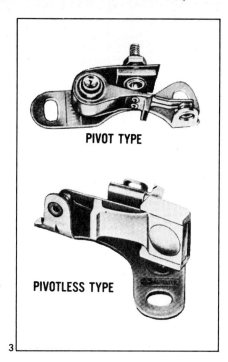

PIVOT TYPE

PIVOTLESS TYPE

3

4

slightly for a better grip and scrape away any obvious corrosion with a nail file, pipe tool or penknife. Make sure all wires are tight and have good connections. Just by cleaning up a lot of little things, you can often pick up several thousand additional volts at the plugs.

If the engine cranks over fast but still doesn't start, don't waste the battery's valuable remaining voltage; get out and check that spark! Pull the high-tension cable from the center terminal of the distributor cap and hold it near a grounded place on the engine. Have somebody run the starter with the ignition switch on. If you have no one to help, you can turn the key on (making sure that the transmission is out of gear) and run the starter by shorting across the two big terminals on the starter relay or solenoid. On some cars even this isn't possible, so you'll have to take off the distributor cap and bump the starter until the points are together, but near one of the cam lobes. You can then turn the breaker plate enough by hand to make the points break and throw a spark from the high-tension cable.

If you get no spark or a weak, yellowish spark, separate the points with a piece of paper. Then trigger the spark by shorting the movable contact to the breaker plate with the tip of a screwdriver. Next, remove the screwdriver. If a good spark is produced, the trouble is the points, which are probably wet, burned or pitted.

You can usually get the points to make better contact—and start the engine—with only a modest amount of cleaning up. After all, the engine has been running on them until now.

A fingernail file or emery board can be pressed into service for this, and in less fortunate circumstances, scraping the contacts with a penknife or burnishing them with a screwdriver blade will probably get most of the crust off them.

In many cases the point trouble turns out to be rubbing block wear that has allowed their gap to approach nil. This often kills the engine while you are driving and is not limited exclusively to a no-start situation. There's no need to panic if you don't have a feeler gauge or dwell meter in your hip pocket. This is an emergency, not a pre-race tune-up. The handle of a fingernail file, your thumbnail or a couple of old ticket stubs can serve as your feeler gauge.

And then there's that old cornball trick of "borrowing" somebody's distributor rotor. If you have that kind of "friends," you can protect yourself from their stunts by carrying an old rotor in the glove compartment for emergencies.

But if you don't have a spare, why give up right away? Be a hero and make your own rotor! Here's where it pays to have a roll of high-quality electrical tape in your car. By wrapping the end of the distributor shaft with several layers of tape, you can insulate it fairly effectively. Then bend a paper clip, safety pin, nail, car key, a bit of wire—anything metallic—into a "J" shape, so that the hook of the J points up in the middle of the distributor cap and the stem of the J reaches out to the contacts in the distributor cap. Tape it in place and you may be able to drive at least as far as the nearest garage. One resourceful driver improvised a rotor from an art-gum eraser and a safety

pin, using only his pocket knife. The amazing thing was that he drove around with it for about a week before bothering to buy a new rotor!

If you're stranded somewhere and a check of the ignition system turns up a carbon track on the coil nose, distributor cap or rotor that's allowing your spark current to escape, you can file or scrape a wide slot through the carbon track so that the conductive path is broken. Never trust such repairs for long, since the carbon nearly always comes back, particularly after the smooth glaze of the insulator has been cut away, but it's better than waiting for road service and having to pay for the call.

Occasionally a distributor holddown bolt loosens and allows the distributor to turn in the engine. The result is spark timing that's so far retarded that the car hardly has the power to move itself. It may not even start. You can retime the engine quite accurately without a timing light by using a piece of thin paper, such as cigarette paper, or a strip of cellophane. Simply turn the engine until the timing mark for the No. 1 cylinder is lined up with the pointer. You may have to take out the plug from the No. 1 cylinder and make sure that the piston is on its compression stroke by placing your thumb over the hole while cranking the engine. However, the distributor probably won't have turned so far that the rotor is not in the general vicinity of the No. 1 terminal.

With the engine positioned on the timing mark, place the strip of paper or cellophane between the point contacts. Turn the distributor to position the rubbing block just before the cam lobe for No. 1 cylinder. Exert a light but steady pull on the paper strip. Now rotate the distributor toward the No. 1 firing position. Stop turning the distributor the instant that the points release their grip on the paper. Tighten the distributor retaining bolt. *Voilà!* The engine is now timed.

It never hurts to carry a spare rotor, condenser, breaker point assembly and some extra plugs in the car, along with a few basic tools and supplies. However, preventing trouble in the first place is far more important than being able to cope with emergencies. Regular tune-ups properly done are the key. Just installing new plugs and a tune-up kit may get you by for a while, but little things like ignition cable tests, timing adjustments, spark advance checks and proper lubrication of all moving parts are what it really takes if you want to keep all the performance that was designed into your car. Some people are happy if their car just runs, but personally, we're not happy unless it's running *right*.

HOW-TO: **IGNITION TUNE-UP**

1. The first step is to remove the air cleaner and examine it for cleanliness. If it's restricting airflow, change it.

2. We're using a Ford truck engine to demonstrate tune-up procedures. Here the mechanic is removing old spark plugs.

3. Now is a good time to run a check on the engine's compression. Cylinders shouldn't vary more than 10-15 psi if okay.

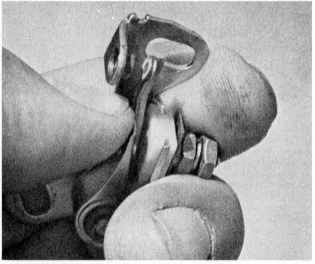

4. If your ignition system still uses breaker points and they are burned as this set is, you'll have to change them.

5. Although you'd probably leave the distributor on the engine, our shop removed it for easier access to the points.

6. Remove points and condenser from the distributor. Before installing new points, use a good cam lube on the cam wheel.

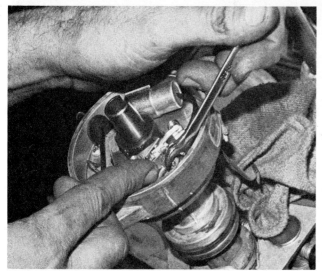

7. Install the new point set and carefully adjust to the proper setting, with the cam follower resting on a lobe.

8. In case you've removed it, reinstall the distributor and tighten the hold-down bolt sufficiently to hold it in place.

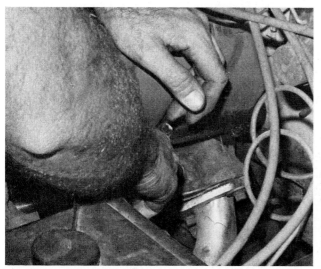

9. Install new spark plugs (don't forget to gap them to your engine's specs) with fingers first. Then tighten with wrench.

10. The cost of this trick timing light is prohibitive, but it tells you dwell angle and timing degrees simultaneously.

11. You may also have to adjust the air/fuel mixture to get engine to idle smoothly. Autolite 2-bbl. has screws in front.

12. A stuck PCV valve can cause rough idling and dirty plugs. Check it by shaking. If it's okay, the valve ball will rattle.

Aftermarket Ignition Conversions

MORE MILES PER GALLON, HIGHER ENGINE PERFORMANCE, MORE MILES BETWEEN TUNE-UPS, REDUCED EMISSIONS—THE BEST OF ALL WORLDS COMES IN A "BLACK BOX."

Whenever a manufacturer wants to sell his latest fancy ignition, he runs a test that shows that his unit puts out more voltage than any other ignition. If you read enough ads with claims of extremely high available voltage, you may begin to think that voltage is the only thing necessary to make your ignition the best in the world. We have been as guilty as anyone else in succumbing to the lure of the advertisements. After all, if ignition A puts out more voltage than unit B, the one we want is A, right? Sorry, but it isn't necessarily so. Unit A may put out more voltage, but is it mechanically more dependable than B? In 99 cases out of 100, the cause of an ignition failure is mechanical, not electrical; you can blame burned bearings, wires that broke, screws that unscrewed, timing that slipped, etc., etc.

The importance of extremely high secondary voltage for more performance has been somewhat overplayed. An ignition system, regardless of type, produces only that voltage necessary to jump the spark plug gap and ignite the air/fuel mixture. In perfect condition, a good rotor, distributor cap and silicone wires can't handle much more than 32,000 volts. If an ignition could produce more than that, then the extra voltage would escape as crossfire in the cap or arcing at the wires; besides, an engine just doesn't need that much voltage. An ignition advertised to produce 40,000 volts may have the potential to do it, but unless the cables are in good condition, only a fraction of that voltage will ever reach the plugs.

Today there are many ignition products on the market that claim increased voltage and performance with lower emissions. These products include coils, magnetos, dual-point distributors, dual-point conversion kits, capacitive discharge (CD) ignition systems and transistorized breakerless systems. Some of them are very good and actually perform as advertised, but others should be avoided as you would an angry skunk.

In most cases, if the engine is kept in perfect tune, the stock factory system provides more than enough voltage for normal street driving. However, there are a few situations in which the aftermarket performance parts will do the job that the stock Detroit parts may indeed be incapable of doing.

As a spark plug's electrodes wear, its gap increases, so more voltage is required before the spark is able to jump across the larger gap. If uncorrected, the gap eventually increases to the point where the plug requires more voltage than the coil can produce. In this situation, the plugs should be replaced; however, a high-output coil or system would probably be able to fire the worn plugs.

Oil- or gas-fouled plugs are difficult for a stock ignition to fire, but not always for a true high-performance setup. Gas-fouled plugs are most common in large, carbureted, high-compression, high-horsepower engines. Whenever these are operated in city traffic or allowed to idle for long periods, they tend to load up and stall unless the throttle is "blipped" from time to time. Oil-fouled plugs are usually a symptom of bad piston rings or leaking valve seals. Using a high-voltage system to fire them would be fighting the symptom, not providing a cure. It's a cheap way of putting off an inevitable engine job.

Until recently, the most common application for high-performance coils, mags, distributors and transistor ignitions was on modified engines built to wind above 7000 rpm. Most conventional stock ignitions are designed to provide a hot spark up to a relatively low engine speed. At higher rpm with the points system, the points open and close so quickly that the coil's primary winding has less time to absorb voltage. As a result,

1. This is Chrysler's breakerless distributor. The circular piece in the center is the reluctor, which has one ridge for each engine cylinder. A sandwich-type magnet attached to a pickup coil is mounted next to it. Each time a reluctor ridge passes the magnet, the attraction is strong enough to be transferred to the pickup. The pickup amplifies the voltage and sends a signal to the control box on the fender; within, a transistor opens the primary circuit and the plug is fired.

2. This exploded view shows you the details of Chrysler's 8-cylinder electronic distributor.

1

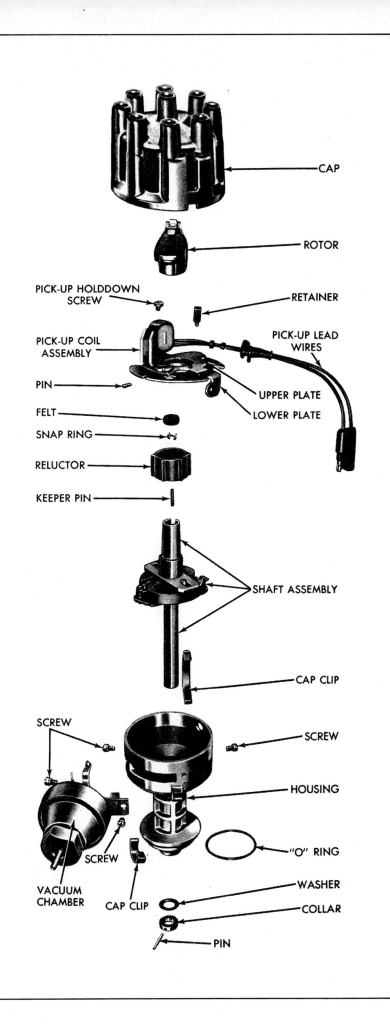

CAP

ROTOR

PICK-UP HOLDDOWN SCREW

RETAINER

PICK-UP COIL ASSEMBLY

PICK-UP LEAD WIRES

PIN

UPPER PLATE

FELT

LOWER PLATE

SNAP RING

RELUCTOR

KEEPER PIN

SHAFT ASSEMBLY

CAP CLIP

SCREW

SCREW

HOUSING

"O" RING

VACUUM CHAMBER

SCREW

CAP CLIP

WASHER

COLLAR

PIN

with the stock points system, secondary voltage to the plugs decreases and the engine sputters just when victory is in sight. However, for most street use, a good stock Detroit ignition provides plenty of spark. It's been found that in many cases the heavy-duty (truck or industrial) version of a stock coil produces as much voltage as many of the so-called super models, or even more.

One of the chief claims of the "super coils" is that they are oil-filled. But many stock coils are oil-filled too. An oil-filled coil transmits heat from the windings to the case more effectively, thereby keeping the windings cooler and lowering the resistance at the same time.

As with many products, the key phrase is "Let the buyer beware!" You should carefully investigate the top-name coils and ignition systems before making a purchase.

YOU, ME AND THE SMOG LAWS

We have reached the point where we all realize the severity of the smog problem and agree that it must be controlled. Congress has passed laws establishing emissions standards and Detroit must equip cars with devices to meet these standards. The Environmental Protection Agency (EPA), a Federal agency, sets up test procedures and approves or rejects emissions control devices on all cars sold in the U.S. As a result, compression ratios have been lowered, and each year the list of power-robbing smog controls increases.

In a time of rising fuel prices, gas economy has dropped and prices for cars have gone up while their power has greatly declined. The new engines are designed for the emissions equipment, so merely disconnecting the devices not only increases pollution but often results in a car that runs poorly or not at all.

Also, in many states it is illegal to disconnect, remove or change your car's emissions control systems. The law is enforced and stiff fines are issued to offenders. California law regarding emissions is most strict, but it usually sets a precedent for other states, so be prepared.

The performance enthusiast has been faced with a dilemma. He can escape the tougher emissions laws by registering his car in a more lenient state, or he can work within the law and modify his car for more power but fewer emissions. The cheapest and easiest way to considerably reduce emissions and raise power is still through a complete tune-up.

However, today an increasing number of manufacturers are producing speed equipment compatible with the stricter laws. It is now possible to perform modifications and not have to tamper with the existing smog equipment—proving once again that performance and cleaner air are much more compatible than many non-automotive-thinking legislators may believe.

Many top-name performance companies are busy designing and testing quality ignitions, manifolds, headers and carburetors, including a sonically controlled carburetor replacement. Detroit and the EPA have taken notice of these developments and are more than casually interested. The performance industry and the hot rodder may just save the life of the internal combustion engine and bring about a renaissance of performance through previously unattainable engine efficiency. Such efficiency would contribute to improved fuel economy and, even more important, much cleaner air.

Anytime you increase the combustion efficiency of an engine, you increase power and lower emissions. One way of increasing efficiency is by increasing the voltage to the plugs. More voltage results in more complete combustion and therefore lower hydrocarbon (HC) and carbon monoxide (CO) emissions. The hotter spark created by a CD ignition can burn through plug deposits and reduce the chances of plug misfiring. Misfiring from plug deposits or worn plugs or points results in incomplete combustion and greater emissions. Higher voltage is essential for better fuel economy. The stock breaker points ignition system is usually fine for everyday driving if kept in perfect tune, but as the points wear, which they do from their first firing, voltage output drops to the point where the ignition misfires or doesn't fire at all. Without spark, there can be no fire, and it's quite embarrassing to shut off halfway to work or play. An aftermarket ignition will provide higher voltage than a stock system at any rpm, which results in more power when needed.

ELECTRONIC IGNITIONS

The latest products in aftermarket high-performance ignitions are the much-improved electronic ignition systems. There are many new ones on the market and many good units are now available, so ask around and consider only name brands before buying. The electronic ignitions are basically of three types: magnetic-pulse transistorized breakerless ignitions, transistorized units using stock breaker points or the capacitor dis-

charge (CD) system with or without points.

A few years ago, similar aftermarket CD and transistor units were introduced, but most met with early failure from electrical breakdown. The bugs have since been ironed out, so many new systems are very dependable, though their earlier reputation is

only now being overcome. Nevertheless, when choosing that new ignition, don't forget that when a breakerless unit breaks, you're stuck. Those units that retain the points can be switched back to conventional use in the event of a malfunction.

The magnetic-pulse—transistor, not CD—breakerless systems sold by

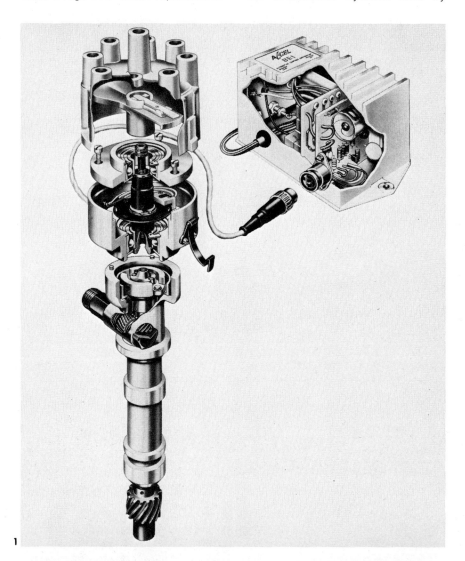

1

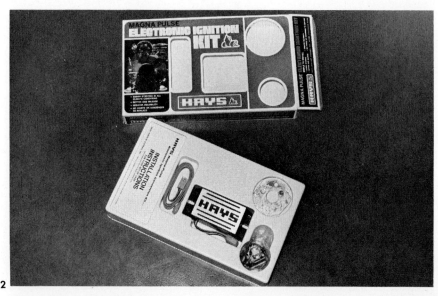

2

speed shops are patterned after Chrysler's electronic ignition. A reluctor is pressed over the cam on the conventional distributor. Like the cam, it has six or eight ridges, depending on the number of engine cylinders. Mounted directly below the reluctor is a plate almost identical to the conventional contact plate, but the pickup coil assembly replaces the condenser and contact points. This pickup coil assembly consists of a permanent rectangular magnet sandwiched between two metal pieces. One metal piece is shaped so that it can anchor the assembly to the contact plate, while the outer piece, or pole piece as it is called, is also part of the pickup coil. As the distributor shaft rotates, the reluctor rotates past the pickup unit in much the same way that the cam passes the conventional contact-point rubbing block.

During one distributor shaft revolution (equal to two crankshaft revolutions), all six (or eight) reluctor ridges pass close to the pickup unit. The reluctor ridges pass closer to the magnet than do its low areas, so magnetic attraction is greatest when the ridges pass. Each time a reluctor ridge passes the magnet, the attraction is strong enough to be transferred through the pole piece to the pickup coil.

This little coil is actually another magnet, but a stronger one due to the large amount of finely coiled wire contained within it. The coil produces

an amplified voltage, which is then sent through the pickup coil leads to the control unit on the firewall or fender.

To simplify things, one could say that a reluctor ridge signals the pickup unit each time a spark plug is to be fired. That is why there is one ridge for each plug.

The signal is received by the pickup coil and sent through the wire to the control unit. Located within the control unit is a power-switching transistor that performs the job formerly

done by the contact points. When the control unit receives the signal, the transistor opens the primary circuit. As with open contact points, this induces the high voltage into the ignition coil's secondary winding and the spark plug fires.

The beauty of the breakerless system is the absence of points, resulting in a maintenance-free distributor. Dwell adjustment is no longer necessary or possible. There are no points to burn, no rubbing block to wear and no condenser.

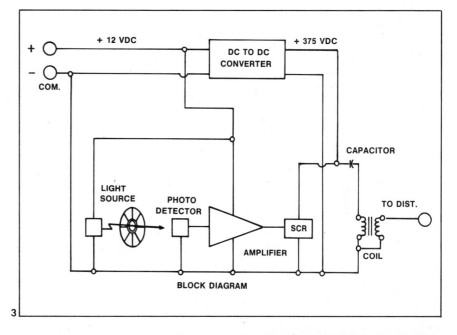

1. This superman's view of Accel's BEI CD gives you a pretty good idea of how it works. The black disc in the distributor is the shutter, which contains one hole for each engine cylinder. It rotates with the shaft and passes through the light-emitting diode. As each shutter hole passes through it, the control box is triggered and voltage is released to the spark plug.

2. Hays makes a Magna-Pulse Street and Strip system for all GM, Autolite and Motorcraft distributors, plus a replacement power module for Chrysler Corp. products. Shown here is the system for Motorcraft distributors. Included is Hays Power Module, custom wiring harness, cap, rotor and a new Motorcraft distributor already converted to an electronic unit. All the parts shown are included in purchase price.

3. Here's a schematic of Accel's BEI. It uses photocell (light-emitting diode) timing, so there are no points to wear out. The control box is CD and it's triggered by diode, which is unaffected by heat or vibration. The unit combines the high voltage and short spark duration of a CD with a maintenance-free distributor. Accel guarantees that its system will not vary more than ± ¼° in timing even at top rpm.

4. One of the neater features of the Accel BEI unit is the instant timing. Just loosen the Allen screw and turn the flat to numeral 1 (arrow).

Conversions

On a conventional system, the points and rubbing block wear; this results in ignition timing changes. Timing at higher speeds fluctuates due to point bounce, so timing accuracy at competitive speeds is reduced as engine speed increases.

This problem is solved with the breakerless system. Since there are no points to bounce, timing at high engine speeds is extremely accurate. More voltage is provided by a breakerless ignition at higher rpm than with a conventional system. As with the conventional system, voltage reaches a peak and then drops off—but it reaches a higher peak than with the conventional system. This ensures voltage when necessary at high speeds, but without the timing wander of either the conventional or CD breaker-point systems.

The ideal setup is now being produced by a few companies. It combines the CD control box with the breakerless system. The price is higher, but it's the best of both worlds.

Of the two systems—with-points or transistorized CD or breakerless—the breakerless is better for reducing emissions. With no points or rubbing block to wear, timing does not change. Ignition always takes place at the correct time (provided that the advance mechanisms and the rest of the engine are operating correctly). As a result, combustion is more complete and doesn't vary as in the conventional breaker-point system. Plugs burn cleaner and there are no points to burn, so the chances of engine misfiring are greatly diminished, thereby reducing emissions and increasing gas mileage.

Avoiding misfiring is especially important in those cars equipped with a catalytic converter. One or two fouled plugs can eventually destroy a converter. For this reason, Detroit has included a breakerless transistor ignition on all cars since '75. A breakerless CD would probably do a much better job, but it's much more expensive to build. As standard equipment, its cost would have to be added to the price of the car. Consequently, the cheaper transistor unit was chosen instead.

Aftermarket CD units have a control box that operates in a manner similar to the Oldsmobile unit of the late '60's, but Olds used a magnetic-pulse distributor and most aftermarket units have stock breaker points. However, there are a couple of good units which, like the Olds, have combined the CD control box with a breakerless distributor. These are discussed later.

The breaker-point CD system retains the points but uses them only as a switch to signal the transistorized control box, or amplifier as Oldsmobile calls it. Point burning is minimal, because a current flow of less than 1 amp passes through the points as compared to the 3 or 4 amps (at low speeds) of a conventional system. The box contains a transformer which transforms 12 battery volts into 300 and stores them in a capacitor, also located within the box. When the distributor points signal the box, the capacitor releases the 300 volts to the primary side of the coil.

During starting, a conventional breaker-point ignition introduces 12 battery volts to the coil's primary winding. Only about 8 volts are delivered while running. This voltage creates a magnetic field within the primary winding. However, when the points open, the magnetic field collapses, inducing approximately 25,000 volts into the secondary winding, which goes on to the plugs. The CD system releases not 8 volts but 300 to the primary, which becomes approximately 40,000 volts at the coil's secondary outlet. The spark gets to the plugs much faster than in a conventional or a magnetic-pulse (transistorized) ignition.

This very fast "rise time" is characteristic of CD systems. Rise time for a conventional ignition is from 75 to 125 microseconds (millionths of a second), while some magnetic-pulse systems are even slower. A CD system has a rise time of only 20 microseconds, enabling it to fire even badly fouled plugs. Spark plugs last longer with a CD ignition than with the others, because the spark duration is very short—about 1/6 as long as a conventional system. The voltage is high, but it stays at the plugs for only a very short time; therefore plug electrode erosion is reduced.

For serious competition, the CD system has an advantage over the transistorized breakerless units. A CD unit increases voltage with rpm, while voltage drops off with a breakerless

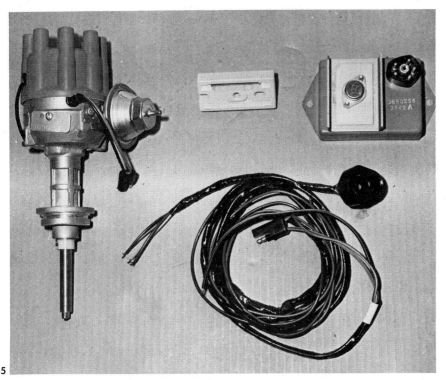

1. Speedatron really puts out the voltage. The manufacturer claims that it can be installed in less than 15 mins. It's also said to produce faster starting, better mileage and a hotter spark, and the claims are backed with a money-back guarantee.

2. From American Racing comes this CD ignition. It uses the stock distributor and breaker points but includes a feature different from any other system. It's an auto theft control device that American calls "safe-t-key." An electrical receptacle is plugged into the box and a flat plastic key imprinted with a circuit is inserted into the receptacle The key completes the circuit to the distributor, and without it the car won't start.

3. Mardek's entry into the ignition field is the Mobelec CD. It's one of the few ignitions that combines CD with breakerless. Installation is simple and one kit will fit any American car—4, 6 or 8-cylinder—and also most imports.

4. Probably the most revolutionary ignition is Autotronics' Multiple Spark Discharge. The box is triggered by the stock points, at which time it emits not just one spark per cylinder but several high-energy sparks. This results in more complete combustion and thus fewer emissions, as well as greater economy and higher performance.

5. For you Mopar fans, this is the best deal in town. You get everything necessary to convert over to an electronic breakerless system. Your local Chrysler parts man will take your order.

magnetic-pulse system. The spark is there with CD no matter what the engine speed.

In addition, the CD system provides easier starting when the battery is low or on cold mornings—without draining much battery current. This feature is made possible by the transformer within the control box. The transformer takes what little battery voltage may be available and greatly amplifies it.

The presence of the transformer makes the CD system better than the breakerless magnetic unit when it comes to firing fouled plugs or saving batteries, but unlike the breakerless unit, most aftermarket CD units utilize the stock distributor and points. The points are usually conventional, and in time, the friction of the distributor cam on the rubbing block wears it down, resulting in timing changes and fluctuations. Of course the breakerless unit doesn't have this problem,

since the points have been totally eliminated for a maintenance-free distributor. The timing on a breakerless unit does not change. It remains the same as when first adjusted and stays predictable throughout the speed range.

For street or strip, the CD unit is becoming increasingly popular because it combines high-rpm strip operation with easier starting and longer point and plug life for street use. Oil- and gas-fouled plugs are no obstacle to the higher voltage of the CD system. The Porsche 911S had an inherent plug fouling problem which was solved by making the Bosch CD its standard ignition. Many fleet cars have also switched to CD units to prolong point and plug life and to maintain the good gas mileage of a fresh tune-up.

The hottest setup is one that, like Oldsmobile's, combines the CD control box with the breakerless distribu-

tor. The result is the best of both systems and a great combination for both street and strip. Unlike the breakerless system, voltage keeps increasing with rpm (the voltage drops off in the breakerless unit) and there are no points to worry about as in most CD units. A magnetic-pulse system or a light-emitting diode replaces the points; therefore timing is predictable and timing changes due to worn points are nonexistent. Fouled plugs fire easily and they last longer, reducing emissions and increasing overall gas mileage. The only disadvantage is price. These combination units are expensive to make, so they cost quite a bit more than the transistorized breakerless systems.

POPULAR IGNITIONS

Some of the most popular electronic ignitions today are made by Hays, Mallory, Prestolite, Accel, Speedatron, Delta and Gaylord Electronics. Hays has an excellent line of kits they call the Magna-Pulse Street and Strip kits. They're designed so that anybody can convert a stock GM or Ford distributor into an electronic unit.

The Hays kits include a transistorized control box with wiring harness, a base plate for the single-pole pickup coil assembly, the pickup coil assembly and a rotating pole piece which fits right over a stock breaker cam. The unit is designed to be used with the original equipment coil, rotor and cap. Installation is a simple task, requiring only a few basic tools. Ford conversion is easiest. Since the Ford advance mechanism is below the breaker cam, the installation can be made without removing the distributor. Delco conversion requires distributor removal, because the advance mechanism is above the cam. However, the results are said to be great and well worth the work.

The unit is maintenance-free and similar in operation to Chrysler's. Some manufacturers install limiters in their control boxes as a means of limiting the amount of voltage output, but Hays' control module has a different type of transistor and no limiters. This permits more voltage at the plugs and accurate timing. The Hays transistor is completely internal to further ensure protection against the ef-

fects of heat, dampness and vibration. These features make it ideal for both street and strip. With no more points and condenser, no dwell adjustments and no timing changes, it's virtually a maintenance-free unit.

The Hays kit does not alter factory settings or emissions equipment and it aids in reducing emissions. Hays claims that starting is easier, gas mileage is better and acceleration is brisker—and they seem pretty confident, for they back their claims with a one-year, over-the-counter guarantee.

Accel has become famous for its line of high-performance ignition products. Most popular among these is their Breakerless Eliminator Ignition (BEI), which is advertised to put out 41,000 volts. Accel bought out Spald-

ing Ignitions and took over production of Spalding's BDI. They are basically the same units, although the parts are not interchangeable.

The Accel BEI is a breakerless CD unit. The control box works in much the same way as other CD's, but the similarity ends there. The points have been replaced by a light beam control device (similar to a camera shutter) rather than a magnetic pulse as in the Olds system. A rotating shutter containing one hole for each engine cylinder passes through a light beam and triggers the control box, at which time the capacitor releases its stored-up current to the coil's primary winding. As in most CD's, voltage rise time is very fast, so spark plug fouling is greatly reduced.

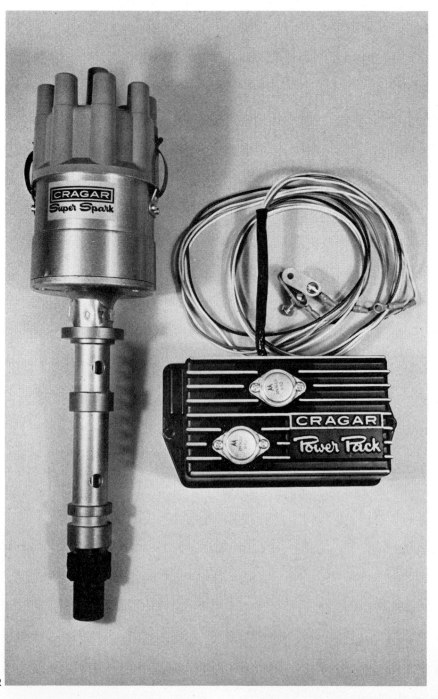

1

2

Speedatron produces a CD control box that uses the stock distributor and points as a triggering device. Their box is advertised to increase voltage to the plugs 10 to 15 times over the stock system. The increased voltage and much faster rise time clean fouled plugs and increase combustion for fewer emissions. However, the stock points are still there, so rubbing block wear can still cause timing changes and make distributor maintenance a hassle. The base unit is a bit expensive, because all you get is the black box. Nevertheless, it does put out a lot of voltage—supposedly more than any other unit on the market.

Unfortunately, the importance of voltage output has been overplayed. Most companies advertise the quality of their systems according to the voltage they produce, but what's more important is the amount of energy (measured in millijoules) that the spark has. This energy or heat or total work that the spark can do is a more realistic measure of system usefulness than voltage, so look for the spark energy rating to know what you're really getting.

The Speedatron unit is considered very efficient (even by its competition) and is rated at a high 120 millijoules. Using that rating as a guide, you can determine the relative power of other systems (most others put out 60-75 millijoules). Speedatron also offers a built-in, adjustable Rev-Limiter which cuts out every other spark plug to eliminate the gas build-up in the cylinders. A Mag-Pulse system, available with the Rev-Limiter, is designed for breakerless distributors.

The Delta Mark Ten is a CD unit which is used with the stock breaker-point distributor. Like so many CD systems, it includes just the control box, so voltage output is high and rise time is fast, but distributor maintenance and timing inaccuracies are still present. Delta claims that the duration of the spark with their unit is only one-tenth that of the conventional system. The fast voltage rise time and the short spark duration are said to clean dirty plugs and result in 3 to 10 times longer plug life. The Delta unit has a good reputation and has been used on many fleet cars.

The short spark duration of the CD system is great for most cars, but for some cars (usually '73 through '75) it could create a problem. A stock coil can accept the super-high voltage of a CD system because of the CD's very fast rise time. The high voltage isn't there long enough to do any damage. The duration of the spark, however, is often too short to ignite the lean air/fuel mixtures of the newer engines. The engine sputters at low rpm and at idle, but as you give it more gas, ignition smooths out because the mixture is richened.

The problem can be cured by going to a heavy-duty coil—although not all coils will do. Accel's Super Coil is recommended because its secondary winding is designed to double spark duration. Some performance coils are built to produce less duration, so choose carefully.

Because of the lean-mixture problem, a few manufacturers have created a variable-spark CD that provides long spark duration at low rpm and shorter duration as engine speed increases. The Compu-Spark CD is one of these. Produced by Gaylord Electronics Inc. of Carson City, Nev., the Compu-Spark is very popular. Secondary output from the stock coil is advertised at 54,000 volts; when engine speed exceeds 2500 rpm, the unit switches to a shorter-duration spark. The stock points are retained.

Some manufacturers include a

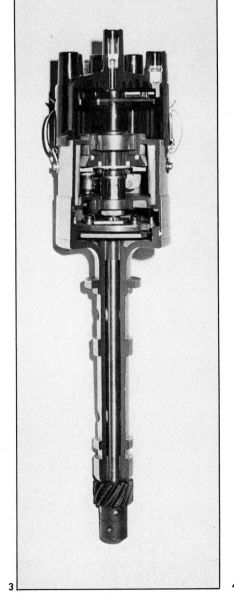

1. The Per-Lux Ignitor, made by Per-Lux of Covina, Calif., does away with black boxes and wiring. A permanent magnet for each cylinder is imbedded in the rotor. The magnets trigger an electronic chip mounted within the distributor. This also eliminates need for pickup coil and large magnet. Installation time is same as for points.

2. From the outside, Cragar's new high-performance distributor and CD ignition look pretty much like any other unit. But inside there is a world of difference.

3. Close-up of a Cragar cutaway shows (bottom to top) the centrifugal advance chamber, then a shaft bearing, the point compartment, a larger bearing and the rotor.

4. Accel's dual-point distributor permits the total advance to be adjusted without removing the unit from the engine. It's available in an economy-priced model designed for the average driver and a performance model for those concerned with competition operation.

heavy-duty coil with their systems or suggest changing to one. For the best results, especially in competition, this should be done. However, if the instructions make no mention of a coil change or if they state that a change is not necessary, then stick with the stock unit. For street use, a Detroit coil is sufficient with most CD and transistor ignitions. Whichever unit you consider, though, investigate thoroughly and choose carefully before spending any cash.

SOMETHING NEW, SOMETHING BORROWED

After 1975, breaker points were no longer available on American cars. Detroit universally adopted the breakerless ignition, and the aftermarket was quick to follow with some new ignitions of their own. Systems by Accel, American Racing, Mardek, Mallory, Borg-Warner, Edelbrock and Autotronic Controls entered the market and their popularity grew. Like anything new, most had a few bugs to be ironed out. Wise buyers stood back and waited until the systems were improved.

The majority of the new products are patterned after those that have already succeeded, with only minor changes in voltage output or perhaps spark duration. There's nothing very new, but the names behind these systems are established and reliable. Unfortunately, electronic ignitions don't offer too many combinations to work with. Until something revolutionary comes along, most makers are sticking with magnetic-pulse systems, a light-emitting diode or a breaker with either the transistor or CD box.

One of Accel's breakerless units is a conversion kit very similar to the Hays setup. A reluctor is pressed over the breaker cam of the stock distributor and a magnetic-pulse pickup coil replaces the points and condenser. The coil is wired to a transistorized control module.

American Racing is producing a CD box that hooks up to the stock distributor; as in most CD's, the breaker points are retained to signal the box. But there's one thing that makes this CD different from any other. It features what American calls "safe-t-key" auto theft control. The wiring harness from the control box is long enough to run through the firewall and into the passenger's compartment, where it plugs into another harness (about 3 ft. long) that leads to a small, flat, electrical receptacle. The harness is long enough to permit the receptacle to be hidden under the seat. A flat, rectangular piece of plastic with an electrical circuit printed on each side comes with the system. This "key" completes the circuit to the distributor. One side is for the CD ignition and in case of failure, the other side is imprinted with a circuit to activate the standard distributor points. A spare "key" with a key chain is provided so the driver can carry it with him. Without the key the car won't start, and this will certainly delay a potential thief. American has 1200 possible key combinations, so it's not likely that anyone could use another key to start your car.

Mardek Corp., at P.O. Box 2860, Newport Beach, CA 92663, produces the Mobelec electronic ignition. The control box is CD and the points and condenser are replaced with a magnetic-pulse triggerhead. Installation is very simple, requiring only a minimum of steps and tools. Unlike most other conversions, the Mobelec can be installed without removing the distributor. A lot of thought has gone

1. Most aftermarket ignitions boost voltage radically upward. Therefore spark plug wires should be in tip-top condition to handle the added load. Many companies market pre-made sets of plug wires (in another chapter we also show you how to make your own). Here Accel's kit with the spark plug ends already in place is shown.

2. The Mark Ten C ignition is a CD unit manufactured by Delta Products. It can be easily and quickly installed with a bare minimum of tools.

3. Don't be frightened off by the huge signs depicting high performance. While they do a large business with racers, most shops such as this one (Service Center, 9536 Firestone Blvd., Downey, CA 90240) also employ personnel who are much more knowledgeable about auto mechanics than the cut-rate parts houses can afford to hire.

2

1

3

into this unit, a fact which becomes even more obvious when you learn that one kit fits all American cars and most foreign cars, whether of 4, 6 or 8 cylinders. An assortment of adapters is included to make this possible. Very few breakerless systems will fit 4-cylinder domestics—and even fewer are made for the imports. Good price, ease of assembly, versatility and dependability all combine with the advantages of a breakerless CD to make Mobelec a name to seriously consider.

Mallory and Borg-Warner offer similar conversion kits which use an infrared light-emitting diode rather than the magnetic pulse of other conversions. The shutter wheel slips over the stock distributor cam and the trigger light screws to the distributor plate. Distributor removal is not required. Both systems use a transistor box rather than a CD, but diode operation is much like Accel's BEI. However, since these systems are conversions and transistorized, their price is naturally much lower than the expensive-to-build BEI CD distributor.

Edelbrock's Thermalspark uses a transistor box and retains the stock points. Point gap is reduced substantially for longer plug life, and spark plug gap is increased by 50% for greater fuel economy and drivability. The box increases spark energy by 200% for reduced emissions and less misfiring.

Probably the most revolutionary new product is the Autotronics (6908 Commerce, El Paso, TX 79915) Multiple Spark Discharge system. The transistor box is triggered by the stock points; when that occurs, a high-energy spark is created and repeated many times after the initial spark. This results in more spark heat (100 millijoules for the first spark, 80 for the others) and more complete combustion, which contributes to lower emissions, greater overall economy and improved performance. The thing really works, and according to reliable sources, the results are very satisfying. Labtronics, Inc. of Ypsilanti, Mich. produces a similar unit they call the Multiple Restrike Ignition.

By way of completing this chapter, we've included a step-by-step how-to section on installing a Mallory aftermarket pointless ignition replacement kit in a Delco distributor. We chose a Delco unit because they appear in all GM and AMC products and are therefore quite representative. Mallory's instructions for the Model 501 kit were very complete; we assume this would also be true of their kits for other distributors. While your distributor may differ slightly from the one pictured, by using our pictures and the kit's instructions (whether the car is Ford or Mopar or the kit is from Accel, Hays, Mallory, Chrysler or whatever), you should be able to proceed with your conversion.

If we were to be restricted to just one hint, it would be this: Take it slow and easy—don't rush. Now, get a cup of coffee, sit down under a bright light with your kit's sheet of instructions grasped firmly in your hand and read it and this chapter. Twice. Carefully.

AFTERMARKET IGNITION MANUFACTURERS

Accel Eliminator Ignition
P.O. Box 142, U.S. 1
Branford, CT 06405

Allison Automotive
1269 Edna Pl.
Covina, CA 91722

APO International
Suite 131, 3003 LBJ Fwy.
Dallas, TX 75234

Autotronic Controls Corp.
6908 Commerce St.
El Paso, TX 79915

Avionics Inc.
1915 No. Bendix
South Bend, IN 46628

Borg-Warner Automotive Parts Div.
11045 Gage Ave.
Franklin Park, IL 60131

Chrysler Parts Division, Chrysler Corp.
341 Massachusetts Ave.
Highland Park, MI 48203

Clifford Research & Development Co., Inc.
102 Kalmus Dr.
Costa Mesa, CA 92626

Echlin Manufacturing Co.
Echlin Rd. & U.S. 1
Branford, CT 06405

General Products
107 Salem St.
Union Springs, NY 13160

Guaranteed Parts Co.
Auburn Rd.
Seneca Falls, NY 13148

Hays Sales
15116 Adams St.
Midway City, CA 92655

Holley Carburetor Div., Colt Industries
11955 E. Nine Mile Rd.
Warren, MI 48090

Judson Research & Mfg. Co.
541 E. Hector St.
Conshohocken, PA 19428

**Mallory Electric Corp.,
Div. W.R. Grace & Co.**
1801 Oregon St.
Carson City, NV 89701

Mardek Corp.
P.O. Box 2860
Newport Beach, CA 92663

Motorola Automotive Prod., Div. Motorola
9401 W. Grand Ave.
Franklin Park, IL 60131

Per-Lux
804 E. Edna Pl.
Covina, CA 91722

Pneumetrics Inc.
19338 Londelius St.
Northridge, CA 91324

Prestolite Co.
511 Hamilton St.
Toledo, OH 43694

Research Dynamics
1150 Tennyson, #10
Manhattan Beach, CA 90266

Rite Autotronics Corp.
3485 S. La Cienega Blvd.
Los Angeles, CA 90016

Slep Electronic Co.
Highway 441, Franklin S., Box 100
Otto, NC 28763

**Speedatron, General
Nucleonics Div. Tyco**
2811 Metropolitan Pl.
Pomona, CA 91767

Springfield Elec. Spc.
500 Belleville Trnpke.
North Arlington, NJ 07032

Standard Motor Products, Inc.
37-18 Northern Blvd.
Long Island City, NY 11101

Sydmur Electronic Spec.
1268 E. 12th St.
Brooklyn, NY 11230

Systematics Inc.
547 N. Wheeler
St. Paul, MN 55104

Tri Star Corp.
P.O. Box 1727
Grand Junction, CO 81501

Wells Mfg. Corp.
2-26 S. Brooke St.
Fond du Lac, WI 54935

Western Controls Inc.
805 W. Madison St.
Phoenix, AZ 85007

HOW-TO: INSTALLING A BREAKERLESS IGNITION

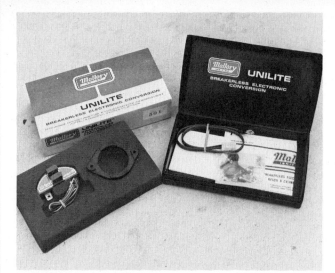

1. Mallory's microcircuitry unit eliminates breaker points and condenser. It installs in minutes and retails for $66.

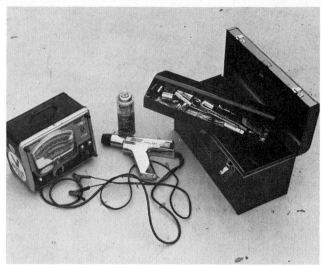

2. It takes all this to do a tune-up on a car with points, but after this conversion, all you'll need is a timing light.

3. Late-model Delco distributor caps (before HEI) are held on with two screw-capped fingers. Remove them counterclockwise.

4. AMC engines have starter relays. Making contact with the two posts indicated by arrows will turn the engine over.

5. Cover the timing mark on the crankshaft pulley with chalk, bring it up to TDC and align the rotor with No. 1 spark plug.

6. Go way overboard when marking the distributor prior to removal. The more marks, the easier it is to reinstall later.

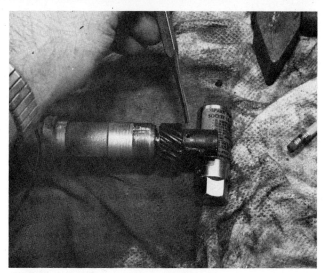

7. Using a Craftsman 5/32-in. drift punch, drive out the indicated pin in order to remove the distributor's drive gear.

8. Mallory provides two new pins (both of which were too long for this particular car) and three shims (arrow).

9. On this car, we needed only one shim and used the old pin to replace drive gear. We then installed the mounting plate.

10. The distributor was then complete and ready for reinstalling. When replacing the rotor, be careful as you tighten the bolts.

11. If you marked everything correctly, you can start the engine immediately and allow it to warm up prior to timing.

12. No more dwell adjustment! Simply time the engine to factory specs. Future tune-ups will consist only of changing plugs.

Batteries

OLD BATTERIES DON'T FADE AWAY—
THEY JUST DIE! PROPER CARE AND MAINTENANCE WILL
PREVENT A PREMATURE DEATH.

Ask the average man on the street what his car's battery does and he'll probably tell you that it stores electricity. In fact, "storage battery" and "accumulator" are the most generally accepted names for this vital piece of equipment. The words "accumulator" and "storage" do not, however, accurately describe the true nature of the beast, since in reality batteries do not accumulate or store electrical energy at all. Condensers and capacitors are the only true accumulators of electricity. The storage battery in your car produces electrical energy by means of an electrochemical reaction. The current drawn from a battery originates in the battery, whether it's the dry cell in a transistor radio or the 6-cell wet unit in your car.

You don't have to be a psychiatrist to understand why the average person assumes that an automotive battery stores electricity. After all, there is an engine-driven generator or alternator in the car to charge the battery, and if the cells go flat after a long and fruitless cranking session, you have to connect the battery to a charger, right?

Still, there's something else that would tip you off that it isn't necessary to deposit electrical current in a battery before you can make a withdrawal; namely, the dry-charge batteries that are sold in many service stations. These batteries are shipped without any electrolyte (the acid and water mixture that you see inside the battery after removing the filler caps). They sit around on a shelf for months, drier than a banker's eyes at a mortgage foreclosure. Then when someone buys one, electrolyte is poured into the cells and an electric current is produced immediately, without any outside electrical charge having been fed into the battery. Sometimes a quick booster charge is necessary to start the chemical reaction, but that only takes a couple of minutes.

The current that a battery produces is the direct result of a chemical reaction within the cells. It is not simply the release of a reservoir of current put into the battery in the way that gasoline is poured into the fuel tank.

HOW IT WORKS

Obviously there are quite a few considerations in the physical design of any battery—its size, weight, cost, materials, intended use, resistance to damage, resistance to temperature extremes and many others. There are, however, only three *electrical* conditions which are important: *voltage, current-delivering ability* and *endurance.* Together these three factors determine practically everything else about a battery. Let's take a look at them and then see how they apply to an automobile battery.

Voltage is determined solely by the materials used in the battery's positive and negative poles. Every metal, every metallic compound and many nonmetals—practically any material which is a conductor of electricity, in fact—has an inherent electrical activity when paired with another conductor. Using this activity, scientists have arranged all known conductors into a table, called the *electromotive series.* The farther apart two materials are in this series, the greater is their electrical potential for doing work, or voltage. Voltage can be directly compared to pressure in a hydraulic system; its name comes from that of Count Alessandro Volta, an Italian physicist who made the first battery in the year 1800.

If more voltage is required than can be provided by a single pairing of materials, then each pairing or "cell" is connected in series with more cells until the desired voltage is reached. That is, the positive terminal of one cell is connected to the negative terminal of the next cell, and so forth. The battery's total voltage is the sum of that produced by the individual cells.

In our automobile battery, the negative material is pure lead, while the positive material is lead dioxide, often called lead peroxide since it contains more oxygen than the more usual lead-oxygen compound, lead oxide. Under ideal conditions, this lead-lead peroxide combination yields 2.2 volts per cell. However, since conditions are seldom ideal, this is usually rounded off to just 2 volts per cell. A

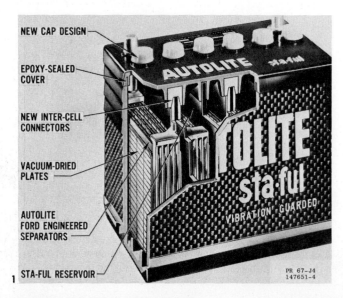

NEW CAP DESIGN

EPOXY-SEALED COVER

NEW INTER-CELL CONNECTORS

VACUUM-DRIED PLATES

AUTOLITE FORD ENGINEERED SEPARATORS

STA-FUL RESERVOIR

AUTOLITE sta-ful

OLITE sta-ful
VIBRATION GUARDED

PR 67-J4
147651-4

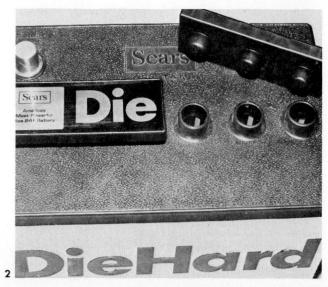

Sears Die

DieHard

6-volt battery, then, has three such cells connected in series, and a 12-volt battery has six of them.

The lead and lead peroxide are arranged in parallel plates. Connecting them electrically is the *electrolyte,* a fancy name for a liquid which is electrically conductive and which also enters into the chemical reaction when the battery is in operation. In our automotive battery, the electrolyte is diluted sulfuric acid, a mixture of sulfuric acid and pure water.

Current-delivering ability depends upon the size of the plates and terminals, but not upon the voltage. For example, the ordinary household dry-cell zinc-carbon flashlight battery which you buy in a hardware store is rated at 1½ volts; connecting eight of them in series, then, would give 12 volts, the same as your car battery. But you could not run your car with eight flashlight batteries. They could not deliver the 25 amps or so needed to operate all the accessories and lights, much less the 125 amps drawn by the starter.

The *endurance* of the battery also depends upon its size. A large battery can maintain a sizable current for a long time; a small one cannot. The current flow is measured in amperes or amps, named after another electrical pioneer, Andre-Marie Ampère, a French physicist who was a contemporary of Volta.

It is customary to rate the endurance of automotive batteries according to the ampere-hour system. A 100-ampere-hour battery is capable of delivering 5 amperes (a measurement of current flow) for a period of 20 hrs. The 20-hr. figure is not mentioned in the rating, but is generally understood with automotive batteries. The greater the plate area in a battery, the higher the ampere-hour rating. There is therefore a close relationship between the number of plates in each cell and the rating fig-

ure applied to the battery. For example, lower-priced batteries are usually 48-ampere-hour units and have four positive plates per cell. Moving up the power scale—and the price range—we find 59-ampere-hour batteries with five positive plates and 70-ampere-hour batteries with six positive plates per cell.

The higher the battery's rating, the more work it can do before it becomes discharged. Cars with few accessories—just a starter, lights, windshield wipers and possibly a heater—can get by satisfactorily on one of the light-duty, low ampere-hour types. But when you start to add a radio, tape deck, air conditioning, power windows, etc. to the battery's normal chores, it takes at least a 70-ampere-hour battery to keep up with the demand.

When a storage battery releases electricity so you can operate your car, it does so through the positive post. The current runs through your electrical equipment and completes its circuit when it returns to the battery via the negative post.

We won't go into the exact chemistry involved here, but the plates in-

3

4

teract with the acid in such a way that there is a flow of electrons inside each cell from the negative to the positive plates. The acid acts on both positive and negative plate active materials to form a new chemical compound called lead sulfate. The sulfate is supplied by the acid solution (electrolyte), which becomes weaker in concentration as the discharge proceeds. The amount of acid absorbed by the plates is in direct proportion to the amount of electricity removed from the cell. During this process, the storage battery is being *discharged,* and it will continue to discharge as long as electricity is being drained from it.

Very small amounts of lead and acid are consumed in the battery discharge process, but because the percentage of acid in the electrolyte is relatively low, the reaction stops long before all the materials are consumed. When all the available sulfuric acid has been absorbed into the chemical structure of the plates, the battery becomes fully discharged. It will then no longer generate electricity, for two reasons. First, the acid content of the electrolyte is depleted. Second, the positive and negative plates have become so much like each other due to their lead sulfate coatings that there is practically no voltage difference between them.

This is where charging comes into the picture. Current directed into the battery's cells reverses the chemical reaction by driving sulfuric acid away from the plates and increasing the acid content of the electrolyte. Once this is done, the battery is ready to start producing electrical current once more.

It should be pointed out that not all batteries are rechargeable; for example, those dry-cell flashlight batteries aren't, which is another reason you couldn't use them in your car. The ability to be recharged is one of the principal reasons the automobile battery is built the way it is.

In actual practice the battery electrolyte is kept at a steady state of acidity by the current delivered by the car's generator or alternator. After running the starter, the amount of acid in the electrolyte is low, since the heavy demand for current has caused it to be absorbed into the plates. The alternator charging system on the car operates the entire electrical system at a constant voltage. When the voltage of the battery is low, as it is after starting, current flows from the alternator into the battery. This is the reason that the ammeter on your car's dash reads higher for several miles after you've run the starter or placed other heavy demands upon the battery's current-producing potential.

1. Cutaway view of a typical storage battery reveals individual parts and assemblies. Note that this battery has internal cell connectors.

2. Latest battery designs feature plastic construction, quick-removal filler cap units. Plastic is less prone to cracking, lighter in weight and allows greater plate and electrolyte capacity without enlarging battery case on outside.

3. Loosening battery cables must be done carefully to keep from damaging the battery. Note how left thumb is braced against the cable to keep from bending the battery post.

4. The proper way to remove the battery cables is to first loosen the nut and then use a cable puller to lift the terminal off the post.

Batteries

Could an automobile battery be made from any other electrode materials? Yes. Theoretically, a battery could be made from any two materials in the electromotive series, many of which have a lot more voltage than the lead-lead peroxide combination. Practical considerations, especially cost, safety, reliability and rechargeability, eliminate most of them. For example, some years ago Ford spent a lot of research money on a sodium-sulfur battery, which put out plenty of power. However, it was quite bulky, had to be maintained at a temperature of 550° F and was very expensive. It was dropped.

In fact, only two other types of storage batteries have ever been successfully developed: the nickel-iron-alkaline type (called the Edison battery) and the nickel-cadmium-alkali or nicad battery. Both are widely used for certain applications and have several advantages over the lead-acid battery, but both cost more and produce less voltage per cell. So the automotive lead-acid battery will be with us for a long time to come.

CONSTRUCTION PRINCIPLES

Automotive batteries consist of either three or six individual cells, depending on whether they are 6- or 12-volt units. As mentioned above, each cell is a battery in itself, producing approximately 2 volts. The cells are connected together in series. The positive pole of the first cell and the negative pole of the last provide the terminals to which the car's battery cables are attached. Each cell has its own "private box" in the battery case, so there is no mixing of the electrolyte from cell to cell.

The manufacture of battery plates starts with a grid cast from high-purity secondary lead with small amounts of antimony and tin added. The antimony makes the metal hard, while lead, the basic material, must be used because it is the only metal capable of surviving in sulfuric acid under storage battery conditions.

The grid is transformed into a plate by filling the open spaces in it with the more chemically active material. The active material is applied as a paste consisting of lead oxide mixed with water and sulfuric acid.

After the plates have dried, they are immersed in a weak sulfuric acid solution and charged. This converts the active material into sponge lead in the negative plates and lead dioxide (peroxide) in the positive plates. In some dry-charge batteries, a few minutes on the battery charger are used for this conversion and to ensure proper polarity of the plates.

If one positive plate were to touch a negative plate, all the plates in that cell would lose their stored energy. To prevent this from happening, thin sheets of porous, nonconductive material known as separators are inserted between the plates. For many years these separators were made of wood, but the growing scarcity of Port Orford cedar brought about a gradual transition to rubber and later plastic separators. Some inexpensive batteries still use wood separators, but this wood is generally fir, which is inferior to Port Orford cedar and much more prone to cracking.

Separators have ribs on the side facing the positive plates to provide greater acid volume next to the positives, which improves efficiency and facilitates acid circulation within the cell. The ribs also minimize the area of contact with the positive plate, which has a highly oxidizing effect on most separators.

Plates of any number and size can be used in a cell, depending upon how much energy is to be stored, but there is always one more negative plate than there are positives, for reasons of improved performance. The greater the plate surface area in each cell, the higher the voltage during battery discharge at high rates and low temperatures.

However, the open-circuit voltage of a fully charged cell, no matter what the size of the cell or the number of plates in the element, is only a little over 2 volts.

Battery cases are formed with narrow rests or bridges at the bottom of each cell compartment, preventing the cells from sitting on the bottom of the case and also producing an area for sediment to settle. Repeated discharging and charging of a battery gradually wears it out. After a time, the active material of the positive plates gradually disintegrates, loses physical contact with its plate and falls to the bottom of the case.

Battery covers are usually of molded hard-rubber construction to provide an acid-tight seal. They are also provided with vent plugs. These plugs are designed to baffle the gases and any electrolyte that may splash against the underside of the cover. They also prevent loss of acid from the cells.

The capacity of the case determines the battery's ampere-hour rating. It wouldn't be much use to add plate area if there weren't enough acid to react with the additional lead.

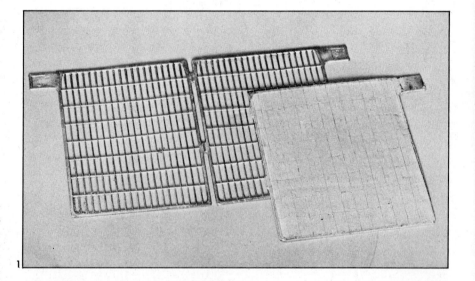

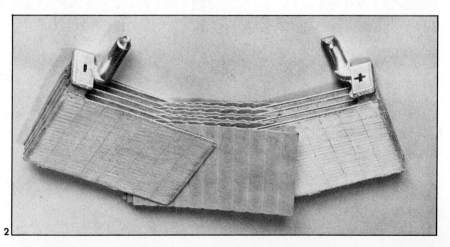

Raising the percentage of acid in the electrolyte would only speed disintegration of the internal battery parts, so the added quantity of acid must be balanced by an added quantity of water. All this takes more space, and automotive batteries conventionally fall into certain limited sizes that allow car makers to standardize battery box designs.

A development which allows increased case capacity is the use of plastics in place of the traditional hard rubber "tanks." The Sears DieHard, which uses a case made of polypropylene plastic, is an outstanding example of this. The use of plastic allows the case to be much thinner, giving more room on the inside without increasing the outside dimensions of the battery.

Conventional battery cases are usually made of reclaimed rubber mixed with sulfur and various fillers to make a container which is acid-proof and mechanically strong—although cracking is not unknown. Cheaper batteries, the kind you see in bargain stores bearing unheard-of brand names, have cases molded with a bituminous binder, such as asphalt, rather than rubber. These are cheaper, but more brittle and a little less acid-resistant. Until recently, plastic cases were not considered to be worth the added cost over rubber, but an increasing number of motorists feel that these cases are actually worthwhile investments.

Cell connectors are welded to the protruding cell terminal posts. They are heavy enough to carry the high current required for starting without overheating. Different methods are employed to connect the cells in series. The conventional method has been to connect the cells by lead straps running along the outside of the case. However, both over-the-partition and through-the-partition methods have proven better, because they provide an acid-tight seal between cells and are a shorter connection, which assures minimum voltage loss.

Automotive battery terminals are of standard sizes, so all positive and negative cable-clamp terminals will fit any corresponding battery terminal. The positive terminal is tapered and is slightly larger (11/16-in. diameter) at the top than the negative terminal (⅝-in. diameter).

The purity of the materials that go into a battery's manufacture is of prime importance to its serviceability. Although impurities seldom cause outright failure, there are occasional instances of trouble, particularly in the real cheapies. The lead used in making the active material must be at least 95-99% pure, with only traces of copper, nickel and silver, in addition to bismuth, the chief impurity. The sulfuric acid must also be of exceptionally high purity, containing at most only a few hundredths of a percent of iron.

The water in quality batteries is distilled water, because distilled water is completely free of any impurities. Water containing iron, chlorides and manganese is seriously harmful to battery life even in extremely small concentrations. These are substances commonly found in everyday tap water, which for this reason should not be used to refill battery cells.

Certain other impurities sometimes find their way into battery cells after the unit has been placed in service. Small bits of copper wire produce copper deposits on the negative plates and lead to the generation of hydrogen. The tolerable amount of hydrogen in a battery is about one-hundredth of one percent. Using the same hydrometer barrel for testing both radiator antifreeze and battery cells may accidentally introduce alcohol or glycol into the battery. The usual consequence is grid corrosion in the first cell tested, while the other cells remain unaffected.

The latest word in battery design is the non-fill battery pioneered by Delco for use in some GM cars. The battery is filled at the factory and permanently sealed; it has no cell openings. The terminals are on the side so that the top is flat and unvented. There are no vents for escaping vapors; even if there were, there's no way to add water. Delco solved this problem by situating a baffled tank in the area above the cells. The vaporized electrolyte gathers in this tank, condenses and then returns to the liquid electrolyte below. The result is reclaimed electrolyte and no water loss through vapor venting.

One of the most significant changes in the past several decades has been the switch from 6-volt systems to 12-volt systems. Prior to 1950, there were no American cars with 12-volt batteries, though a fair number of European cars had them. What caused the switch was the advent of high-compression engines,

1. The plates of a lead-acid storage battery consist of an electrically conductive grid framework in the meshes of which are the active materials. Negative plates are filled with a porous mass of lead so electrolyte can penetrate freely. Positive plates are filled with lead peroxide.

2. The lugs of the positive plates are welded to a common post, forming a positive group, and the negative plates are similarly welded to form a negative group. Thin sheets of nonconductive, porous material called separators are inserted between the plates to prevent their touching. If they touch, all plates will lose their stored energy.

3. The number of the graduation that is even with the surface of the electrolyte in a hydrometer tester indicates the state of charge of that particular cell. Numbers on the scale indicate the specific gravity of the electrolyte.

4. Hydrometers are calibrated to read accurately at 80° F. At higher or lower electrolyte temperatures it is necessary to adjust the specific gravity figure by using this chart.

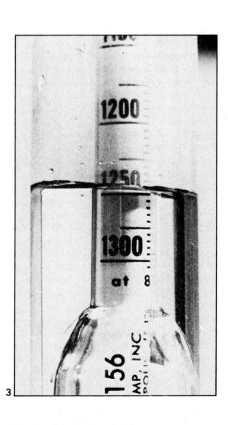

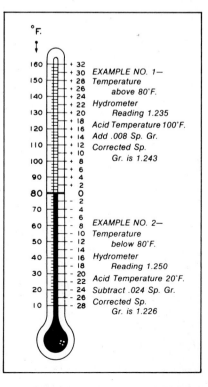

°F.

EXAMPLE NO. 1—
Temperature
    above 80°F.
Hydrometer
    Reading 1.235
Acid Temperature 100°F.
Add .008 Sp. Gr.
Corrected Sp.
    Gr. is 1.243

EXAMPLE NO. 2—
Temperature
    below 80°F.
Hydrometer
    Reading 1.250
Acid Temperature 20°F.
Subtract .024 Sp. Gr.
Corrected Sp.
    Gr. is 1.226

Batteries

which needed a lot more power from the starter motor to turn them over. Now, the power (in watts) from an electric motor is defined as the voltage multiplied by the current. If battery voltage remained at only 6 volts, the only way to obtain more starter motor power would have been to increase the current flow, which could only have been done by enlarging the size of all the wiring in order to reduce its resistance. This would have made the starter (and generator) both much bulkier and much more expensive, since thick copper wire isn't cheap. By doubling battery voltage, the necessary extra power was obtained, yet wiring and electrical components were kept at a reasonable size and cost.

HYDROMETER TESTS

Since the percentage of acid in the electrolyte is less when the battery is discharged, the relative acidity of the solution provides an extremely accurate picture of the battery's state of charge. Service stations and garages, as well as the majority of home mechanics, use a device known as a *hydrometer* to measure this. The hydrometer measures the *specific gravity* of the electrolyte solution—specific gravity being the weight of the solution compared to the weight of an equal volume of pure water. There is a small float inside the barrel of the hydrometer, weighted in such a way that its scale projects upright through the surface of liquid drawn into the instrument's glass body. If pure water is drawn into a battery

hydrometer, the 1.000 line will rest even with the surface of the liquid, showing that the specific gravity is exactly that of water (1 times the weight of water). If, however, there is acid in solution with the water, as in battery electrolyte, the weight of the liquid will be greater than that of pure water, since sulfuric acid is considerably denser than water.

The electrolyte of a fully charged battery usually contains about 36% sulfuric acid by weight or about 25% by volume. This corresponds to a specific gravity of 1.270 at 80° F. In other terms we can say that the electrolyte in a fully charged battery would be 1.27 times heavier than pure water if equal amounts of each substance were weighed at the same temperature.

When the battery discharges, sulfuric acid in the electrolyte combines chemically with the plates, so the remaining electrolyte becomes lighter in weight. A reading of 1.250 is usually considered good, while a fully discharged cell will test only about 1.150. The scale on the average hydrometer extends, therefore, from 1.300 down to 1.100. A cell in fair conditon produces a reading between 1.225 and 1.250. Anything below 1.225 is considered poor. If a cell is found with a specific gravity below 1.150, the battery is for all practical purposes dead.

Hydrometer readings also provide a "window" through which the mechanic can get an inside look at the battery's physical condition. When one or more of the cells produces a reading that is .050 or more below that of the others, it's a pretty good indication that the low cells are short-

ed. Also, if charging can't get the battery up to at least a 50% charge (about 1.200), it's time to install a new battery in the car.

Tests made with a hydrometer must be carried out under the proper conditions in order to get a true picture of the battery's health. A reading taken immediately after adding water to the cells would indicate a specific gravity much lower than it should be, since the electrolyte is diluted and the newly introduced water has not yet thoroughly mixed with the electrolyte in the cells. Conversely, after a long, high-speed trip the hydrometer reading would be considerably above the figure that's truly representative of the battery's condition.

The most accurate hydrometer readings are obtained two or three days after water has been added to the cells and the car has been left parked for several hours or overnight following a period of normal service. The engine should be started, switched off and the battery given a five-minute rest to "recover." Hydrometer readings taken at this time give the most precise indications of actual battery condition.

Most automotive batteries are designed for discharge cycles of not greater than 25%. Prolonged or frequent operation with the battery discharged to this level or below can damage it, so try to maintain it at a full charge level.

The temperature of the electrolyte has a definite effect on the figures recorded by the hydrometer. In summer, when the solution is apt to be warmer, lower hydrometer readings will be obtained. In cold weather the readings are higher. For absolute ac-

curacy, electrolyte temperatures should be measured before hydrometer testing. Some of the more expensive hydrometers have built-in thermometers for this purpose, but in most instances a separate immersion thermometer is used.

Hydrometers are calibrated to be precisely accurate⁴ when electrolyte temperature is 80° F. For every 10° above 80°, .004 must be added to the hydrometer's actual reading. Similarly, .004 must be subtracted from the reading shown on the hydrometer scale for each 10° that the electrolyte's temperature is below 80° F. Thus a cell that produces a reading of 1.220 might not be as unhealthy as this reading would seem to indicate—if the temperature of the electrolyte is 100° F when the reading is taken. The true specific gravity, allowing for the temperature, would be 1.228, a more promising figure.

OTHER TESTS

In former years a special voltmeter for testing individual cells was in wide use in battery shops, service stations and garages. These voltmeters had two sharp prongs that could be jabbed into the bar-like cell connectors joining the individual cells of the battery. Connecting the prongs was a high-resistance metal strip or coil that placed a heavy load on the battery's current capacity. The prongs were held in contact with the two poles of each cell for 10 to 15 secs. and the reading on the voltmeter carefully noted. Individual cells could produce a full 2 volts when the tester was first applied, but if cell voltage fell rapidly to 1.5 volts or less within the first 10 secs., the battery would not have enough stamina to start the engine reliably even though the cells could be fully charged. This type of test was called a high-discharge voltage check.

High-discharge voltmeters have become obsolete for testing individual cells, since modern hardtop battery construction makes their use impossi-

ble. Most present-day batteries employ internal cell connectors that are placed so far below the top of the case that even if someone did jab a cell tester through the top, there would be nothing for the prongs to contact. No attempt should ever be made to test batteries that have internal connectors by this method. Hydrometer testing is now universally recommended by battery makers for testing the individual cells.

However, a high-discharge voltage check can be made of the entire battery, and for this purpose the modern service garage employs a battery tester with an ammeter, voltmeter and variable resistor built into its cabinet. As with any high-discharge test, the cells must be charged to produce a specific gravity of at least 1.220 for conclusive results. In fact, if all the cells do not have at least a 50% charge, a high-discharge test can seriously damage the battery.

A standard 12-volt battery should be able to produce a minimum of 9.5 volts for 15 secs. at a current draw rate equal to three times the ampere-hour rating of the battery. If the battery is not charged up, put it on a slow charge for as long as possible before testing it.

CHARGING

By passing an electric current through the battery in a direction opposite to that of discharge (from negative to positive), the lead sulfate formed in the battery plates during discharge is made to decompose. As the sulfate is removed from the plates and returns to the electrolyte, the battery is gradually restored to its original strength. This process can be accomplished through your car's alternator or generator system or with a battery charger.

When a storage battery has been severely discharged and you hook a battery charger onto it, lead sulfate decomposition in the plates is greatly speeded up. As this sulfate is removed from the positive and negative plates through electrical charging, hydrogen and oxygen gases are given off when the plates approach the fully charged condition. These gases result

from the decomposition of water, caused by an excess of charging current not utilized by the plates.

These hydrogen and oxygen gases are highly explosive. *Precautions must be taken to ensure that no arc, spark or flame comes into contact with the generated gases.* The possibility of explosion is always present if the battery is exposed to sparks or flame, but the end of the charging period is particularly hazardous. If a battery explodes, it is a violent explosion, with acid spraying everywhere. In all automotive battery cells small quantities of hydrogen gas are even given off at the negative plates even when the cells are not being charged. It must therefore be assumed that explosive mixtures of hydrogen gas are present within the cells at all times.

If your battery is low or dead and requires charging, wash all dirt from it and clean its terminals before placing it on charge, but do not allow dirt to get into the cells. Bring the liquid level in the cells to the correct level, using distilled water. If a battery is extremely cold, let it warm up before adding water, because the water level will rise as it warms up.

A battery may be charged at any rate which does not raise the electrolyte temperature of any cell above 125° F and does not cause excessive loss of the electrolyte. Where the battery is badly sulfated (really dead), it must be charged at specified low rates. The constant-current slow charging method is recommended where the internal cell condition is not known and where a diagnosis of trouble is being made.

To properly charge your dead battery, connect the positive lead from the charger to the positive terminal of the battery and the negative lead to the negative terminal. A safe rate for bench charging is 1 ampere per positive plate per cell. For example, in a battery with 11 plates per cell (or a total of 66 plates for the whole battery), 5 plates in each cell would be positive, so the charge rate would be 5 amperes for the battery.

Hydrometer readings should be recorded hourly for each cell of the battery as soon as it approaches the

1. Fancy hydrometers like this cost more, but they have a direct-reading scale which makes temperature corrections unnecessary.

2. The advantage of a charger like this is speed. If you have the time, a smaller (and less expensive) charger will do the job. This charger will also start cars with completely dead batteries.

3. There are many small home battery chargers on the market. This one will charge either a 6-volt or 12-volt battery at 6 amps. It's perfect for keeping a battery perked up during the winter.

4. A larger and more complex home charger such as this one can charge at 20 amps; it puts out enough current to actually start an engine.

fully charged state. A battery is fully charged when the cells are all gassing freely and the specific gravity reading stays the same for three successive readings taken at hourly intervals. Most batteries can be recharged at normal rates in from 12 to 16 hours. Excess charging decomposes water and is harmful to the positive plates.

High-rate chargers (quick chargers) cannot be expected to fully charge batteries within an hour, but they do charge the battery sufficiently so that it can continue to give service commensurate with its condition and state of charge. We strongly recommend that *only* slow chargers be used, however.

Sulfating is a condition in which large areas of the plates become blanketed with extra-heavy thicknesses of lead sulfate as a result of inadequate charging. A long, slow charge is the only way to completely displace the acid from the sulfated areas and restore the battery to full capacity. Shorter periods of charge may return the battery to service temporarily, but they will not remove the sulfate.

Four characteristics that can be observed during charging are indications of a sulfated battery: (1) there is a rapid increase in electrolyte temperature while charging; (2) the battery produces gas excessively even at normal charging rates; (3) excessive voltage is required to obtain a normal charging rate; and (4) charging increases the specific gravity very slowly or not at all.

Usually a battery can be slow charged in from 12 to 16 hours; however, if the battery continues to show an increase in specific gravity after that time, the charging process should be continued even if it takes 24 hours or more. Safe slow charging rates are determined by allowing 1 ampere per positive plate per cell. The number of plates per cell can be determined from the ampere-hour rating of the battery. At no time should the temperature of the electrolyte be allowed to exceed 110° F. If it reaches this level during slow charging, the rate of charge must be lowered.

The quick charger featured in many service stations can put as much as 80 amperes into a 100-ampere-hour battery. The rate of charge that a battery is capable of accepting, however, is limited by its capacity and state of discharge. As the battery's state of charge rises, it will accept less current from the charger. Therefore, quick charges are only practical on greatly discharged batteries. On others, the result will be overheating and battery damage.

Quick charging should be reserved for those rare instances when time is not available for a slow charge. A quick charge of about an hour will enable the battery and alternator to continue carrying the car's electrical load. However, the battery may be damaged beyond repair if certain precautions are not observed. First, the temperature of the electrolyte must never be allowed to rise above 125° F during a quick charge.

Also, as the battery approaches full charge, the electrolyte in each cell will begin to gas or bubble. Excessive gassing must never be allowed. If there is no significant change in the hydrometer reading after an hour of quick charging, the high charge rate must be discontinued and the slow charge method applied. Some of the better battery chargers have built-in thermostatic controls to limit the time and charge rate automatically.

Home battery chargers are highly satisfactory, as long as they are used for their intended purpose: keeping the battery safely charged under adverse service conditions. They should not be purchased in an attempt to wring a few more weeks of service from a dying set of cells. The money would be much better spent as a down payment on a new battery.

CARE AND LONGEVITY

With proper care, high-quality batteries can provide four or five years of flawless service. Neglected and misused, they may die a sudden death in less than six months. However, most of the threats to an automotive battery's long and happy existence come as a result of improper voltage regulator functioning.

Sulfating, for instance, is the direct result of the battery being in a constantly undercharged state. Sulfated areas which remain unchanged chemically for a sufficient period of time become so permanently hardened that their chemical convertibility is lost. Usually there are warnings that the battery no longer has its old stamina, and if the cells are given a long, slow charge, the battery may be restored to its former vigor, but the cause of the chronic undercharging must be eliminated if continued service is to be expected.

Contrary to popular opinion, overcharging is as bad as undercharging. As we have seen, a battery can only accept a charge equal to the amount it has been previously discharged. When the cells are developing their maximum voltage output and the specific gravity is up at about 1.260 to 1.280, the cells can accept no additional charge. If the regulator is set to give a little extra charge under these conditions, the only result will be elevated temperatures in the electrolyte and cracking and disintegration of the plates.

Due to the effects of temperature on battery chemistry, a cold battery has more internal resistance, so it takes a higher charging voltage to charge a cold battery. Voltage regulators therefore have a thermostatic compensator built into them to adjust the charge rate to the prevailing thermal conditions. Still, on a long-distance trip in the heat of summer, the battery often gets a bit of an overdose. For this reason, some motorists make it a practice to switch on their headlights during the day to minimize the possibility of overcharging.

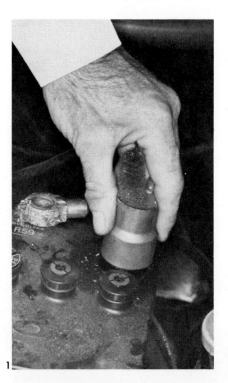

1

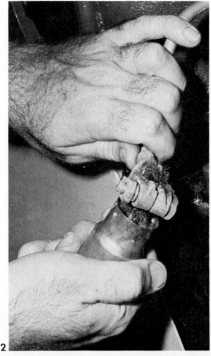

2

Extreme fluctuations in the battery's state of charge can also result in serious damage. Usually this occurs only in cases where the driver is ignorant of the effect it can have on his car's battery. These extreme fluctuations in the state of charge daily loosen active material from the grids of the battery's positive plates. This not only decreases the plate's current production potential, but the broken bits fall to the bottom of the battery case and short out the cells.

For a healthy battery, it is absolutely necessary that the charge rate be maintained within strict boundaries. If your car has an ammeter, be on the lookout for anything peculiar that might indicate changes in the voltage regulator's operation. If an idiot light is all you have, you're all set up for trouble—especially if an extreme overcharge condition develops. Buy an ammeter and have that regulator checked regularly. It's the only way to make sure that those precious cells are being fed a proper diet.

One of the best ways to keep a sharp lookout for overcharging is to check the electrolyte level in the battery frequently. During charging, some of the water in the battery evaporates and escapes through vents in the filler caps. This leaves the electrolyte with an overconcentration of acid. If, through neglect, the electrolyte level becomes very low, the battery will begin to lose power, since part of each plate will be above the water line. Not only does this keep the rest of the plate overworked, but the higher acid concentration begins to eat away at the grids. In addition, the tops of the plates start to dry out and harden. This is a sure way to assassinate a good battery, and once it's happened, the plates will have lost most of their ability to accept a charge and produce electricity.

Normally a battery requires the addition of water about twice a year. If your battery seems to be thirstier than an alley cat who's eaten a pound of salted herring, it's a good bet that the cells are receiving an overcharge. If only one cell seems to be losing water, though, the trouble is more likely a cracked battery case that's allowing electrolyte to leak from that particular cell. If the specific gravity of this cell becomes increasingly lower after adding water several times, the problem is definitely leakage, since acid is obviously being lost as well as water.

Most batteries are built with some kind of water level indicator. This is usually a tube-shaped filler that extends down into the case. Many have slotted sides or a diamond-shaped bottom to mark the point where the maximum electrolyte level should be. Never fill the cells beyond this point. Generally speaking, the electrolyte

level should be maintained about ¼-in. above the tops of the battery plates.

The type of water used in filling batteries is important too. Distilled water is the only kind that should ever be added to a battery. Every water system in the country contains its own particular brand of battery poison. Those with a high iron content—including iron picked up from rusty water pipes—are deadly in a battery cell. Furthermore, the water in battery electrolyte gradually evaporates, leaving behind its content of minerals. So every time you add tap water to your battery, you are increasing the concentration of minerals. With the cost of distilled water as low as it is, you'd be foolish to use anything else.

Caring for the outside of the battery is just as important as attending to the inside. Whenever dirt and acid salts are allowed to accumulate on top of the battery, a conductive layer

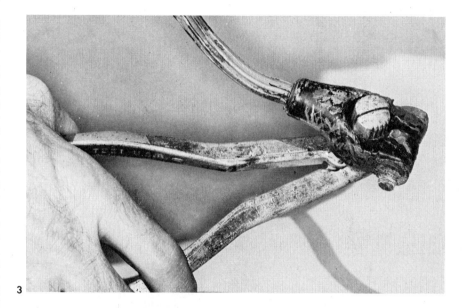

3

1. The post brush has been around for a long time, and it works in most instances. Inspect the post carefully, though. There may be a hard deposit that will have to be scraped off with a knife or sanded.

2. The other end of the brush is used to clean cable ends. Advantage of brush is that it doesn't remove too much lead, but sometimes it doesn't remove the corrosion deposits either. When using brush, turn eyes away, because deposits tend to fly upward.

3. Battery pliers are another well-known tool. They are used to scrape the insides of the terminal clamp clean and also spread the clamp jaws.

4. A bath with baking soda and water or household ammonia will remove the conductive salts that gradually accumulate on top of the battery. These conductive salts can grow to the point where they are draining off much of the battery's electrical energy.

4

Batteries

is formed that puts a constant discharge drain on the cells. This condition can become so advanced that in damp weather it can completely discharge the battery overnight. Further, growths of conductive salts sometimes form on the battery posts, which can ruin their effective electrical contact with the cable terminals.

A bath with a mixture of baking soda, water and dish detergent about three times each year goes a long way toward keeping external battery losses at their minimum. After cleaning the battery, remove the cables and brighten the posts and terminals with a battery cleaning tool or sandpaper. Once they are clamped firmly

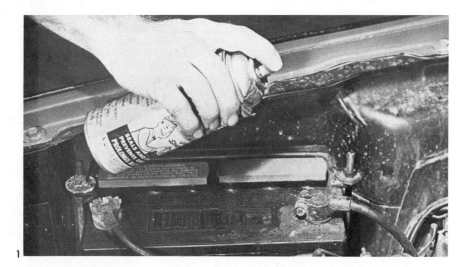

back into place, a *light* coating of Vaseline spread over the terminals will prevent future corrosion.

Corrosion of the cable terminals is a major cause of battery ills. Not only does the poor contact and consequent high resistance greatly diminish the voltage delivered to the car's electrical system, but sometimes makeshift repairs to correct this condition are responsible for major damage to the battery itself. For example, when contact has become so poor between the battery cables and the battery posts that there is not enough voltage available to run the starter, a desperate driver will sometimes get himself going again by pounding on the terminal to restore contact temporarily. In many cases the internal connections of the battery or even

the plates themselves are damaged by such wanton carelessness.

Having to pry or twist cable connections away from the terminals can also break the post's internal bond with the plate connectors. A special battery-terminal-pulling tool, which resembles a small gear puller, should always be used in cases where terminals have become stuck.

Loose battery mounting bolts are another common source of damage. Batteries that have lived through a collision or have endured punishing service in off-road vehicles are also likely to have active material shaken from their plates. However, in the quest for firm battery mountings, do not tighten the hold-down bolts so much that the case is cracked or deformed. Also, the battery should sit level in the battery box, with no unsupported areas that can suffer as a result of a sudden jolt or constant jiggling.

Cracked cases are frequently the result of a frozen battery. This can happen when the battery is allowed to become almost completely discharged, as in cranking a non-starting engine in below-freezing weather and then letting the car sit out after the battery has been run down. When the battery is fully discharged, practically all of the acid is absorbed by the plates and its antifreeze effect in the electrolyte is nil. The almost-pure water left in the cells then freezes and cracks the battery case.

Acid corrosion leading to partial destruction of the cable greatly reduces the current that the battery can make available to the starter. The cross section of the battery cables is determined by the amount of current flow that they must carry. Current flow (amperage), not voltage, is what gives the starting motor the power to do its backbreaking job. Cables for a car with a 6-volt battery are heavy, because extremely high current flow is required to crank an engine at such low voltages. Twelve-volt cables are smaller, but the current flow is still immense by everyday standards. Common cable used for wiring electric stoves and other pieces of household equipment would soon burn up if it carried the high-amperage starting current in an automobile. A kitchen range draws a maximum of about 20 amperes going full blast. On a very cold morning the average starter in a car draws in excess of 200 amperes getting that frozen iron to budge.

When cable strands are eaten away by acid corrosion, the cable loses its capacity to carry enough current. Overheating of the remaining strands further increases the cable's resistance to current flow. Proper care of the cables and their terminals is as important as maintaining the battery itself, and on a cold morning it can make the difference between a quick go and a no-start.

BATTERY JUMP STARTING

Jump starting a car can be defined as the transfer of battery current from a charged battery to one that is in a discharged state. The transfer is made through a set of battery jumper cables. Using cables is a simple matter, but certain precautions should be taken to avoid electrical damage.

The first rule is to connect like terminals. Connect the positive to positive and negative to negative even if one car has a positive-ground system and the other a negative.

To avoid a shower of sparks which could explosively ignite a gasoline leak or a hydrogen gas leak from the battery, always connect the ground terminals *last* and disconnect them *first*. The battery supplying the charge should be of approximately the same capacity as the one being charged. To prevent alternator diode damage, disconnect the alternator leads before connecting the two batteries. In this way, if the batteries are connected improperly (which is a possibility when done in the dark), alternator damage wilh be avoided.

Handle those cables carefully! Do not let them touch each other or another metal object, especially a fender, after connecting them to one battery. The car with the good battery should be left running anytime the cables are connected; otherwise both batteries will soon be dead. If misused, jumper cables can cause more trouble than the problem they're designed to solve.

BATTERY TROUBLESHOOTING

Warnings of impending battery trouble are rare. There may be noth-

1. Corrosion can be slowed down or eliminated by coating the battery terminals with grease or one of these special sprays.

2. No car owner should complain about the cost of using distilled water in the battery, because it is available at low cost in any market. Two quarts should last two or three years and will result in added battery life, better operation.

3. Battery filler holes have a tube extending down to the proper electrolyte level. This one has a roughly triangular bottom to indicate the fill level.

4. Starting in cold weather is made much harder due to the fact that available battery power grows less with falling temperatures, while the power required by the starter goes up as temperature drops. You must keep your battery in good condition during winter.

ing more than a few sluggish starts, which are usually ignored anyway. Turning the ignition key one fine evening, however, you may be greeted with a sickening clicking sound or a few slow attempts at starting that get slower with each try. You just may be able to get started if you have a few basic tools, such as a screwdriver, a pair of pliers and maybe a spark plug wrench.

First you must determine whether or not the culprit is the battery. Turn on your headlights. If they seem dim (along with your dash lights), especially during starting attempts, then the battery is being discharged. Another indication may be a sick-sounding horn or one that doesn't work at all, or even an FM radio that won't play while the AM does.

Turn on the headlights again, raise the hood and visually check the cables and terminals for dirt, moisture or corrosion. Insert a clean, dry screwdriver tip between the battery post and the cable end. Jiggle it around. If the lights grow brighter, the problem is dirty cables and posts. If you have an assistant, have him or her try to start the car while you hold the screwdriver in place. Be sure to work from the side of the car, just in case the car is in gear. A plastic-handled screwdriver is best, because it ensures insulation from shock.

The screwdriver tip creates a clean

3

connection between the dirty post and cable end. If you're lucky, the car just may start. If so, allow it to recharge somewhat by operating the engine at a high idle for a few minutes. Then carefully put it into gear and make for home, where the battery can be cleaned and properly charged.

If the lights grew brighter when you touched the screwdriver tip between the post and the cable end but the car failed to start, remove the cables from the posts and scrape them both lightly with a screwdriver, penknife or nail file until shiny. A corrosive film that's hardly noticeable accumulates on these contacts. In time, the film resists the flow of current. By scraping the inside of the cable end and the outside of the battery post, the resistance is reduced and metal-to-metal contact is restored.

Hopefully, there's still enough charge left to start the car. Wait at least half an hour before trying again. Allowing a low battery to sit sometimes results in a partial rejuvenation. If possible, while it's "resting," clean and scrape the connections to the frame (which are usually overlooked as a source of poor contact) and the starter solenoid. Your challenge is to lower electrical and mechanical resistance as much as possible in order to increase current flow. You want to get all contacts clean and dry, because every bit of resistance puts a further strain on the battery. Inspect the cables and wiring for bad connections and worn insulation and fix if possible.

Check the cells for electrolyte level, because one low cell can cause a problem. If water is handy (clean rain water works well) and one or more cells is noticeably low, add to the low cells. After adding water, wait a while to let it mix with the acid.

After doing all the above, go back and try starting the car again. It may turn over much faster now, but perhaps not quite fast enough. If this is the case, don't continue cranking; instead conserve what charge there is.

If there's no steep hill around for push-starting, there is a last-resort

Temperature		Starter Power Required	Battery Power Available (Full Charge)
°F	°C		
80	27	100%	100%
50	10	133	82
32	0	165	65
10	−12	210	50
0	−18	250	40
−10	−23	310	33

4

Batteries

tactic. Engines are hardest to start when cold, especially those with high compression. The moving parts and the thick oil resist movement. Remove the plugs, clean the electrodes and lower their voltage requirement by decreasing the gap somewhat. If this doesn't help, remove three to four plugs from every other cylinder in the firing order and place their cables where they will not be grounded or throw a spark. This will not only reduce mechanical resistance and speed up the engine's cranking speed, but will increase coil saturation enough to noticeably improve the spark.

If all this fails, lock the car and start walking, bearing in mind that proper battery care could probably have prevented it all. For additional troubleshooting tips, see the ''Ignition Emergencies'' heading in the ignition tuning chapter.

If you live in a section of the country that gets so miserable during the winter months that you keep your car garaged for the duration, here's how to keep that battery alive. Carefully remove it from the car by loosening the ground terminal first. Corroded parts can be cleaned with a mixture of sodium bicarbonate (baking soda) and water, along with some scrubbing with a stiff brush. Don't place the battery on a concrete deck, but set it on a bench or wooden blocks. Attach a charger to it every couple of months or whenever a hydrometer check shows the cells are getting low. When you reinstall the battery in your car, clean the terminal clamps and battery posts with a wire brush.

NEW BATTERIES

When you buy a new battery, make sure you select one of a size and amperage at least equal to the battery you've replaced. In instances where an engine has been swapped, an air conditioner installed, etc., choose one that's appropriate for the job at hand.

The drain on the battery of a modern car can be very high when the engine is not running. High-capacity alternators or generators carry the electrical load when the engine is running, but too small a battery may be discharged so much by a stereo or radio in use when the car is parked that starting is seriously impaired. An electrically oversize battery is therefore highly desirable. It provides a factor of convenience and safety. A larger battery also has longer life and more starting power and can therefore be a worthwhile investment. Cars equipped with air conditioning definitely require larger batteries. So when buying, go for a high ampere-hour rating.

An accompanying chart reveals typical load requirements of many automotive electrical components. If you are going to buy a larger battery, check the size of your battery tray *and* the clearance above it. All batteries are not of the same height; if you select one that is taller than stock you may run into trouble.

When installing a battery in your car, note which terminal post of the old battery is connected to ground before removing it. If your engine is equipped with an alternator, then the rectifiers, vehicle wiring or other components of the charging system can be damaged by hooking the battery up backwards.

One of the most important factors to consider regarding battery installation is proper choice of cables. Battery cables must carry the extremely heavy starting current with a minimum loss of voltage, since the speed of cranking is dependent on the voltage made available at the starting motor. In instances where a battery is located some distance from the starter motor, the proper choice becomes very important. The cable running to the starter motor should be as large as possible.

Where the battery is installed within three cable-feet of the starter and the load on the battery will be reasonable, No. 4 gauge cable is sufficient for a 12-volt battery and No. 1 gauge for a 6-volt battery. Where the battery is remotely mounted or the demand on it will be great (such as an air conditioner), then No. 0 gauge is recommended for both. Copper cable is

1

TYPICAL CURRENT LOAD OF MODERN CARS
(in Amperes)

Switch	Accessory Switch Load	Max. Vehicle Operating Load
Parking	4 to 8	—
Low-Beam Headlamp	8 to 14	—
High-Beam (4) Headlamp	12 to 18	18
Heater	6 to 7	—
Windshield Wiper	2 to 3	3
Air Conditioner	10 to 15	15
Radio	0.4 to 1.8	1.8
Ignition—Standard	3	—
Ignition—Transistorized	8 to 12	12
Alternator Field	3 to 5	5
Total		54.8 Amps
Summer Starting	100–400	Amperes*
Winter Starting	225–500	Amperes*

*Values vary with engine size, engine temperature and oil viscosity.

2

the way to go, because it is an ideal conductor of electricity. Some modern cars are equipped with aluminum-core cables, but it takes a larger size cable to carry the same load as a smaller copper cable could.

In retrospect, the best advice we can give is to purchase a battery that offers more capacity than you actually need. It will cost a few dollars more initially, but it will save you money and give you more satisfaction and dependability in the long run.

SPECIAL BATTERIES

If you're a restorer of old cars or a hot rodder, you may have a 6-volt system, yet wish for the advantages of a modern 12-volt system. This is especially likely to be true if you've modified the engine or substituted a newer one, since high-compression engines require a lot more oomph at the starter motor. Probably one of the most logical things to do, since 12-volt electrical systems are now so common, is to change to a 12-volt starter. It is not, however, absolutely necessary to convert the remainder of the car's electrical system to 12-volt specs. The solution is a 6/12 system. The key device in such a set-up is an automatic voltage converter switch. You merely add a second 6-volt battery and connect it through the special switch to the starter.

This system automatically delivers 12 volts to the starter for cranking the engine, but does not alter the 6-volt current supplied to the rest of the electrical system. There are also conversion kits available that allow entire 12-volt engines to be fitted in 6-volt cars. It is not even really necessary to change the original 6-volt starter, because briefly supplying 12 volts to a 6-volt starter motor will not hurt it.

Even problems of battery space shouldn't deter anyone from this choice, since dual-voltage batteries are also available. These are 12-volt units built as though they were two small 6-volt batteries. The dual-voltage setup comes with the automatic switch installed on the battery, and the entire unit will fit into standard 6-volt and 12-volt battery boxes.

For that competition car, starting may not be a particular problem, but weight probably is. A solution is to adapt a motorcycle battery. Something else to remember in push-started cars is that since there is no starter circuit, much lighter-gauge wire can be used for the battery cables.

The battery is the heart of your car's complex, extensive electrical system. As with your own heart, if you take good care of it, it will take good care of you. ♙

1. Most batteries are furnished with labels that furnish the consumer with sufficient data to guide him in choosing the battery for his needs. This unit is a group 24 battery with 66 plates that's rated at 70 ampere-hours. Always pick a new battery with an ampere-hour rating at least as high as that of the old battery you're replacing.

2. The high current load of a modern car loaded with accessories is shown by this chart. If you add accessories which were not originally on your car, you should install a larger battery.

3. The Delco Energizer battery is permanently liquified and sealed at the factory. It was designed with the Vega in mind and permits new Vegas to be shipped by rail standing vertically rather than resting on their wheels. This allows room for more cars, and once the destination is reached, cars can be driven away, because electrolyte has not spilled out.

4. This dual-voltage battery installed on an old Packard is really two 6-volt batteries in one case, connected externally by the solenoid on top of the case. When the starting circuit is engaged, the solenoid is activated and connects the two 6-volt halves in series, sending 12 volts to the starter motor. As soon as the engine starts running, the solenoid flips back and connects the two battery halves in parallel for 6 volts. A godsend for old 6-volt cars, the dual-voltage battery provides quick starting without the necessity of converting the car's entire electrical system.

Starters

TURN ON, BUT IF IT WON'T TURN OVER,
DON'T TURN IN YOUR STARTER—
IT'S USUALLY NOT TO BLAME.

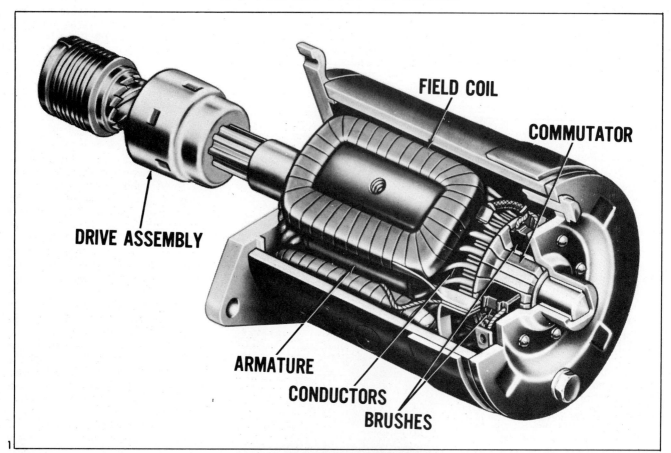

FIELD COIL

COMMUTATOR

DRIVE ASSEMBLY

ARMATURE

CONDUCTORS

BRUSHES

1

The introduction of the electric starter has been hailed by some as the greatest automotive development of all time — right up there with the "neckers' knob" and the swan hood ornament with light-up plastic wings. In terms of making the automobile acceptable to the masses this is probably true, but had earlier developments in carburetion (so the driver didn't have to get out and prime the cylinders) and ignition (high-tension systems instead of low) not taken place, the electric starter might have had an even longer wait before it became a satisfactory alternative to the hand crank. Perhaps even more necessary to the successful application of the electric starter was the development of a storage battery to provide current for its operation.

Some early starters were permanently engaged and, when not being used for starting, were driven by the engine and acted as generators. Although this wasn't a bad idea in principle, the design was not compatible with high engine rpm and eventually had to be shelved. In modern practice, the

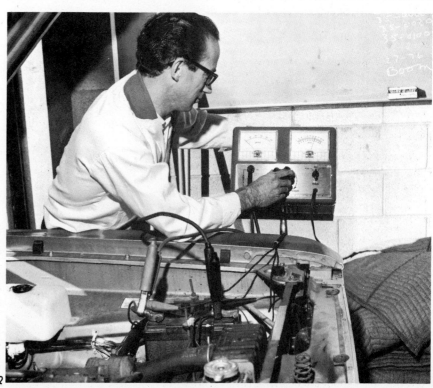

2

starter drives the engine's flywheel by means of a small pinion gear which engages a large ring gear that is fitted around the flywheel's circumference. Since the ratio between the starter pinion and the ring gear is something like 12 or 16 to one, the starter would be driven at something in the neighborhood of 50,000 rpm if it were permanently coupled to an engine turning four grand. Obviously, this speed of rotation would cause the starter to literally explode from the developed inertia! For this reason, there is a device incorporated in the starter drive to disengage it as soon as the engine is operating under its own power. The generator, on the other hand, is prevented from overrevving by its relatively large drive pulley and the only slightly larger pulley on the engine's crankshaft.

At the time of the electric starter's invention, there was nothing about the design of the motor itself that was not already well known to engineers. After all, powerful direct current motors were a common source of motive power for streetcars well before the turn of the century. It was the development of a satisfactory drive mechanism that ultimately made electric starting a reasonable substitute for a bent piece of iron twirled vigorously by hand.

STARTER DRIVES

The starter drive used in modern-day cars has a number of necessary duties to perform. First, it has to be able to couple the starter motor to the engine in such a way that starter operation will cause the engine's crankshaft to rotate fast enough to start the engine. It must also be able to absorb the shock of the sudden application of torque against the inert mass of the engine's movable parts. Lastly, it must be able to uncouple the starter motor from the engine as soon as starting has been accomplished. While there have been other types of starter drives used at one time or another, there are basically two types in common use today. Both of these, however, have undergone a great deal of development since their introduction, and it appears that one of these types is slowly losing ground to the other in the actual number of vehicles equipped with it.

The first starter drive type is the so-called Bendix drive. It is also variously called an inertia drive, or self-engaging drive, as well as by various brand names such as "Folo-Thru." An example is shown which is currently being used on some Ford products. Bendix drives are also found on many English cars, and on older Plymouths, Studebakers and American Motors cars. Thirty-five years ago Bendix drive starters were used almost universally in the U.S. and throughout the world, but their

end appears to be fast approaching. The most important feature of its operation is that it will engage itself with the engine's flywheel gear using no other power then that provided by its inertia against the sudden rotation of the starter motor. There is a spiral-cut sleeve fixed to the armature shaft of the starter motor. Around this is the pinion gear's driving sleeve which engages the spiral grooves that turn with the starter motor shaft. A light spring keeps the pinion assembly pulled back from the flywheel when the starter motor is at rest, but when the starter is operated, the inertia of the pinion assembly's mass causes it to be thrust forward along the spiral splines before its rotation can catch up with that of the motor itself. By this time the teeth of the pinion are in engagement with the flywheel ring gear. There is also a very heavy spring — commonly called a Bendix spring — that serves to absorb the sud-

SEAL ASSEMBLY

SWITCH

3

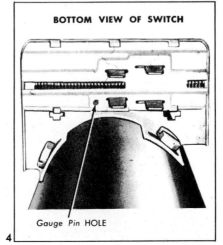

BOTTOM VIEW OF SWITCH

Gauge Pin HOLE

4

den impact and application of torque.

In its original form, as developed by Bendix, there was nothing more to the unit than is described above. However, as years went by, it became obvious that there were some definite shortcomings to the system. The foremost was that the heavy Bendix spring was asked to carry the entire load of the torque being applied by the starter. The result was that the spring fractured rather frequently, close to the bolts holding its "eyes" to the drive assembly. This was overcome by relieving the spring of its torque-transmitting duties except by the friction between itself and the drive. It still serves, however, to absorb the impact of engagement.

Another annoying habit of Bendix drive starters was the tendency to disengage themselves the first time the engine fired, even though the engine was not yet ready to run under its own power. It is often necessary for the starter to help the engine through several revolutions after the cylinders have started to fire — particularly during a cold-weather start. With some of the old Bendix drives, even a very small increase in crankshaft speed was enough to reverse the pinion on its splines and disconnect the starter. The problem was solved by adding a lock pin that would slip into a detent cut into the spiral sleeve. The lock pin is loaded by a carefully calibrated spring that holds it in the detent until crankshaft speed reaches a level sufficient to keep the engine running under its own power.

A backfire, or accidental engagement of the starter while the engine was running could still make mincemeat out of the flywheel gear or the starter drive. Perhaps one of the reasons that Ford has continued to use this type of starter drive for so long is that their Folo-Thru unit has completely overcome all the problems inherent in the original concept of the design. The latest Folo-Thru drives incorporate an overrunning clutch and a sealed-in rubber cushion that serves to protect the drive and flywheel gears from damage under conditions of malfunction or inept operation.

1. This is the old Ford Folo-Thru starter, which did not have a movable pole shoe. The shape of the drive is the easily recognizable element.

2. Battery and starter testing go hand in hand. This Allen Battery-Starter tester will put a load on the battery and measure the voltage at the same time. It will also tell you how much current the starter is going to be drawing in operation.

3. Chrysler has used this neutral safety switch for years. It screws into the side of their automatics.

4. Pin hole in this GM neutral safety switch is for proper positioning of the switch in its slotted mounting.

Starters

In all fairness, it must be pointed out that Bendix drives do have many attractive advantages not shared by other types. For one thing, they generally take a little less current to operate since no separate electrical unit is required to engage the drive. Also, they are more compact, cheaper to build and to service, and—since the starter is already in motion when the gear engages — can sometimes "bump" an engine into life when the battery has become too discharged to do a real job of cranking. The chief reason that they seem to be losing favor is that large, powerful, high-compression engines appear to cause drive breakage.

The other type of starter drive found on contemporary automobiles is the overrunning-clutch, or positive-engagement system. Until about 1949, many GM cars still had foot-operated starters. When the pedal was depressed it first shoved the starter pinion into engagement with the fly-wheel, and then actuated the starter's electrical switch. These were, in effect, the original positive-engagement, overrunning-clutch types. Later, Delco began placing a heavy solenoid atop the starter which performed the task of engaging the drive and switching on the starter current. Some earlier starters of the foot-engaged type used Bendix type springs to absorb the sudden torque load of the starter motor, but eventually this gave way to an overrunning clutch. Since the starter drive is held in engagement electrically, it will not be disengaged un-

til the driver releases the key (or dash button). To keep the running engine from over-speeding the starter, an overrunning clutch is an indispensable means of preventing damage to the starter motor. The overrunning clutch allows the starter gear to turn freely on its shaft when being driven by the engine's flywheel, yet locks up solidly when the starter motor is cranking the engine. Naturally, as soon as the driver releases the key, the drive gear is disengaged by a spring.

One of the things that makes the positive-engagement starter more suitable for cranking high-powered engines is the extra bearing it provides for the starter shaft beyond the drive assembly. This serves to take much of the cranking load off the starter motor bearings. However, the American Motors Bendix drive starters incorporated this feature into their design as well. Nevertheless, recent years have seen this unit dropped from AM products in favor of the Delco and Autolite positive-engagement starters.

The solenoid used on most positive-engagement, overrunning-clutch starters does increase the voltage required to operate the starter somewhat. However, Ford's positive engagement starter employs a rather clever arrangement that eliminates the need for a separate solenoid — one of their "better ideas," no doubt! When the key is turned to the start position, current is sent through one of the starter motor's field coils, which is grounded at its other connection. This causes a magnetic field to be set up in and around the coil.

There is a movable iron pole shoe mounted beside this field coil that is attached to the starter drive actuating lever. The pole shoe is naturally attracted by the magnetic field and is drawn into the core of the starter coil. When this happens, the starter drive is thrust into engagement with the flywheel gear and, as the movable pole shoe seats itself, it switches on the current to the remainder of the field windings and places the starter in normal operation. A small holding coil is used to keep the movable pole shoe in the fully seated position during the time that the starter is turning the engine.

This unit has proven quite trouble-free and easy to service, since the only electrical parts that are not an integral part of the starter motor itself are the contacts that switch current to the windings. The cover for the starter drive actuating lever is held in place on the motor by the brush cover band. By loosening just one screw it is possible to get at both the brushes and the actuating contacts for servicing or testing.

Chrysler Corp. dropped Bendix drives from Plymouth starters when their existing design proved unable to cope with the demands of their newer, more powerful engines. The positive-engagement starter used on Chrysler cars other than Plymouth was different in detail only from the Delco starters found on GM cars. But in addition, a special positive-engagement starter was developed that incorporates a reduction gear for use on models having more powerful engines. In this starter, the motor bearings are spared the punishment of carrying part of the load of sudden drive engagement. Also, since there is about a four-to-one reduction ratio between the motor shaft and the shaft on which the drive mechanism is mounted, the motor turns more freely and at a higher rpm. Since motors draw more electrical energy when turning slowly, the windings are not so likely to become overheated, and less current is demanded from the battery. Unfortunately, the design is bulky and rather complicated, which does not make it one of the all-time favorites with service personnel. Other than the unique use of reduction gears, however, the drive mechanism is not unlike that of any other overrunning-clutch type.

THE STARTER MOTOR

The starter motor is a direct current motor operating on electrical current from the car's battery. Because it is a direct current design, only one cable need be attached between the battery and the motor, since the battery's opposite pole (usually the negative) is coupled to the motor through the chassis of the automobile.

The outer part of the starter motor is

known as its frame. On the outside of the frame you can see four screws, which are quite large. While on some starters these screws are slotted in the ordinary way, some have square recesses in their heads. These are the pole shoe screws which hold the heavy iron pole shoes in place inside the starter housing. Around the pole shoes are the field windings. When electrical current passes through the field windings, a magnetic field is produced which converts the pole shoes into powerful magnets.

On the shaft of the starter motor is mounted the armature, a round assembly consisting of soft iron laminations wound with heavy copper wire. At one end of the armature windings is the commutator, which is made up of brass segments to which the wires forming the armature windings are soldered. The brushes ride against the commutator providing current to the armature windings while in motion.

Each pair of pole shoes is directly opposite one another in the starter frame. When current flows through the field windings, one of these becomes a north pole magnet and the opposite one a south pole magnet. One of the principles of magnetism is that north poles are attracted to south poles, and vice versa, while like poles tend to repel each other. The windings of the armature are arranged in such a way that it too becomes a magnet. Its north pole is attracted to the south pole of the field while being repelled by the field's north pole. The armature's south pole is similarly affected by the other field poles, but in the opposite manner. As a result, the armature turns on its shaft in the direction of magnetic attraction. But, before the poles of the armature can align themselves with the poles of the motor's field, the motion of the commutator has cut off current to that part of the armature's windings, and has routed it to the next set of windings.

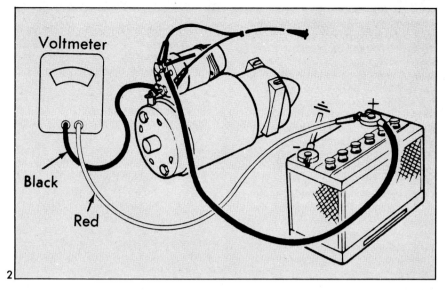

2

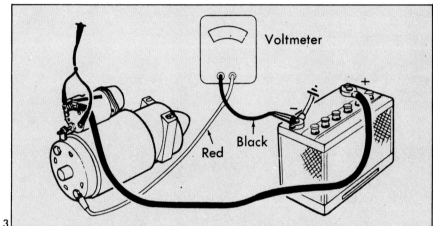

3

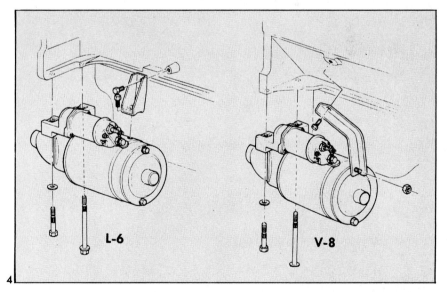

4

1. Starter relay on Chrysler products is firewall-mounted. Note fusible link, which protects circuits that get their power from this source.

2. Battery-cable-to-starter test on Delco-Remy system. Gadget hooked to solenoid is auxiliary start button. You must be very careful when making voltage drop tests to keep from blowing up your voltmeter, if you use the low scale. Switch to the low scale only when engine is cranking, and then switch back to the high scale before the cranking stops.

3. Ground circuit test on a Delco-Remy system. The danger of blowing the voltmeter is not as great here, but it is still a good idea to take first readings on the high scale.

4. Starters are usually located low on the right side of the engine. On most late-model V-8's, they must be serviced from under the car.

Therefore, the magnetic field of the armature remains almost stationary — in a constant state of attraction to the field poles — while the armature itself is made to rotate.

There are two basic types of direct current motors and several derivatives that result from combinations of the two principles. The first is the shunt-wound motor, which is used in wiper motors, and other types which operate at a steady and controlled rate of speed. The other is the series-wound motor. This is the type used for automobile starters.

In a shunt-wound motor, current is supplied directly to the field coils as well as directly to the armature windings, but the armature current in a series-wound motor first passes through the field windings. Series-wound motors therefore make the most efficient use

Starters

of the electrical energy available to them since they perform double duty, so to speak. They are also the type of motor best suited to starting and moving heavy loads. Since the series-wound direct current motor uses the same current to magnetize the field poles as to energize the windings of the armature, the current from the fields must be routed through brushes to the commutator. Two brushes form the electrical connection with the field coils (which receive current from the battery's positive pole) while the other two connect to ground.

In the early years of electric starting, motors of the "pure" series-wound type were used. These were not unlike the larger series-wound motors that had been in use for many years as traction motors for trolleys and electric railroads. The early starter motor therefore shared one of the basic characteristics of all series-wound motors. Unless a load is placed upon them, their speed of rotation will increase rapidly until the point . is reached where something

breaks. Since broken starter drives were not uncommon in the old days, more than one motor accidentally over-revved to the point where inertia caused the armature windings to tear free of the rotor or commutator. For this reason, modern starter motors are usually lightly compounded series-wound motors, which means that there is a third (or fourth) pole that has shunt windings, *i.e.* they draw their current directly from the battery rather than in series with the other field coils. This fourth pole has windings that are generally smaller than those of the other field poles. It serves to augment the starter's power at normal cranking speeds while limiting it should the load be suddenly removed. The shunt coil in Ford positive-engagement starters doubles as the starter drive actuating coil and holding coil. When performing this latter duty, the movable pole shoe that actuates the starter drive becomes the starter's shunt-wound pole.

STARTING CIRCUITS

Each make of car has its own typical layout for the starting system. This is largely determined by the type of starter and drive used, but is also partly due to the car maker's design philosophy and may be further influenced by the transmission type and the optional accessories offered.

General Motors, for example, has used the same basic Delco starter for many years and the system has generally become a fixed concept that shows few changes from year to year. The solenoid on Delco starters is mounted directly on top the starter motor itself, and serves not only to engage the starter drive but to close the internal contacts that make the final connection between the battery's positive pole and the starter windings.

On the end of the solenoid's dust cover are three terminals. The largest of these is connected directly to the battery by a heavy cable. In addition there are two smaller terminals. One of these is connected to the dash control and actuates the starter when the key is turned to the start position. The other is the ignition terminal. The resistance wire used as ballast in the ignition system connects between the ignition switch and the coil, with a spliced wire running to this terminal on the solenoid. When the starter is operated, the solenoid contacts send full battery voltage to the coil via the spliced wire — current that is picked up directly from the large cable connecting the starter to the battery itself.

After the engine has started, the solenoid disengages the starter and cuts off the current flow from the battery. Current for the ignition system must then flow from the ignition switch on the dash by way of the resistance wire. Connections between the resistance wire and the plain wire have been handled differently through the years. Some cars run two wires to the coil, one being the resistance wire from the ignition switch, and the other the plain wire from the starter solenoid. In later models it is easier to make the wire loom if the resistance wire ends at or near the starter and a single plain wire runs from there to the coil. When doing any repairs to wiring, you must have the wiring diagram for the car, as furnished in the factory shop manual or by an independent publisher in the field.

All later model GM cars have two cables connected to the battery's positive pole. The larger of the two serves only the starter, while the smaller cable supplies the remainder of the car's electrical system. This small cable passes first to the horn relay, from which radiate the wires that conduct electricity to other parts of the system — including the ignition switch on the dash. Since some Ford trucks and the majority of American Motors 6-cylinder engines use the Delco starter, there is some similarity in the appearance of their

1   CONTACT FINGER — PLUNGER — SOLENOID — RETURN SPRING — SHIFT LEVER — SPIRAL SPLINES — BUSHING — PINION STOP — OVERRUNNING CLUTCH — ASSIST SPRING — ARMATURE — FIELD COIL — INSULATED BRUSH HOLDER — BRUSH SPRING — GROUNDED BRUSH HOLDER — BRUSH — GROMMET — BUSHING

2

starting systems to that of a General Motors car. However, the circuits serving these are often quite different from those used at GM. It's always better to check the wiring diagram for the particular make and model before doing any modifications, trouble-shooting or repair.

Since no Ford Motor Co. passenger cars employ a solenoid-operated starter drive, there is no need to mount the starter relay (also variously called a solenoid or magnetic switch) on the starter motor. The starter relay on Ford products is therefore a separate sealed unit mounted in most cases on the firewall or fender housing inside the engine compartment. There is just one heavy cable between the relay and the positive terminal of the battery that supplies both the starter and the remainder of the electrical system.

The FoMoCo starter relay has two large terminals and two small ones. The cable from the battery's positive pole is connected to one of the large terminals, and a similar cable connecting the relay to the starter motor is affixed to the other. One of the small terminals is connected to the ignition switch on the car's dashboard and, when the key is turned to the start position, current is directed from the dash control to the relay, causing it to close the main circuit between the battery and the starter motor. Current to the dash switch, as well as to the rest of the car's electrical system, is drawn from a wire attached to the large terminal on the relay to which the battery cable is connected. The other small terminal on the relay is the ignition terminal, which supplies full unballasted battery current to the ignition coil during starting.

As we've seen, GM starting systems have a solenoid at the starter, while FoMoCo products have their starting relays located elsewhere. Chrysler Corp. goes a step further and places a solenoid on the starter in addition to a remotely located relay. Whether this is a carry-over from the days when Plymouths had Bendix drive starters, or whether the philosophy of keeping the starting system independent is at the root of this practice is hard to say. In any case it does give the solenoid just one job to do, and that's operate the starter. Also, the relay is not asked to carry the heavy starting current load in addition to the rest of the car's current demands.

The action goes something like this: when the ignition key is turned to the start position, the starter relay bypasses the ignition ballast and energizes the solenoid on the starter. Current for the entire electrical system is drawn from a terminal on the starter relay which has its own connection with the positive pole of the battery. The solenoid at the starter merely couples the starter motor to the heavy cable that leads to the battery's positive pole. After the engine has started, the ignition key is returned to the on position and the relay no longer supplies the ignition system — although the remainder of the electrical system does continue to draw current from the "Batt." terminal of the relay. The ignition now takes its power through the ballast resistor which receives its electrical energy from the "Ign." terminal on the alternator regulator.

Although American Motors has used Delco, and Prestolite (Chrysler) starters in recent years — and still does on some recent 6-cylinder engines — the majority of their current output is equipped with the Ford-Autolite positive-engagement starter described in detail earlier. Since it's the AM V-8's that are of greatest interest to the hot

3

1. Delco starters such as this are used on all GM products, as well as on many AMC cars and some Ford cars.

2. Prestolite starter used on American Motors cars is similar to Delco design, with overrunning clutch.

3. To remove the solenoid from a Prestolite starter, disconnect the shift pin at the front end, then the lead at the other; remove mount bolts.

4. Electric contacts show wear from a lot of starting. Bolt can be turned, and contact washer flipped over, for new surfaces, as on Delco units.

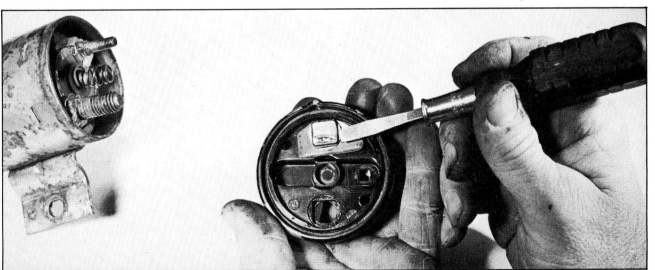

4

rodder and drag racer, the system which most concerns us is the Ford positive-engagement starter setup. The circuitry for this system is almost exactly like that described for FoMoCo products and should cause no special problems for those familiar with Ford starters.

Among the foreign cars there are the Volkswagen overrunning-clutch and Lucas Bendix drive starting systems to contend with. On VW's there is just one cable from the positive pole of the battery that connects to the large solenoid terminal. Another wire connected to the same terminal supplies voltage to the ignition switch and thence to the light switch and the remainder of the electrical system. The ignition system is un-ballasted and takes its current from the ignition switch at all times. When the key is turned to the start position, current is directed to the solenoid's single small terminal which actuates the starter. There is a lock-out in the ignition switch that prevents using the start position more than once without first returning the key to the off position. This is a very good idea that could well be copied by other car makers since it prevents the starter from being accidentally engaged while the engine is running.

The Lucas starters found on most British sports cars are unusual in respect to the majority of American-made units in that they are in most cases purely series-wound. The motors have four field windings that are built in pairs. Each pair is connected at one end to battery current and at the other to the starter's insulated brushes. The current from the field windings is thus sent into the armature windings via the commutator and returned the same way through the two grounded brushes. In most English cars the electrical system — including the ignition switch — draws current from the battery terminal of the starter relay. However, in many of the older sports cars there was a manual starter switch rather than a relay. On these cars the driver pulled a knob on the dash which connected the heavy battery cables through the manual switch to the starter motor. The operation of the switch was exactly like that of a relay, but the work was accomplished by muscle power instead of electro-magnetism. Many Lucas starters have a square extension to the armature shaft that can be turned with a wrench in case of a jam in the drive mechanism — a rather quaintly-British touch of "being prepared for anything."

STARTING SYSTEM TROUBLE

If the starter operates sluggishly, the chances are definitely in your favor that

the trouble is in the battery or its connections and not in the starter itself. However, even in cases where the starter does not turn the engine, the trouble often results from defects that are not in the motor. One of the quickest ways to get on the trail of starting ills is to perform a series of simple headlight tests. But before even attempting this step, the battery should be checked with a hydrometer to make sure that the cause of your troubles is not simply a "flat batt." A weak battery will make any starting system test produce faulty or inconclusive results and prevent you from ever pinpointing the actual cause of the trouble. After you've assured yourself that the battery is in good condition, switch on the headlights and attempt to operate the starter. The result will be one of three things: first, the lights may go out and the starter will not operate; second, the starter will make "working" sounds, but the lights will dim considerably and any actual cranking will be very slow; lastly, the headlights may remain bright but no cranking will take place.

If the lights go out when the starter is switched on, look for poor connections between the battery and the starter motor. Corroded battery termi-

nals are the No. 1 suspect, but don't overlook the ground strap where it fastens to the engine block or car body. Some cars have the battery grounded to the body of the car and a separate ground strap between the body and the engine. This may be located under the car in the area of the transmission or starter mounting. A loose bolt here can kill the voltage available to the starter just as quickly as a loose battery clamp. Another rather offbeat cause of poor contact between starter and battery is paint — either between the starter motor and the engine's bellhousing, or under the ground strap mounting. This trouble is usually associated with new cars or rebuilt and renovated engines. The cure is simply to remove the paint layer with sandpaper and bolt every-

4

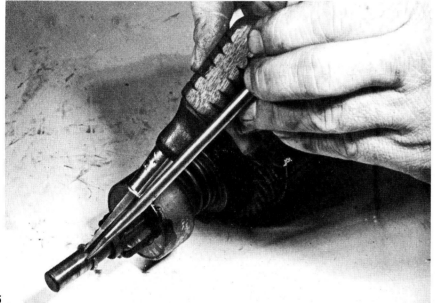

5

1. With through-bolts removed, drive end housing will come off, including fork and armature on Prestolite starter.

2. Shift fork pin is driven out with a few light taps. If fork looks good, there's no need to remove it.

3. This fork is definitely bad. One side is almost completely worn away (arrow). New fork is shown at top.

4. To expose locking ring, collar is driven back with a socket.

5. Getting the ring off involves a little fussing and cussing. Try not to bend it too much, because you will have to use it again.

bypass it with the jumper wire (making sure that the transmission is in neutral). If the ignition key will now operate the starter, the trouble is in the neutral safety switch. Chrysler Corp. automatics have a neutral safety switch that grounds the starting circuit whenever the transmission is in neutral. These switches have only one terminal and can be bypassed by simply grounding the wire.

If these tests of the control circuit fail to provoke any action from the starter, you can try connecting a heavy booster cable jumper directly from the battery's hot side to the terminal on the starter motor. If this causes the starter to operate, the trouble is in the solenoid or starter relay. If the starter does not run when the booster cable is connected, the trouble is in the starter motor itself.

If the relay or solenoid makes a clicking sound when the key is turned to start, and the starter does not run, but does run with the booster in place, it is not necessarily an indication that the relay or solenoid is OK. In many cases the internal contacts are burned, making it impossible for the solenoid to switch on the heavy starter current. Some solenoids can be repaired, but in the majority of cases this trouble calls for a replacement.

If you have a voltmeter you can do a better job of checking out your starting system. The first thing you should do (and which should be a part of every tune-up) is check cranking voltage. Just hook your voltmeter to the battery in correct polarity and crank the engine in the normal way. Battery voltage should not fall below 9.0 volts on a 12-volt system, or 4.5 volts on a 6-volt system.

While the engine is cranking, you should check the cranking speed, either by listening to it, or with a tachometer. Cranking speed on most 12-volt systems is about 180 rpm, or better. On a 6-volt system it is about 125 to 150 rpm. Your ear is really the best judge of whether an engine is turning over fast enough. If it sounds sluggish, you have problems.

The battery must not only be in good condition, but also up to the job. You can't start a 400-inch engine with a

thing back together tightly. All cables in the starter circuit must be secure and in good condition in order to provide an adequate supply of current for cranking the engine.

If the lights dim noticeably when you operate the starter, and cranking action is sluggish or unable to turn the engine at all, there is something throwing an unusually heavy load on the starter and imposing a high discharge rate on the battery. Probably the most frequent cause of such trouble is having too heavy an oil in the crankcase. This is, of course, usually a problem associated with cold weather. Newly assembled engines will sometimes place an undue drain on the battery because of tight clearances. It could also be a case of excessive spark advance. If the initial advance has been set too high or if the advance mechanism of the distributor is not working freely and correctly, the cylinders may be firing before the piston reaches the top of its stroke. The engine tries to run backwards, fighting the action of the starter.

If the lights stay bright, but there is no response from the starter, there is an open circuit in the starting system. This could be in the starter motor itself (possibly worn-out brushes), in its wir-

ing, the starter relay, or in the ignition switch and its wiring. The ignition switch gets a lot of wear and tear, being used at least twice every time you go somewhere — once starting up at home, and again to get you back. This can add up to hundreds of "clicks" every month and, in time, the internal contacts may become too badly worn to work properly. This is probably the first thing to check, and a lot of mechanics would have saved an awful lot of time if they had bothered to look under the dash before tearing into the starter. You can make a small jumper cable to test the control circuit using 14-gauge wire and two alligator clips — or do it the crude way using a screwdriver. Make contact between the main (large) terminal on the starter relay or solenoid and the small terminal that receives the wire from the ignition switch's starter control. If the starter runs, the trouble is in the dash switch or its wiring.

On cars with automatic transmission, there is a neutral safety switch that allows the ignition key to actuate the starter relay only when the transmission selector is in the park or neutral positions. This might also be causing your trouble on cars equipped with an automatic. Locate the switch and

Starters

$7.00 battery — at least not very often. Be sure the battery is in good shape and powerful enough to do the job.

If the trouble is indicated by low voltage while cranking or slow cranking speed, make voltage drop tests. These voltage drop tests check only the wiring and connections, but they are necessary to eliminate one source of trouble. Voltage drop tests indicate the amount of electricity being used in the portion of the circuit you are checking. Any time you check a switch, a wire, or a connection, you should get a very low reading. Theoretically you should get a zero reading, because a switch or wire should be a perfect connection and use no electricity at all. But every conductor has a little resistance to the flow of current, so it uses up some electricity. Approximately one- or two-tenths of a volt is a normal reading on each connection or short length of wire. Through experience you will find that some connections always draw more than they should, but that is normal for that model car. You may get high readings on some voltage drop tests when the starter is bad and is drawing an extra heavy load out of the battery. In that case you would probably find that the wires and connections were getting hot from carrying so much load.

If the voltage drop test doesn't pinpoint anything and you know the battery is good, then the trouble must be in the starter. Remove the starter, take it apart, and you will probably be able to see the trouble just by looking. Starters take a tremendous load, and their bearings can easily wear enough to let the armature drag on the field pole shoes. When that happens, the starter is fighting itself, and it pulls large amounts of current out of the battery.

The field coils should be checked for continuity and the armature should be checked on a growler for shorts. Because you will seldom use one, it isn't worthwhile to buy a growler, but your local garage will have one. Some growlers have a two-position switch that should be in the starter position for starter armatures. It makes the growler more sensitive and catches shorts that other growlers might miss. If you have access to the equipment, an armature can also be checked for shorted loops, and a simple test light will catch a grounded armature. All of these tests are really not conclusive, however, because an armature can have a flying short that only shows up when the armature is turning. You do the best you can, and if it doesn't work when you put it back on the car, you get another starter.

Rebuilt starters are OK if you know they come from a reputable firm. There

is only one right way to rebuild a starter, and it includes a torque test on a test bench to see if the starter really puts out.

For just about any starter motor trouble other than worn brushes it may be wise to replace the entire unit with a new or rebuilt starter. This is particularly true if the trouble appears to be a combination of several different growing defects. On a brand new car it may pay to replace only the armature or the field windings if these prove to be faulty, but in older motors it is likely that the brushes, bearings, brush springs and internal insulation are also just about on their last legs. The difference between $12 for a new armature and $24 for a new starter might seem to be an important saving, but if something else in the starter packs it up soon after the new armature is installed, that $12 is money down the drain.

Actually, the starter motor is a very reliable and rugged part and is seldom a troublemaker. When something goes wrong internally, it is usually a result of placing abnormal demands on the starting system. Cars that are chronic hard starters due to a poorly maintained ignition system can be death on starters. If the starter has to work three times as long as it should really need to each time the engine is started, it is obvious that the useful life of the unit will be at least two-thirds shorter than it should be. In actual practice its life is reduced even more due to the damaging effects of excessive heat build-up which may eventually break down its internal insulation.

OTHER TROUBLES

Occasionally an engine will refuse to turn over even though the starter is

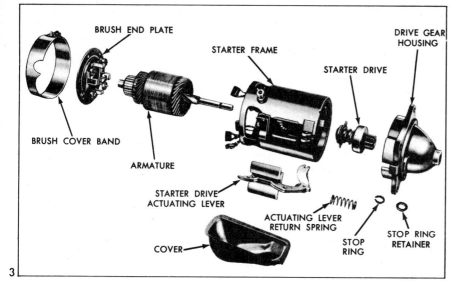

BRUSH END PLATE · **STARTER FRAME** · **DRIVE GEAR HOUSING** · **STARTER DRIVE** · **BRUSH COVER BAND** · **ARMATURE** · **STARTER DRIVE ACTUATING LEVER** · **ACTUATING LEVER RETURN SPRING** · **STOP RING** · **STOP RING RETAINER** · **COVER**

3

making obvious working sounds. The trouble could be hydrostatic lock. This occurs when one or more of the cylinders become partially filled with some liquid. Liquids will not compress — that's what makes hydraulic brakes possible — and if a leaking head gasket or a stuck carburetor float has filled a cylinder with enough coolant or fuel, the starter will not even budge the crankshaft. Should this seem a possible source of your trouble, pull out the spark plugs and try the starter again. If the engine turns over normally — and there's a gush of liquid from one of the plug holes — the culprit was hydrostatic lock!

Acute oil run-down can cause similar troubles. This frequently happens when poor-quality or over-age oil is used in a car that is being operated at high speeds on a hot day. Many motorists on turnpikes will find that after stopping for fuel their car's starter can only turn the engine very slowly. At first sight it appears to be a case of a weak starting system, but in reality the engine has lost its lubrication, making it almost impossible to turn. After all those hot miles with weak or worn-out oil in the crankcase, the lube has about the same viscosity as unused mouthwash. What's left of the oil will run off the cylinder walls of the hot engine moments after the key has been turned off, leaving them drier than the inside of a scorpion's palms. Of course the right thing to do would be change oil right then and there. But if you just want to get going again, remove the air cleaner and pour some SAE 10 motor oil slowly into the carb intake while someone attempts to start the engine. The cranking action will quickly speed up and the engine will start.

Another cause of slow cranking on a hot engine can be the cooling system. We have seen many a starter changed in a desperate attempt to fix a starting system that actually had nothing wrong

4

5

1. A bent cotter pin pulls the brush spring back so that the brush can be slipped out, on Prestolite starter.

2. The usual tests should be made, for grounds, shorts, or opens. This is the ground test shown here.

3. Ford's positive engagement starter requires no separate solenoid to engage the drive. Starter actuating lever is operated by a movable pole shoe using the magnetic attraction of the shunt windings for engagement.

4. Ford starter with movable pole shoe is a little tougher to take apart than others. Brushes must be removed from their holders through slot openings in the frame.

5. After brushes are out, through-bolts can be unscrewed and the end plate will come off. Check the bushing for signs of wear.

with it. The cooling system was the culprit. After a few thousand miles, rust deposits can pile up around the cylinders, particularly around the rear cylinders where there may be poor coolant circulation. The accumulation of rust and just plain old crud allows hot spots to develop in the cylinder walls. When the engine is shut off after a hot run, those hot spots grab hold of a piston skirt tighter than a miser holds a ten dollar bill. Sounds incredible, doesn't it? But clean the cooling system thoroughly and the starting difficulties will go away.

There is yet another brand of cooling system starting trouble caused by seeping anti-freeze. Ethylene glycol in oil causes high friction, and can sieze an engine so tight you'd think somebody welded the crank to the block. In mild cases, the seeping anti-freeze will only cause one or two pistons to stick a little. If your engine starts sluggishly after sitting for several hours, it may be because the long rest has allowed anti-freeze to seep into the cylinders. Drain the cooling system and refill with pure water for a test. If starting improves, use a good stop leak preparation and then put in new anti-freeze. You must use anti-freeze in all late model cars (except Volkswagen) to get the proper cooling needed.

In extreme cases of anti-freeze contamination, just draining the cooling system isn't enough. You also have to get the anti-freeze out of the oil. A preparation called Butyl Cellosolve can be purchased at auto parts stores and used in the engine oiling system to remove the anti-freeze. It's tricky to use, but if you follow the directions carefully you'll prevent engine damage.

A rubbing, grinding or bumping sound from the starter motor during cranking usually means a loose pole shoe that is dragging against the turning armature. On rare occasions this will jam the starter. The starter should be inspected to see if the windings, armature or insulation have been damaged by the loose part, and if not, the pole shoe can be tightened and the starter returned to service.

If the starter motor seems to be faulty there are several defects other than worn-out brushes that can be spotted visually. These are important things to know if you are buying a used starter, since they can be the tip-off that a particular unit isn't worth the trip home. Burned segments on the commutator are a possible sign of faulty windings in the armature — providing that the segments on either side of the burned one appear normal. Sloppy fitting bearings should also be an obvious fault, but if everything else seems OK it may be

possible to get new brushes and bearings and renovate the unit yourself. One sure sign of miseries is a ring of molten lead that has solidified on the inside of the brush inspection band. This may be accompanied by one or more loose wires on the commutator, since the molten lead is the solder that once held them in place! Starters that have been this greatly overheated are probably best used for anchors on small boats or for throwing at persistent bill collectors. Charred-appearing insulation on the field windings should be also grounds for immediate rejection.

DRIVE TROUBLES

If the starter motor appears to run normally when the key is turned to start, but the engine does not crank over, there is probably something wrong with the drive mechanism. Simi-

larly, if there are horrible grinding noises — either with the starter turning or failing to turn the crankshaft — the drive unit should be given your immediate attention. If you're lucky, the trouble might be only a broken overrunning clutch, pinion assembly or spring. If the stars are against you, it might be a stripped flywheel ring gear — which means pulling the transmission, clutch and flywheel.

Occasionally — particularly on Bendex drive units — the starter will have its drive jam in the engaged position. This is usually the car's way of giving notice that it's time to replace the drive unit; however, you can usually free such jams (unless the car has an automatic transmission) by placing the transmission in high gear and rocking the car forward and backward — with the emphasis on backward. A lack of proper lubrication may be at the bottom of

1

2

such a malfunction, and a thorough cleanup followed by an application of the specified lube could be all that's needed to make life rosy again. Some overrunning clutches, such as those used by GM and VW, have permanent lubricants packed into them at the factory. These units must not be cleaned in solvents since this could destroy the lubrication. Most starter drives that are not factory-lubed are either to be assembled without lube, or are to be lubricated with engine oil. Car maker's specifications should always be noted before applying any greases or oils to starter drives.

Late model General Motors starters with vertical mounting bolts sometimes have shims between the starter and the block. Those shims determine the mesh of the pinion teeth with the flywheel. If they are left out, the pinion will end up too close, and may jam in the engaged position. If shims are put in when they aren't needed (it happens) the pinion will be too far

from the flywheel, and will make horrible noises as the pinion teeth skip over the flywheel teeth, resulting in destruction of either the pinion or the flywheel ring gear. Before removing any starter with vertical bolts, make a check of the pinion-teeth-to-ring-gear clearance. Engage the drive by disconnecting the battery and running a wire to the solenoid only. Be sure that the new or rebuilt starter goes on with the same pinion teeth clearance as the old starter had.

HOT ROD ACCESSORIES

There's nothing to be gained in performance from hot-rodding the starting system, but it is frequently necessary to modify it to make possible custom engine installations and to get reliable starts from highly modified power plants. Your friendly neighborhood speed shop won't have any hopped-up starter motors on its shelves, but there is something almost as good waiting at the nearest

parts store or wrecking yard: namely, a truck starter. The majority of truck engines are based on passenger car blocks. Since this is the case, heavy-duty commercial starters will bolt right onto most of the blocks that are popular with hot rod builders. By checking the exploded-view drawings for the various starter units in the dealer's truck and passenger car catalogs you can quickly find out what will fit. Commercial starters have a greater current demand than those commonly installed on passenger cars, so it's necessary to use a more powerful battery to get the full benefit of its design. This is a step that you should consider when planning the starting system for your rod.

In addition to the 6-12 systems that we talked about in the chapter on batteries, there are also several conversion kits that permit using entire 12-volt engines in 6-volt cars and 6-volt engines in 12-volt cars. Six-volt starters can also usually be found that will fit engines that originally had 12-volt jobs. However, a 6-12 battery system, or converting the car's electrical system to 12 volts, will get you much more in the way of reliable starts than swapping the 12-volt starter for a 6-volt unit.

The starter motor can sometimes create an interference problem on some engine swaps—and, unfortunately, this interference is usually with the steering system. When dropping a Cadillac or an Olds block into an early Ford, the starter can be moved to the other side with a speed shop adapter; however, on other engines, the clearance must be made some other way. The steering can be moved, the starter motor housing can be ground or cut or the motor can be turned upside down—or you can make your own adapter.

We've come a long way since the days of the hand crank, and the starting system of the modern automobile has reached a point where it is both well up to its task and one of the most trouble-free parts on the car. Given half a chance—and some preventive maintenance in the area of the battery and its cables and connections—it will provide sound and reliable service for the life of the car ♨

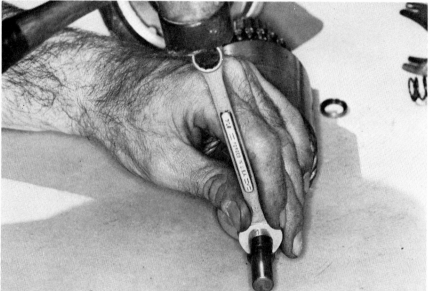

3

4

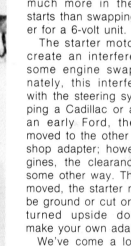

1. Pivot pin is all that keeps the movable pole shoe in place. It slips out easily. Don't lose it.

2. Slots in fork slip over drive and shift it into the ring gear on the flywheel. Drive won't come off yet.

3. This is not recommended by Ford, but it seems to be the easiest way to get the ring off the armature shaft.

4. Armature lathe is used to renew commutator. Small wheel (arrow) is used to undercut mica.

HOW-TO: STARTER REBUILD

1. Working at Ivan's Generator Exchange in Hollywood, Calif., we begin the starter overhaul by attacking the solenoid first.

2. After removing all its screws, the solenoid is twisted slightly to unlock a flange that attaches it to the starter case.

3. Next, unbolt the long through-bolts. The armature can then be slid out of the case. Watch out for the big solenoid spring.

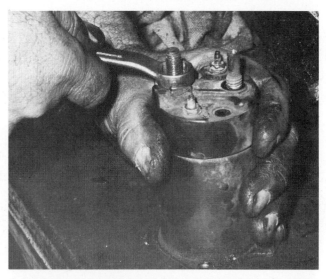

4. Removing two screws and these two terminal nuts allows access to the electrical components of the solenoid.

5. The solenoid operates by pushing back the round copper disc so that it contacts the two square copper boltheads.

6. If in good shape, the copper disc and bolts are cleaned up and reused. If badly burned or pitted, they are replaced.

7. Here are the refurbished components of the solenoid. Reassemble them and set them aside until later.

8. Now let's look at the armature. The Bendix assembly can be slid off the shaft once this snap ring has been removed.

9. Off comes the Bendix assembly. First a spacer and a retaining sleeve have to be removed, after snap ring comes off.

10. The armature's commutator is then lightly turned down on a lathe. This one is useless; note the broken commutator bar.

11. After being turned down, the commutator's insulators must be carefully undercut so that they do not foul the brushes.

12. To make sure that all commutator connections are soldered, the end is carefully dipped into a pot of molten solder.

HOW-TO: **STARTER REBUILD**

13. The armature is then checked on a growler machine to determine its electrical continuity and magnetic flux continuity.

14. After tapping out the old bushing from the Bendix nose housing, the new bushing is test-fitted to the armature shaft.

15. Using a shouldered drift punch of exactly the right size, the new bushing is tapped into the Bendix nose housing.

16. The copper bushing in the front cover is also replaced. Then the Bendix unit is replaced. A new snap ring is included.

17. Remove the small screws that hold the brushes in brush holders. Next, field windings are checked for continuity.

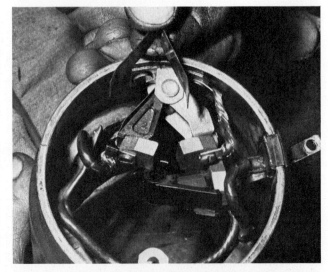

18. If you removed the V-shaped brush springs, they must be replaced behind new brushes. This is tricky—be careful.

19. A pivot pin holds each spring and brush holder. Make sure electrical leads do not interfere with brush movement.

20. With its Bendix side down, the armature is fitted into the nose housing. The Bendix clevis must engage the collar.

21. These fiber washers have to be fitted at the commutator end of the armature before slipping on the case.

22. With thumbs holding the brushes apart so that they will slip over the commutator, case is lowered over the armature.

23. The front end of the starter looks like this before the cover is bolted back on. Now install the rebuilt solenoid.

24. Ivan's adds this final nicety: a dressing stone touches up the commutator while the starter is spun with external power.

Solenoids and Switches

THOSE SMALL ITEMS CAN MEAN BIG HEADACHES IF THEY LET YOU DOWN. HERE'S HOW TO CHECK 'EM OUT AND SET 'EM RIGHT.

All large electromagnetic switches controlling the flow of battery current to the starter motor are commonly called solenoids, yet a few of these are not, in the strictest sense of the word, solenoids at all. To make matters even more involved, the car manufacturers' service publications sometimes use other terms for electrical devices which are, literally speaking, solenoids. While the whole picture may look as confusing as a Japanese road sign, we may be able to straighten it out a little bit in your mind — even though you'll probably have to keep on using the word solenoid to describe virtually any starter switch just to make yourself understood by the neighborhood mechanic. For the purpose of simplification we will discuss starter-circuit controls under four specific names: solenoids, relays, magnetic switches and manual switches. Whether you're trying to understand a manufacturer's service manual, or just attempting to communicate with your mechanic, a discussion of these terms will help you to understand what it is that they're talking about.

ELECTROMAGNETIC ATTRACTION

The ancient Greeks knew that the mineral lodestone — a naturally magnetic form of iron oxide — would attract iron as well as other pieces of lodestone. Yet it wasn't until about 1000 years after Christ that somebody finally came up with a practical use for magnetism: the compass. Further, it was not until about 800 years after that important event that any significant understanding of magnetic attraction was gained. It remained until about 75 years before the invention of the motor car itself for the first electromagnet to be developed. Virtually all that we know about — or accomplish with — electromagnetism is the result of 20th-century development.

About 1825 it was discovered that an electrical current passed through a coil of wire wrapped about a piece of iron would cause the iron to become a magnet. Later, it was learned that even without an iron core, there was a magnetic field produced inside such a coil. Various shapes of coils were found to radiate different field patterns. A wire coil wound in the form of a cylinder or helix was discovered to produce a field

which had almost perfectly straight lines of magnetic force extending through the center of the coil. Such a coil was called a solenoid, derived from the Greek word *solen:* a channel. When electrical current is passed through a solenoid, extremely powerful magnetic attraction is exerted upon a piece of iron that is placed partially within the coil. The iron is drawn suddenly and powerfully along the parallel lines of force until it rests within the strongest part of the magnetic field. Such arrangements have the ability, therefore, to exert leverage and do mechanical work at the push of a button. The starter solenoid found in GM and Chrysler starter circuits consists of such a solenoid coil with a spring-retracted iron plunger resting partly inside the core of the windings. When the ignition key is turned to the start position, current is directed to the windings of the solenoid. The resultant magnetic field draws the plunger home, engaging the starter drive mechanism and closing the heavy contacts that complete the circuit between the battery and the starter motor.

The term relay can be properly applied to a solenoid — since a relay is any electro-mechanical device used to switch current on and off at a point remote from the operator. However, not all relays are solenoids, in view of the fact that the term solenoid applies only to electromagnetic coils wound in a cylindrical pattern. For example, the

drive-engagement unit on a Ford positive-engagement starter cannot properly be termed a solenoid since the windings are circular in pattern rather than cylindrical.

A cylindrical coil wound about an iron bar — which in turn is used to produce a magnetic attraction between the magnetized core and a movable armature that serves to close a set of electrical contacts — would appear to be justifiably called a solenoid. However, since the coil is not being employed as a solenoid coil, but simply as a means of magnetizing a fixed iron core it is, in reality, an electromagnetic relay. Such relays are used in the control circuit of Chrysler Corp. starting systems. To be absolutely proper, devices with a fixed core and movable armature are relays, while those with a cylindrical coil having a movable iron core to do the work are solenoids.

Occasionally you will see the term magnetic switch used in service manuals — particularly those relating to Bendix drive Plymouth, Dodge and American Motors starting systems. A relay is in truth a magnetic switch. The term was introduced to avoid confusing those who might not know what a relay was, but could grasp the meaning of magnetic switch.

SOLENOID & RELAY CONSTRUCTION

The movable-pole-shoe system employed in Ford positive-engagement

starters to engage their overrunning-clutch drive mechanism is probably the most practical way to design a magnetically engaged starter drive. However, the separate solenoid as used, for example, on the Delco starter is an understandable alternative when you stop to think of how and why the design evolved in the first place. So long as foot-operated starters were the norm, starter drives could be engaged merely by the action of depressing the foot pedal. But jockeying the manual choke, accelerator, and — with the same foot — the starter pedal, called for a bit more skill and coordination than some people possessed. This, along with heavy clutches, unsynchronized gears, and manual spark advances explains why about 85% of our grandmothers never learned to drive. The men in Detroit decided that if they could make an automobile that anybody could learn to run, they'd eventually be able to sell at least one car to every citizen of legal driving age. So-o-o, the foot-operated starter and the manual choke had to go. When the question came up at GM as to how the drive could be engaged, it was solved by bolting a solenoid onto what was basically the same old starter in such a way that it could take over the tasks formerly performed by muscle power. This system did the job, and darned reliably too.

The movable iron plunger in starter-mounted solenoids is what pulls the starter drive into engagement. In addition, as the plunger is pulled into the solenoid's core, it strikes a rod that projects into the solenoid from the opposite direction. This rod passes through the closed end of the solenoid housing and provides the movement required to switch battery current into the starter motor windings. An insulated contact disc is attached to the end of the rod and, as the rod is moved outward by the

2

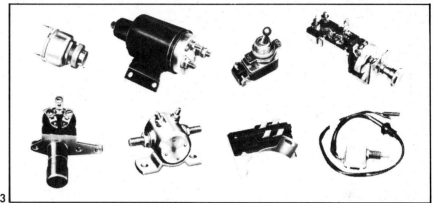

3

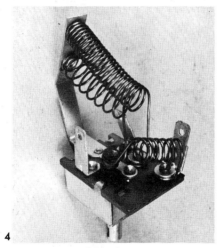

4

5

1. The large solenoid at the left is the type used to engage the drive on Delco starters. Notice huge size compared to starter relay in Bendix drive starters.

2. The solenoid plunger is a heavy piece of iron which is drawn into the core of the solenoid by magnetic attraction when current is fed into the solenoid windings.

3. A selection of Autolite switches. Any one of these can be tested as outlined in the text. In some cases you may have to rig up jumper wires to make the proper connections.

4. This air-conditioning switch has seen better days. It overheated and burned up the contact. Some switches do this repeatedly because they don't have enough current carrying capacity.

5. Magnetic engagement mechanism on Ford starters cannot properly be called a solenoid due to its construction. A separate relay similar to that used with Bendix drive starters is used in conjunction with this.

6. Old Ford solenoids were all metal. The good ones had a button on the bottom so you could work the starter from the engine compartment.

6

Solenoids and Switches

striking action of the solenoid plunger, it presses the disc into contact with two large brass terminals set into the bakelite cover of the solenoid assembly. One of these terminals is connected to the heavy "hot" cable coming from the battery, the other to the windings of the starter motor itself.

Key starting was more easily accomplished on cars having Bendix drive starters. During foot-start days, there had been a small button on the floorboards similar in appearance to the headlight-dimmer switch. Depressing this pedal simply closed an internal contact that routed battery current to the starter motor. All that was needed to convert these cars to key starting was a relay to make the battery connection when it was energized by current supplied by the ignition switch. The relay did not need to be a heavy and powerful device as in the overrunning-clutch starter, since there was no need for it to engage the drive mechanism.

Ford automobiles and American Motors cars using FoMoCo starters are the only makes in the United States currently employing remote relays for switching the starting current. These units can quite properly be called solenoids due to their construction; however — also properly — they are described as relays in most service manuals. FoMoCo starter relays are sealed assemblies which can be serviced only by replacing the entire unit. Commercial replacements available for similar relays formerly used on Dodge, Plymouth, Willys and Studebaker can, however, frequently be disassembled for the purpose of cleaning or replacing the contacts. In construction, they all employ a rather short solenoid of small diameter. The iron plunger that is drawn by magnetic attraction into the core of the solenoid has an insulated contact disc affixed directly to it which bridges the gap between the relay's heavy internal terminal contacts. In the case of relays found on 12-volt cars, there is an additional terminal that draws current directly from the contact disc to supply the ignition coil with unballasted current during starting. On Ford units this terminal is marked "I"

for "ignition." A similar small terminal marked "S" (for "start") receives the solenoid-energizing current supplied by the ignition switch when it is turned to the start position.

The starter relay found on current Chrysler Corp. products is a simple electromagnetic relay — not a solenoid. It does not need to handle heavy battery current since there is a drive engagement solenoid mounted on the starter for this purpose. The relay consists of a coil of light-gauge wire wrapped about an iron core. When the ignition key is turned to the start position, it energizes the coil which in turn causes the iron core to become a magnet. A flat movable iron armature is attracted towards the magnetized core, closing a set of contacts in the process. These contacts control both the current used to energize the starter solenoid and the unballasted voltage delivered to the ignition system during starting.

The manual starter-pull found on some older British sport cars is functionally nothing more than the primitive foot switch once found on American cars with Bendix drive starters. The only

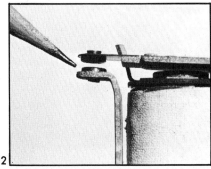

1. Late Ford solenoids are plastic with a metal bottom. They are ordinarily not repairable.

2. Principle of the electromagnetic relay is completely different from that of a solenoid. Movable armature is attracted by magnetic iron core in coil, motion of armature closes contact points (pencil). Such relays are useful only for light currents.

3. The contact disc eventually becomes badly pitted, sometimes does not make a good connection. In rare instances it may weld in place, disabling the solenoid.

4. Rivets on bottom of Ford solenoids can be drilled out if you insist on repairing instead of replacing.

5. Contact disc assembly from Ford starter relay shows spiral spring-brass connection between disc and "S" terminal. Corrosion under terminal connection or broken connector sometimes disables the entire unit.

6. Contact disc assembly is here being removed from starter relay. After drilling out rivets, replace them with self-tapping screws.

7. Badly worn stationary contacts such as this can be turned over and reused. Although FoMoCo relays are "sealed," such repairs are practical for the persistent.

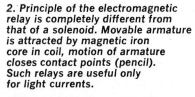

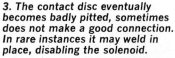

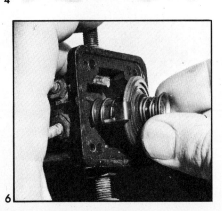

real difference is that it is operated by hand, rather than by the driver's foot — thereby freeing that member for more useful activities such as jockeying the accelerator. Many of the first U.S. cars to abandon foot-operated starter controls adopted a button on the dash to switch current to the solenoid or relay windings. These have now all given way to key-start systems.

WHY RELAYS ARE NECESSARY

The contacts in the ignition switch would be quickly burned out by a current only one-tenth as strong as that needed to operate the starter motor. An extremely heavy switch is required to handle the 150-200 ampere current which the starter motor may draw from the battery under cold-weather starting conditions. The low-amperage current from the starter/ignition switch is therefore used simply to energize a solenoid, which in turn can do the job of closing the heavy switch and engaging the starter drive. It would seem that the task of engaging the starter drive alone would be too great a load to place on

the ignition switch and its wiring, and this would probably be true if a simple electromagnet were used. However, the very electromagnetic princples governing the operation of a solenoid and plunger come to the rescue to multiply the power produced by the electrical energy supplied by the starter's dashboard control. This added strength is derived via a phenomenon commonly known as "cooperation of currents." Whenever a magnetic field is produced, there are patterns of motion created in the electrons of the magnetic material called electron spins. It is the movement of electrons that creates the magnetic fields exerted by the magnetized object. Such electron flows are called amperian circuits, after Andre Marie Ampere, the French physicist who was the first to theorize their existence.

A solenoid and plunger takes advantage of these amperian circuits and the currents which they generate to multiply the strength of the basic magnetic field set up by energizing the windings of the solenoid. When the ignition switch is turned to start position by the driver, the solenoid establishes an ini-

tial magnetic field that attracts the iron plunger. In the process, the magnetic field transforms the plunger into a magnet. The important thing is that the electron spins in the plunger produce amperian circuits that imitate those in the solenoid windings. The plunger, therefore, becomes the equivalent of another solenoid.

The electron currents in the plunger are everywhere the same as those in the nearest part of the solenoid windings. Since like currents tend to flow parallel and in the same direction, the plunger is drawn into the solenoid. This motion closes the starter switch and, in most cases, is also used to engage the starter drive. As this happens the amperian currents in the plunger become progressively more coincident with the current in the solenoid. As a result, the cooperation of the currents in the plunger and the solenoid increases, greatly multiplying the attraction that would be possible due to the battery-supplied current alone. A solenoid and plunger, therefore, exerts a considerably greater force in relation to the current supplied to it than does a simple

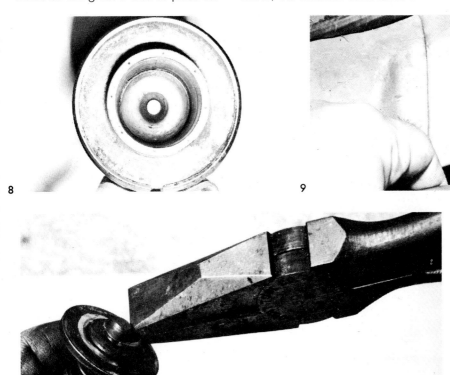

8

9

10

11

12

8. Looking inside the solenoid after the plunger has been removed reveals the tip of the contact shaft projecting through the solenoid's end piece. When plunger strikes the contact shaft on this Delco-Remy starter, battery current is switched to the windings of the starter motor.

9. Mechanical starter control such as this has been used on many British sports cars. Its function in the circuit is similar to that of a starter relay worked by muscle instead of magnetism.

10. The contact disc can be removed from its shaft on Delco solenoids by taking a metal clip off. Disc can be turned over, or a new one installed.

11. Delco solenoid disassembled. Note one nut (arrow) that does not have to be removed for disassembly.

12. It is also possible to loosen the retaining nut and turn the stationary contact(s) 180 degrees to place their unused side against the contact disc. Note the soldered wire that may break if you aren't careful.

Solenoids and Switches

electromagnetic relay. Without the principle of cooperation of currents, we'd probably still be saying "step on the starter."

MAINTENANCE & REPLACEMENT

The prime maintenance consideration in caring for starter-mounted solenoids is cleanliness. Many solenoids are put out of commission by oil leaks that allow engine oil to coat and saturate the solenoid and starter. Oil seeping into the windings or onto the electrical contacts eventually will serve to break down the insulation and promote burning of the electrical contacts. Also, any dust settling in the oil is retained and — in severe cases — such a heavy accumulation of sludgy grime develops that the plunger becomes jammed, or the switching mechanism no longer makes proper electrical contact.

Most do-it-yourselfers are too conscientious about the condition of their machinery to ever run afoul of such troubles. However, in the natural course of everyday usage the solenoid may begin to give trouble. In nearly 100% of the cases, solenoid trouble is the result of wear, burning, or pitting of the main contacts and contact disc. There are rebuild kits available for about $2.00 that will service most types of Delco and Autolite solenoids. The kit consists of new terminals, contacts, gaskets and everything else likely to be at the root of a malfunction. It is only necessary to remove the solenoid, take off its end cover, and install the new parts. It's always best to thoroughly clean the outside of the solenoid before taking it apart to avoid having dirt fall into the coil or working parts.

Sometimes you can get by "on the cheap" simply by rearranging the positions of the various electrical contacts. The battery terminal contact is usually the one which receives the most wear and tear and, by loosening the nut holding it in place in the solenoid end cover, it can be turned 180 degrees to place its unused side under the contact disc. The motor connector strap's terminal is sometimes welded to the solenoid winding's lead-in wire and cannot, therefore, be turned. But since wear at this point is generally less, it can often be filed smooth and left as is. Similarly, the contact disc can be removed from the plunger rod and turned over to place its new side toward the terminal contacts.

As mentioned earlier, most relays that are located remotely from the starter are sealed units that are not supposed to be serviced, but only replaced. This, perhaps, depends upon just how determined you are. By removing the four rivets holding the bottom

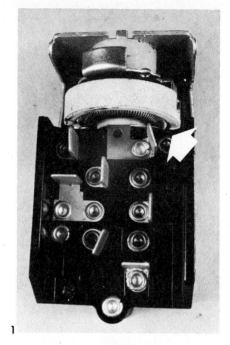

1

3

4

5

1. This is what the underside of a headlight switch looks like. Circular coil (arrow) is part of resistance unit that dims instrument lights.

2. Ignition switches are supplied by parts stores without the key or lock. Locking parts can be reused.

3. Push on this button and you will be able to remove the knob and stem from the light switch, a necessary step before removing the switch.

4. Another type of ignition switch with shielded terminals to prevent shorts. Large center post is for accessories, but don't pile too many on or you will overload switch.

5. You can fix anything if you are stubborn enough, but this type of dimmer switch would probably be ruined if you try to take it apart.

6. The small terminals on FoMoCo starter relays are marked "I" for "ignition" and "S" for "start." In some cases the letters are not too distinct, but they're there all the same.

7. Ignition switches with this type of connector are designed to foil car thieves. Older open types could be bridged simply by holding a quarter against the back of the switch.

8. This illustration of a Dodge starter shows the relationship of the moving core—or solenoid plunger— with the drive shifting fork and the overrunning clutch assembly.

9. Drive housing doubles as the solenoid case on Chrysler reduction gear drive starters, makes unit somewhat more compact, allows separate replacement of solenoid windings.

10. On most starters the solenoid plunger remains attached to the starter drive when the solenoid is removed. Some units, such as this Chrysler, retain their plunger upon removal.

cover on the FoMoCo relay, it is possible to restore the contacts in the main circuit rather easily. The cover can then be replaced with the help of four self-tapping screws obtained from the local hardware store. The terminals in Ford-made units can be loosened and turned over to present their unused side to the contact disc just as in starter-mounted solenoids. It is not out of the question to turn over the contact disc as well — even though this is riveted in place and requires more than casual effort to perform the operation. Also, if the trouble is in the ignition terminal circuit, the cause of the failure will be immediately apparent upon taking the cover off the unit. Often, it is only corrosion — although a broken conductor is not out of the realm of probability. In an emergency, a bit of solder may produce a fix that might otherwise have had to wait until the car could be towed to a repair shop. The person who'd rather not spend the bucks for a new relay, or who

finds himself grounded at a time when the parts stores are closed, will find it wise to attempt a fix. If you wreck the unit in the process, you still haven't lost a thing.

If the jumper cable or voltmeter tests outlined in the starter chapter seem to indicate that the solenoid winding is defective and is preventing the unit from being energized by current from the dash control, it does not necessarily mean that the assembly is beyond repair. By removing the solenoid's end cover you will be able to inspect the wire connecting the windings to their terminals. In some cases, what have appeared to be burned-out solenoid windings have been repaired simply by soldering a broken wire. If a broken wire is not evident, you can still test the windings with a voltmeter or with a battery-operated circuit testing light. These tests will sometimes reveal that the windings are intact, but grounded. A careful inspection of all visible insula-

tion might lead you to the source of the electrical trouble.

When reassembling a solenoid or relay it is very important to make sure that the plunger or contact shaft works smoothly and effortlessly. A stuck or binding contact can shoot down the solenoid unit just as quickly as a burned-out winding. If you've left the drive-engaging plunger attached to the starter's shift arm, don't tighten the bolts holding the solenoid onto the side of the starter motor until it has been aligned to allow the plunger to move effortlessly. A starter relay can be bench-tested following repairs by connecting its start terminal to the hot side of the car's battery using a jumper cable, and then grounding the relay case against the engine or frame. Starter-mounted solenoids, of course, must be tested in place on the starter. When the connection is made, there should be a click as the plunger moves into the contact position and another click when the

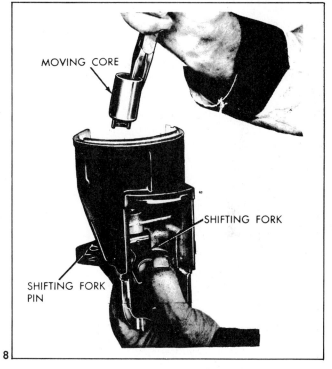

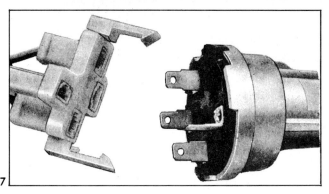

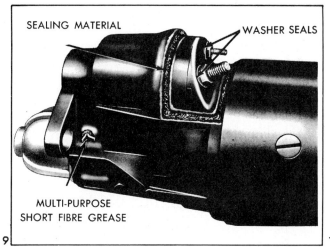

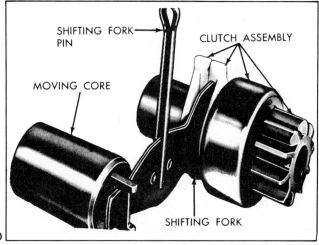

Solenoids and Switches

connection is broken and the spring causes the plunger to retract. If there is no click, the windings are defective and obtaining a new relay or solenoid is probably the only way out. Chrysler Corp. reduction-gear starters can have the windings replaced separately since the solenoid case is a part of the drive housing casting.

Should the starter's control-circuit relay give trouble on a Chrysler-built

car, it may be possible to return the unit to service with simple home repairs. If the unit can be heard to click when current is directed to it, it is possible that the cause of the malfunction is burned or dirty contacts. On the other hand, should no sound be produced, the device probably has faulty windings and will undoubtedly have to be replaced. The cover on such units must be taken off to inspect the condition of the contacts. If they are found to be burned or fouled by deposits of one kind or another they can be cleaned off with crocus cloth or a small file.

MISCELLANEOUS SWITCHES

Whether you use the term solenoid, relay, magnetic switch, toggle switch or headlight switch — as far as the electricity is concerned, it is only a switch that turns something on or off. Switches are designed for most jobs according to the amount of current they will carry. Any time a switch is replaced, the new switch must have enough capacity to carry the current. If not, it might burn out the minute you turn it on.

If a switch is made so it can be taken apart, then all you have to do is look at

SOLENOID

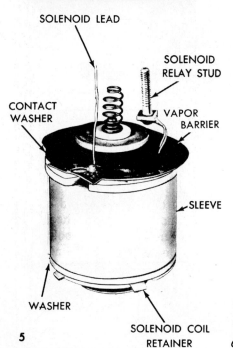

SOLENOID LEAD

SOLENOID RELAY STUD

VAPOR BARRIER

CONTACT WASHER

SLEEVE

WASHER

SOLENOID COIL RETAINER

5

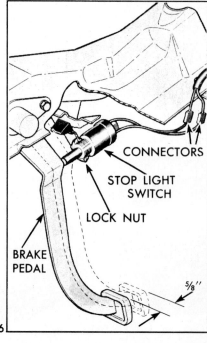

CONNECTORS

STOP LIGHT SWITCH

LOCK NUT

BRAKE PEDAL

5/8"

6

1. You'll see a lot of these contact washers if you take apart many Delco or Prestolite solenoids. Note how posts are pushed to one side so that washer and plunger can be removed.

2. Prestolite starter with exposed shift lever. Solenoid removal is easy, but in most cases there isn't room to do it in the car. You have to remove the entire starter.

3. Delco solenoid, showing wires that are exposed when end cap is removed. If these wires break, get a new solenoid.

4. On most cars the solenoid can be removed without disturbing the starter motor. Replacement units, overhaul kits and rebuilt parts are available at low cost and are very simple to install.

5. Solenoid assembly of Chrysler Corp. reduction gear starter can have its coil unit replaced separately. This is cheaper than buying an entire solenoid as on some other types.

6. This stoplight switch has a lock nut. Others are a friction-fit, and the switch is slid back and forth to adjust it.

7. Accessory fog light switch has a fuse on the back, and a bracket for mounting on the lip of the instrument panel. This switch can be used for controlling many other accessories besides fog lights.

8. This little beauty screws into the side of a Chrysler automatic transmission. If you accidentally send full battery current through it, it will burn up quicker than you can blink.

9. Solenoids for overrunning clutch starters must be mounted directly on the starter unit. It is necessary to remove the starter to service most such solenoids.

10. Next to the headlight switch, the ignition switch probably controls the most wiring circuits. Faulty units can be replaced. Some have a small hole into which a pin must be inserted to remove the lock cylinder from the switch.

11. Dimmer switches are much easier to replace on late cars because the wiring is above the floorboards. Older switches required two people, or one with very long arms.

the contacts to tell if they are in good shape. But if the switch cannot be disassembled, then you will have to test it with a voltmeter.

The best way to test a switch is to have current flowing through it in actual operation. The battery supplies electricity to one side of the switch, and the electrical load (a light, motor or whatever) is connected to the other side. Never connect a switch directly across a battery without a load. The switch will burn up instantly. Connecting solenoid or relay windings across a battery is OK, because those windings are an electrical load in themselves. But if you also connect the battery across the electrical contacts that the solenoid or relay operates, then say goodbye to the unit. Whenever making any connection, you must stop and consider whether you have a load in the circuit.

With the switch connected between the battery and the load, it's a simple matter to connect a voltmeter across the terminals of the switch and read the voltage drop on the meter. The reading on the voltmeter indicates the amount of electricity you are losing because of resistance in the switch. If the switch was perfect, you wouldn't lose anything and the meter would read zero. Even the best switch has a little resistance, however, so we expect the meter to read something. Most switches will carry the amount of current they were designed for with only about two tenths of a volt drop. If you get more than that on the meter, either the switch is making poor contact, or there is too much current going through the switch, more than it is supposed to carry.

When making voltage drop tests, do not connect the voltmeter to the switch until after you have turned the switch on. Remove the voltmeter before turning the switch off. These precautions will save your meter. Do it any other way and you will put full battery voltage through the meter, which is OK if you are on the 12-volt scale. If you are on a 1- or 3-volt scale, it's rough on the meter to have 12 volts go through it all at once.

Most small switches cannot be taken apart, so if you find a bad one, you will probably have to replace it. Removing most of them from the car is easy if you look for screwdriver slots or other obvious ways of getting the switch out of the instrument panel. Headlight switches can be tricky. They usually have a button on the body of the switch behind the instrument panel. Depress the button with your finger, then gently, and with a turning motion, pull the switch knob and shaft out of the body of the switch. After the knob and shaft are out, just unscrew the bezel and the switch will fall out the back of the panel. When it does, it will probably blow all the fuses if you haven't disconnected the battery. When testing, you have to use the battery for the test, but when disassembling or removing anything electrical — especially when working behind the instrument panel — always disconnect one cable from the battery, preferably the ground cable.

As with any sealed or encased electrical component, the starter solenoid or relay can seem like a pretty mysterious piece of equipment. Once you've taken one apart, the mystery disappears and its faulty operation is no longer cause for any particular feeling of horror. By reading this chapter you should have gained an excellent understanding of the electrical principles behind the operation of such devices, as well as a new confidence in dealing with them either for purposes of repair or when developing a starting system for your hot rod or custom car. A basic understanding of solenoids can also give you the needed insight to get yourself going again should one of these indispensable bits of machinery let you down some sunny day. No matter how you look at it, fixing it yourself is always a desirable alternative to paying for an expensive tow!

7

8

9

10 RELEASE-PIN HOLE

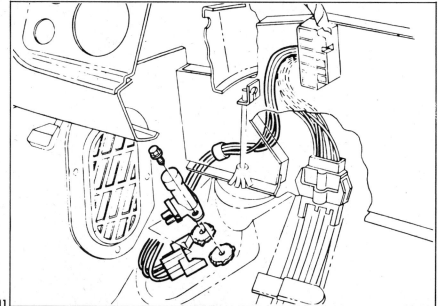
11

Solenoids and Switches

IGNITION SWITCHES

The once-simple ignition switch for making and breaking electrical contact has advanced in complexity over the years to become a sophisticated, multiterminal device that does a great deal more than just complete a single electrical circuit. In fact, the modern "ignition switch" provides several mechanical actions in addition to routing current in several directions at once. It has up to five positions to which the ignition key can be turned and held. The ignition switch, it seems, might more appropriately be termed a trigger, since it is the key (pardon the pun) to so many electrical and mechanical actions.

The simple dash-mounted, on/off ignition switch began to get complicated when manufacturers decided to mount it on the steering wheel column, where it was ostensibly easier for the driver to reach. This meant that all the wires running to and from the switch had to be encased inside the mast jacket (the steering column's outer tube). There the wires were virtually inaccessible in case of a broken wire or faulty insulation on a wire that could cause it to short against some grounded metal part.

Then, as if someone suddenly remembered the old Ford ignition lock switch so popular on Fords of the Thirties and early Forties, manufacturers began designing switches that would not only direct electrical current, but which would also lock the steering shaft when the key was removed. This move was made in the interests of preventing vehicle theft. The theory was that a thief would be foiled even if he shorted the ignition under the hood, since he couldn't turn the steering wheel to maneuver the car after he got it running. Lobbyists for the insurance companies had been behind this move, and in the late Sixties they further confounded Detroit engineers by making it mandatory that manual-shift cars be shifted into reverse before the key could be removed. This would theoretically prevent the car from being towed away by ripoff artists unless the whole vehicle were lifted bodily off the ground by a derrick.

These "advancements," plus several more, served to change the lowly ignition switch from the former simple make-and-break device to a complex assemblage of wires, terminals and contacts, plus rods and linkage, all of which had to be routed down through the mast jacket and exit from that shaft on the engine side of the firewall. We all know how the addition of extra automotive parts and components increases the possibility of malfunctioning, so let's look at one maker's example of an ignition switch system and gain some insight into the whys and wherefores of troubleshooting the mechanical and electrical portions of the modern driver's "trigger."

AN INSIDE LOOK

Like any other mechanical device, an ignition switch can go sour—usually just when it is needed the most. This failure can happen when internal contacts within the switch body become corroded, damaged or just worn out.

The typical ignition switch has five key positions, usually labeled ACC (accessory-on position), LOCK, OFF, ON and START. The key lock cylinder also controls the mechanism which provides a positive lock for the transmission linkage and steering shaft. On late-model Ford-built cars with an automatic transmission, the ignition key can be removed from the lock cylinder only when the shift lever is in

1. The modern key lock has five key positions, each identified as on this typical example ("Accessory" is usually abbreviated "ACC").

2. This is the so-called pin-type connector ignition switch and related assemblies as used on '75-'76 Ford Comets, Mavericks and Lincoln Continentals. Note that the ignition switch itself is on lower part of steering assembly (engine side of firewall) and connects to the key-lock cylinder by an actuator rod. The actuator rod may often need adjustment.

3. A somewhat different version, the blade-type connector ignition switch, was used on all '75-'76 Ford cars except those noted above in caption No. 2.

4. This is a typical electrical continuity test when checking for an ignition switch electrical fault. All auto manufacturers include such a testing diagram for all car models in their respective shop manuals.

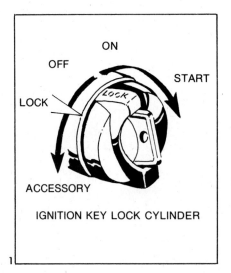

ON
OFF
START
LOCK
ACCESSORY
IGNITION KEY LOCK CYLINDER

1

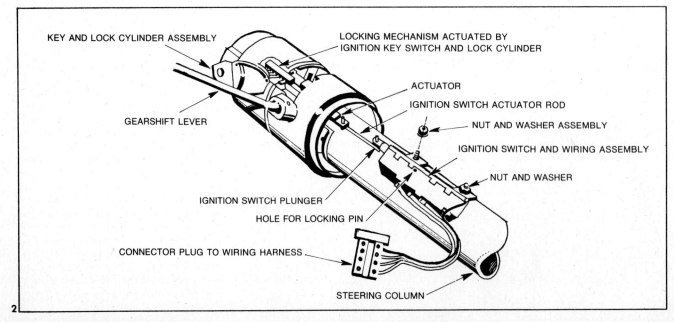

KEY AND LOCK CYLINDER ASSEMBLY

LOCKING MECHANISM ACTUATED BY IGNITION KEY SWITCH AND LOCK CYLINDER

ACTUATOR
IGNITION SWITCH ACTUATOR ROD
NUT AND WASHER ASSEMBLY
IGNITION SWITCH AND WIRING ASSEMBLY
NUT AND WASHER

GEARSHIFT LEVER

IGNITION SWITCH PLUNGER
HOLE FOR LOCKING PIN

CONNECTOR PLUG TO WIRING HARNESS

STEERING COLUMN

2

park position and the key is turned to the LOCK position. The ACC position operates while the steering and transmission systems remain locked, in case you want to shut off everything but the radio while you're parked in front of your girl's house.

Turning the key to the OFF position shuts off battery current to the ignition coil *without* locking the transmission or steering. With manual transmissions and floorshift automatic transmissions, the pushbutton on the left side of the steering column must be pushed inward before the lock cylinder can be rotated to the LOCK position and the key removed. On all Ford-built models for '75 and '76, the ignition switch is connected to the lock cylinder by an actuator rod, since the actual switch is located far down the mast jacket on the engine side of the firewall. This switch has

blade-type terminals that engage with two multiple connector plugs. They are held to the switch by snap-type locking tabs. These tabs must be disconnected before unplugging the connectors.

To troubleshoot this kind of ignition switch when you suspect it of foul play, disconnect the switch's multiple plug connectors by lifting up on the retaining or locking tabs while pulling the connector off the switch itself.

To test electrical continuity through the switch, connect a battery-powered test light or ohmmeter between the plug terminals for each switch position, as shown in an accompanying drawing.

If the ignition switch is proven faulty or if for some reason the lock cylinder mechanism at the top of the mast jacket has to be replaced, some adjustment will be necessary to make

sure that the actuating rod, the steering column and transmission lock assemblies, the ignition switch and the lock cylinder itself work harmoniously.

To adjust the position of the ignition switch, rotate the ignition key back and forth to either side of the LOCK position until a drill bit can be inserted through the locking pin hole to a minimum of ⅜-in. The lock pin holes and drill bit sizes for '75 and '76 Ford products are as follows: On blade-type ignition switches with a plastic switch housing, the locking pin hole is on the top surface of the ignition switch between the terminals marked "Al" and "B." The hole takes a 3/64-in. drill bit. However, on blade-type switches with a metal housing, the lock pin hole is next to the mast jacket on the right side of the switch. Use a 5/64-in. drill bit. Finally, if the late Ford product has a pigtail-type switch, the locking pin hole is at the uppermost part of the switch at the junction between the metal and plastic parts of the assembly and requires a 3/32-in. drill bit.

With the switch locked, loosen the two ignition switch mounting nuts. Turn the key to LOCK—you'll feel the detent position—and remove the ignition key. Next, move the ignition switch up and down on the steering column to locate the midpoint of rod lash (or free play) and tighten the mounting nuts. Remove the drill bit from the locking pin hole. Plug in all the electrical connectors. Insert the key in its cylinder and turn it through all of its positions—while watching all the instruments, gauges and of course engine-start and engine running conditions.

Ford made only minor refinements to the above system for the '77 model year. While other manufacturers have somewhat different versions of the ignition, all cars work in pretty much the same way. Even if looking at a factory service manual convinces you that you don't want to trace any malfunctions in the ignition switch and its related systems, at least you now know why your agency or local mechanic had your car torn apart for so long and why you were charged as much as you were.

As noted earlier, the simple ignition switch has come a long way, and so, necessarily, have repair procedures. But remember that no matter how complex a system may seem, it can be still be reduced to just a few simple mechanical and electrical functions. This alone makes ignition switches and interlocks fodder for the do-it-yourselfer, but if you doubt your handiwork in any way, head straight for your car agency. After all, you wouldn't want your car's steering to suddenly lock up on you while you're driving, would you?

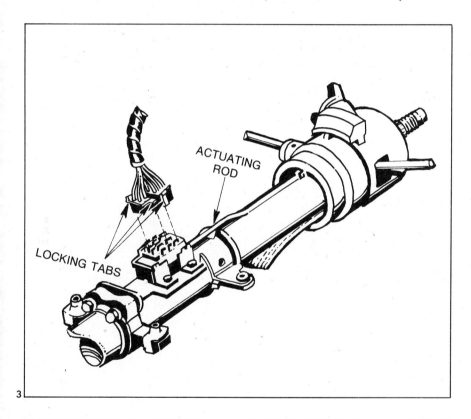

3

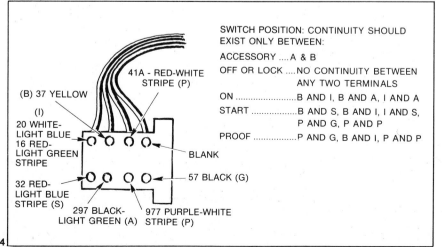

SWITCH POSITION: CONTINUITY SHOULD EXIST ONLY BETWEEN:

ACCESSORY ....A & B

OFF OR LOCK ....NO CONTINUITY BETWEEN ANY TWO TERMINALS

ON ....B AND I, B AND A, I AND A

START ....B AND S, B AND I, I AND S, P AND G, P AND P

PROOF ....P AND G, B AND I, P AND P

41A - RED-WHITE STRIPE (P)

(B) 37 YELLOW

(I)
20 WHITE-LIGHT BLUE
16 RED-LIGHT GREEN STRIPE

BLANK

32 RED-LIGHT BLUE STRIPE (S)

57 BLACK (G)

297 BLACK-LIGHT GREEN (A)

977 PURPLE-WHITE STRIPE (P)

4

Generators & Alternators

THE HARDEST WORKING COMPONENTS IN YOUR CHARGING SYSTEM WILL GIVE THOUSANDS OF TROUBLE-FREE MILES IF CARED FOR PROPERLY.

Under the hood of your car is a miniature dynamo. Its function is to supply the necessary current to keep all the electrical accessories in your car humming merrily along, and at the same time, supplying nourishment to the heart of the system: the battery. It is likely that your car is fitted with an alternator, which is an AC generator that is better equipped for the task of supplying increased electrical power to today's complicated electrical systems. However, if you are driving one of the older, more simple automobiles (bless you and take care of it) it's probably still purring along quite nicely with its generator. Here is some basic information that will help you keep either system functioning properly.

GENERATORS

The day may soon be at hand when the generator will have become as rare as Indian villages and steam locomotives. Although generators have been an accepted part of the automotive scene for well over four decades, the horseless carriage's second half-century is fast becoming the age of the alternator. Nevertheless, a few cars are still being marketed with generator-based charging systems, and there are thousands of other vehicles still on the nation's highways that were built before the alternator took over.

The automotive generator is a highly refined device designed to convert a small part of the engine's mechanical power into electric power for the purpose of charging the car's battery. The means by which it does this is quite similar to that employed by a magneto in generating its electric energy. Both are machines based on the principle that an electrical current can be produced in a coil of wire by rapidly changing the number of magnetic lines of flux linking the turns of its windings. If, for example, you were to take a simple horseshoe magnet and place one side of a wire coil between the two poles, a sensitive voltmeter attached to the coil would register no current so long as the coil is held stationary. Yet, when the coil is moved deeper into the horseshoe, the voltmeter will register a current. When the coil is withdrawn, it will also indicate a current, but one of the opposite polarity (positive or nega-

1

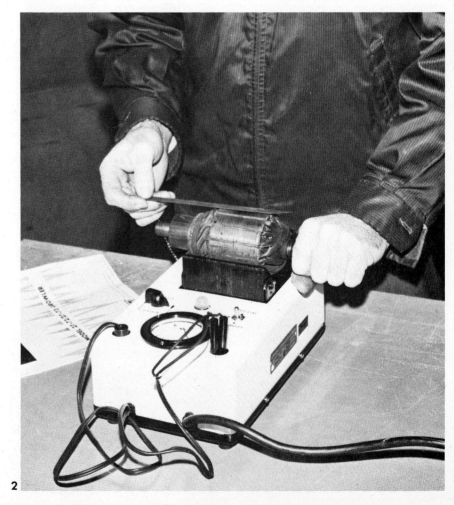

2

tive). The reason for this phenomenon is that when the coil is in motion, the lines of flux extending through its windings are constantly changing. As a result, an induced electric current flows from the windings of the coil.

The generators used on standard production cars in recent years have all been shunt-wound, two-pole units. A shunt-wound field is one which is connected directly to the battery current without having any common circuit with the windings of the armature. The generator is therefore dependent upon current from the battery to make it operate. The two large poles within the frame of the generator have circular windings wrapped about them. When the battery current is fed through these windings, the iron pole shoes are converted into strong electro-magnets. One pole shoe becomes a magnetic north pole and the other a magnetic south pole.

The generator's armature rotates in the space between the two pole shoes. The windings of the armature are therefore subjected to a constant change of magnetic flux, which causes an electrical current to be induced within them. The current in the windings is alternating current—that is, it changes its direction of flow twice during each revolution of the armature. If a voltmeter were attached to the armature windings, the maximum voltage peaks recorded would be alternately positive and negative separated by periods of zero voltage as the windings aligned themselves momentarily in a position parallel to the magnetic field's lines of flux. Alternating current, however, cannot be used to charge a battery. The windings of the armature are therefore attached to a segmented commutator in such a way that the ends of each coil connect to segments that are opposite one another on the shaft. Two brushes are kept in contact with the commutator, and located in such a position that each is in contact only with those segments producing straight positive or straight negative current. In actual practice there are about 14 overlapping windings in most automotive generators, and about twice that number of commutator segments—one attaching to either end of each individual coil. The brushes, therefore, make contact only with those windings producing maximum voltage during each fractional degree of armature rotation.

The insulated brush picks up the current off the commutator. Then the current goes to the armature terminal on the generator, which is connected to the various accessories and lights on the car, and also to the battery. Everything that receives current, including the battery, is grounded. The current goes through the ground into the frame or body of the car, travels along until it comes to the generator frame, enters the ground brush and completes the circuit to the armature.

Most car generators have only two poles, which means they only need two brushes to make a circuit for taking current off the armature. However, since the brushes are only picking up and delivering current to the armature for a very few degrees of armature rotation, it is possible to put more poles and more brushes around the armature to get more current. A generator can have four, six or eight poles and brushes.

CURRENT CHARACTERISTICS

The voltage delivered by a direct current generator increases with both its speed of rotation and with the strength of the current supplied to its field windings. Since the generator is coupled directly to the car's engine, it goes through wild speed variations. Early generator-equipped cars would frequently burn out their headlights when the engine was revved too high. Not only was the constant variation of overcharge and under-charge harmful to the battery, but the stronger the battery became, the higher the voltage it sent to the generator's field windings. As a result, generator output increased at the very time when the battery needed less voltage. It soon became apparent that something would have to be done to the generator to limit the amount of voltage it could deliver to the battery.

GENERATOR CONSTRUCTION

The frame of most generators is cast iron, partly for strength and economy, and partly because in most generators the magnetic lines between the field poles pass in a return

1. Most late model generators have done away with the end slots and cover band. Brush inspection is a little more difficult, but can be done with a small mirror.

2. A growler checks armatures for shorted coils. The better growlers, such as this Allen, have a meter for checking the armature loops individually for open circuit.

3. Spring-loaded arms keep the brushes in contact with the commutator. Although the carbon brushes have a long life, worn-out or sticking brushes are the major cause of generator trouble.

4. Generators can be completely dismantled for inspection, cleaning and repair by removing the two long through-bolts (arrow) that pass from one end of the unit through to the other.

5. Large screws pass through the generator frame to hold the heavy pole shoes and their field windings in place inside the housing.

6. The position of the commutator is almost 90 degrees off from the windings to which the individual segments connect. Note that the wires are spiraled between the armature core and the commutator bars.

3

4

5

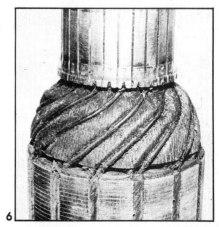

6

Generators

circuit through the unit's housing. The end pieces, on the other hand, are generally of some non-magnetic material such as aluminum alloy. The pole shoes used in automotive generators are generally of mild steel and may retain a considerable degree of residual magnetism even when not energized by battery current. The pole shoes are held in place in the generator's frame by large screws not unlike those found in starter motors. The steel plates from which the pole shoes are made are flanged at their outer edges, which serves to hold the generator's field windings in place.

The coils surrounding the poles of an automotive generator are interconnected so that current passes first through one coil and then the other. One end of the wire forming the field coils is attached to the "field" terminal on the outside of the generator housing. This terminal is insulated from the generator frame by a fiber insert and washer. In most cases this terminal is marked "Fld." or "Field" with letters stamped into the generator housing. The wire leading from the generator's field terminal attaches to the "field" terminal on the voltage regulator unit, which completes the circuit for battery current needed to energize the electromagnetic poles of the generator. When the car's engine is not in operation, no battery current is delivered to the field windings because the cutout unit in the voltage regulator breaks the circuit, thereby automatically shutting off the generator when the car is not in use. But that's another story we will get into in the chapter devoted to regulators.

The armature found in the majority of automotive generators is relatively long in proportion to its diameter. This design reduces the effect of inertia on the armature windings at high rpm. The core consists of from about 60 to 75 laminations stacked up on the armature's steel shaft. Each lamination is about 1/16-inch thick, although in some cases they are made even thinner. These laminations are of soft iron which does not retain magnetism well, but will accept it temporarily.

There are grooves cut into the surface of the armature core which serve to retain the windings. The wires forming the windings are insulated to prevent their making contact electrically with one another or with the laminated core of the armature. They are wound back and forth through the grooves in the armature according to a precise and rather complex pattern so that the portion of their length exposed directly to the magnetic field between the genera-

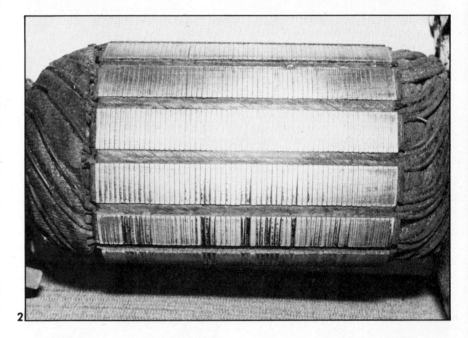

tor's poles is parallel to the shaft of the armature. Such armatures are said to be "barrell wound."

Each coil of the armature's windings is connected at either end to two opposing segments on the commutator. The segments are insulated from one another as well as from the armature shaft by strips of mica or a synthetic substitute. Brass is generally used in the commutator's construction because of its superior conductive ability and its comparative resistance to corrosion. The armature windings are soldered in place on the commutator segments; however, the position of the commutator is almost 90 degrees off from the position of the related windings on the armature

core. The brushes are therefore in electrical contact with those loops of wire in the coil traveling fastest in relation to the magnetic flux lines—i.e., those midway in their semi-circular course between the poles of the field. It is these windings that are developing the maximum voltage at any given time.

The brushes that ride against the commutator in an automotive generator are of a different design and material from those found in electric starter motors. Starter brushes are cut from a metallic copper-based material, but those used in the generator are of carbon. Although carbon brushes could not carry the extreme current loads for very long in a starter, they have, nonetheless, several virtues all their own. Chief among these is their extremely long life when used in friction with a brass commutator. Generator brushes commonly last well over 50,000 miles, even though the generator is in constant operation. A starter, on the other hand, is required to run only in short bursts and remains idle for the rest of the time.

One of the generator's brushes is connected to a terminal—usually in the end of the unit—which sends the current produced in the armature to the battery via the voltage regulator. This terminal may be marked "A" or "Arm." for armature, but in most cases its location alone is sufficient to prevent confusion. The other brush is grounded directly to the frame of the generator. Polarity of the ground brush is the same as that of the grounded side of the battery. The charging system's circuit is therefore completed through the frame of the automobile.

The armature runs in bushings or bearings set into the end plates of the generator. In the past, these had to be oiled every thousand miles or so to prevent excessive friction and possible failure. However, later generators are often equipped with ball or roller bearings—at least at the drive end—which are pre-packed with a permanent lubricant at the factory, while the commutator end of the armature shaft still requires periodic oiling on many generators. Ruined gen-

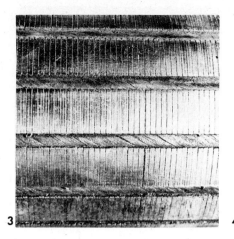

3

erator bearings and broken drive pulleys are often the result of excessive fan belt tension. Incorrect tension is always a prime suspect in cases where bearings fail in spite of proper lubrication.

QUICK TROUBLE CHECKS

The generators on most contemporary V-8's (except Ford) are mounted high on the engine, making them a snap to test or remove for repairs. Once they're off the engine, disassembly usually consists of nothing more than removing the drive pulley, unscrewing the brush wires, and taking out the two long bolts that retain the end plates on the generator frame. Before you start taking anything apart, however, it should be determined definitely whether the fault is in the generator or whether it lies elsewhere.

Generator problems are much more easily detected if your car is equipped with a dashboard-mounted ammeter—although those types of trouble normally associated with the generator itself will usually be caught by even an "idiot light." Overcharging, low-charging, or a fluctuating charge are most likely the result of a malfunctioning voltage regulator. Intermittent charging or no charging are the troubles that most often originate in the generator itself.

Low charging and *no charging* are, perhaps, the most common forms of charging system trouble. If the ammeter begins to register a constant and steady discharge while you're driving, or if the generator light comes on and stays on, the generator may be delivering no charge at all. Take a quick look at the water temperature gauge. If the cooling system's temperature is rising, the cause of the no-charge condition is probably nothing more than a broken fan belt.

Your attention may be attracted by an ammeter needle that dips suddenly into the discharge zone and then returns an instant later to a reading well up in the charge range—even at a steady engine speed. This is an in-

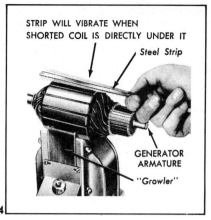

STRIP WILL VIBRATE WHEN SHORTED COIL IS DIRECTLY UNDER IT
Steel Strip
GENERATOR ARMATURE
"Growler"

4

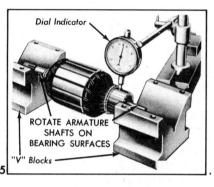

Dial Indicator
ROTATE ARMATURE SHAFTS ON BEARING SURFACES
"V" Blocks

5

dication that charging is taking place only part of the time. A winking idiot light can tip you off to the same problem. Troubles such as this—as well as those discussed in the preceding paragraph—are the types normally produced by generator defects. But before attacking the generator, check the condition of the battery and its connections. A loose battery connection that is making poor or intermittent contact can cause the generator light to flicker or the ammeter needle to take dips.

The next step is to determine if the defect lies in the generator or in the voltage regulator unit. This can be done quite simply by eliminating the regulator from the circuit. On most General Motors and Chrysler Corp. cars ("A" circuit systems) you can do this by removing the field wire from the regulator, then grounding the field terminal at the generator. If you don't remove the field wire you will burn up the regulator if it is the double-point kind. Ford uses a different wiring setup ("B" circuit system), so you have to run a jumper wire from the armature terminal to the field terminal, either at the generator or at the regulator, and it's not necessary to remove the field wire.

You can perform this test in emergencies with the blade of a screwdriver. The engine must be running of course, and great care should be taken not to accidentally get your hands or tools into the moving fan blades. If eliminating the regulator increases the ammeter reading to a high level,

1. A close-up of the commutator shows that it is formed by brass segments separated by insulating strips—usually mica. Rectangular areas are holes filled with solder that hold the winding leads in their proper place.

2. Generators are of small diameter in relation to their length, which minimizes inertia at high speeds that might otherwise damage windings. Windings pass through grooves cut into core, holding them in place.

3. The core of the armature is made up of from 60 to about 75 laminations. Note that the windings are wrapped with insulation to keep them from electrical contact with the core and with one another.

4. Defective armatures can best be tested in a well equipped automotive electrical shop. Test devices include a growler which quickly finds shorted windings—when operated as shown here by a skilled mechanic.

5. Whenever brushes are changed the commutator must be checked for runout and smoothness, and the part turned true in a lathe. In most cases the mica insulation must also be undercut.

Generators

the trouble lies in the voltage regulator. But if it does not increase the output, the generator is at fault.

When making this test be sure that everything in the car is turned off except the ignition. Run the engine just fast enough to see if the generator is going to put out, then turn the engine off. An uncontrolled generator puts out a lot of voltage, and you can blow a stereo or radio or even a dome light if they happen to be on.

Many people think that the generator is charging only when the ammeter needle is on the charge side of the zero position. That is not true. The ammeter is hooked into the circuit so that any time the needle is on the plus side of zero, it shows the amount of charge that is going into the battery, not the amount that is coming out of the generator. You can test this yourself by turning on lights and accessories with the engine at idle. The ammeter needle will show a discharge of the amount of electricity being used from the battery. As you bring the engine speed up, the generator will supply electricity to run the things you have turned on, and the needle will move toward zero. The generator is putting out enough electricity to take over operation of the lights and accessories from the battery. If you run the engine faster, and the generator has any output left, the needle will move to the plus side of zero. That means the generator is running all the lights and accessories, and putting some electricity into the battery besides. Just because you see a zero reading on the ammeter, it doesn't mean the generator is not charging. The generator might be working like a dog, but not have anything left to put into the battery.

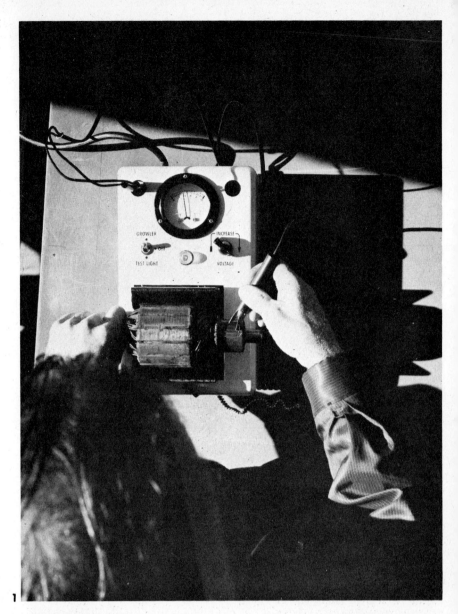

1. *Using a growler to check for open loops. Probe is held against the commutator, and the armature rotated. Meter reading should be the same all the way around the commutator.*

2. *The poles of the generator are really large electromagnets. Two-pole, shunt-wound generators have always been the most common type for automotive use.*

3. *In some alternator designs, one brush is inside the housing. A hole is provided in the end frame so that a rod or drill bit can be slipped in to hold up the brush while the alternator is assembled.*

4. *Most alternators have foolproof connections so you can't get the wires crossed. If you use homemade wiring, be careful, because many of the terminals look alike.*

5. *Early Ford design, with the brushes and diode plate in one assembly.*

In the vast majority of generators that won't charge, the trouble is worn-out generator brushes. If you're lucky enough to have a generator with a removable inspection band at one end, it can be snapped off for the purpose of checking the brushes. Of course if your particular generator does not have a removable inspection band, the unit would have to be taken apart or a mirror used to check the condition of the brushes. Should inspection reveal that the brushes have worn to less than half their original length, they are in definite need of replacement.

In some cases, the brushes may be found merely to be sticking in their holders. This is particularly true if the generator has become very dirty and perhaps oil-soaked. Sticking brushes usually call for nothing more than a good cleaning, but if the commutator has become burned and glazed due to the effects of the poor electrical contact, the unit should probably have the brushes and commutator renovated as a precaution against further trouble. Whenever brushes are replaced, the commutator should always be turned in a lathe to make sure that it is concentric with the shaft and that the segments have a smooth, level surface for the brushes to ride against. The mica between the commutator bars should be undercut

so it won't interfere with the brushes New brushes should be sanded after they are in place in the generator to insure proper contact, which can be done by drawing a strip of fine sandpaper between the commutator and the brushes with the abrasive side against the contact area of the brush. The sandpaper should be pulled through four or five times in the direction of armature rotation to make a good job of it.

The presence of individual burned commutator segments means open circuits in the armature. This and other troubles involving the wiring of the generator are probably best left to a shop with the proper equipment for quickly determining the extent of the trouble existing within the unit. If it's a relatively new generator, it may be economically sound to replace individual parts such as the armature, end plates, or field windings. However, in the case of older units, any trouble more serious than worn brushes is often just the first in a series of failures that may be logically expected. Before investing any money in the repair of an older generator, have it checked out by a competent automotive electric shop and, if a rebuilt or replacement unit is recommended, you'll probably be better off in the long run by taking them up on the offer.

Generator testing is done pretty much the same as starter testing. Of course the first thing you have to be sure of is that the generator is bad. In most cases you can do this on the car, either by electrical testing or by looking into the generator with a small inspection mirror.

When the generator is disassembled, look first for signs of the armature hitting the field coils or the pole shoes. If hitting is evident, it's a sure sign of a bad bearing or bushing. If the bearing is bad, replace it by removing the pulley and any dust shields or plates. If the bushing is bad it's more of a problem because the hole in the endplate does not extend completely through. Some garages stock endplates that have new bushings already installed. You will find a very few shops that have the tools to remove the old bushing.

Armatures should be tested for grounds, shorts, and open windings. Grounds are detected by using a battery or power-operated test light and touching the test leads to the commutator and the armature shaft at the same time. If the light goes on, the armature is grounded, which it shouldn't be because its electrical parts are supposed to be insulated from the armature shaft.

To test armatures for a shorted winding, put them on a growler and hold a steel strip such as a hacksaw blade lengthwise over the armature. Rotate the armature in the growler at the same time. If you feel any vibration or attraction of the steel strip, the armature is definitely bad.

Testing an armature for open windings is best done with the type of growler that has a meter. When used according to directions, the meter measures the induced voltage in the armature, one winding at a time. If some windings give a low reading, they are probably open or have a bad connection where they are soldered into the commutator bars. Another way to check for an open winding is with a test light or high-frequency current on adjacent commutator bars.

3   ⅛ INCH Rod

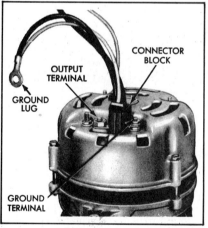

4   OUTPUT TERMINAL   CONNECTOR BLOCK   GROUND LUG   GROUND TERMINAL

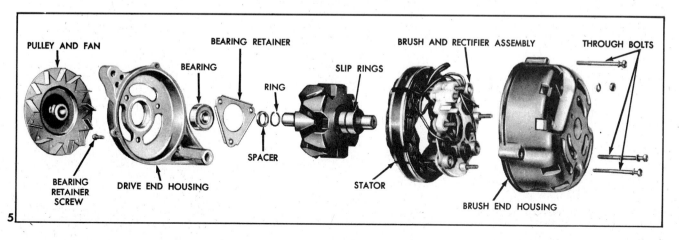

5   PULLEY AND FAN   BEARING RETAINER   BEARING   RING   SLIP RINGS   BRUSH AND RECTIFIER ASSEMBLY   THROUGH BOLTS   SPACER   STATOR   BRUSH END HOUSING   BEARING RETAINER SCREW   DRIVE END HOUSING

Generators

A variation in the brightness of the light or arcing of the high-frequency current indicates a bad connection or a break in one of the windings.

Most generator troubles are caused by the armature, but that doesn't mean you should ignore the fields and other parts. Field coils should be checked to see if they are grounded, shorted, or open. If the field is grounded in the generator, as on Fords, you will have to disconnect the ground wire before using the test light. To check for short or open, use a low-reading ammeter with battery voltage to see how much current the fields will draw. If they draw too much and burn up the ammeter, you can be pretty sure they are shorted.

And you may even find some automotive electricians who don't bother with such testing because they get their replacement generators from a rebuilder.

With the high cost of labor today, very little electrical testing is done. It's much easier and faster to throw away a bad generator (or other electrical part) and put on a new one, than to waste time with a lot of testing.

To finish up your generator testing, you should check the insulated brush holder with a test light to see if it is grounded. Then clean the endplate with solvent, not gasoline. Be very careful with solvent around the fields. They soak it up like a sponge, and it could cause a short later on. The generator frame and fields are best cleaned with a dry brush.

POLARIZING THE GENERATOR

After the generator is back together, but before it is started up, you must polarize it. Polarizing can be done before or after the generator is installed on the car, but it must be done before the engine is started. It is possible that while installing the generator a couple of wires may have been crossed for an instant, giving the generator reverse polarity. For that reason, polarizing is best done after everything is hooked up, before starting the engine. To polarize the generator, just touch the wire between the battery terminal and the armature terminal to take care of all situations. Remember, it only requires a touch of the jumper wire. If you leave it connected for more than a fraction of a second, you may very well burn up the regulator. Always polarize a direct current generator after installing either it or a regulator.

Most of the generators supplied on late-model American cars have an output in the neighborhood of 32 to

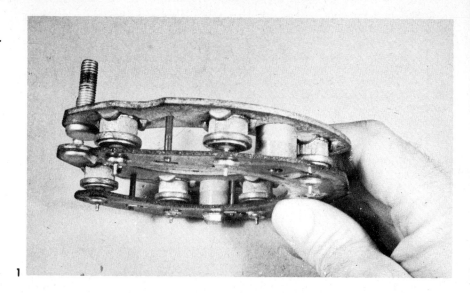

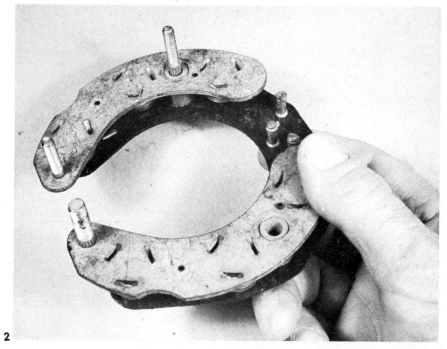

35 amperes. This output is controlled by the regulator unit so that only the amount of current that the generator can safely put out will be produced at any given time. Under normal conditions the generator is seldom required to produce a charge greater than about seven to ten amps in a 12-volt system. This does not place any great physical strain on the generator and for this reason it seldom offers trouble in the well-cared-for automobile. On the other hand, neglected batteries and malfunctioning voltage regulators can place a load upon the car's generator that far exceeds the capacity of its normal charging rate. When a generator is called upon to operate almost constantly at its highest possible level, its useful lifetime may be significantly shortened.

Very often the deadly combination of high summer temperatures, high speeds, and an improperly function-

1. When diodes are mounted in a plate, they are usually soldered in. Even if you could buy individual diodes, putting them into the plate would be quite a tough job.

2. Some alternators have diodes that are removable one at a time, but those designs are fast disappearing. Most alternators have all six diodes mounted in a plate, with individual removal not possible.

3. Late model Ford alternator has brushes separate from diode plate (rectifier). If one diode burns out, all should be replaced.

4. Two views of the brush end of the 60-ampere Leece Neville alternator supplied on "special-equipment" Ford products. Note the finned aluminum heat sinks holding the diodes. Bottom photo shows same view but with stator assembly in place.

5. Big Prestolite alternator is used on trucks, will put out a lot of current, but isn't much bigger than an ordinary alternator.

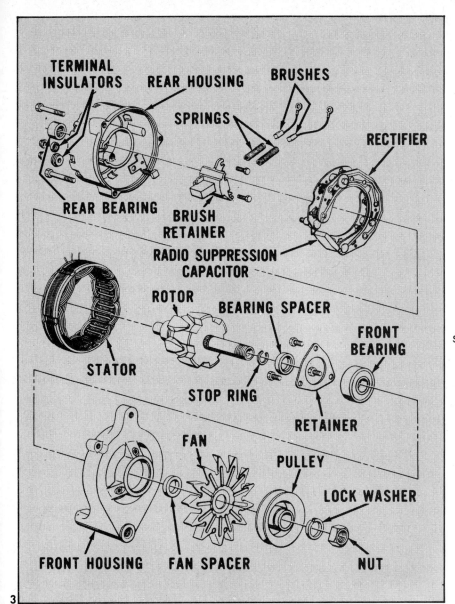

TERMINAL INSULATORS · REAR HOUSING · BRUSHES · SPRINGS · RECTIFIER · REAR BEARING · BRUSH RETAINER · RADIO SUPPRESSION CAPACITOR · STATOR · ROTOR · BEARING SPACER · FRONT BEARING · STOP RING · RETAINER · FAN · PULLEY · LOCK WASHER · FRONT HOUSING · FAN SPACER · NUT

3

HOUSING AND HEAT SINK-RECTIFIER ASSEMBLIES

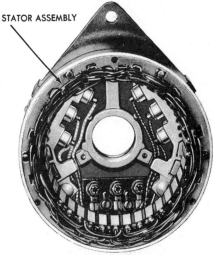

STATOR ASSEMBLY

4   **HOUSING, HEAT SINKS AND STATOR**

ing regulator will spell death not only for the car's battery, but for the generator as well. A cool generator is a happy generator. The air vents in the endplates and the fan built into the drive pulley have a vital job to perform. If air vents are allowed to become clogged with grime, or if the fan vanes are bent or broken, a rather drastic reduction in the unit's life expectancy can be expected.

Over-charging, with its resultant destructive effect on both battery and generator, should be considered one of the most serious of possible charging system malfunctions. If your car has only an idiot light, one of the best five bucks you'll ever spend would be for the addition of an ammeter to your machine's dashboard. Extreme accuracy is not so important. A gauge that will give the driver an indication of excessive charging or an abnormal charge rate that progresses up and down the ampere scale in direct proportion to engine speed is all

5

that's really needed. That little red light won't tip you off to either of these conditions—*ever*. You'll never know anything's wrong until it's too late.

ALTERNATORS

As surprising as it may seem alternators have been used on the highway for several decades—in motorcycles. The two-wheel set discovered long ago what Detroit has only recently begun to appreciate; namely, that alternators are lighter, more compact, require a less complicated regulator, and do a better job of charging the battery. One of the things which slowed the advance of the alternator to its rightful place on the automotive scene was the need for a separate rectifying unit to convert its alternating-current output into direct current for battery-charging purposes. The selenium rectifier used to be the only practical means for accomplishing this, and such devices were expensive, fragile, sensitive to heat, and difficult to produce easily in in quantities large enough to keep up with the contemporary automobile production rate. The alternator has become a practical replacement for the direct-current automotive generator in recent years mainly because of the revolutionary developments that have been made during the last decade in solid-state electronics. The modern automotive alternator employs a number of positive-negative diodes—a basic form of transistor—to rectify its alternating-current output into direct current. They are relatively durable and can be produced in quantity at low cost by many existing solid-state electronic component manufacturers.

As a device for converting mechanical power into electrical power, the alternator has certain distinct advantages over the generator both in efficiency and durability. The same principles of magnetism employed in magnetos and generators are also used in designed alternators; however, there are certain very noticeable differences in their actual construction. As was observed in our earlier discussion of the magneto, it is possible to induce an electrical current in a coil of wire either by moving the coil and allowing the magnetic field to remain stationary, or by leaving the coil stationary and moving the magnetic field. The important thing is that some means must be employed to change the number of magnetic flux lines passing through the coil windings.

In the generator, the magnetic field remained stationary while the armature's coils were rotated. This is the most practical way of designing a direct-current unit which must be made compact, since many coils are needed to produce a steady supply of direct current. Direct-current generators therefore require a segmented commutator so that voltage of the right polarity can be picked up from whichever coil in the windings is developing the most power. If, on the other hand, alternating current is desired, the current produced in all the windings at all times is acceptable for use. In an alternator the aim is not merely to tap the maximum voltage of one particular polarity, but to use the entire output—regardless of the fluctuating voltage. In order to obtain a sufficiently high average voltage, however, a greater number of cycles must be generated.

An alternating-current cycle is the length of time that it takes for the current output to rise from zero voltage to maximum positive voltage, return to zero voltage, proceed to maximum negative voltage, and again fall to zero. Normal house current is said to be 60-cycle AC, which means that it completes this cycle pattern 60 times per second, giving 120 voltage peaks that are alternately positive and negative.

Current flow alternates in the windings of a direct-current generator's armature, but the brushes pick up only the current from those coils having the correct polarity at any given time. The alternating current in the individual coils of an automotive DC generator changes direction twice with each turn of the armature. This means that if such a two-pole machine were used as a source of alternating current it would only produce one cycle for each turn of the armature. On the other hand, the automotive alternator usually has about 14 magnetic field poles and produces seven AC cycles for each rotation of the shaft. It is true that a DC generator could be built that would duplicate this feat, but the unit would need to

1. Chrysler alternators require a special tool to remove. Pulleys are an interference fit and have no other retaining means. Pressing pulley back on (shown here) is done before assembling alternators so that shaft will take the press load.

2. To separate the drive end shield from the stator on a MoPar alternator, remove through bolts and pry between components with a screwdriver blade, carefully separating the two halves.

3. Note in this cross-section of an alternator how the rotor or field windings are inside the stator or generator windings. It is just the opposite of a common generator.

4. The insulated brush can be removed separately from Chrysler Corp. alternators. Note also the three diodes in their externally-mounted heat sink next to the terminal in the rear.

5. In the Ford alternator, a tiny drill bit (arrow) must be used to hold up the brushes while the alternator is assembled. When drill bit is pulled out, brushes drop into contact with slip rings on rotor.

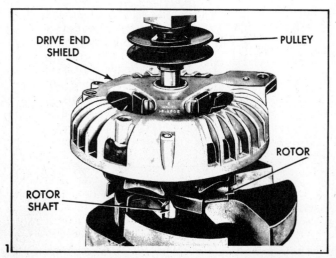

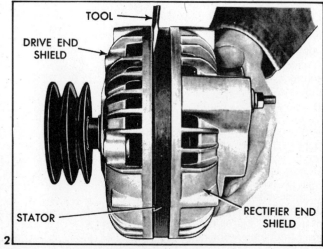

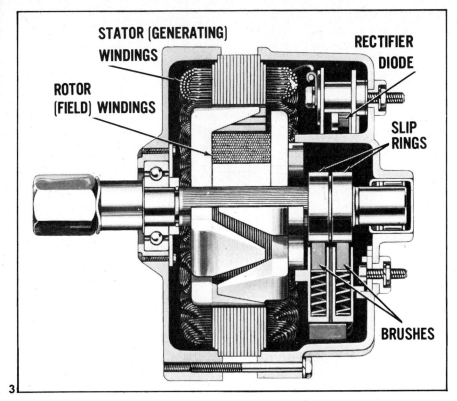

STATOR (GENERATING) WINDINGS

ROTOR (FIELD) WINDINGS

RECTIFIER DIODE

SLIP RINGS

BRUSHES

3

INSULATED BRUSH ASSEMBLY

4

5

be so large and complicated that it would scarcely fit into the engine room. The most important fundamental difference between the automotive DC generator and its AC successor is that in the alternator it is the field magnets that -otate while the current-producing windings stand still.

To avoid confusion, different terms are commonly used to describe the parts of the alternator than for describing their counterparts in the DC generator. The rotating part of an 'automotive generator is called the armature. The rotating part of an alternator is called its rotor. The rotor contains the magnetic field coil in an alternator. The stationary windings of the alternator, which correspond to the armature windings in a generator, are called the stator. Since the rotor forms the magnetic field in an alternator, it only needs to be supplied with a steady source of direct current from the battery. It has no segmented commutator such as that found in generators, but only two smooth brass slip rings. The slip rings have brushes riding against them—one supplying the field coil with current of positive polarity and the other providing a negative ground connection.

The practice of employing a rotating field in alternators has a history that begins with the very first attempts at making alternating current a usuable form of electricity.

Even though the voltage output of the automotive alternator is quite low and does not present the danger of flash-over between the slip rings, the scheme employed in larger AC generators is retained for very practical reasons. Since the windings in the stator are producing alternating current, and direct current is needed to charge the battery, a means of retifying the current output is mandatory. It is much simpler to couple the stator windings to the rectifying diodes than it would be to connect diodes to the rotating windings by means of multiple brushes.

CURRENT CHARACTERISTICS

Alternating current can be transmitted over a single wire and used in conjunction with a common ground, while direct current requires two conductors of opposite polarity. Some primitive light systems—such as those used in early rural electrification—employed single-line transmission with individual ground rods at homes and farms that could be wired to the other side of the lamps. In modern-day practice, two-wire transmission is the accepted rule, with one wire being a ground obtained at the source of power generation. Alternating current can be handled in this manner since the electrical power results from a constant reversal of flow and polarity rather than from the unidirectional flow of direct current. The alternator's stator coils, therefore, need only one wire between them and each pair of diodes.

For the sake of maximum efficiency it is desirable that the wave form of AC voltage is a *sine* wave—the voltage pattern giving the smoothest transition, fastest rise and longest peak possible from the alternator's

rotary motion. Wave form is controlled by the spacing and winding lengths of the stator coils and by the air gap between the poles of the stator and rotor. Commercial power generators normally produce 60 cycles per second, which is still rather "peaky" in its voltage levels for maximum power. The AC generators in large power plants are therefore designed to produce *three-phase* alternating current. That is, the voltage output is picked up at three points in the stator windings to produce three overlapping sine waves. Large electric motors used for industrial purposes are frequently wound for three-phase operation and must therefore be served by four wires—one for each of the AC phases and one for ground.

Automotive alternators need only be of single-phase construction since they produce current in the neighborhood of 3000-3500 cycles per second even at idle speeds. This may increase to as much as 50,000 cycles at top engine rpm. With this number of voltage peaks being reached each second, there is ample power available to handle the electrical system's demands.

Generators

The introduction of the alternator has also made it possible to greatly simplify the regulator. Although alternatorator voltage output is—like that of the generator—proportional to rpm and field strength, its current output (amperage) is much more stable. In addition, since it produces near-maximum current at low speeds, the voltage-regulating function has a more uniform requirement throughout the engine's speed range. Some of the first alternator systems employed a regulator not very different from those used with DC generator systems, but in the course of the past several years various developments in both alternator design and regulator construction have served to simplify and miniaturize the regulator to the point that some cars no longer even have a separate regulator but only a small transistorized regulating device incorporated into the alternator itself. Now that solid-state electronic components are becoming an economical alternative to electromagnetic relays, transistorized regulating circuits are growing in their popularity with car makers. In the properly maintained electrical system such units have an indefinite service life, while all-relay type regulators sooner or later begin to suffer from burning and deterioration of their contact points.

Unfortunately, some car makers are going back to mechanical regulators because their transistorized units can't stand booster-battery starts. When a booster battery is removed after starting a car that has a dead battery, the voltage will shoot up to such a high value that it kills the transistor in the regulator. This can be avoided by turning on all the accessories and lights in the car before disconnecting the booster battery, but very few emergency road servicemen know this.

CONSTRUCTION

One of the most striking features off alternator construction is the simplicity of the rotor. The field poles are two—usually identical—star-like pieces of mild steel having their points bent over so that they will interlock. These produce a series of magnetic poles of alternating polarity all around the rotor's circumference. One field winding serves to magnetize both the poles. It is coiled in a simple manner about an insulated spool which slips over the iron core on the rotor shaft separating the two pole pieces. Each end of the rotor's coil attaches to an individual slip ring, both of which are insulated from the rotor shaft. The materials and their lay-out in the assembly produce an extremely strong unit which is, incidentally, much more able to stand high rotational loadings than the armature used in normal DC generators.

Small carbon brushes ride against the slip rings to provide current to the rotor's field coil. In many units—including all Chrysler alternators and the larger options offered by Ford and General Motors—the brushes can be removed for replacement and inspection without disassembling the alternator. Even the smaller General Motors "Delcotron" (which must be taken apart for access to the brushes) has these vital components mounted in a separate brush holder for ease in servicing. One brush is connected through the regulator unit to the hot side of the battery. The other is placed in contact with ground—often simply by being wired to the alternator housing. The field relay in the regulator shuts off current to the rotor automatically when the ignition switch is turned off. In some designs there is no field relay and the ignition switch must then control the field current.

Chrysler products commonly have an alternator with only two terminals, one for the field current and one to transmit the diodes' positive current to the battery. All other parts of the circuit are grounded internally. Ford and GM cars employ, in most instances, alternators with four terminals. Two of these connect the brushes with separate terminals on

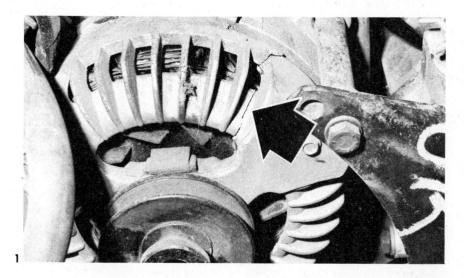

1. Alternators are aluminum, and will break easily if mistreated. This housing (arrow) was probably broken in a collision. A generator might have come through unharmed.

2. GM "Delcotron" alternators have a hex recess in the rotor shaft to hold it while the pulley retaining nut is removed.

3. Chrysler Corp. diodes are removed with these press tools. Try it without them and you'll probably ruin the alternator.

4. Autolite's integral regulator is on the way out. It seems that booster battery starts will knock the regulator out unless lights and accessories are turned on in the car before removing the booster battery. Servicemen take note.

5. A diode tester will allow you to test the diodes without disassembly on some alternators. With a test light or ohmmeter, you not only have to disassemble, but unsolder.

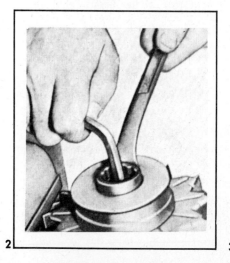

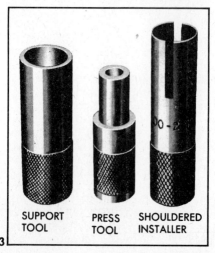

SUPPORT TOOL   PRESS TOOL   SHOULDERED INSTALLER

the regulator for control of the field current, while the other two connect the unit's output to ground and to the battery's hot side. Even those GM and FoMoCo alternators with integral regulator units require four terminals for the purpose of supplying the regulator with battery current.

Like the armature of the DC automotive generator, the stator of most alternators is built up from many laminations which in turn hold the windings in place. Although the windings in the stator may appear to be complex, they are in reality simply coils overlapping one another in a simple chain pattern. At the present time all common automotive alternators have their stator coils in multiples of three—such as 12, 18, 24. These are linked together into three basic interconnected circuits which feed current from their juncture points to the three rectifier diode-pairs.

Since the frame—or housing—of the alternator has no function in the magnetic field of the unit, it is not necessary to construct it of a ferrous metal. Aluminum, lightweight sheet metal, and various light alloys are commonly used for the purpose. This tends to make the comparative weight of an alternator much less than that of a

DC generator. The housing serves principally to hold the stator in place, provide a mounting point for the unit, and supply bearing support for the rotor. As with the generator, ample openings are allowed for the passage of cooling air and a fan is incorporated into the rotor and shaft assembly to improve its circulation. The bearings which support the rotor shaft are of the permanently lubricated ball bearing type in the vast majority of cases, although plain or needle bearings prepacked with lubricant are common on the smaller units at the brush end. This serves to make the alternator virtually service-free and is in keeping with the trend toward longer service intervals for passenger cars.

Perhaps the only really unique factor in automotive alternator design is the use of rectifying diodes that are self-contained parts of the unit. Rectifying diodes are a simple type of transistor that have the unique property of permitting electrical current to flow through them in only one direction. As mentioned in another chapter, such a diode is commonly a part of transistorized ignition system to prevent current back-flow from arcing across the breaker points or damag-

ing the switching transistor. The Motorola alternator supplied on American Motors cars has an additional "isolating" diode for similar reasons which is not necessary to the production of an electrical current.

These are six rectifying diodes in the alternator that are supplied with alternating current from the stator windings. Three of these diodes permit the passage of negative-polarity current and three allow only positive current to pass. Alternating current leaves the alternator windings and goes directly to the six diodes. Three of the diodes feed current to the battery and electrical parts of the car. The other three diodes are grounded in the alternator, and act as a return path for the electricity that has done its work at the battery, lights and accessories.

The windings of the stator overlap, and while the result is not exactly like that of the three-phase electric power generator, the voltage peaks produced by the three diode-pairs do overlap. However, their output is fed into a common wire so that the end result is either positive or negative current of relatively uniform voltage. Much has been made of diodes as an "Achilles' heel" in alternator systems; however, there is no cause for them to be considered as such except in cases where ignorance (the real Achilles' heel) has been responsible for their destruction. The two causes of damage to which the diodes are most susceptible are heat and reversed polarity.

For protection against excessively high temperatures diodes are commonly mounted in some type of heat sink. This is usually an aluminum casting—often finned for better heat

4

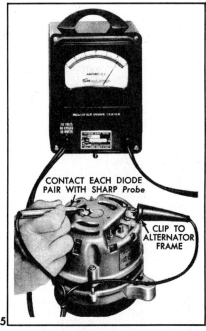

CONTACT EACH DIODE PAIR WITH SHARP *Probe*

CLIP TO ALTERNATOR FRAME

5

Generators

dissipation—which is mounted by a thin "neck" that allows little heat to be conducted to the diodes from the other parts of the alternator. However, a far more damaging source of heat results if improper procedures are used when the lead wires of new diodes are soldered into place. To safely solder the diode leads, a heat dam (a small metal clamp that absorbs excess heat) must be clipped onto the diode wire during the soldering operation. Another possible source of diode damage is vibration. This is seldom a problem with the unit in normal service, but in cases where mechanics have attempted to

remove a "dud" diode by hammering rather than pressing it out, the shock of the blows has often sounded the death knell for the other diodes in the assembly as well. In all probability, alternators will present far fewer troubles than generators ever did—once mechanics become used to dealing with them.

As a final word of caution, never continue to drive a car that has evident charging system trouble. Should the problem be a loose connection that opens the charging circuit, unregulated current of the wrong polarity may be allowed to enter the battery or the alternator diodes. Nor should you ever short across or ground any of the terminals on the regulator or alternator on alternator-

equipped cars—even though such practices are part of the troubleshooting routine used with generator systems.

QUICK TROUBLE CHECKS

Brushes last a lot longer on an alternator than on a generator, but they can wear out. The quickest way to check for this trouble is to pull the field connection off, since it is usually in the form of a plug connector. The "F" terminal uncovered by pulling the plug is the one leading to the insulated brush. Using an ohmmeter with the selector set on the X10 position—or a 110-volt bulb with two test probes—it's possible to check the circuit through the brushes and field windings for continuity, with the engine off. Touch the test probes to the field terminal and ground, and the ohmmeter should register little measurable resistance (or the test lamp should light up). If considerable resistance (or a reading of infinity) is indicated,, or if the bulb fails to light

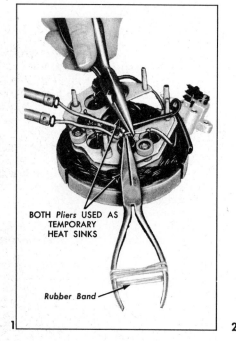

BOTH *Pliers* USED AS TEMPORARY HEAT SINKS

Rubber Band

1

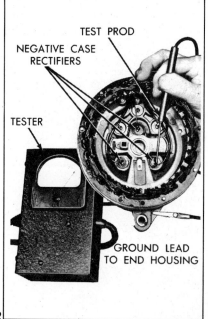

TEST PROD

NEGATIVE CASE RECTIFIERS

TESTER

GROUND LEAD TO END HOUSING

2

1. A heat sink made from a pair of pliers will protect the diodes if you have to solder their leads.

2. Chrysler Corp. diodes can't be reached without taking the alternator apart. A diode tester eliminates the need to unsolder the leads. These diodes are replaced individually.

3. Test hook-up to measure voltage output of alternator.

4. Parts location of GM Delcotron alternators. Unit at left must be disassembled to get at brushes, while the one at right has a separately removable brush holder.

5. Exploded view of typical FoMoCo alternator showing parts location.

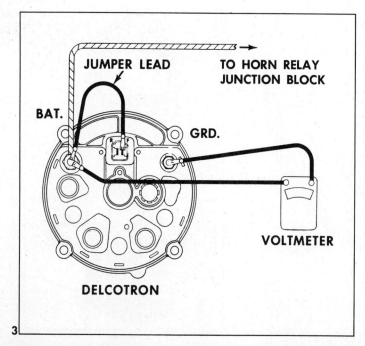

JUMPER LEAD

TO HORN RELAY JUNCTION BLOCK

BAT.

GRD.

VOLTMETER

DELCOTRON

3

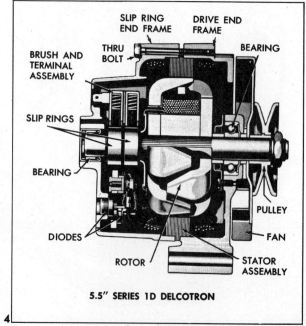

SLIP RING END FRAME

DRIVE END FRAME

THRU BOLT

BEARING

BRUSH AND TERMINAL ASSEMBLY

SLIP RINGS

BEARING

PULLEY

DIODES

FAN

ROTOR

STATOR ASSEMBLY

5.5" SERIES 1D DELCOTRON

4

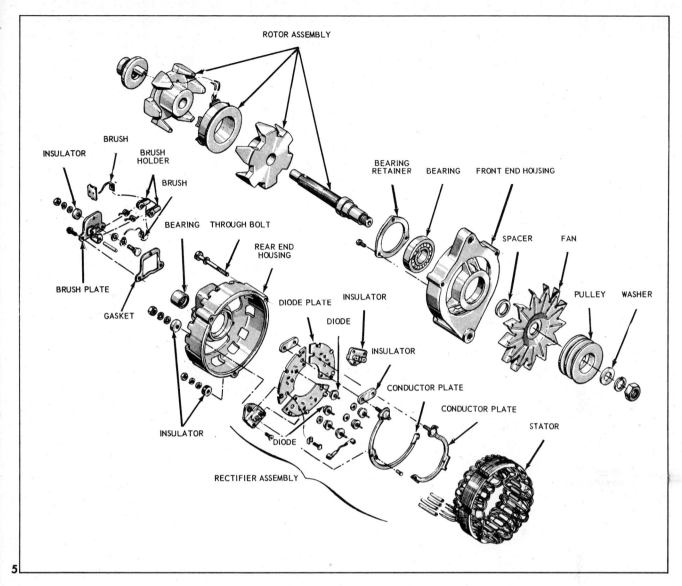

ROTOR ASSEMBLY

INSULATOR
BRUSH
BRUSH HOLDER
BRUSH
BEARING THROUGH BOLT
BEARING RETAINER
BEARING
FRONT END HOUSING
SPACER
FAN
PULLEY
WASHER
BRUSH PLATE
GASKET
REAR END HOUSING
DIODE PLATE
INSULATOR
DIODE
INSULATOR
CONDUCTOR PLATE
CONDUCTOR PLATE
STATOR
INSULATOR
DIODE
RECTIFIER ASSEMBLY

5

at all, there is probably poor contact between the brushes and the slip rings. Actual resistance of the field winding can be as high as 12 ohms, depending on design. However, you are not interested in the resistance value as much as in finding a bad connection or broken wire, which would be indicated by a very high reading on the ohmmeter.

On some of the alternators used by Chrysler it is possible to remove the brush holders individually. Sometimes, by wiggling these brush holders with the engine running the unit can be made to charge temporarily. This is a sure indication that the brushes need attention. On most other alternators the housing will have to be taken apart to get at the brushes should the initial ohmmeter check indicate possible poor contact. Once this is done it will be possible to duplicate the test at the slip rings. If the windings are intact, the trouble has to be worn-out or sticking brushes.

Should the brushes be making good contact and the rotor windings are also OK, the diodes should be

tested. This is not a hard job once the housing is apart, but the diode leads must be disconnected. The diodes can be tested either with a three-volt battery-powered test light, or an ohmmeter or "VOM" containing a 1.5-volt battery. Higher voltage should never be used since it will ruin the diodes. The test lead probes are touched to the wire and the case of each disconnected diode, and then reversed to check current flow in the opposite direction. A good diode will light the lamp or produce a low resistance reading in one direction but not in the other. If both readings are about equally high or low, or if the light will (or will not) light in either direction, the diode is bad. Individual diodes can be replaced using one of the inexpensive diode-fitting tools available or by replacing the entire heat sink in which the diodes are mounted.

An even faster on-the-car check can be carried out by disconnecting the battery ground cable and taking ohmmeter readings in both directions

across the output and ground terminals of the unit. Test results will be similar to tests of individual diodes but will not pinpoint which diodes are faulty. Garages have a diode tester; a small unit that will test the diodes after the alternator is taken apart, but without disconnecting the individual diode leads.

It may also be possible that there is more serious trouble in the rotor. Grounded windings can be detected merely by testing between the slip rings and the rotor shaft. There must be absolutely no electrical contact between these parts. Grounds in the stator windings can be found only by disconnecting the coil leads from the diode terminals and testing between one of the wires and the stator frame. A higher voltage is needed for this, and most electrical shops use 110-volt house current and a regular light bulb for such testing. If the lamp lights when the test leads are applied, the stator windings are grounded. Shorts in the stator are difficult to detect unless you have special equipment. However, if everything is OK

Generators

and alternator output still remains low, shorted stator windings are probably at the root of the problem. Some alternators have a condenser. It can cause trouble, and can be tested by a condenser tester.

ALTERNATOR FACTS

With the trend in recent years toward loading the electrical system with more and more accessories, it is not difficult to understand why the alternator has been steadily gaining in favor with the auto makers. Basic transportation like the VW probably doesn't need any extra low-speed charging capacity since there are only the lights, ignition, and possibly the radio or windshield wipers to draw current. However, when you add a heater and additional lights (those four-eyed American cars do use more current), the drain on the battery can become acute in city traffic where a great deal of time is spent with the engine idling at traffic signals, and speeds are generally below 25 miles per hour. Even without such electrical extras as tape decks, power windows, and four-way seats, an alternator is almost a must under such driving conditions—unless the driver foregoes the pleasures of radio music and warm air.

The fact that an alternator can charge at idle is by far its most outstanding virtue. Furthermore, extra-high-output alternators can be supplied as options on "loaded" cars that will fit into little more spaces than the standard dynamo. This would not be the case with a DC generator, the cost of which would likely also be higher. The standard

40- and 42-ampere alternators supplied on Fords and Mercurys, for example, can be replaced with a 60- or 65-ampere unit to handle extra equipment. Ford trucks are sometimes equipped with 100-ampere alternators which are not even nearly twice as big as the little "40's." The standard 37-ampere Delcotron on General Motors cars can have units of 42- or 62-ampere rating substituted in its place for more heavily laden electrical systems. Chrysler products are generally equipped with alternators ranging from little 26-ampere units on stripped models to 40-ampere or larger jobs on special-equipment models.

When building a hot rod or adding custom electrical accessories to any car it may be desirable to consider revising the charging system for the sake of increased capacity. This is basically a three-part undertaking. The first step is to obtain a higher-rated battery, which is an absolute *must* if you expect to gain the full value of the charging system improvements. Secondly, the alternator must not only be switched for one of greater output, but the regulator also has to be exchanged for the proper unit to match the alternator. Even if the components of the new system come from the same make and model car as your own, it will not always be possible to merely switch the two major components, since the wiring between them may be different. This is particularly true of Ford products which use Ford-built alternators for most standard models and Leece Neville 42-, 60- and 65-ampere units on special-equipment models. The regulators have a different number of terminals and are wired into the electrical system in different ways. The only way the job can be done is to consult

the schematic diagrams in an official shop manual and if the systems differ significantly, you must re-wire the connections to suit the plan for the larger alternator.

If most of your driving is done in the warmer areas of the country, the standard charging system is probably adequate even if you add quite a few accessories—at least on the average American car. Your battery won't be fighting the debilitating cold or suffering the rigors of winter starting—you probably won't be using the heater very much either. It's when you add several voltage-consuming extras that a revamping of the charging system is likely to pay off. Of course if you're building a rod from scratch, you have a very free hand in setting up the charging system to match the proposed electrical equipment. If the primary object is red-hot performance for street or competition, you may even want to go the other direction and find the smallest, lightest and lowest-powered alternator that is available.

If you pick up a used alternator (or generator, for that matter) from a salvage yard, you may—depending on its age—save yourself a lot of trouble later by starting right off with a rebuild, replacing all the parts that may have been subjected to considerable wear and tear. New bearings for most alternators and generators cost from about fifty cents to $2 depending on the type and size. Complete rebuilding kits that contain bushings, brushes, springs, and even new diodes and tools for installing them are available from many sources—including some of the large mail order houses. An extra five or six bucks can often make what was just a used alternator into a reliable like-new

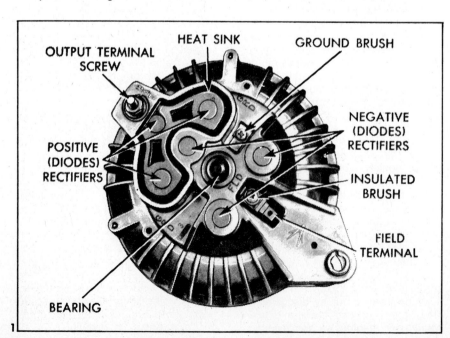

OUTPUT TERMINAL SCREW

HEAT SINK

GROUND BRUSH

NEGATIVE (DIODES) RECTIFIERS

INSULATED BRUSH

POSITIVE (DIODES) RECTIFIERS

FIELD TERMINAL

BEARING

1. This illustration is of a '66 MoPar alternator as used on Dodges. The specific features of this type of unit are pointed out.

2. Typical terminal location on GM alternators.

3. Typical terminal location on FoMoCo alternators.

4. It is relatively simple to check a GM alternator stator to determine if the windings are open or grounded. A 110-volt test lamp or an ohmmeter is used.

5. Hot terminal (arrow) on this Delco alternator is covered for a reason. It is hot all the time and will throw some fine sparks if it is accidentally grounded by a wrench.

6. How's this for a neat alternator drive, right off the driveshaft? Major fault with this setup is that it won't charge at idle, but a show car like this won't be found at any stoplight or drive-in.

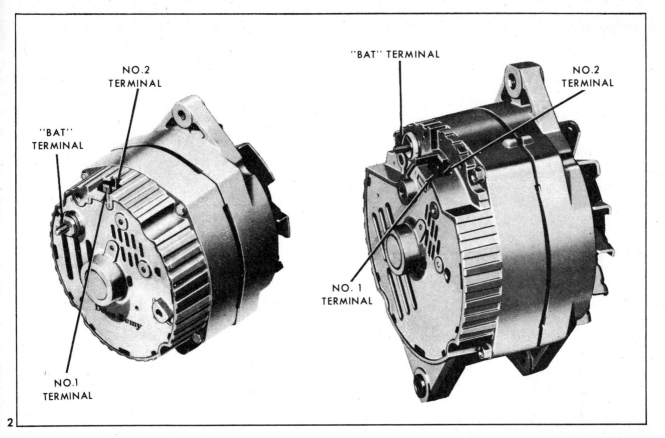

"BAT" TERMINAL

NO.2 TERMINAL

"BAT" TERMINAL

NO.2 TERMINAL

NO.1 TERMINAL

NO. 1 TERMINAL

2

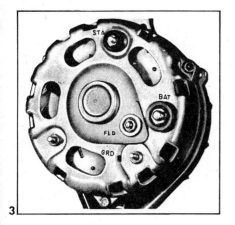

3

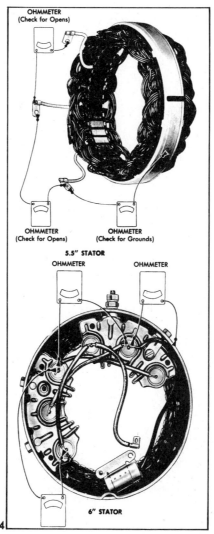

OHMMETER
(Check for Opens)

OHMMETER
(Check for Opens)

OHMMETER
(Check for Grounds)

5.5" STATOR

OHMMETER

OHMMETER

6" STATOR

4

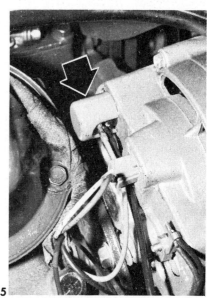

5

6

piece of equipment. Even if the dynamo came from a relatively late-model car it's still always best to check it thoroughly before pinning the fate of your electrical system on it. This is especially true if the alternator is suspected to have been in a collision, which might have given the diodes and their mountings more than just a love tap.

On the whole, the alternator is a much more satisfactory piece of hardware than the generator and nobody should have cause to grieve that the one has replaced the other. The increase in electrical system reliability alone is well worth any changes in service procedures that mechanics have had to learn. The most amazing thing is not that the DC generator has almost disappeared in the last few years, but that it didn't happen sooner!

HOW-TO: **GENERATOR OVERHAUL**

1. A Delco-Remy generator overhaul is old hat to a shop like Ivan's Generator Exchange, located in Hollywood, Calif. Disassembly begins by removing the two long bolts which extend through the case and attach the front cover to the rear cover.

2. The rear cover will now drop off. Grasp the front cover and pull it forward, carefully withdrawing the armature and commutator. Slight tapping with a plastic hammer may be necessary here. The brushes and field windings remain in the case.

3. Field coils are checked by passing current through them. A common problem in old generators is that the rear bushing becomes so worn that the whirling armature hits the field windings, damaging field and armature. Check field insulation.

4. After removing the nut on the front end of the shaft, the pulley and fan must be removed. The best way to do this is with a bench press, shown here. You can use a small gear puller, but be careful not to damage the fan or belt pulley.

5. With pulley and fan off, the front cover can now be slipped off the shaft. There are several spacers and a sleeve here, as well as the Woodruff key which located the pulley and fan; make a note of where they all go upon reassembly.

6. The armature is checked for shorts on a "growler," a test fixture which lights up and really does emit a growling noise in operation. Inspect the wire connections around the base of the commutator bars; they must be resoldered if loose.

7. The surface of the commutator should be clean and perfectly round, so it is customary to take a light cut off the surface with a lathe. Commutator bars are of thick copper and can take many light cuts before a new armature is needed.

8. After a light cutting on the commutator, the mica insulators between the commutator bars must be cut down below the level of the commutator. Otherwise they will touch the brushes and prevent proper conversion of AC current into DC.

9. Getting the old shaft bushing out of the rear cover can be a real problem, because it's fitted in a blind hole. Ivan's has a special bushing puller, but you'll have to use a hammer, drift pin and a cold chisel, preferably a diamond-point chisel.

10. The new rear bushing is pushed into the cover with a press. Now don't you wish you had let Ivan rebuild the generator? Removing these three screws and the retainer plate allows access to the front bearing, which must be tapped out.

11. Before installing the new front ball bearing, put in this felt washer and metal shim first. Then press in the new bearing. Be careful to get it in straight, not cocked. Next, replace the retainer plate and the three screws.

12. Install new brushes. Replace the front cover on the armature shaft, then the fan and pulley. Don't forget the Woodruff key. Carefully slide the armature into the case, pulling the brushes aside. Then the rear cover bolts back on.

HOW-TO: ALTERNATOR OVERHAUL

1. At Ivan's Generator Exchange in Hollywood, Calif., disassembly of a Delco-Remy alternator begins with removal of belt pulley and fan. An impact wrench is the only good way to loosen the nut; no screwdrivers in the fan blades, please.

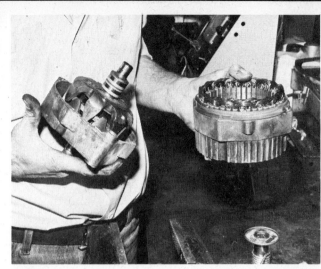

2. Mark the two halves of the case so that they can be properly realigned upon reassembly. Then remove the four bolts holding the case together. The rotor, containing the field windings, now easily pulls out of the front case half.

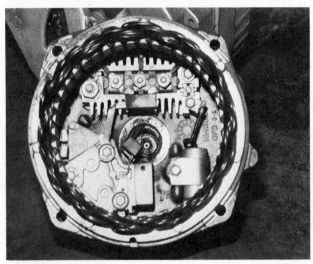

3. The stator housing contains all of the electronic goodies. At top center is the diode carrier/heat sink assembly, and mounted on that is the small diode bridge. At the bottom are the voltage regulator, the brush carrier and a condenser.

4. Disconnect the stator's three internal connections and lift out the windings. Next comes this brush carrier, attached with three bolts and mounted on top of the voltage regulator. The brushes ride against the rotor's slip rings; replace them.

5. In the Delco unit, the regulator has two blade terminals which extend out through the case and connect to the wiring harness. Regulator now lifts out easily, since it was attached by the same three bolts which held the brush carrier.

6. Next to come out is the little black diode bridge, attached by three nuts to posts on the diode carrier. By removing one nut and two capscrews, the diode carrier/heat sink assembly itself can then be lifted out.

7. Here's the alternator completely disassembled. A quickie overhaul would replace only the brushes and bearings, but all electronic components should be checked. At Ivan's all such components are replaced, including the stator windings.

8. Unless this technique is used, it is practically impossible to reassemble the alternator with new brushes in it. A long, thin pin is inserted into the brush holder to hold the brushes back; the holder has two holes in it for this purpose.

9. To get at the front ball bearing, its cover plate and these three capscrews must be removed. Old bearing is then tapped out from the other side with a large drift pin and a hammer. Care is needed because the housing is aluminum.

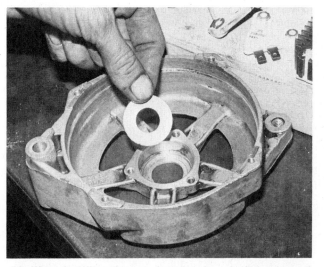

10. When installing the new front bearing, don't forget to replace this shim first. Ideally new bearing should be installed with an arbor press. Using a hammer is asking for trouble, because bearing can go in crooked and ruin the case.

11. There's another shim (arrow) on the rotor shaft which must be fitted before the rotor can be reinstalled in the front case half. Then replace the needle bearing in the rear case half and bolt the two case halves back together.

12. The rebuilt alternator is then run up on a test machine and thoroughly checked out. This is one reason you should let a really professional shop like Ivan's rebuild your alternator; they have the equipment to make sure it's right.

Lights

SOME BASIC INFORMATION ABOUT HEADLIGHTING WILL KEEP YOU FROM BEING LEFT IN THE DARK.

It would be nice if we could report that there have recently been many revolutionary improvements in the headlights installed on American cars, but unfortunately we can't. It's not that there is no room for improvement or, more important, the *need* for improvement. Certainly anybody who does much driving after dark will agree that the headlights supplied by car manufacturers are somewhat less than marginally adequate for many common night-driving situations.

The changes that have taken place in automobile headlights since World War II are limited to a few lens modifications, a modest increase of 3000 candlepower in 1955, the switchover to four-light systems on large American cars beginning in 1958, and the sudden shift to rectangular headlamp styling pioneered by GM for 1975.

Right at the root of our present dilemma is the "safety" legislation of 1940—the year when sealed-beam headlights were made a legal requirement in all states. The bulb-and-reflector headlights used until the late Thirties were not basically inferior to the sealed beams, but the automakers and lamp manufacturers decreed that they had to go. Their only serious problem was that the reflectors tended to tarnish with age and owner neglect. The average driver, being what he is, usually kept right on driving with them even when their capacity for illumination had diminished to approximately that of a jar filled with fireflies.

Another curious situation prevailed in those days which no doubt poisoned the minds of many legislators when specifications for sealed-beam lamps were laid down. About the time when grandpa was buying his first beam-axle V-8 flathead, it was a popular trick to blind oncoming drivers with bright lights. Many drivers went out of their way to not only aim their headlights to hit other drivers right between the eyes, but also invariably added at least one swivel-mounted spotlight.

As a result of this kind of horseplay, the various state legislatures passed laws that limited the power and type of headlights, as well as specifying the permissible number and legal aim for auxiliary lights—sometimes banning them altogether.

The red tape resulting from these old laws makes it almost impossible for a car maker to revise the lighting equipment installed on his product even if the change would be in the interest of safety. It took a tremendous amount of effort just to get all the states to approve the four-light systems—which have, incidentally, some disadvantages as well as advantages in comparison with two-light installations.

Some of the highly potent aftermarket and European auxiliary lights, which in most cases have proven to be a real night-driving asset, are not legal in some states—and some are not legal in any.

For years Detroit played around with rectangular sealed-beam units, primarily on their "dream" or advanced-concept idea cars, but for a long time buggy-era regulations eliminated their use on production vehicles. It took the might of GM to obtain the go-ahead for the use of rectangular units on some of their cars beginning in 1975. However, the corporation promised the bureaucrats to discontinue the lights if for any reason car buyers frowned on them or if they created any service problems at dealership levels. Thus was born the greatest change in headlighting in many decades, thanks to the stylists who insisted on the new shape in order to design "tighter" front-end

sheetmetal with lower hoodlines. Rectangular lights are now very nearly the universal choice of our domestic car builders.

However, it is interesting to note that only the *shape* of the sealed-beam lights has changed. Candlepower limits are the same as before, but because of the units' smaller sizes (in total area), their illuminating beams have actually been reduced.

Whether square or round, grouped on the prow of a car in pairs or as quads, headlights function much as they always have, and changing a bulb is pretty nearly the same now as

1

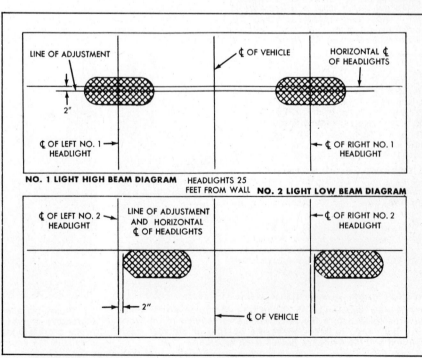

2

NO. 1 LIGHT HIGH BEAM DIAGRAM   HEADLIGHTS 25 FEET FROM WALL   NO. 2 LIGHT LOW BEAM DIAGRAM

it was when the sealed-beam units first came along.

HEADLIGHTS

The headlights supplied on two-light cars have a twin-filament system for dimming. Four-light systems have two sealed beams with both high- and low-beam filaments, plus two additional sealed beams with high-beam filaments only. These last units go out completely when the headlights are dimmed, and since the diameter of the remaining two lamps is less than that of the 7-in. sealed-beam units on two-headlight cars, the result is poorer visibility with the lights dimmed than is offered by the two-unit setup in the same mode.

Quartz-iodine bulbs, on the other hand, cannot be dimmed by using two filaments—at least not practically nor economically. The tungsten filament in these bulbs is enclosed in a quartz glass tube with iodine vapor. The gaseous iodine makes the vaporized tungsten from the filament redeposit itself on the filament rather than on the glass parts of the lamp. This not only keeps the lens and reflector clear, but extends filament life considerably. A hotter filament gives more light, but in ordinary bulbs this only makes it burn out sooner. Because quartz-iodine lamps redeposit the tungsten on the filament, the erosion rate is low despite the higher temperatures. Quartz is used for the encasing tube due to the high temperatures developed.

The Europeans have devised an electromagnetic shutter which is incorporated into the rectangular quartz-iodine headlights. By electrical means, the shutter can be dropped down to mask some of the reflections for low-beam driving. It should be obvious that this complicated means would be unnecessary with four-light systems, but the American driver would be well advised not to hold his breath until these superior headlight systems become legal here.

Many states have gone so far as to deny the car owner the right to aim his own headlights, although there are still many parts of the country where this work can be done at home. Shops that specialize in headlight aiming generally use a headlight aimer that attaches directly to the lens of the sealed-beam units. It does not require the use of a wall screen except for calibration. These devices are quick, compact and require little shop space for their use. But unless the mechanic using them understands their operation thoroughly and takes the time to perform a conscientious job, the results are sometimes none too accurate.

For home mechanics, an improvised aiming screen is probably the best way to go. The most important factor is having an area available which allows the car to sit absolutely level, with the headlight faces at a distance of 25 ft. from the screen. The screen should have four lines drawn upon it. First, make a horizontal line across the screen that is parallel to the ground and at exactly the same height as the centers of the car's headlights. Now draw three vertical lines across it. One should be in the exact center and the other two equidistant from it at an included width equal to the distance between the car's headlight centers. If the car has a four-unit headlight system, a separate set of lines should be drawn for each pair of lights.

The sealed beams used on cars with two-light systems, as well as the combination high-beam, low-beam sealed beams used with four-light systems, are designated Type 2 units. These are ordinarily identified by a numeral "2" molded into their lens. The high-beam-only sealed beams used for two of the lamps in four-light systems are called Type 1 units

3

1. Most cars, whether fitted with one or two pairs of either round or rectangular headlamps, require that the bezel or surrounding trim be removed to gain access to lamp adjustment screws or, in case of bulb replacement, retaining screws.

2. Draw this diagram on your garage door and you can do your own headlight adjusting right in your own driveway—provided the pavement is level.

3. It took GM's might to pave the way for rectangular headlights on some of their '75 models, but style is now widespread throughout the industry, as shown by this '77 Versailles.

4. The once-simple headlight is now a complex system of dual headlamps, parking lights and turn-signal lamps, all in a huge housing with a bezel and other retainers to keep it together. This is a '77 Seville.

4

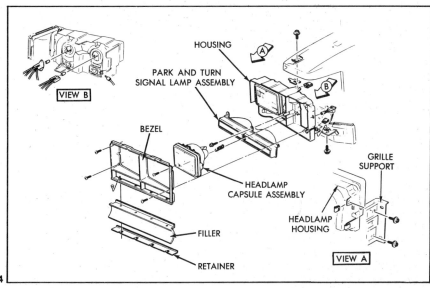

VIEW B

HOUSING

PARK AND TURN SIGNAL LAMP ASSEMBLY

BEZEL

HEADLAMP CAPSULE ASSEMBLY

FILLER

RETAINER

GRILLE SUPPORT

HEADLAMP HOUSING

VIEW A

and are correspondingly marked. Type 2 sealed beams can also be recognized by the fact that they have three terminals on the back, while Type 1 units have only two.

To aim the headlights, the car must be positioned 25 feet from the aiming screen so that the center vertical line on the screen is exactly in line with the center of the car. The quickest way to do this is to shift the screen from side to side until it is lined up with the center of the car's hood. If the car has no distinct line at the center of the sheet metal, you can locate the center by using a tape measure and then placing a small suction cup at that point for a "front sight." The "rear sight" can be the joint in the middle of the rear window molding, or a yardstick held straight up from the trunk lock. The car should be rocked from side to side several times and allowed to settle into its normal position before making the adjustments.

The Type 2 units are adjusted on low beam only. This will assure adequate illumination with the lights dimmed, and the built-in angle between the high and low beams will take care of the aiming for the "brights." Type 1 units are aimed separately in reference to their own lines on the screen. Only the light to be adjusted should be allowed to shine on the screen; the others should be covered to prevent their interfering with your work. To assure a good job, have the tires properly inflated and make sure that all grille, fender and headlight assembly bolts are tight. Some car makers specify that the lights be aimed with a half-tank of gas and a person in the driver's seat. Others say a full tank and no one in the car, but all agree that there should be nothing in the trunk and no passengers on board. The aiming charts appearing in the illustrations show where the light beams should fall in relation to the lines on the aiming screen.

Older cars using the two-headlight systems had 5000-series bulbs that are still seen in some areas. They are most easily recognized by lack of the the three points around the rim, which all the later bulbs have for use with mechanical aimers. The 5000-series bulbs are aimed on the high beam only. Lights are aimed so that the hot spot of the light hits the aiming screen exactly in front of the light, but with a two-inch drop at 25 feet. Some states may require more drop. Aiming the high beams in that manner automatically takes care of the low beams. That is exactly opposite to the later Type 2 units, which

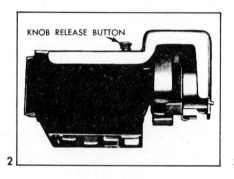

KNOB RELEASE BUTTON

will fit in place of the 5000 series. If your car has one of each bulb, aim each one according to its own particular specifications.

Certain non-standard sealed-beam units are available that have a greater intensity than the normal units. These are usually meant to be installed in place of the Type 1 units in four-light systems. There are also high-power replacements for seven-inch Type 2 units. Some of these are rated as much as 200,000 candlepower. They're great for high-speed night driving in the wide-open spaces, but are definitely illegal in every state. If you live out in a wild and wooded country where the most important traffic on the roads at night is straying livestock, you might want to investigate some of these non-standard replacements. But if you try to use them in most places they'll earn you a quick trip to the "cop shop" faster than a trunk full of un-cut heroin. There are also iodine replacements for your sealed beams and, if used discreetly, their 65,000 candlepower (as opposed to the 37,500 candlepower of standard units) might not get you into trouble.

OTHER LAMPS

When you flip on the headlights there are a number of other less noticeable lamps that light up as well. These include parking lights, side lights, tail lights, and the bulbs illuminating the instrument panel. A look at the average main light switch assembly on most American cars will show that this little piece of equipment is only slightly less complicated than the latest IBM computer. It controls more individual circuits and performs more varied tasks than any other electrical part on the car. First of all, it switches on the parking lights, instrument panel lights and other small bulbs. Pull it out a little further and you get the headlights too. If it's turned from side-to-side a rheostat dims or raises the intensity of the instrument panel bulbs. Turned all the way clockwise, it turns on the passenger compartment domelight.

In many cars the headlight switch also contains a circuit breaker which replaces the headlight circuit fuses that were used on many older cars. If there is a short in the lighting system, the circuit breaker cuts out momentarily—a much less nerve-racking situation than having the whole illuminating system go dead while descending a mountain pass at a very sneaky 70 mph. If any of the many and varied functions of the headlight switch ceases operation, the whole unit must be replaced. The car makers—probably frightened to death of tying up their dealer's service departments on these things—have made exchanging them an easy task. Most late cars have a pushbutton on the switch that, when depressed, frees the control knob so that it can be pulled out of the dash. Then all you need to do is un-plug the multiple connector and unscrew the mounting ring-nut.

1. *Shown here are a variety of headlamp switches. Some are factory units, the others are replacements.*

2. *FoMoCo headlight switch, like GM's, contains dash light rheostat, dome-light switch and circuit breaker for the headlight circuits. Note connector terminals at bottom.*

3. *These headlight beam selector switches—dimmer switches to most—are coupled to the lighting system through a multiple connector on most late-model cars. They permit choice of high or low beams.*

4. *This is a stock Chrysler product fuse block that mounts under the edge of the instrument panel. This type of fuse block has much more protection against accidental shorting, because the clips and fuses are sunk in little wells.*

5. *For '74, Chrysler made several engineering improvements with the mechanic in mind, and this fuse block was one. The block eliminates the usual hassles of checking fuses, since it swings down from the dash.*

6. *Turn signal switches come with their wiring permanently attached. The steering wheel must be removed to get the switch out.*

7. *Typical turn signal circuit. When the rear turn light is blinking, the stop lamp on that side is disconnected from the stop lamp switch by the turn signal switch.*

Whenever you're working on this or any other part of the lighting system, the ground cable of the battery should always be removed. Hint No. 2: Before condemning the headlight switch, make sure that the real trouble is not a loose or corroded multiple connector.

The headlight beam selector switch mounted on the floorboards also has a multiple connector on most late-model cars. Headlights that "mysteriously" become inoperative are frequently caused by this connector being kicked loose or by its becoming corroded by water or snow from the driver's shoes. As in the case of the main headlight switch, the dimmer pedal switch can be replaced but not repaired.

The dimmer switch has three terminals. One receives battery current from the headlight switch when it is turned on; the other two terminals are connected to the headlights. One of these goes to a terminal on both the Type 1 and Type 2 sealed beams and provides current for the high beams. The other connects to the low-beam filament terminals on the Type 2 units only. The remaining terminals on the sealed beams connect the filaments to ground. Whenever the driver depresses the dimmer switch, it redirects battery current from one set of lamp filaments to the other.

SECONDARY LIGHTING SYSTEMS

Besides those circuits controlled by the main headlight switch there are circuits for the turn signals, stop lights, back-up lights, four-way flashers and courtesy lights—all operating independently. Each of these systems has its own switches, its own particular type of bulbs, and is generally protected by its own individual fuse. On some cars, only the headlights themselves are wired through the circuit breaker, all other circuits—including the taillights and parking lights—having fuses. Many newer cars have dropped fuses entirely in favor of circuit breakers.

The switches controlling the various secondary lighting systems are nearly always completely different from one another in their construction, location and manner of operation. In addition, turn signal and four-way flasher circuits have a relay in them that switches the current delivered to the lamps on and off automatically.

Flasher and turn signal relays are small electromagnetic switches that operate on thermo-electric principles. When the turn signal or four-way

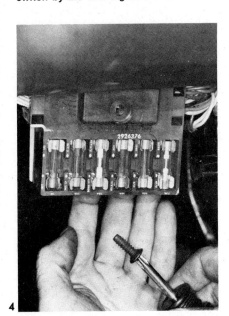

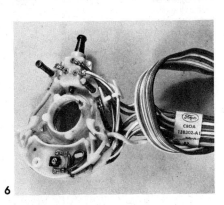

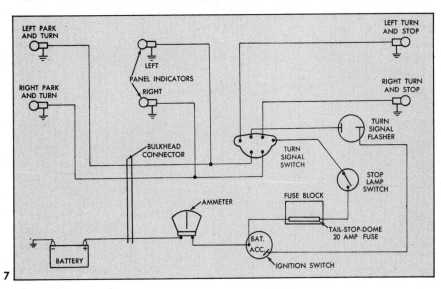

flasher switch is closed by the driver, current is sent through a fine wire inside the relay housing. Since the fine wire produces a short circuit, it begins to heat up. As with any other metal object, the heat causes the wire to expand and lengthen. A set of spring-loaded contact points is anchored open by this wire and, as the wire expands, the points are allowed to come together. This permits battery current to pass through the windings of the relay rather than through the fine wire. The relay energizes, drawing a second set of contacts together which route current through the signal bulbs. However, once the current load is no longer on the fine wire, it begins to cool and contract, opening the points and deenergizing the relay. This causes the signal lamps to go off again. The fine wire once again receives battery current and starts to heat up. The entire cycle has begun all over. Nearly 100% of flasher failures result from the fine control wire burning or breaking off.

When replacing a faulty flasher unit you will find that most parts stores carry "standard" and "heavy-duty" flasher relays. The heavy-duty type is intended primarily for trucks and other vehicles which have many high-wattage bulbs in the flasher or signal circuit. On most cars, the load is too light for these units and the fine control wire does not cool enough to release the relay. The signals will simply go on and stay on without flashing. If you have a trailer that is equipped with stop lights, turn sig-

nals, flashers and taillights which are coupled into the front circuits of the tow car, you may find that the flashes produced with a standard flasher are of very short duration and quite widely spaced. Here's where the heavy-duty type flashers come into their own. Since the heavy-duty flasher relays have the same terminal arrangement as the standard-duty numbers, it's a simple job to just unplug one and insert the other when either towing or when "running light."

In most instances where turn signals go on and stay on without flashing the cause is a burned-out bulb. Since the flasher relay control wire is coupled in series with the signal lamps, it depends on their resistance to absorb the current and allow the control wire to cool. If the balance in the system is very critical, a burned-out dash indicator bulb may cause the signals to go on and stay on, or—depending on the circuitry—transform the signals into four-way flashers.

There are various conversion kits available to modify cars with conventional lighting arrangements to produce a four-way flasher system. Conversion kits vary in price from about $3 to $10 and come complete with easy-to-follow directions. There's no complicated wiring, and it's possible to make your own conversion simply by wiring all four turn signals to an additional flasher and control switch. The switch, however, must be of the two-pole type so that the left and right signals are connected electrically only when the four-way flasher switch is closed.

Stop lights and back-up lights are commonly operated by mechanical switches, although a few cars still re-

tain the hydraulically operated type that was common on American cars about 25 years ago. Before the advent of hanging brake pedals, mechanical stop light switches were a constant source of trouble since they had to be located under the car, where they soon became rusted or water-soaked by spray thrown from the wheels. Now, with the stop light switch located inside the car on the pedal mouting assembly, they are practically trouble free. Hydraulic switches were never subjected to the water and corrosion problem, but they're still a headache to change since the brake system must be bled after the new switch is installed.

Back-up light switches—even those screwed directly into automatic transmissions—are all mechanically operated. Their location varies from make to make, but the majority are mounted somewhere on the shift lever linkage. Those that are screwed into the transmission are actuated by an internal cam that moves whenever the driver puts the trans into reverse.

LIGHTS FOR SPORTS & RODDING

Even though state laws prohibiting "originality" in headlight systems will probably remain on the books for a long time despite technical advances (old laws never die, they just get in the way), there are a few "loopholes" which can get you better lighting for your car. High-candlepower outputs alone do not create a problem for other drivers, but rather the amount of *glare* inherent in the design of the unit's lens and reflector. Most sealed beams are, unfortunate-

1. *A 3-prong flasher. The best of these are the heavy-duty types that will flash with any number of lights.*

2. *There is quite a variety of stoplight switches available, and the type of wire connectors they employ is also varied.*

3. *Driving light placed at the 24-inch level is legal in all states, and the low limit in some. It places the light out of harm's way, but leaves it on almost the same level as the regular headlights—which may not be very attractive on some cars.*

4. *This Courier pickup truck has been fitted with four quartz-iodine driving lights. Though illegal for highway use, they are designed to be used strictly off-road. They perform far better than any American driving light.*

5. *Top photo shows how the road looks through the windshield with only the car's standard high beams on. Lower photo shows the difference with just one 100,000-candlepower quartz-iodine driving light.*

5

permit their being mounted conveniently on most cars. Placing their centers at about 24 inches above the road will usually protect them from "park by ear" drivers much better than mounting them just above bumper height.

When mounting your auxiliary lights, it's a good idea to do so by drilling the minimum number of holes possible. Unless you plan to sell the lights when you trade the car, you can bet that any open holes bored into the bodywork won't add one cent to its resale value. Often, a through-the-grille bracket can be made that may be anchored to one of the grille or radiator bolts so that no drilling will be necessary.

There are several important things to be considered when wiring auxiliary lights. First off, driving lights are meant to be used with the high beams only, and most states specify that they switch off automatically when the headlights are dimmed. It is therefore necessary that they draw current from the wiring that leads to the car's high-beam units. A separate switch should always be incorporated in the wiring for the driving light(s) so that the driver can completely deactivate them if he wishes to.

Fog lights are generally used with the headlights on low beam to minimize reflections from snow, rain or fog. It is therefore unnecessary to wire them into the headlight circuit. It is desirable, however, to pick up current for them from either the headlight switch or the ignition switch so that the fog light(s) will not be left burning accidentally when you leave the car.

Anytime that an auxiliary light is wired to a power source other than the headlight circuit it should be provided with a fuse or circuit breaker control to prevent fires in the event that the unit becomes shorted. Most production cars have a blank space or two in their fuse panel, and you may find it desirable to wire the light(s) through one of these. However, in-line fuse holders are readily available which permit such circuits to be fused individually.

A combination installation of fog and driving lights will assure you of having the best available illumination regardless of weather conditions. In all probability, auxiliary lights are going to get more and more emphasis in the next few years. You can get ahead of the game by "updating" your lighting system now; but no matter what type of installation you decide upon, make sure that you follow the laws of your state. The misuse of powerful lights will only delay the general acceptance of these vital safety accessories. 🦅

ly, rather high in glare for the amount of light they put out. This is undoubtedly one factor that has held back the legalizing of higher-powered replacements. Some of the high-intensity headlight replacements are relatively low in glare production, but offer better long-range lighting than standard sealed-beam units do.

French-made "Optique" headlights are available in the U.S. and are built in both 7- and 5¾-inch sizes to replace sealed beams in either two- or four-headlight cars. They can be had with regular or quartz-iodine bulbs, and even though they are almost twice as powerful as "legal" headlights, their glare and dazzle production has been cut down. They are illegal on public highways, but a jeep-type or off-road vehicle could really use them.

There is, however, an even better solution to the long-range night vision problem—namely, auxiliary driving lights. Driving lights are not only extremely practical pieces of equipment, but are a great custom touch for any car. They are available in various power outputs ranging from about 35,000 candlepower to as much as 300,000. Most of these units are of overseas manufacture and can be had with sealed beams (some have

aircraft landing light units), regular incandescent bulbs, or quartz-iodine elements.

As to what's legal and what isn't, things are rather confused. The states that have laws limiting the type of driving lights which can be used usually require that the manufacturer seek state certification for his product before it can become a legal accessory. Only one unit, the California-made "Perlux," is actually approved in all states. However, many areas—such as Ohio, Oklahoma, Maine and Wisconsin, as well as a number of other states that are also primarily rural—have no specific requirements for driving lights. Some states permit two driving lights, others only one. None permit them to be mounted above 42 inches; but the minimum mounting height varies from 12 to 24 inches—although here again, some states do not specify standards.

Fog lights are a handy accessory during rain, snow and foggy driving conditions. They are also quite useful for "balancing" a driving light appearance-wise in states that limit cars to only one such fixture. Nearly all driving light manufacturers make a matching fog light for such installations. Fog and driving lights come in various shapes and thicknesses to

Regulators

REALLY JUST A RELAY, A REGULATOR IS THE SIMPLE SECRET BEHIND THE HAPPY TEAMWORK OF GENERATOR AND BATTERY—IF IT'S WORKING RIGHT.

Unless you're in the income bracket in which the cost of a new battery every few months means nothing, you should be mighty thankful that somebody invented the voltage regulator. A battery fed a steady diet of raw current from the alternator would be boiling one moment from an overcharge and dying the next under the burden of the electrical system's entire current load. When alternator output is adequate, the main load of the electrical system is carried solely by the generated current, with only the "surplus" being used to charge the battery—providing it needs it. It's only when the alternator output falls below the demands of the electrical system—or when the starter is in use—that the battery becomes the prime source of the car's electrical power.

Yes, you can generalize and say that the charging system is "just for charging the battery," since without such a system the battery would soon be flatter than a dead cat on a city street. But most of the time the charging system is actually carrying the electrical system's load virtually by itself. All of this requires a fine balance between charging system output and current demand. Making sure that the dynamo is neither putting out too much power nor draining the battery dry is the job of your automobile's regulator.

BATTERY-ALTERNATOR CIRCUITS

An alternator or generator alone

1

2

FIELD RELAY   VOLTAGE LIMITER

3

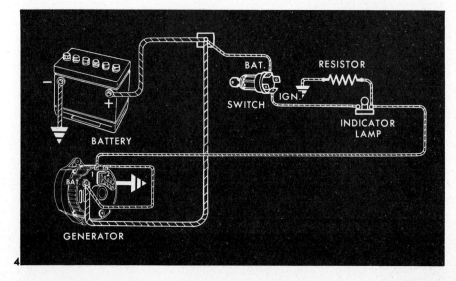

BAT. SWITCH   IGN.   RESISTOR
INDICATOR LAMP
BATTERY
BAT.
GENERATOR

4

1. Regulators have changed in size, if not in function, over the years. Grubby one on the left is out of an early Ford, small one at the bottom is the transistorized version out of a much later model.

2. Even the earliest transistorized regulators represented a great saving of size and weight over their electro-mechanical predecessors.

3. Many cars still on the road are equipped with units like this—an electro-mechanical regulator for an alternator system. The ignition switch sends current to the field relay, which then energizes the alternator's field.

4. Simplified circuit shows relation of main components in charging circuit. This manufacturer refers to alternators as "AC Generators."

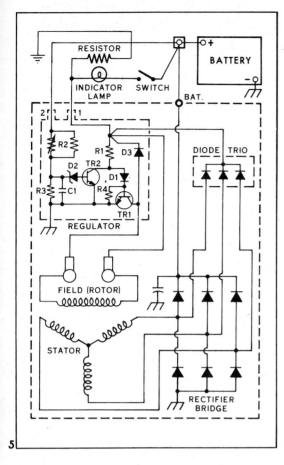

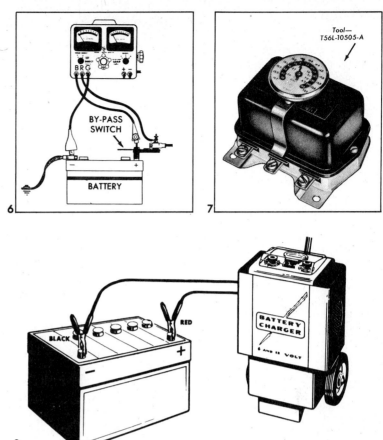

5. *Schematic wiring diagram shows what components go into the circuit of an alternator/transistorized regulator system. Everything within the dashed lines is inside the alternator housing.*

6. *Terminal adaptors make it possible to test the charge and discharge rate of the battery while the engine is running. This is a must for checking operation of voltage regulator.*

7. *Voltage regulators contain a temperature sensing unit to limit charging on hot days. When a unit is calibrated, the mechanic must make sure it is at the proper temperature with the cover in place.*

8. *Have you considered that maybe all your regulator troubles are the result of a defective battery? The battery controls the charging rate by its counter-voltage. If the battery is old and weak, the full job of controlling the charge rate is heaped on the regulator, overloading it, and possibly causing voltage fluctuations. Charge the battery, then test it, before you touch regulator.*

would obviously be an extremely poor power source for the automotive electrical system. First of all, it would not be able to provide current for starting, since electrical power is not produced unless the engine is already running. Even if it could generate electricity without the engine's mechanical power to turn it, such a generator would have to be a huge affair to supply the immense current demands of the starter motor.

A battery alone would be a far better power source for an automotive electrical system than just an alternator would be. However, the battery would then have to be recharged frequently from some outside source. The ideal setup is for the battery and the alternator to work together as partners, the battery carrying the load when the engine is not running—or running very slowly—and the charging system taking over the job as engine speed builds up.

Our accompanying diagrams show only the battery-alternator circuit. The details of the car's starting and electrical systems have been eliminated in the interests of clarity.

The basic wiring diagram and circuit diagram show a General Motors system, in which the regulator is built into the alternator case. To further add to the confusion of today's technical terms, GM refers to their alternator as an "AC Generator." The basic system is the same for all cars, even though Ford and Chrysler products have the regulator mounted separately from the alternator and call the alternator by its rightful name.

We show a system using an idiot light, since, unfortunately, most cars are equipped that way today. When the system is turned on with the ignition switch, current from the battery flows through the light to the number one terminal on the alternator. This is part of the regulator circuit, and current flows through resistor R1, diode D1, and the base of transistor TR1 on its way back to the battery through the ground connection. This current flow turns the transistor on, allowing current to flow through the alternator field coil and the other side of TR1 before flowing back to the battery. A resistor in parallel with the indicator lamp reduces the total circuit resistance to provide a higher field current for initial voltage buildup when the engine starts. The powerful battery current that goes to the starter does not appear on either diagram, since it is electrically outside the charging circuit.

Once the engine is running and the alternator turning, AC voltages are produced in the stator winding in proportion to the movement of the rotor. The diodes in the rectifier change the alternating current across the "Bat." terminal and ground. As alternator speed increases, more voltage is provided for charging the battery and operating accessories.

With the alternator operating, the same voltage appears across the "Bat." terminal and the number one terminal, and the indicator lamp goes out, showing that the alternator is producing voltage. The number two terminal is also connected to the battery, but the high resistance of R2 and R3 limit the discharge current. As the speed of the alternator increases, and the voltage output in-

Regulators

creases, the increased voltage between R2 and R3 allows the Zener diode D2 to conduct, turning off transistor TR1 and turning on transistor TR2. With TR1 off, system voltage decreases, until TR2 turns off again and TR1 turns back on, increasing the voltage again. This cycle repeats many times per second, keeping output voltage to a predetermined value.

The other elements of the system shown include a capacitor to smooth out the voltage across R3, a resistor to limit the current through TR1 at high temperatures, and a diode that prevents high induced currents in the field windings when TR1 turns off.

In an alternator system, then, the regulator controls the voltage allowed into the system at all times, protects the battery from an overcharge, and keeps battery current from flowing into the stator during periods of low output.

BATTERY-GENERATOR CIRCUITS

At first glance, the generator system looks much simpler in the diagrams. It can be simplified more, and has fewer components, but actually it is prone to more troubles—which is why car makers have dropped it in favor of the alternator system with full electronic control.

In our simplified diagram, the engine is started by turning on the ignition (part of the electrical system load) and operating the starter by closing switch "Sol." The generator relay shown in the simplified regulator remains open, since there is not yet sufficient current being produced by the generator to operate the relay that controls it. Therefore, the powerful battery current directed to the starter ("St.") will not be shown on the ammeter ("Amps") since it is outside the starting circuit electrically.

There will be some deflection of the ammeter needle, however, since the solenoid (also part of the electrical system load) requires some current to operate.

Once the engine is running, the generator action increases with engine rpm until it begins to put out current. This causes the regulator relay to energize and close the cutout contacts, so that current flows through the ammeter into the battery. The reversal of current flow through the ammeter causes the needle to swing from the discharge zone (battery doing the work) to the charge zone. (charging system doing the work). Once the charging system has taken over, current is driven not only through the ignition and other components included in the electrical system load, but also through the battery. The current flow therefore divides at connection C1—as the arrowheads indicate—and rejoins at connection C2, the battery ground.

If the engine is slowed down, the charging system output weakens and the ammeter needle gradually returns to "zero"—the point where the charging system is just meeting the needs of the electrical system load and no more. If the engine is allowed to idle—especially when several electrical accessories are in operation—the ammeter needle will swing down into the discharge zone indicating that the current flow has reversed and the battery has assumed some (or all) of the electrical system's load. Should charging system output fall very low, current would obviously be drawn back through the cutout into the generator windings. This would not only be wasteful, but might possibly damage the generator windings. The cutout relay prevents this by opening to switch off the generator and isolate it from the battery. The cutout relay has, therefore, two basic functions: 1) When the engine is not operating, the contact points are held open by spring tension to prevent battery current from flowing to the generator windings. 2) It switches the generator output "on the line" when the voltage being produced is slightly above 12

volts (6 volts in a 6-volt system).

ALTERNATOR SYSTEMS

Most cars produced in recent years use alternator systems with transistorized regulators, as described above. These systems allow no adjustments of a regulator, or at most only an adjustment for maximum voltage. If the regulator proves bad, you throw it away and buy a new one, and that's that. Older cars, however, used a conventional electro-mechanical regulator in conjunction with their alternators, and before that, with their generators. Many cars still on the road have this system, and there is consid-

1. This is what they mean when they mention a riffler file for cleaning regulator points. The tip of the file can dig all the crud out of the points so that they'll work properly.

2. Some aftermarket electro-mechanical regulators offer quality features not found on factory equipment. These features include adjusting screws, multiple tungsten alloy cutout contacts, fuse wires, etc.

3. To make their operation smoother, electro-mechanical regulators do not actually break the circuit to the field. They merely insert a resistance into it. The resistors are usually at the bottom of the regulator, as indicated by the arrows.

4. Basic Delco-Remy generator circuits with single-and double-contact regulators. Note that in both circuits the field windings are grounded in the regulator. That is known as an "A" circuit. Systems with a "B" circuit have the field grounded in the generator.

5. If you can't figure out why a regulator doesn't work, maybe this fusible wire (at pencil point) has melted. Some regulators have them to protect the unit in the event of a current overload.

6. Typical layout of a regulator for generator-based charging systems.

7. To adjust most Ford regulators, you bend this hunk of metal underneath the point spring.

8. Pliers will work, but this Snap-On bending tool is just the thing for setting Ford regulators.

RIFFLER FILE

OXIDIZED CAVITY
EXAGGERATED VIEW

1

2

6 VOLT
8 63 899

3

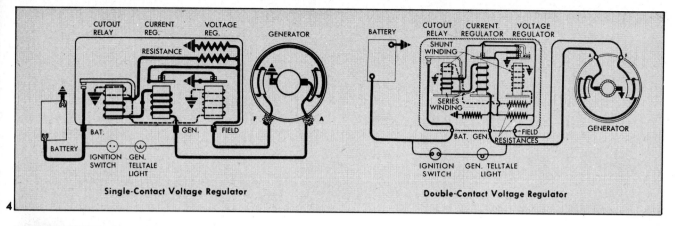

CUTOUT RELAY CURRENT REG. VOLTAGE REG. GENERATOR

RESISTANCE

BAT. GEN. FIELD

BATTERY

IGNITION SWITCH GEN. TELLTALE LIGHT

F A

Single-Contact Voltage Regulator

BATTERY

CUTOUT RELAY CURRENT REGULATOR VOLTAGE REGULATOR

SHUNT WINDING

SERIES WINDING

BAT. GEN. FIELD RESISTANCES

IGNITION SWITCH GEN. TELLTALE LIGHT

GENERATOR

Double-Contact Voltage Regulator

4

5

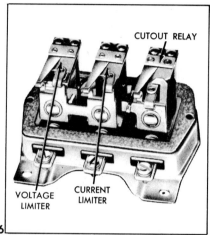

CUTOUT RELAY

VOLTAGE LIMITER CURRENT LIMITER

6

7

8

together. When this happens no current is sent to the field windings, and alternator output ceases.

Each progressive movement of the movable contact results in lowered output of the alternator, which means that the coil controlling the regulator armature puts out less magnetic force. Less magnetic force means that the movable contact will move up to its previous position. When it gets back to that position, the regulator coil gains strength, so the movable point goes down again.

Delco voltage regulator relays are constructed opposite to those of Chrysler and Ford. In the Delco design the double points are on the armature, and the single double-faced point is stationary. The coil and spring arrangement is different also. The result is that the resistor contact is the lower one, and the shorting contact is the upper one. In any event, the effect on the alternator (or generator) output is the same with either design.

In reality, these contacts usually stay busier than a watch dog in a fire hydrant factory. They seldom ever come completely to rest in any one position, but are in constant vibratory motion. When there is a fair electrical system load, and the engine is running slowly, the armature vibrates against the resistor contact. In doing so, it alternately sends *full current* and *resistor-reduced current* to the field coil. The varying proportion of one to the other determines the strength of the rotor's magnetic field, and hence the alternator's output. Since the voltage limiter's coil is sensitive to electrical system load, it varies the rate of vibration to change the alternator's field strength in direct proportion to the electrical system's load. If engine speed is high and there is only a light electrical system load, more current is made available to the relay windings, and the armature begins to vibrate against the shorting contact. This means that it will be alternately supplying resistor-reduced voltage and "zero" voltage to the alternator field. The alternator's

erable leeway for repair or any necessary adjustments.

All regulators used with alternator systems commonly employ double-contact, voltage-limiting relays—unless this function is transistorized. The Chrysler Corp. and Ford relay armatures have a double-faced contact with stationary contacts mounted above and below it so that the contact on the movable armature may touch one or the other of these depending on the armature's position. When the upper contacts are closed, full voltage is supplied to the field

windings, and the alternator is permitted to produce its maximum output. If the resultant voltage exceeds the demands of the electrical system, the relay core begins to build up a magnetic field, thereby attracting the relay's armature. When the armature floats between the upper and lower contacts, the field current is lowered by forcing it to flow through a resistor located under the regulator's base. If the magnetic attraction is strong enough to pull the armature even further against its controlling spring tension, the lower contacts are brought

Regulators

output is therefore reduced considerably for the protection of the battery, lights and various accessories.

To prevent the regulator from being subjected to electrical surges while the limiter relay is vibrating, there is a resistor of about 50 ohms connected from the regulator's field terminal to ground.

On Delco-Remy circuits that use an indicator light without a separate relay, the path of the electricity gets a little tricky. Instead of using current from the ignition switch to close the field relay, actual charge current from the alternator is used. When the ignition is switched on, battery current flows through the indicator lamp and a low-ohmage resistor wired in parallel with it. From here it proceeds through the relay contacts of the voltage regulator to the field coil of the alternator. This small current is adequate to lightly magnetize the field poles of the rotor and initiate the production of electrical current. The low-powered current that results serves only to close the field relay, which then allows the voltage limiter to supply full battery current to the alternator's field windings. Since the main load of the charging system's field current is now being transmitted through the regulator from the battery, the charge indicator light consequently goes out.

The alternator's regulator uses bi-metal hinges and/or springs to compensate for temperature variations which affect the charging needs of the battery.

TRANSISTORIZED REGULATORS

The use of transistors to control the limiting circuits in alternator system regulators was spearheaded by General Motors with their introduction of a regulator containing twin diodes. This device still relied on the use of electromagnetic relays to carry out the actual voltage-regulating and field-control operations—the diodes being incorporated solely to prevent current backflow. They were, in effect, merely solid-state switches. The trend in later years has been to make even conventional regulators "sealed" units which are not to be adjusted, but only replaced in the event of malfunction. The latest transistorized regulators also follow this pattern, but at least in the case of those supplied on some newer models, there is an adjusting screw that makes it possible to control voltage output.

Since there is no way to take these regulators apart to work on them—indeed, no reason to even contemplate the necessity—there is little use of going too deeply into precisely how their circuits function. However, two or three general points should be discussed.

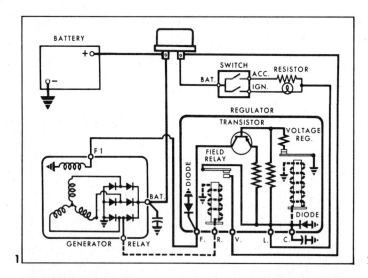

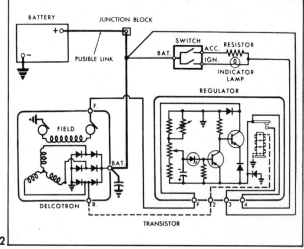

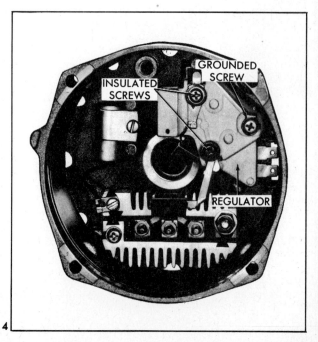

1. *Earliest GM transistorized regulators—starting in 1963—still had two functions carried out through the use of mechanical relays; single transistor carries out part of the voltage-limiting function.*

2. *In intermediate versions of the GM transistorized regulators, the entire voltage-limiting function is transistorized, and the relay only controls field current. Compare this with the latest version shown near the beginning of the chapter.*

3. *Mechanical regulators may be located anywhere in the engine compartment, but are usually on a vertical surface, so that weight of the armatures does not affect their operation.*

4. *In many recent systems, the regulator is inside the alternator case. These fully transistorized regulators almost never need service.*

5. *Increasing the spring tension increases the voltage on all models of electro-mechanical regulators. Check the direction of bend needed to produce the required change.*

6. *Three-unit regulators are usually for generator systems. Only a few special alternators have three-unit regulators in their control systems.*

7. *Most regulators are adjusted by bending the tabs holding the relay springs and gap limiters. Adjustments should be carried out according to recommendations in the manufacturer's service manuals.*

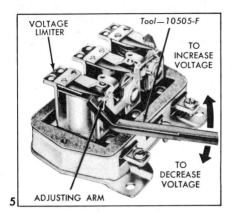

5

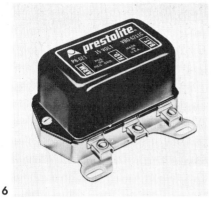

6

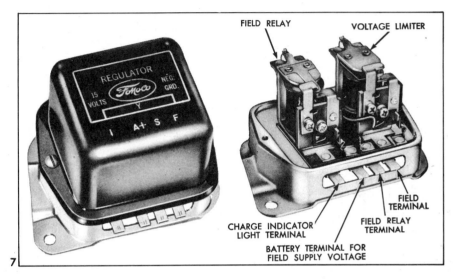

7

The first is that the circuits between a transistorized regulator and the alternator are exactly the same as those associated with conventional relay-controlled regulator units. Secondly, the transistors controlling the field current strength are generally triodes which can vary the electrical flow through two of their connections in proportion to the strength of the current fed into their third connection. The precision of their operation and their inherent long service life in comparison to mechanical contact points give them obvious features of superiority over the conventional electro-mechanical devices. Lastly, in those units having a screw permitting adjustments to the charging rate, it is a mistake to assume—as some mechanics have—that they are "adjusting a transistor." Transistors are not adjustable. The adjustment actually controls a variable resistance—or rheostat—that determines the strength of the voltage delivered to the triodes.

GENERATOR SYSTEMS

In actual practice there is considerably more to the voltage regulator than the simple cutout relay shown— at least in this day and age. Generator systems commonly have regulators containing two other additional relays as well. These are designed to

correct various other conditions that might be harmful to either the battery or generator. As we pointed out in the chapter on generators, charging system output increases with engine speed. For this reason there is another relay which limits the unit's total voltage output. This *voltage limiter relay* keeps the generator's output below a predetermined level by controlling the amount of electricity supplied to the field coils. When the charging system output begins to approach higher voltages than would be healthy for the car's light bulbs, battery and accessories, the voltage limiter relay must "apply the brakes" on the generator's production capacity.

There is also a *current limiter relay* in regulators used with generator-based charging systems. Its job is to protect the generator's armature windings by limiting the maximum amount of the electrical system's load that can be assumed by the generator. Like the voltage limiter, the current limiter performs its function by controlling the amount of current delivered to the generator's field coils. The current limiter therefore serves to protect the generator when the electrical system load is high, while the voltage limiter protects the battery, lights, etc., when the electrical system load is low.

A visual inspection of a generator-system regulator unit will show that each of the three relays is different from the other in appearance as well as function. The cutout relay is easy to spot since it has a large-diameter coil made up of very heavy copper wire. The cutout is also the only relay which has its contact points held open rather than closed by spring tension. Most cutout relays also have either an extra large contact—often consisting of two heavy tungsten alloy squares—or dual contacts that, while round in cross section, are quite large in diameter. The heavier contacts of the cutout relay are necessary since they must carry the generator's entire output to the battery and electrical system.

A more detailed examination of the cutout relay will show that there is also a fine wire leading to its coil. This is because there is another smaller coil made up of fine windings concealed beneath the heavy copper wire of the exterior coil. The smaller coil is connected from generator output to ground. When the generator starts to charge, no current can go through the large coil because the cutout points are open. But current can go through the small coil to ground, and it is the magnetism from this small coil that closes the cutout.

Regulators

When the cutout points close, current flows through the large coil, and its magnetism is added to that of the small coil, holding the points closed that much tighter. If the engine is idled or shut off, battery current will start to flow back into the generator because it is not turning enough to put out. When the current flows in a reverse direction through the heavy coil, the magnetism reverses, and the cutout is kicked open.

The current limiter relay is wound only with large-diameter copper wire, while the voltage relay has many turns of fine wire about its core. Both relays have relatively small contacts which are more than able to handle the field current delivered to the generator's stationary coils through them. Some regulators have a fusible wire connecting the field contacts of these two relays to prevent the generator windings from damage in the event that one of the limiters' contact-"weld" together. The contacts of both the voltage limiters are in almost constant vibration. By this action they control the amount of current available to the generator's field. A resistance between the regulator's field terminal and ground "damps out" the electrical surges produced by these vibrations to further protect the system from any damage.

Voltage regulator relays can have either single or double contacts. The double contact units are more precise in their control of generator voltage, as explained earlier in this chapter under Alternator Systems. Voltage regulators operate in the same manner, whether they're used with a generator or an alternator.

It will be noticed that the flat springs and/or hinges used in the relay armatures (their movable parts) are stamped with words, letters, numbers or abbreviations. These are metallurgical indications of the type of material from which the springs and hinges are made. Generator regulators are designed to provide automatic compensation for temperature variations as well as for changes in electrical conditions. The springs and/or hinges are therefore cut from a bi-metal plate which changes its degree of tension in precise relation to ambient temperature. As we observed in the battery chapter, a higher charging-system output is required to handle the car's electrical system and battery-charging load in cold weather, while a corresponding reduction of the charge rate is dictated by a return to warmer temperatures.

It is extremely important that, for the sake of the battery, any warm

1. Two different types of early GM regulators. The double-relay type is on the left and the first type of transistorized regulator is on right.

2. Typical two-unit regulators used with alternators. Since alternators are self current-limiting, only a voltage-limiter relay is necessary.

3. This regulator is adjusted by means of a bendable spring post. Best tool for the job is the special one made by Snap-On.

4. Some regulators have a Phillips-head screw which is used for adjusting spring tension.

5. Adjust the early GM transistorized voltage regulator air gap as shown.

6. The metal tab must be bent on early GM transistorized regulator to adjust voltage-control relay.

7. On this Delco-Remy regulator, you bend the upper contact arm to adjust the point opening.

8. Most early Chrysler products with alternators have single-relay regulators. The unit draws battery current from the ignition and controls voltage by regulating the field current.

9. As in generator systems, there are resistors under the base of alternator-system regulators. Their function is to prevent electrical surges which may result from regulator functions.

10. Inside view of early Chrysler Corp. single-relay regulator. Double contacts are used, as in most alternator-system voltage limiters. Two wires at left side of contact-mounting post are fuse wires.

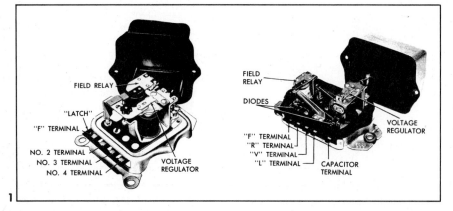

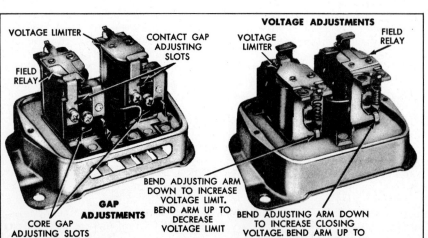

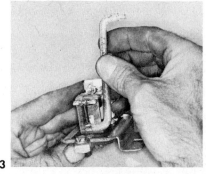

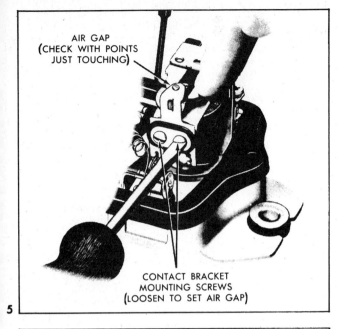

5

AIR GAP
(CHECK WITH POINTS
JUST TOUCHING)

CONTACT BRACKET
MOUNTING SCREWS
(LOOSEN TO SET AIR GAP)

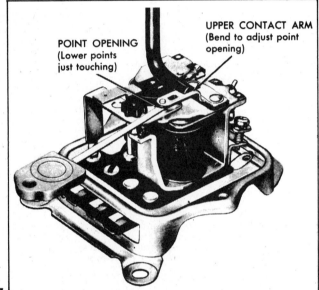

7

POINT OPENING
(Lower points
just touching)

UPPER CONTACT ARM
(Bend to adjust point
opening)

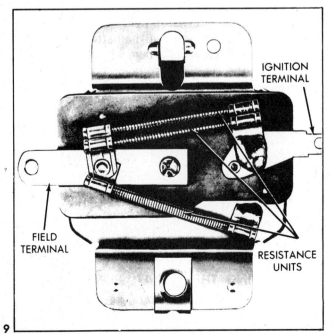

9

IGNITION
TERMINAL

FIELD
TERMINAL

RESISTANCE
UNITS

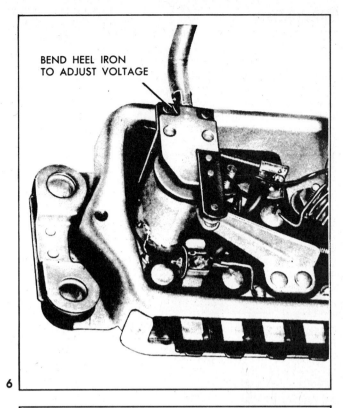

6

BEND HEEL IRON
TO ADJUST VOLTAGE

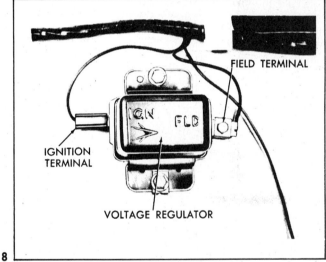

8

FIELD TERMINAL

IGNITION
TERMINAL

VOLTAGE REGULATOR

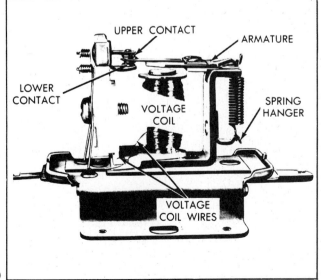

10

UPPER CONTACT

ARMATURE

LOWER
CONTACT

VOLTAGE
COIL

SPRING
HANGER

VOLTAGE
COIL WIRES

Regulators

weather overcharging be prevented. Whenever voltage regulators are readjusted, the unit must first be warmed up until its temperature has stabilized at a normal level. Most car makers specify that the unit's prescribed voltage output be achieved at a temperature of from 70° to 80° Fahrenheit. Further, it will usually take at least ½-hour of operation in the car to reach the regulator's own stable operating temperature. If attempts are made to adjust the regulator without taking temperature into consideration, it is impossible to expect the battery to receive the proper ''dose'' under all sorts of varying temperature conditions.

TROUBLESHOOTING & ADJUSTMENTS

Unless the field circuit and brush tests described in the preceding two chapters turn up an obvious source of trouble, it's advisable to give the regulator at least a casual inspection before bothering to remove and disassemble the generator or alternator itself. Certain other troubles that definitely indicate regulator malfunctions can often be spotted by the behavior of the dash-mounted ammeter. One of the most common symptoms is an ammeter needle that proceeds up and down the scale from a high charge rate to a low discharge in direct proportion to engine speed. This condition is very harmful to the battery and should be corrected immediately. Since the cause is usually either a burned-out resistance in the regulator or a faulty relay winding, the only practical cure is to install a new regulator. Actually, the only regulator troubles that you should attempt to correct by repair and/or adjustment are those involving incorrect

charge rates or a no-charge condition. If this is the case, the regulator should be calibrated exactly to the car maker's specifications and, if such adjustment proves impossible, the unit should be scrapped in favor of a new one. It's just not worth taking a chance that by trying to save $20 on a regulator, you may end up ruining at least $100 worth of battery and generator.

A no-charge problem—if caused by the regulator—is limited to two possibilities. First, the contacts controlling current to the alternator or generator field may not be making contact. An inspection of the contacts' condition will usually determine if such is the case. Secondly, the regulator may contain fuse wires which are designed to melt under abnormally high charging conditions for the protection of the alternator or generator. The regulator should be inspected visually to see if it has fuse wires, and if so to determine whether they have separated. The cause of the burned-out fuse wire probably lies in the regulator itself, so it's a must that it be thoroughly tested according to the car maker's instructions before renewing the fuse wires and returning the regulator to service. For the protection of the alternator, these wires must be replaced with fusible wire of the proper material.

A low charging system output, usually accompanied by a low battery, probably results from improper calibration of the regulator. The unit's charge rate should therefore be readjusted to bring it within the manufacturer's specifications. A low, unsteady charging rate is usually caused by a high resistance somewhere in the charging system or its connections—including the battery posts and terminals. In some instances this may result from the formation of oxidation deposits on the regulator contacts.

The presence of dirt and deposits is usually apparent upon taking the cover from the regulator unit. The relays can normally be cleaned and the contacts lightly burnished with a ''riffler'' file without upsetting the unit's standard adjustment.

An excessive charge rate is the most dangerous condition that can develop in the electrical system. In some cases the regulator may merely be set too high. This could be the result of recalibrating the unit without first bringing it to the proper operating temperature. It can also stem from non-functioning relays or regulator contacts which have stuck or welded together. Both of these conditions call for replacement of the regulator unit. Another common cause of excessive charge rates is a poorly grounded regulator. Some cars do not have a separate ground connection for the regulator, which must then depend on having its base in good electrical contact with the body of the car. Try connecting a jumper wire between the regulator base and a clean spot on the car's body or chassis. If the charge rate then be-

1. Alternator circuit used on some earlier Ford and Lincoln-Mercury products had the field grounded in the regulator instead of in the alternator. More recent Fords no longer have the regulator mounted on the alternator.

2. Many Chrysler product regulators have fusible wires to prevent damage to units in event of an overload.

3. Transistor technology has allowed a considerable reduction in size and weight of regulators, along with a quantum jump in their reliability.

4. Converting an early-model engine to use late-model alternators and regulators will increase efficiency and reliability of its electrical systems and allow the use of a number of electrical accessories.

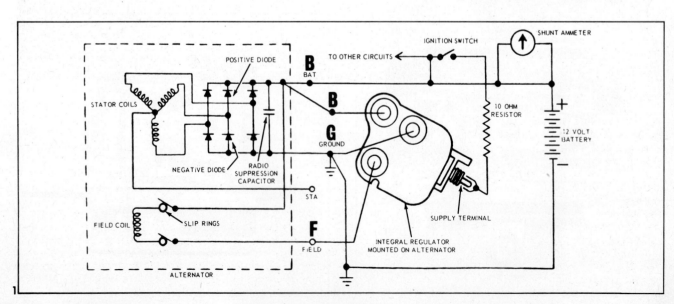

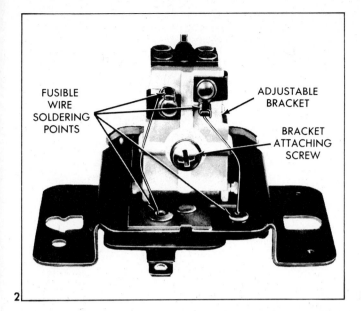

FUSIBLE WIRE SOLDERING POINTS

ADJUSTABLE BRACKET

BRACKET ATTACHING SCREW

2

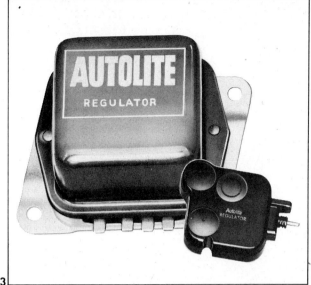

AUTOLITE REGULATOR

3

comes normal, it is only necessary to correct the regulator's contact with ground.

When installing a new regulator on a generator-equipped car it is of the utmost importance that the generator be polarized before starting the engine. If this is not done, the generator—or regulator—will be burned out in the first few minutes of operation. This is especially important on cars having only idiot lights. An ammeter will show a no-charge condition when the engine is started without first polarizing the system; the light may not. Should you accidentally reverse the system's polarity and start the engine, remove the battery ground cable before shutting off the motor to save the generator from possible damage due to unregulated battery current flowing "backwards" into the windings. When making an engine swap, polarizing the generator and regulator is sometimes overlooked in the confusion of taking care of so many other important details. If you're the rod-building type, don't neglect this important step before firing up for the first time.

The generator must be polarized before starting the engine. All you have to do is momentarily touch a jumper wire between the generator (Arm. or Gen.) terminal and the battery terminal of the regulator. The jumper should only be connected for a fraction of a second. If you leave it on any longer, you will burn up the points in the voltage regulator on some double contact regulators. If you want to be 100% safe, remove the field lead from the regulator and ground it, then flash between the armature and battery terminals to polarize any generator with an "A" circuit.

An "A" field circuit is one that has the field grounded at the regulator. A "B" circuit has the field grounded at

4

the generator. As a general rule, all generators are "A" circuit, except Ford generators which are "B." All alternators are "B" circuit, except integral regulator types which are usually "A" circuit. You have to know which is which so you can hot wire current to the fields when making tests on either alternators or generators, and when polarizing generators.

Alternator systems are never polarized. They do not depend on residual magnetism in the field. If you ever memorized a no-no, now is the time to do it: *Never*, under any circumstances, should you make any attempt to *polarize an alternator*.

To sum up, a regulator is an amazing little device that probably does more to keep the electrical system functioning properly than any other single component. It's not an item that the hot rodder will want to modify or improve upon, but it's one piece of equipment that no hot rod, custom or passenger car can get along without. Keeping a check on its operation is the best insurance you can have against premature battery or electrical system failure.

Instruments

THE CARE AND FEEDING OF THOSE NECESSARY TELLTALES

A driver's dashboard instruments are his main line of communication with the car's engine and electrical system. Anyone who has not learned the importance of instruments or who has not made it a part of his driving technique to scan their readings periodically is a person subject to surprise by "sudden" failures and malfunctions. When somebody tells you that his car's alternator or regulator has burned out "for no reason at all" or that its engine has incurred major damage "without warning" due to overheating or lack of lubrication, you can bet your last dollar that he has not formed the basic good driving habit of keeping a constant check on the dash gauges.

In past years, mechanical gauges of one sort or another were used for indicating fuel level, oil pressure, water temperature and engine rpm. Although such instruments are not completely unknown today, they are becoming about as rare as hip flasks at a weekly meeting of the Ladies' Aid Society. Mechanical fuel gauges were the first to go—especially after the invention of a reliable fuel pump allowed the high-mounted gas tanks of the Model A era to be stowed safely and conveniently under the rear of the car. However, converting the other common instruments to electrical operation has been done more for convenience and reliability than out of sheer necessity.

The electrical instruments normally found in production automobiles are not intended to be highly accurate, but their indications are nonetheless relatively precise, considering their simplicity and low cost. They are designed so that their readings change in proportion to the resistance in an electrical circuit that is wired through them. To prevent the fluctuations in their readings that might be induced by changes in the electrical system load, a voltage limiting device is incorporated into the system which assures the gauges a stable source of electricty. Many early fuel gauges were electromagnetic in operation and did not need a voltage limiter—only a steady resistance. But since they registered every ripple in the surface of the fuel supply, they were often more useful as accelerometers than as gas gauges. Currently, most gauges are of the thermal type; they react slowly to current changes and produce more steady "average" readings.

VOLTAGE LIMITERS

The voltage limiter keeps the current delivered to the instruments at a steady level. Actually, its output fluctuates between 0 and 7—sometimes 10—volts, but since the instruments react slowly, the effect is the same as constant current of approximately 5 volts. The voltage delivered to the instruments is kept well below the 12 volts at which the battery is rated. That way, when voltage in the electrical system drops due to the burden of lighting and accessory loads, it is still well above the minimum figure that is required to operate the necessary gauges accurately.

The operation of the voltage limiter is controlled by a bimetallic arm which flexes when heated, opening a set of contact points. Surrounding the bimetal strip is a coil of fine wire that receives battery current as long as the contact points are together. When the ignition switch is turned on, current is sent through the contacts and the fine wire heating coil. When the

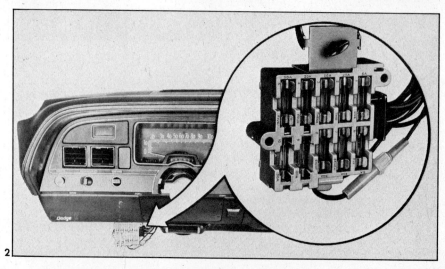

coil has raised the temperature of the bimetallic strip to a precise level, the strip bends to open the contacts. This cuts off current to the heating coil as well as to the instruments. As the strip cools, the contacts come together once again and the cycle is repeated. When the car is first started, it sometimes takes a bit longer for the bimetal strip to reach its cutout temperature, so the gauges ascend to an abnormally high reading for a few seconds before returning to their correct level.

Cars equipped only with a fuel gauge commonly have the voltage limiter built right into the gauge itself.

1. If you're lucky, the gauge faces on your car are accessible by snapping off the outer bezel and cover. You can't do much to the instrument itself from this side, but at least you can reach the light bulb (arrow).

2. Chrysler one-upped the industry for '74 with a handy fold-down fuse block for easy accessibility.

3. Old cars had a nearly flat panel that formed the dash, and the gauges came out from the back side after undoing hard-to-reach screws or nuts. Engineers have helped the at-home tinkerer now, though, by making most gauges and dials accessible from the car's front seat—after removal of any trim panels (like the lower skirt shown here) and the cluster bezel. This allows gauge access within the cluster carrier.

4. The owner of this car installed accessory or aftermarket gauges to augment his idiot lights. Add-on panels are available that contain anywhere from one to up to four gauges.

5. AMC Pacer owners will find that their idiot lights are accessible by snapping off the instrument cluster bezel. There aren't even any screws to take out. Gauge cluster also comes out from the front.

Cars that have additional instruments occasionally use the gas gauge limiter to supply stable current to the other dials as well; however, in most instances multiple gauges are served by a common voltage limiter that is a unit by itself.

THERMAL GAUGES

The thermal gauges used for fuel, water temperature and oil pressure are usually identical in construction, but have different faces and sending units. Their operation is similar to that of the voltage limiter itself, being controlled by a bimetallic strip which flexes in proportion to the heat it receives. Here, however, the strip does not operate a set of contacts, but is coupled directly to the gauge's indicator needle. The reading produced by the needle is directly proportional to the degree of flex in the bimetal strip. The sending units for the gauges vary the resistance of each control circuit in precise relation to

whatever is being measured. Current passing through the gauges' heating elements is therefore varied according to the condition sensed by the sending units.

In the case of the fuel gauge, a movable float located in the gas tank controls the position of a wiping contact against a semicircular resistance coil. This is actually a simple rheostat. When the fuel level falls, the resistance is increased, allowing less current to flow from the voltage to the sending unit's ground connection. Since this reduced current also passes through the gauge, its bimetal strip cools proportionately and moves the needle to a lower reading on the dial. Resistance is lowest when the tank is full, and the resultant increase in current flow heats the gauge's bimetallic strip to produce the maximum reading.

The oil pressure gauges installed on some present-day automobiles are of the type operated mechanically by

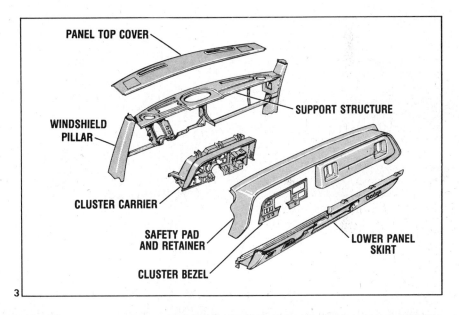

PANEL TOP COVER

SUPPORT STRUCTURE

WINDSHIELD PILLAR

CLUSTER CARRIER

SAFETY PAD AND RETAINER

LOWER PANEL SKIRT

CLUSTER BEZEL

3

4

5

Instruments

an oil line attached to the engine's lubrication system. However, most cars have switched to electric oil pressure gauges in recent years. Electric oil pressure gauge sending units generally consist of a small sealed cylinder that has a diaphragm or piston inside which engine oil can bear against when under pressure. The piston is spring loaded and connected to a variable resistance that functions similarly to that found in the fuel tank sending unit. The greater the oil pressure the lower the electrical resistance and the higher the gauge's reading.

Water temperature gauges have a different sort of sending unit since the quantity being measured (heat) cannot be converted directly into mechanical motion as can fuel level and oil pressure. The means of varying the resistance in the water temperature sending unit must therefore be different. A disc of heat-sensitive material is incorporated in the temperature sending unit that changes its level of conductivity in proportion to its temperature. When the engine is cold, the resistance of the disc is high and little or no current is allowed to pass through the gauge circuit. As engine temperature increases, the disc becomes more and more conductive, permitting a greater current to pass through it to ground so that the flow through the dash gauge is strengthened. Many older American cars, as well as some current foreign machines, have a mechanical temperature gauge which employs a copper tube to couple the engine with the gauge. There is a sealed bulb containing a volatile liquid suspended in the cooling system, and as the temperature increases the liquid begins to expand and fill a metal bellows that moves the indicator needle on the gauge. Since vibration will often cause the copper tube to eventually break, the change to electric temperature gauges has been a most welcome one.

AMMETERS AND IDIOT LIGHTS

Of the common dashboard instruments, the ammeter alone is different in its operation from all the others. Most ammeters used in sensitive electronic equipment applications have an electromagnetic coil which moves a piece of iron attached to the indicator needle or, in others, a movable coil that is deflected when its magnetic field reacts to a fixed magnet or piece of iron. The ammeter on the dash of your car comes closest to being of the movable iron type, but it is very greatly simplified. The wire serving the ammeter is, in most cars, not connected electrically to the meter but merely passes through a loop by the back of the instrument. A small magnet inside the gauge is affected by the passage of current through the wire. When current is flowing from the charging system into the battery, the magnet moves the pointer in the "charge" direction. When the battery takes over the electrical system's load, current flows in the opposite direction and the pointer is drawn into the "discharge" zone.

Indicator lights are often used in conjunction with gauges for the purpose of attracting the driver's attention when something abnormal is taking place so that (hopefully) he'll take time to check the dials and find out what's wrong. The only flaw in this scheme is that drivers who do not bother to check their gauges are just

1

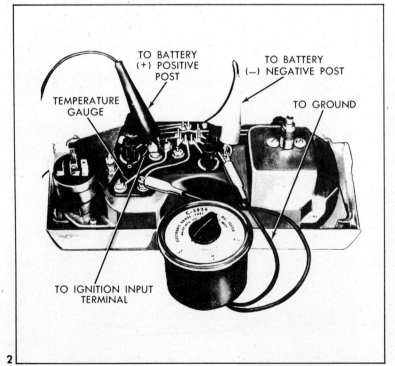

TO BATTERY (+) POSITIVE POST

TO BATTERY (−) NEGATIVE POST

TO GROUND

TEMPERATURE GAUGE

TO IGNITION INPUT TERMINAL

2

3

as unlikely to look for little winking lights. Even if the light does draw his glance toward the instruments, it's not likely that he'll understand what they're telling him anyway. If he did, he'd have been watching them in the first place.

Cars with only warning lights for oil pressure, coolant temperature and battery charge, place the driver in a very poor position for anything other than normal, conservative driving. Even if the car never sees a drag strip or a road race course, regular high-speed freeway driving can create conditions that may completely wreck an engine or electrical system before the lights tell you anything at all. For example, some generator warning lights do not even begin to glow until the battery is being discharged at a rate of from 10 to 15 amperes. Worse yet, none of them will warn the driver of overcharging. Regulator failures that can destroy the battery or generator often go undetected at high speeds until it's too late to make any difference.

Oil pressure warning lights are often set to stay off until pressure has

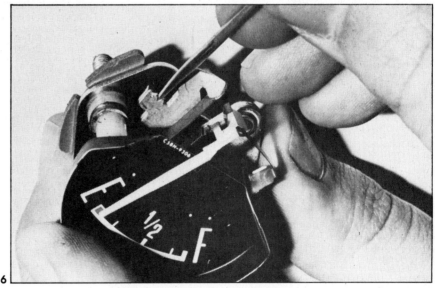

1. HI Enterprises offers custom instrument panels for many vans, all fitted with Sun instruments.

2. A variable-resistance unit like this is used to test gauges in shops that handle this work. Note the printed circuit instrument panel—a common practice on many late-model cars.

3. Mounting with a modern, modular look is possible with S-W's new gauge housing modules, available with or without the mounting "foot." This one houses a Stage III vacuum gauge—definitely a popular gauge with today's economy-minded drivers.

4. It isn't easy to get your hands up there to do instrument work. One trick is to remove the radio and work through the opening. You can do a lot through the ashtray, too.

5. Sun Super Tach uses a sending unit such as this. Two terminals serve tach; one connects to coil primary and the other is for ground. The "black box" also contains tiny replaceable mercury cells that actually power the tachometer.

6. This gauge has a toothed rack used at the factory for calibrating. The instrument can be readjusted as shown with a small screwdriver.

7. Mounted here in a three-gauge panel from their Super Sub-Panel line are Smiths performance vacuum and oil temperature gauges. In the center is one of their unique dual-reading gauges that shows both oil pressure and water temperature. The others are vacuum and oil temperature.

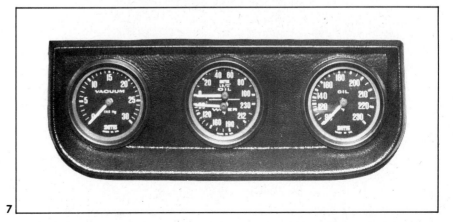

dropped to less than 7 psi. A bearing that's starting to go or an oil pump that is losing its bite will not show up on such a gauge. If you happen to be cruising the turnpike at 55 mph, you'll probably be ripe for a complete engine rebuild long before the light comes on.

Temperature indicators are generally more satisfactory—providing they indicate both hot and cold conditions. But even here, an overheating condition may already have become critical before you are warned that anything is amiss.

AFTERMARKET GAUGES

Keeping the foregoing in mind, it should not be surprising to anybody that ammeters and oil pressure gauges are among the hottest-selling accessory items on the automotive market. Additional instruments are available from new car dealers, parts stores, speed shops, mail-order companies, discount stores, the five-and-ten and—so help me—drug stores. In all probability there's a friendly neighborhood tavern somewhere that sells them across the bar.

Prices can range from about $20 for an inexpensive three-dial ammeter, oil pressure and water temperature combination to almost the same amount for individual gauges. The difference in price from the least expensive to the most expensive instruments reflects variations in both appearance and construction. The lower-priced units are comparable in quality to those supplied by car makers as original equipment and are accurate enough for highway use, even if their appearance is generally none too elegant.

The more expensive gauges are usually more accurate. Some are of a quality suitable for such precision work as calibrating the voltage regulator or adjusting oil pressure bypass valves. Many of the more refined instruments are electromagnetic rather than thermal in operation, and have a small rotating armature that is controlled by a magnetic field. These units generally include a damper mechanism to prevent erratic pointer movement.

For the most part, the difference in price between one set of instruments and another is strictly a matter of price versus engineering. Pay a little more and you'll get a little more in the way of accuracy. If you're just looking for reasonably accurate and attractive instruments that can be added to a stock passenger car dashboard to replace or supplement the idiot lights, stick to the lower-

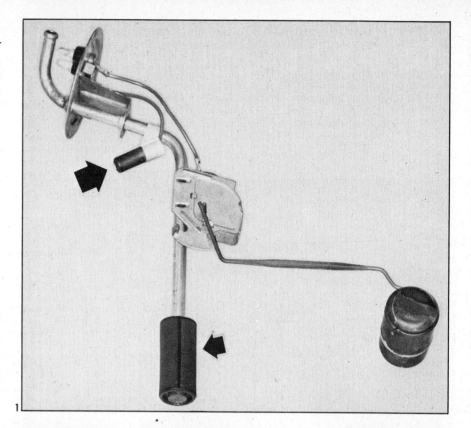

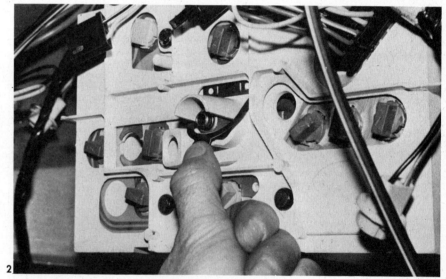

priced models. After a couple of years you won't feel so bad about trading them with the car. (Getting around to removing them always seems to take more effort than their installation did.) Find a set that offers fairly neat appearance at a modest price and you'll probably discover that their accuracy level is more than adequate for highway driving.

Many of the less-expensive gauge sets come installed in small panels suitable for under-dash mounting. The location makes them a bit hard to see, but the instrument panels on most production cars do not readily lend themselves to in-the-dash mountings.

There are a number of complete instrument panels available for custom installations, and these are definitely worth the car owner's consideration. However, many attractive custom mountings are also made possible by some of the accessories sold for use with standard 2 1/16-in. and 2⅝-in. gauges. These include recessed mountings and angle-mount bezels, to name just two.

For the really mechanically minded enthusiast, there are additional instruments not normally thought of as standard on automobile dashboards. Some, such as altimeters, inside/outside thermometers, accelerometers and air speed indicators, are of very limited use in a car, but are nevertheless sometimes installed for appearance or for the sheer love of gimmickry. However, voltmeters, transmission or differential temperature

gauges and vacuum gauges can be of definite value to the driver.

A voltmeter, for example, tells the driver a bit more about the condition of his car's electrical system than an ammeter does. The ammeter merely indicates whether the battery or the generator is doing more of the work in the electrical system. It also tells the driver whether the charging system is functioning normally. It does not really give a very good picture of the actual condition of the battery in terms of its power; a voltmeter does. When the voltmeter begins to indicate lower-than-normal "pressure" in the

system, it's time to check the battery and voltage regulator. Battery failures are predicted in advance this way.

TACHOMETERS

Probably one of the most useful instruments that you can add to a car is a tachometer. Tachs are offered either as options or standard equipment on many cars, but these factory-supplied instruments are sometimes of very dubious quality. Worse yet, they are usually sealed units that cannot be repaired when they quit working.

1. Fuel warning light on dash hooks to sending unit (large arrow). When unit is covered with fuel, light stays out. Other arrow shows filter.

2. Here's how to disconnect a speedometer cable on most late-model cars. Thumb-operated tang allows cable connection to be pulled straight off.

3. A few cars still use mechanical oil pressure gauges. They are also available as an accessory. Pen in photo points to connection on back of gauge, which must be connected by an oil line to the engine's lubricating system. The large hole is for illuminating light.

4. Some Chevy V-8's have their temperature sending unit screwed in low on the side of the head, in order to get a better reading.

5. Cal Custom/Hawk makes this fully transistorized wide-sweep tach. It's designed for 4, 6 and 8-cylinder cars. The gauge is a good one, but the mounting location on this VW is definitely too low for safe reading.

6. Accurate and rugged, the top of the Stewart-Warner line is the Professional series of black and white gauges, available in 2 1/16-in. or 2⅝-in. sizes. Mechanical gauges like the one at right feature a 270° scale.

Instruments

If you need a tach, check those available at nearby specialty equipment stores. You'll find that even superlative instruments sell for less than most of the factory-installed options. Furthermore, you'll probably get a worthwhile guarantee. When shopping for your tach, find out if the unit can be serviced—either by returning it to the factory or by turning it over to a shop specializing in such repairs. You can check the classified ads in the back of major automotive magazines such as *Hot Rod* and *Car Craft* if you wish to find addresses of dealers handling a full line of gauges. It might even pay you to contact one of these businesses and ask them which tachs they are equipped to service and which makes, in their opinion, offer the greatest reliability.

There are dozens of tachometers on the market, and some of them are none too good from either the durability or accuracy point of view. It doesn't help you very much to find a brand that's $10 cheaper than the tach you'd really like to have if the cheaper model turns out to be a short-lived dud that cannot even be fixed.

Tachometer dial layouts get a lot of attention in the instrument makers' advertising, but often get too little from prospective buyers. The greater the sweep of the needle, the further apart the dial calibrations can be, making for greater accuracy and ease in reading. However, some units which advertise a 250° to 270° sweep can do so only because their scale extends to 10,000 rpm. This means that on the average passenger car—which is all used up at about 5000 rpm—half the scale will be useless. You'll really have only a 125° or 135° sweep instrument. A wide sweep of about 250° on a 7000-rpm scale is what's really needed for most ordinary cars.

REPAIRING AND RECALIBRATING GAUGES

If you check most of the official service manuals, you'll find that nothing is said about repairing or recalibrating gauges. Frankly, it's neither simple nor advisable to attempt adjusting them in some cases. The basic reason that the car manufacturers advise replacement rather than repair is that it would cost more in labor to adjust a set of damaged gauges than it would to replace them. In the majority of cases in which the gauges have stopped working altogether, the problem is somewhere in the wiring. Usually a wire has broken, or there is corrosion under the terminal nut on the sending unit. Thermal gauges themselves simply don't contain many parts that can go haywire.

Instruments mounted in plastic instrument panels are sometimes damaged by losing their ground contact. Ground is often provided to the instrument panel via one of the wires leading to a dial-illuminating lamp. If this is pulled out to replace a bulb with the ignition turned on or if it falls out while driving, the voltage limiter is no longer grounded. It therefore sends full battery current to all the instruments it serves. Their pointers are then forced far above the normal scale and the bimetallic strips that control them may be deformed per-

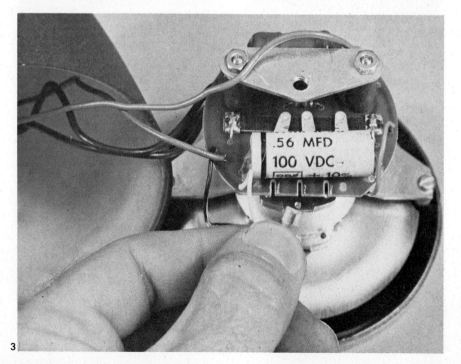

1. *Auto Meter offers custom electric speedometers in either 160- or 200-mph calibrations. These units match their high-performance line of tachometers. They are not odometer-equipped.*

2. *The back of this temperature gauge requires that insulating washers be placed over the studs to keep the terminals from contacting the case. The terminal on the left is upside down, producing a direct short to ground that will probably ruin something.*

3. *S-W "ET" tachs can be shifted for use on 4, 6 or 8-cylinder cars by moving terminal inside case.*

4. *Voltmeters are also popular add-on instruments. They give an accurate indication of battery condition and also detect abnormal loads placed on the battery by shorts.*

5. *This fuel pressure gauge, made by Auto Meter, is one of the best on the market today.*

6. *One of the best tachometers available is this Auto Meter 270 series model. The sender is mounted inside the chrome cup.*

7. *The top of Hawk's instrument line is the VFG (Very Fine Gauges) series. Built to take even the vibration of a funny car or fuel dragster, these instruments are some of the only gear-driven gauges on the market today.*

8. *These are the "works" in a common thermal instrument. Notice the fine heating wire wrapped around the bimetal strip. Due to the low voltage and light current load, this kind of gauge lasts practically forever.*

manently to a slight degree. After proper ground is restored, the damaged instruments will record readings that are far from normal, usually quite a bit lower than they actually should be indicating.

Most gauges have to be calibrated at the factory before they are installed. For this reason there is usually some means of adjusting the pointer position. It may be that a metal tab must be bent, or the gauge assembly may have a gear-toothed rack or screwdriver slot for the purpose. Their manufacturer adjusts them by coupling the gauge to a known output source and turning or bending the adjustment provision until the pointer indicates the correct figure. If your gauges have become accidentally damaged so that their readings are no longer accurate, take them out and inspect them. It may be possible to correct the condition yourself.

The best procedure is to set the pointers at zero and then attach them to the car's wiring once again without actually installing them in the dash. Operate the engine until it is thoroughly warmed up and check the gauge readings. They can then be readjusted slightly until they once again register the figures that you have learned are their normal reading. For more precise recalibration, you can adjust their pointers to match the figure recorded on a shop-tested ammeter or oil pressure gauge.

Since the gauges rely on a precise amount of heat to make them function properly, their fronts must be covered by the glass or plastic lenses just as they are when the instruments are installed in the dash. Otherwise, heat will escape, lowering the readings. The gauges must also be held in an upright position and properly grounded. Fuel level gauges can be set to just barely indicate a full tank immediately after gassing up the car. This will allow you a safe margin for error when approaching the empty position. When fuel gauges stick or give consistently misleading or incorrect readings, the trouble is generally in the sending unit rather than the gauge. ♔

Wiring

UNDERSTANDING AUTOMOTIVE WIRING MAKES IT EASIER TO SPOT TROUBLE, ADD ACCESSORIES OR HITCH UP TO A TRAILER.

Today automobile wiring diagrams are relatively easy to read and understand, compared to what they used to be, but the average person may still find them almost as baffling as a map of the New York subway system. There are a number of traditional symbols which are commonly used by engineers when drawing up electrical system blueprints. At one time, the diagrams presented on the pages of official auto shop manuals were simply copies of these prints.

Unfortunately, most mechanics, unless blessed with a significant background in blueprint reading, often found such diagrams more confusing than helpful. The wiring diagrams supplied by some foreign car manufacturers still retain many of the symbols used by electrical engineers. But for the most part, American car makers have adopted a more pictorial approach for the benefit of the mechan-

ic who has a car to fix right now and obviously can't take time out for a crash course in the vagaries of electrical engineering.

The most noticeable difference between engineering blueprints and shop manual wiring diagrams is that components like switches, batteries, generators, gauges, etc. are represented in auto diagrams by drawings of the part itself rather than a schematic rendering of its circuitry. Simple drawings of an alternator can be understood at a glance, while a collection of looped lines and little arrows (the windings and diodes) may mean almost nothing to the mechanic who's only interested in determining which connection is the field terminal.

Still, certain engineering symbols are indispensable, regardless of how realistic you try to make a wiring diagram. There are times, for example, when the actual circuits of some electrical system component must be

shown in more complete detail. When trying to show exactly how a voltage regulator works, a straight blueprint presentation of the coils, contacts, diodes and resistances shows their relationship much more clearly than a drawing of the actual regulator would. A double-wound relay coil and its core could not be presented as an ordinary picture. You just wouldn't be able to tell for sure whether it had a hidden internal winding or not. Yet this precision is not normally required in an ordinary diagram of a standard wiring system.

The most common symbol found in automotive wiring diagrams is the one used to represent ground. Obviously it would be very confusing if wires that are connected to the car's chassis were shown in the diagram as merely screwed to an undistinguishable hunk of metal. The ground symbol can be seen throughout automotive wiring schematics. It indicates wires

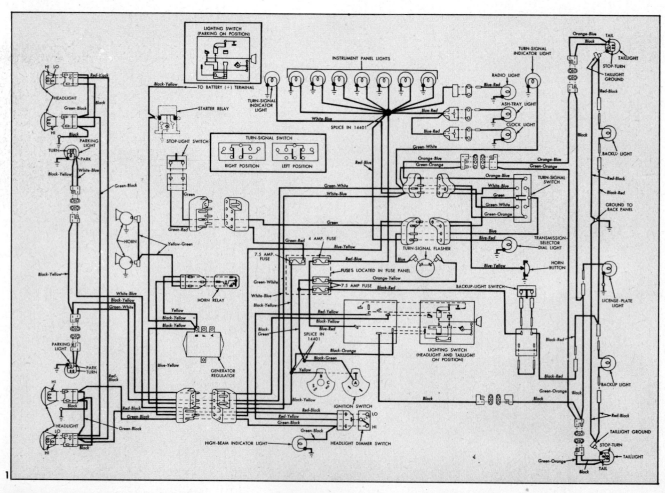

that are in contact with the grounded side of the electrical system via the chassis of the car.

The symbols for positive (+) and negative (−) are generally known, but when they are presented at either end of something that looks like a clump of lines, it may be difficult for the uninitiated to grasp exactly what is meant. Actually, it's only a battery. Most service manual wiring diagrams have an actual picture of the battery, but sometimes—especially where space is limited or where the battery does not play an important part in the circuit—the symbol for a battery is used instead of a picture.

Lights are normally shown as simple loops in blueprints, but shop manual wiring diagrams usually modify this by adding a circle for bulbs and a pictorial approximation for sealed beams. The symbol for a switch is nearly always omitted in favor of a drawing of the actual unit. Ford Motor Co. manuals contain the most traditional wiring diagrams and symbols. Chrysler, GM and American Motors manuals are much more pictorial in their approach to the subject.

To help mechanics locate the various wires that are shown in diagrams on the actual automobile, the wires are color coded. You've no doubt noticed that the insulation on the wires in your own car come in many different colors. Some wires are sheathed in solid colors, while others are combinations of two or more hues. Textile-covered wiring may have various distinguishing patterns woven into the outer sheath.

Even a casual look at a representative wiring diagram will show that beside each wire a color or combination of colors is listed. Some diagrams use abbreviations such as "BW" (black-white) or "G" (green). However, the mechanic probably could not tell if BW meant black-white or blue-white, or whether G meant green or gold. A table is therefore included in one corner of the diagram to tell what color(s) each abbreviation represents. Sometimes a symbol such as "LW" is used for blue-white wires to avoid confusion with BW (black-white). The L, obviously, is not the first letter of the color it indicates.

Some of the newer manuals use longer abbreviations such as BLK, BRN, or DK GRN, LT GRN, the latter meaning two shades of green. Usually a number is also included, such as 14, 16, 18, etc. This number indicates the thickness or gauge of the wire. The gauge can be disregarded unless you are replacing the wire in question, in which case the gauges must match.

CIRCUITS—TESTING AND TRACING

It's fairly easy to follow circuits on most present-day wiring diagrams, but things can get a bit confusing where the wires are shown to pass through an intermediate switch or accessory before reaching their ultimate destination. The following example may serve to illustrate this problem. Let's assume that all four of your car's headlights have stopped working and you have no idea at all where the trouble may be. Trying to find the source of the malfunction by simply checking over the car itself could be a long, involved job. If you inspect the wires coming from the headlight switch, you may discover that their color does not match any of those that you can see attached to the headlights. To further confuse the situation, the wires between these two points are encased in a harness which appears to lead to and from a great many interconnected components. You'd probably spend hours trying to make sense out of it.

The solution to your problem is to consult a wiring diagram. It's amazing how easily you can figure out which wire goes where by spending a few minutes checking the chart. Let's refer to the Ford lighting and horn diagram and assume that this is the diagram for your car. Since all four headlights are inoperative, we can rule out a loose ground connection at the lamps. Starting at the headlights, it can be seen that only two wires serve the four sealed-beam units: a red-black and a green-black. Tracing these from the lights backward into the electrical system, we see that they pass through a multiple connector—one possible trouble spot. Looking beyond the connector, we find that the red-black and green-

1. This Ford lighting and horn wiring diagram is for use in following the hypothetical tests that are described fully in the text.

2. These are some of the many symbols found in wiring diagrams. Note the six cells in the battery. This indicates that it is a 12-volt. A 6-volt battery would have only three cells indicated.

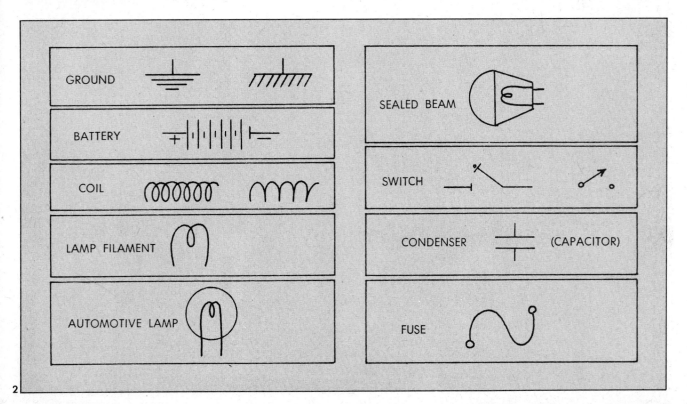

GROUND		SEALED BEAM	
BATTERY		SWITCH	
COIL		CONDENSER	(CAPACITOR)
LAMP FILAMENT			
AUTOMOTIVE LAMP		FUSE	

Wiring

black wires both lead to the dimmer switch, still another potential troublemaker. The only other wire leaving the dimmer switch is a red-yellow one which, sure enough, leads right to the headlight switch.

Your first step is to find out whether current is reaching the multiple connector on the firewall. Pull out the connector and turn on the headlight switch. By inserting the test probe of a test light or voltmeter into the indicated holes in the female connector, you can determine whether current is reaching this point or not. If it is, then the trouble is in the connector plug (which may be misaligned or corroded) or in the wiring to the lights (although it's highly unlikely that both wires would break at the same time).

If no current is reaching the multiple connector, move your point of investigation to the dimmer switch. If current is reaching the switch by way of the red-yellow wire but none is leaving via the red-black or green-black wires, the switch is defective. Here again, the trouble may be a mis-aligned or corroded connector. If no current is being delivered from the main headlight switch, take a look at the taillights. If they're burning normally, the trouble is probably a worn contact in the headlight switch. Another possibility is a break in the red-yellow wire that connects to the switch.

If the taillights are not working either, check the diagram to find the color code of the wire coming from the battery to the headlight switch. You'll see that it is a black-yellow. You can follow this wire all the way from the battery to the starter relay, the generator regulator, the multiple connector and right up to a splice where it changes to black-orange and goes into the headlight switch itself. Using the diagram, you'll know where to make your tests. Without it, you'd have to do a good bit of head-scratching before you were even able to figure out where to hook up your voltmeter.

However, if headlights and taillights both are not working, yet the dashboard lights are, the problem is most likely a defective main light switch or corroded terminals. Examine, clean and tighten all the terminals and check the lights once again. But be prepared to replace the offending switch.

Unfortunately, there may be times when either you are far from home (and your trusty wiring diagram) or you simply have no wiring diagram to work from. There's no really quick and easy way to determine exactly which wires serve the circuit that's out of commission. In the case of the preceding example, you could simply check the more common lighting-system trouble areas, such as the dimmer switch and the multiple connectors. But what if the failure is in the domelight, backup light or some other obscure circuit?

Probably the best way to find the correct wire when you don't have a diagram is to trace the circuits with a test light. The test light should be equipped with alligator clips that can be snapped onto a ground or the component being checked.

Let's suppose that you are trying to locate the wire under the dash that conducts electricity to the backup lights. The lights don't work, and a voltmeter or test light check at the switch or the transmission shows that no current is reaching that point. The

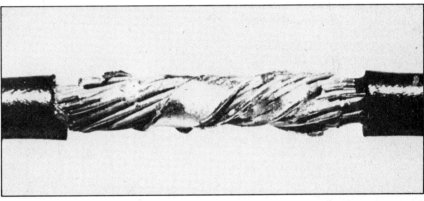

1. We dug into our goodie box for a selection of terminals. Middle pair lock together for connecting two wires, but can easily be disconnected with a simple twist.

2. Shown here are a pair of firewall or flooring quick-disconnect wiring connectors, available from trailer supply houses. These are ideal when pulling an engine or even removing a body from the chassis. Connectors for 6, 8 or 10 wires are stocked.

3. Rosin-core solder is flowed onto the strands for a permanent splice. A piece of shrink tube, rather than tape, would complete the job.

circuit's fuse is all right, but no current seems to be reaching it either. Therefore the trouble is obviously between the fuse block and the current source. However, no wire leaving the fuses corresponds in color to the one leading to the backup light switch. Without a diagram, you don't know which wire to trace from the fuse block back to the battery.

With the ignition switch and headlight switch off and the transmission in neutral, clip the positive lead of a test light to the fuse holder and the negative lead to a good ground somewhere nearby. Now take a short jumper wire that has a large pin or needle soldered to one end and an alligator clip soldered to the other. Attach the clip to ground. The needle of the jumper wire can then be used to probe the wires leading to the fuse block. When you probe the correct wire, the test lamp will light. You'll then know which wire to trace from the fuse block to the source of battery current.

If you are using this method to find a wire that may be continuously connected to the car's battery or if you are going to have to touch some "hot" wires in your process of elimi-

nation, remove the car's battery connections. If the wires being checked have inline connectors, these can be pulled apart and touched with the needle so that you will not have to force it through the insulation.

Simply speaking, tests made with a test light and a jumper allow you to apply current to a known part of a circuit so that you can find the same circuit elsewhere. By eliminating the car's battery, you can be sure that only one circuit has current in it.

Another method of circuit testing uses a non-powered test light. These test lights have a light bulb in the handle, a sharp probe at one end and an alligator clip at the end of a wire on the other end. With the car's battery, energize the circuit you wish to find. Attach the test light's clip to a good ground. When the probe's point finds a "hot" circuit, the test light will come on. When examining a light circuit, always work backward from the nonfunctional light bulb; that is, toward the car's battery.

WIRING CIRCUIT TERMS

The terms "series" and "parallel" are easy to understand if you think of them as ways of describing a road

map that the current is going to travel. For example, if you talk about connecting one electrical unit to a battery, it's just as if you were describing a road between Kansas and California. The electrical unit is simply connected to the battery, and that's really all there is to say about it.

But when you connect a second electrical unit to the battery, you must consider whether you are connecting it in series or parallel. Suppose our second unit is Nevada, and we connect it so that it is on the same road that we originally had running to California. In order to get to California on that road, we now have to go through Nevada, so we can say that Nevada is in series with California. The current that operates our first electrical unit, California, now has to pass through Nevada before it can reach California.

Nevada, as we all know, has certain attractions which we won't discuss here. Let's say that the electricity becomes slightly tired as it goes through Nevada, so that when it reaches California it doesn't have enough push to do the job it's supposed to do.

In order to let our electricity do its

job better, we build a second road from Kansas directly to Nevada, and we route our first road so that it bypasses Nevada and goes straight to California. Now we have a parallel circuit. Electricity can go directly from Kansas to California without the exhausting experience of passing through Nevada. And our Nevada unit receives electricity directly from the battery also. The result is plenty of electricity to operate both our electrical units without their disturbing each other.

No matter how many electrical units there are, they are all connected to the power source either in series or parallel when considered in relation to some other unit. How about the relation between the two headlights? They are in parallel. How about the headlights and taillights? Parallel. All four turn signals? Parallel. What about the headlight switch and the headlights? That's a series connection, because the electricity goes through the headlight switch before it gets to the headlights.

Switches are always wired in series with the load they control. The word "load" means anything that uses up electricity, such as a light bulb, a relay, resistance, electric motor or anything that does work. A switch is not a load. It is supposed to pass on the electricity without any losses. If it doesn't, it starts to heat up, which means that it is using electricity because it doesn't have enough capacity for the load it is feeding. Dirty contacts or a switch that is too small for the job make the switch heat up.

The word "shunt" is another way of describing a parallel circuit. A shunt is a branch from a wire feeding some other unit. Suppose there is a wire feeding the taillights. We break into that wire somewhere in the vicinity of the trunk and connect an additional wire to an auxiliary taillight. Electricity goes through both taillight to ground. It is correct to say that the taillights are wired in parallel, but because we tapped into the original taillight wire instead of coming directly from the battery, our auxiliary taillight is actually shunt wired. Both the stock taillights work in parallel, each receiving an equal supply of electricity, but we have increased the load by adding a light to the original wiring. If the original wire is not large enough to carry the added current, both taillights may burn too dimly because they are starved for electricity. By the way, taillights have a tendency to fill with water, causing the bases of the bulbs and sockets to corrode. A poor ground results.

A ground is nothing more than a

return path for the electricity after it has done its job. The ground strap on the engine provides a return path for the ignition and starting current on an engine that is rubber mounted. If you think of electricity and wiring as similar to cars traveling a road, you will be a long way along your own road to understanding wiring.

WORKING WITH WIRING

One of the most frequent mistakes made by car owners is to add electrical accessories without giving careful thought to where to pick up the current for them. In some cases the car's battery and generating system may be just barely adequate to sup-

ply the electrical system's original current needs. Even the addition of a pair of driving lights can sometimes put an overload on the charging system. In a few cases, the charging system may not be able to keep up with the added current demands at all, which means that the battery will be under a steady discharge.

Before adding any really big current consumers, it's a good idea to take a voltmeter reading of the entire electrical system with all existing lights and electrical accessories in operation. First make sure that your battery is fully charged. Then, with the engine dead, turn everything on and see how much the load drags the battery down. If the reading is

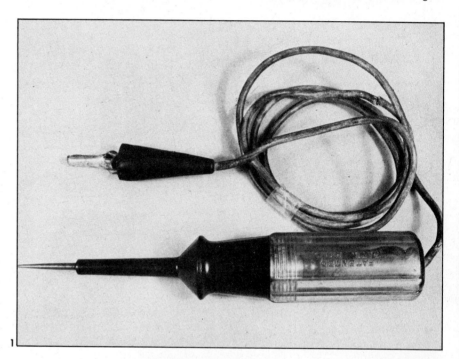

1

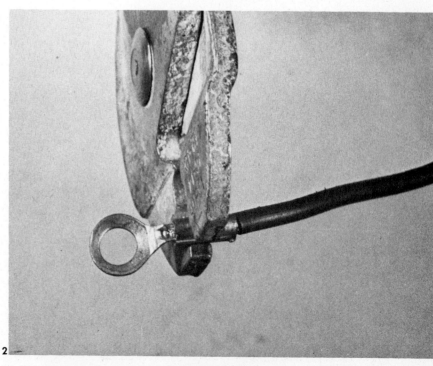

2

11.5 volts or less, you'd probably better think twice before wiring in anything else. An even better test is to insert a test resistance equal to the load of the proposed accessory into the circuit and then make a check of the charging system's ampere output with everything in operation. If the load is continuously above the factory specs for the generator or alternator, you'll need a higher-output charging system to handle the proposed load.

For this reason new cars destined for trailer towing are equipped with heavy-duty electrical systems. Alternators in such systems have almost double the usual amperage output. Chrysler recently included a unit rated at 117 amps in their trailer-towing

1. This is an old, reliable, nonpowered test light. The light bulb is inside the handle and can be changed easily when it burns out. To use, ground the clip, then touch the point to any terminal to see if it's hot.

2. Solderless terminals should be applied with a pair of terminal pliers. The pliers secure the wire by properly pinching the terminal.

3. You won't need this much wiring just to wire a trailer plug, but extra wire is always handy to have around. While 16-gauge is the most common for lights, you'll need more than one color for trailer wiring, along with enough 12-gauge to run the length of the tow vehicle and for ground wires.

package. The on-board battery and clearance lights of a trailer or camper can quickly overtax a standard generating system.

Careful thought must also be given to where to attach your new accessory in the wiring plan of the car. If you hook it into a circuit that already serves another electrical component, you may overload its fuse or circuit breaker. Worse yet, you may overload the wiring. Wire sizes are measured by the gauge system: the higher the number, the smaller the wire. Eighteen-gauge wire is the lightest type used in automobiles, generally for such things as instrument-panel illuminating bulbs. The heaviest is usually 10-gauge, which is reserved for main charging system connections and the current supply to the headlight switch and fuse panel.

In some circuits you will find 12-gauge wire used for some of the charging system connections, but 12-gauge is most frequently installed between the fuse block and the more current-hungry lights and accessories. Fourteen-gauge wire generally serves such things as the headlights, radio, horn and cigarette lighter. Taillights, brake lights, parking lights and other small bulbs are normally provided with 16-gauge wire, as are the gauges, heater and interior lighting.

In all such wiring applications, the fuse size corresponds closely to the size of the wire. There are light-duty fuses for light-gauge wire and higher-amperage-capacity fuses for heavier-gauge wire. The greater the current demand of the electrical component being served, the heavier the wiring and fusing must be.

The most common wear points in automotive wiring systems are at the terminals and where wires are exposed to weather or to mechanical abrasion. Terminals that are loose tend to erode due to both corrosion and the arcing of electrical current. Very often wire flexing induced by mechanical vibration is greatest where the terminal joins the wire, causing it to break at that point. If the rest of the wire is in good shape, a new terminal can be added. If the wire has broken somewhere in the middle, it's possible to make a good permanent splice.

New terminals in various styles and sizes are sold at all automotive supply stores. Some are of the crimp-on variety, and are available in kits including the special plier-like tools used to install them. Others slip onto the wire and are already tinned so that they can quickly be soldered into place. The better terminals have short pieces of plastic tubing slipped onto them which can be slid down to cover the exposed portion of the terminal's stem as well as slightly overlapping the wire's insulation.

The first thing that must be decided when breaks occur in the middle of a wire is whether to replace the whole wire or just repair the break itself. The wire can probably be kept in service if the insulation is neither soft and spongy nor hard and cracked. If its general condition is poor, however, it's wise to remove it and put in a new piece.

Broken wire ends should not be merely twisted together, since vibration and corrosion would ultimately turn this makeshift joint into a high-resistance one. The wire should be spliced either with solder or a crimped-on sleeve. Soldering is usually the neatest and most practical method of splicing the multistrand wire used in car wiring. Brighten the strands lightly by pulling a piece of fine emery cloth over them a few times; then intersperse them and give a twist or two. Apply a small amount of solder to the tip of the soldering iron and touch the iron to the joint. As soon as the solder has flowed into the wire strands, remove the iron. Overheating the joint damages the surrounding insulation.

While soldering is a good way to splice two wires together, the existing joint must be protected with some form of insulation. Plastic electrical tape is commonly used, but it's not recommended. Exposed to heat, oil, weather and gasoline fumes as they are, these tapes tend to either harden and crack or become soft and gummy, sliding away from the joint they were intended to protect.

What is recommended is the use of electrical *shrink tubing,* a material widely used by knowledgeable wiring specialists. A strip of shrink tubing long enough to cover the entire splice (or shank of a wire end terminal) and a reasonable section of wire insulation at either end protects the splice from possible shorts. First slip a piece of shrink tubing over a splice or terminal end. Then heat it (a match or hair dryer will do). The heat makes the material shrink, creating an extremely tight fit over the splice or terminal end.

We mentioned a crimped-on sleeve as an alternative to soldering a wire splice. Actually, there is a choice here too. One type, known as butt connectors, is plain and crimps onto wires butted together in its open ends. A shrink tube must be used to protect this butt connector. You can also buy butt connectors that are preinsulated. Finally, you can buy crimp-on bullets that fit onto the wire ends. These plug into insulated connectors and offer the advantage of being able to disconnect the ''splice''

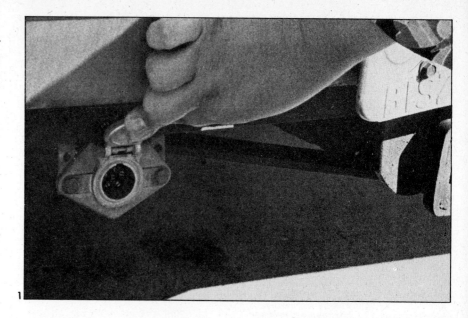

REAR LIGHT WIRING COLOR CODE

	AMC	GM	CHRYSLER*
Taillights	Blue	Brown	Brown
Left turn signal	Orange	Yellow	Yellow
Right turn signal	White	Dark green	Light green
Backup	Brown	Light green	Black
Ground wire	Black	Black	At lights

*Chrysler Corp. cars have a pigtail wire harness at each light that is dark green for brake lights, black for taillights and violet for backup lights. This pigtail harness color code is the same on all lights and then returns to the proper color code at the first connector plug.

at any time by simply pulling one bullet or the other from its end of the connector.

A wiring system in good condition is like a healthy circulatory system. If the wires are of the correct capacity, properly fused and have tight, well-insulated joints and terminals, your car should enjoy a long and efficient electrical lifetime. One thing bears mentioning here: You can always use wires of a larger gauge than necessary in any wiring circuit; nothing can be hurt by it and the added cost for the wiring is minimal. But never try to skimp on your wiring by going to a wire gauge one size or more *smaller* than specified or attempt to justify this act by saying that that circuit won't be used very much. If you reduce the wire size, you increase the load on the wire—and that's how fires start. So if you're going to wire your car, do it the right way. Otherwise you'll have the time of your life trying to locate shorts and other hidden problems, problems you built into your car by negligence.

TRAILER WIRING

Many people, some very knowledgeable mechanics included, become very nervous and agitated when trailer-towing wiring is mentioned. In many cases, the neophyte has an advantage, since he doesn't have any preconception that hooking up a trailer plug receptacle is difficult or complicated. So he goes ahead and connects it in the easiest, most straightforward manner he can and wonders what all the fuss is about. When he's finished, all the circuits work, and this is as it should be. There is really no mystery about how or why trailer lights work, but many people choke up and create problems. In other words, they make things more difficult than they actually are.

We'll start with the easiest circuit and expand from there. All automotive electrical components must be properly grounded in order to operate correctly. This includes trailer lights and appliances. Therefore a ground wire must be run to a frame member on both sides of the trailer plug. The plug fixture mounting screws can be used if the fixture is mounted directly to either the frame or bumper of the car. Drill a hole in the framework of the trailer's tongue. Then use either a sheetmetal screw or nut-and-bolt arrangement to secure the ground wire on the trailer.

Finding which wire activates the taillights is easy when you know how

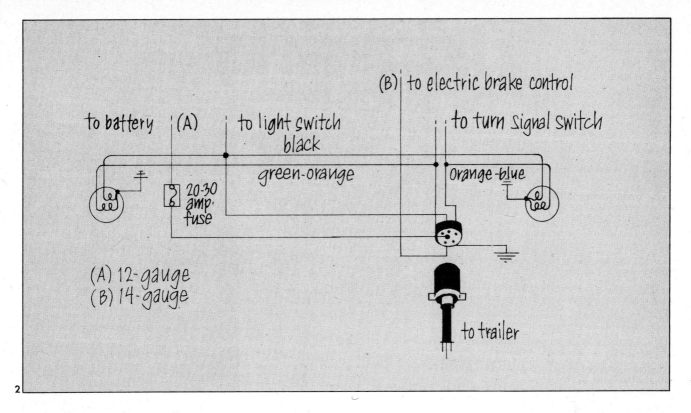

to battery | (A) | to light switch

(B) to electric brake control

to turn signal switch

black

green-orange

orange-blue

20-30 amp. fuse

(A) 12-gauge
(B) 14-gauge

to trailer

2

1. This is a 6-way plug already mounted next to the hitch platform. Even though four circuits may be all that are needed, a 6-way plug is preferred over the cheaper 4-way.

2. This mini-diagram (fully explained within the text) is a close-up of part of the Ford horn and lights wiring diagram that was shown previously.

to look and what to look for. Using the same Ford diagram referred to earlier as an example, the black wire that runs the width of the car activates the taillights. It also energizes the license plate light and side marker lights. It can be spliced into at any one of numerous points. However, before you cut the wire or strip back any insulation, turn on the parking lights and use a circuit tester to make certain that that wire is indeed the taillight circuit. Match the gauge of the existing wire and splice your new wire into the circuit, following the splicing instructions given earlier in this article. Cut the new wire about a foot longer than necessary, let it hang and turn off the lights.

Using the Ford diagram once again, we find that the left turn signal circuit is color-coded green-orange and the right one is orange-blue. Not all Fords, by the way, will correspond with our sample Ford color code; check the wiring diagram for your own year and model.

As for GM, AMC and Chrysler car owners, an accompanying chart gives color codes for those makes. If your car does not match any of the various color codes included here, locate all four wires for the rear lights (you'll probably find them in the trunk). You

will see wires of four colors, two of which will extend the width of the car. These two circuits are for either taillights or backup lights; determine which with your circuit tester. Of the remaining two wires, one will go only to the left and one to the right. These are your combination turn signal/brake light circuits. European-style rear lights with separate brake and turning lights are covered later.

After determining which wire is which, splice and route the new wires to the plug. Again, cut them about a foot longer than needed.

Rather than go into details on wiring for trailer brakes or wiring for appliances within the trailer itself at this time, we'll first cover wiring the trailer plug. We recommend using a 6-way plug. This unit will accept six different circuits rather than just four. While it's true that for a boat, motorcycle or utility trailer you only need four circuits, you may decide to expand to a larger unit at a later date, and it would cost you time and money to change over then. Besides, with a 6-way unit, you have two stand-by terminals in case one of the four goes bad. Each receptacle, regardless of type or brand, will have the mating terminals marked correspondingly on both the male and female pieces. Just follow these for location. Strip off about ¼-in. of insulation before inserting the wire. Insert the bare wire and tighten down the screws.

For those who wish to install a "hot" lead to supply the trailer with continous juice for recharging the on-board battery, running appliances or both, you'll need enough 12-gauge

wire to run the length of your tow vehicle. Prepare one end to attach directly to the car's battery, to a relay (available at any trailer supply store) or to the starter relay if your car is so equipped, but don't attach the wire to a power source until the circuit is complete.

About a foot from the attachment point or wherever it's convenient, cut the wire and attach an inline fuse holder of either 20- or 30-amp magnitude. You can then route the wire along a frame rail, attaching it to the frame with nylon tie-straps. Attach it to the trailer plug in the same manner as previously mentioned. Mount the brake control box if you're wiring to tow a Class II trailer or larger. Wire it according to the accompanying factory instructions. If you wish to form a harness of the two full-length wires with a piece of shrink tubing, do it before attaching either wire to a frame rail.

Those who own autos with European taillights and separate turn and brake lights have two choices. Either equip the trailer with additional lights or equip your car with a device called an MME. The MME is a diode-controlled device which allows the use of single double-filament light bulbs on the trailer but multiple lights on the car. It is extremely sensitive to shorting out and should be used with great care. The MME is available from Hitch Master, 7254 Woodley Ave., Van Nuys, CA 91406.

If you follow these instructions, you'll have no trouble with trailer wiring and you'll save yourself some loot to boot. 👑

Accessories

ELECTRICALLY POWERED COMFORT/CONVENIENCE GOODIES ADD A TOUCH OF LUXURY—BUT ONLY IF THEY'RE WORKING PROPERLY.

When you stop to think about it, there is really an appalling superabundance of electrically operated gadgetry on the modern automobile. Electric door locks, self-raising antennas, automatic headlight dimmers and speed-monitoring auto-pilots are just a few of the less-often-thought-of accessories drawing current from the car's electrical system. Some accessories—such as six-way power seats, convertible top lifters and power windows—are major assemblies only slightly less complicated to engineer than an entire automobile was 50 years ago. It's not difficult to understand the recent improvements in charging systems and batteries, nor why auto makers are showing a continuing interest in their further development. The fully loaded luxury car of today has a mass of accessories that would have brought the charging systems of 1949 to their knees in a matter of minutes. Obviously, it would take an entire chapter about each one of these accessories to cover every function in detail, but we'll do our best in the space of a few pages to at least set down the general engineering and construction features of each one, and to define their place in the many circuits of the electrical system.

MOTOR-DRIVEN ACCESSORIES

You may recall from our discussion of the starter that there are several types of direct-current motors which differ from one another in the way their windings are connected to battery current. *Series-wound* motors—such as those used in starters—have their field windings connected to the armature brushes so that current must pass through the field windings before reaching the armature. Such motors are best suited to moving heavy loads that have to be started slowly. They must, however, be kept under load to prevent their speed from building up to the point where they may damage themselves.

Shunt-wound motors provide current to the field windings independently from that supplied to the armature coils. This is the best type of motor for use where constant speed is required at varying loads.

Compound-wound motors have series windings as well as shunt windings. As we observed in the chapter on starters, most modern series-wound direct-current motors have at least one small shunt winding to keep them from running away if the load is suddenly removed. Units of this type are generally termed *lightly compounded* motors.

Compound motors are often used in general industrial applications to drive tools equipped with heavy fly-wheels, such as shears and presses. This is not only because they can handle heavy starting loads, but because compound motors can draw energy from the flywheel to meet load peaks, and then return it when the peak is past—a process made possible by self-varying speed characteristics that allow them to match their output to the load. Its ability to pro-

duce steady power at varying speeds makes the compound motor a natural for such automotive accessories as windshield wipers. By controlling the armature and series-winding voltage with a rheostat, variable-speed wiper action can be obtained. Nearly all multi-speed motor-driven automobile accessories are equipped with compound-wound motors.

Compensated compound-wound motors are seldom found in automotive applications. Basically, these motors are shunt-wound, but contain several light series windings as well. Compensated compound motors are used in fixed-load applications where steady speed is required, but where there is considerable inertia to be overcome upon starting. Their main use has been to drive rolling mills and mine hoists.

Permanent-magnet motors have no field windings, but rely on permanent magnets to provide this function. Units of this type should be no mystery to slot-car enthusiasts. Their torque characteristics are similar to that of a shunt-wound motor, and therefore tend to be a bit weak at low speeds since speed control is accomplished simply by varying the voltage delivered to the armature windings. "Per-mag" motors are sometimes used to operate various types of automotive accessories.

Direct-current motors have another valuable characteristic that AC motors do not possess. Their direction of rotation can be reversed simply by changing the polarity of the current

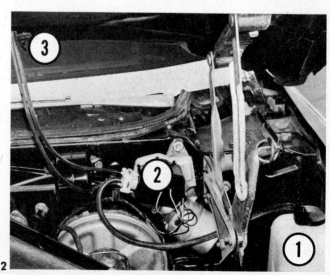

delivered to them. This is frequently taken advantage of in the design of various motor-driven auto accessories such as self-raising radio antennas.

Windshield wipers are perhaps the most important motor-driven accessory on the car. Years ago, wipers were often operated by engine manifold vacuum and, before that, by hand! Today most cars have electric wiper motors. All electric windshield wiper systems are motor-driven and wired to operate only when the ignition switch is in the "On" or "Acc." positions. There are, however, many details of windshield wiper construction that vary from one make of car to another. Each car maker has at least one single-speed and one two-speed —or multi-speed—wiper system in his

catalogs. The single-speed units are standard equipment on some base models, while multi-speed types are options, or standard on higher-priced models. In the case of most American-made automobiles, the wiper motor is protected by a circuit breaker located in the dashboard-mounted wiper control switch. This serves to prevent damage if the wipers are turned on while frozen to the glass or in the event of a wiper circuit overload or electrical short.

Chrysler Corp. uses permanent-magnet motors on their two-speed systems and compound-wound motors on their three-speed systems. Two different sets of brushes are used for the speed control in the two-speed units, and a resistance in the shunt field circuit controls speed on the three-speed units. The switch also has a provision for reversing the motor's polarity when the unit is turned off. This causes the motor to run backwards briefly to park the wipers in their lowest position before a cam-operated switch breaks the circuit completely to shut the current off.

GM uses a similar system for parking the wiper blades on all its units. They are all powered by compound-wound motors, and are two-speed on all models except Cadillac, where a three-speed motor is used. Heavier motors are used on those models where the wipers are parked in a depressed position, out of the line of sight of the driver. The non-depressed-parking units are provided with a flat-shaped motor instead of one with a round cross section.

Ford uses permanent-magnet motors on all models. Speed control on two-speed models is obtained by using different brushes on the motor Parking is obtained by reversing the rotation of the motor, the same as on other makes.

Windshield washers are also usually motor-driven. In the case of General Motors cars, the wiper pump is screwed directly onto the windshield wiper motor and drive mechanism. When the "wash" button is depressed by the driver, a relay engages a cam drive that is turned by the wiper motor as it works the windshield wipers. This cam operates a bellows-type pump that delivers water to the washer jets. The resulting flow is a series of pulse-like squirts as each cam lobe passes under the pump unit's plunger. After one complete cam cycle, the washer mechanism disengages itself automatically.

Constant-delivery washer pumps, such as those used by Chrysler and other makers, have a positive-displacement pump which functions somewhat like the engine's oil pump

1. "I'm stuck in traffic, but should be home in half an hour." Just pick up the mike and let the people at home or office know where you are. CB radio units are only one of the many aftermarket accessories that draw from a car's electrical system.

2. Plastic reservoir (1) supplies windshield solvent to washer pump (2), which pumps it through hoses to nozzles (3) to squirt glass. Washer pump and wiper motor are built into same unit, but can be repaired separately as long as motor works.

3. Provision is made on wiper motors for adjusting end play in the worm gear drive.

4. Ford uses permanent magnet motors for all windshield wiper applications. This is a basic single-speed unit. Two-speed is similar, but has three brushes in motor for speed control.

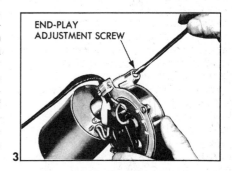

END-PLAY ADJUSTMENT SCREW

3

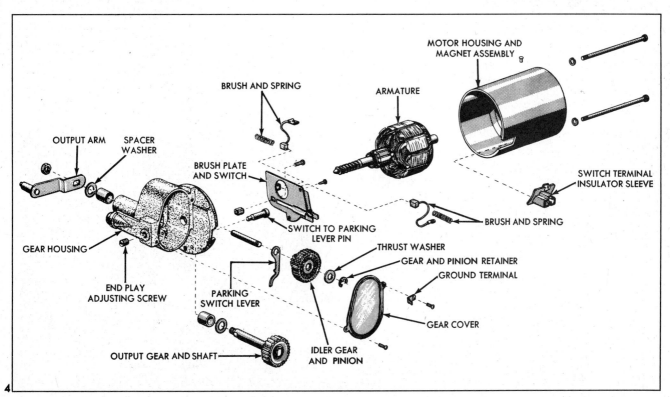

OUTPUT ARM SPACER WASHER BRUSH AND SPRING ARMATURE MOTOR HOUSING AND MAGNET ASSEMBLY BRUSH PLATE AND SWITCH GEAR HOUSING SWITCH TO PARKING LEVER PIN SWITCH TERMINAL INSULATOR SLEEVE BRUSH AND SPRING THRUST WASHER GEAR AND PINION RETAINER GROUND TERMINAL END PLAY ADJUSTING SCREW PARKING SWITCH LEVER GEAR COVER OUTPUT GEAR AND SHAFT IDLER GEAR AND PINION

4

or a Rootes-type supercharger. This device is driven by a small shunt-wound electric motor and provides washing water whether the wipers are in operation or not. In most cases, washing continues only so long as the driver continues to press the control button.

Heaters, defrosters, ventilating systems and *air conditioners* are often integrated affairs sharing the same motor-driven blower. Sometimes there is a separate defroster or air conditioner fan and, in cars having a rear-window defogger, it too usually must be equipped with its own electric motor.

Compound-wound motors are often used to power fans and blowers, but it is not unusual to find shunt-wound units as well. Their speed may be controlled by a rheostat that allows rpm to be varied over a wide band, or by a switch that provides two or three fixed speeds. This last system is more common today and consists of a number of resistors that can be cut into the blower motor's circuit at the driver's discretion. When the switch is in the low-speed position, more resistance is inserted into the motor circuit than when the intermediate speed is selected. High-speed operation is usually achieved by removing all resistors from the circuit.

In cars equipped with air conditioning, the complexity of the ventilating system wiring becomes markedly greater. A switch and circuits must be included to provide low, medium and high air-conditioner output in addition to a fan-driven supply of unrefrigerated air. The operation of the air conditioner's refrigerating compressor is also electrically initiated by energizing a magnetic clutch included in the unit's drive pulley. Further, the relatively heavy current needed to accomplish this demands that a control relay be included in the circuit to take some of the load off the dashboard-mounted control switch. This relay is also controlled thermostatically so that the compressor is switched on and off automatically to keep the temperature in the passenger compartment at the desired level.

The magnetic clutch on the air conditioning compressor is a stationary electromagnetic coil mounted between the pulley and the compressor housing. To eliminate the need for brushes and slip rings, the coil is not allowed to revolve with the pulley—as is sometimes done in similar drive units—but is mounted rigidly onto the end of the compressor. It acts as a short solenoid, drawing the pulley and shaft-driving plate into engage-

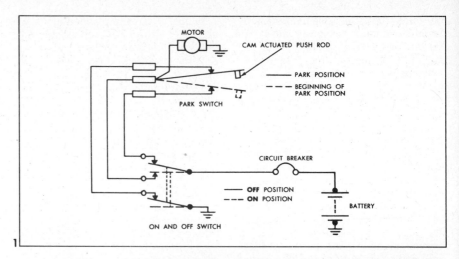

1

2

3

1. Simple circuit diagram shows how a typical single-speed wiper unit operates. A cam on the motor-driven pinion gear shuts off the motor when the blades have reached the park position.

2. Climate Control is complicated, but not as frightening as it looks. With a shop manual, you have a good chance of getting it into shape. On later versions, provision is made for fresh air without running the compressor.

3. Blower motor on many car heaters (or air conditioners) is mounted off to one side, can easily be removed without removing rest of heater.

4. Terminals (arrow) on GM air-conditioning compressor are exposed at side of plug for easy testing.

5. Heater electrical circuit shows how resistors are arranged in the switch to provide different speed settings. Rheostats are seldom used in such applications today.

4

ment so that the car's engine will be able to effectively operate the air-conditioning compressor.

Power seats come in two varieties: two-way seats that provide movement fore and aft, and six-way seats that add up-and-down and tilting movements. General Motors uses series-wound motors for both types of seats in their cars—a simple reversible set-up for the two-way seat, and a solenoid-operated, electrically shifted transmission for changing mode in the six-way versions. Reversing the motor changes the direction of movement on all seats. Ford and Chrysler use permanent-magnet motors in their power seat systems. Two-way seats have a single motor connected by cables to the gear drives on each seat rail. Six-way seats use what is called a ''three-armature'' motor, which amounts to three motors in the same housing. One of the armatures is connected to the front edge up-down gears, another to the fore-aft gears and the third to the rear edge up-down gears. With this system, more than one motion of the seat can be operated simultaneously. The GM system requires a six-wire cable to the controller for the six-way system, while the Ford and Chrysler systems require an eight-wire cable.

Some older cars have four-way power seats, but the principle of operation is the same, with a reversible motor operating sets of gears on both sides of the seat. In addition, some cars have split seats, in which one side may have a six-way adjuster and the other a two-way adjuster. All this means is that there are that many more parts to give trouble and that many more motors to add to the strain on the electrical system.

Power windows are wired so that

they can be raised and lowered from the master control panel on the driver's door or by single switches located at the individual windows. Since initial loads may be high, series-wound motors are universally used. There is a separate motor at each window, and those used by GM have their own internal circuit breaker in addition to the one provided for the entire system. This keeps one stuck window from disabling the whole power window system.

Each motor receives two wires. The position of the operating switch determines their polarity and therefore the direction of motor rotation. Although power window motors only draw between 5 and 10 amperes of current, the circuit breakers commonly have a capacity of about 30 amps. This is fine for forcing the windows loose when they're stuck by ice and snow, but it can be murder if you get your nose caught in one.

Convertible tops are raised and lowered by means of a hydraulic system having a motor-driven pump. The motor is a series-wound reversible unit and is part of an assembly that includes the motor, a pump and the hydraulic fluid reservoir.

Raising convertible tops is pretty rigorous work, and while the hydraulic system provides a tremendous mechanical advantage, the motor is still under a considerable load. Most draw about 35 amperes of current, although this may reach 50 or more when almost stalled. The engine of the car must therefore be speeded up when raising the top so that the charging system can take over the

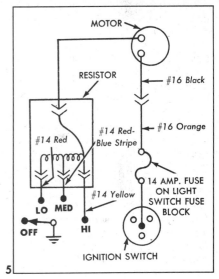
5

added current demand. The motor is usually protected by its own circuit breaker, which cuts out at about 70 to 75 amps. Sliding sunroofs are available with electric power on some GM and Ford models. These are operated by a reversible motor mounted above the windshield header. A 25-amp breaker is part of the circuit.

Self-raising radio antennas are motor-driven units that usually operate automatically as soon as the radio is switched on or off. Series-wound motors are used for these, and their direction of rotation is reversed by changing the polarity of the battery current delivered to them.

In all, it may be possible for a car to have from 12 to 15 electric motors in addition to the starter! With the seemingly endless proliferation of

Accessories

power accessories, this number will likely keep increasing despite the almost overwhelming complexity it adds to the wiring of the electrical system as a whole. However, electrical accessories do not stop with those operated by motors. Here are some of the other devices—electromagnetic and otherwise—that also draw current from the battery and charging system:

Overdrive transmissions are commonly controlled by means of a large, electrically operated solenoid. Essentially, an overdrive is just a two-speed planetary transmission—related to that found on the venerable Model T—that is bolted onto the back of a conventional three-speed box. Rather than using bands, like those found in automatic transmissions (and the T), overdrives employ a pawl and balk ring to lock the ring gear, thereby stepping up the speed of the output shaft's rotation. It's the solenoid's job to engage the pawl when overdrive is needed and disengage it when its operation is not desired. With the overdrive engaged, engine rpm is reduced by almost 30% over that required to drive the car at similar speeds without overdrive.

The electrical operation of the over-

1

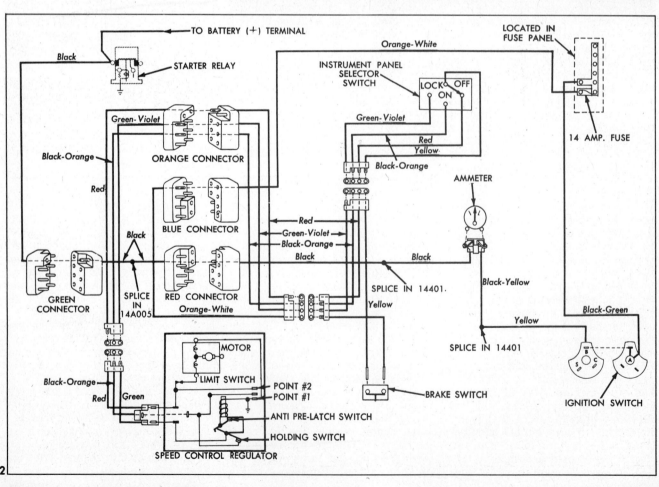

2

drive unit is controlled by a governor that is driven by the speedometer cable. This controls the action of the overdrive relay. When the car reaches a speed of approximately 28 mph, the governor contacts close, completing the relay's field circuit to ground. Operation of the relay switches bat-

1. Early type cruise control unit had electric motor to control throttle position. Current units use vacuum for the same application, are more reliable and simpler.

2. Schematic of an electrical cruise control unit. They can be repaired, but it takes time and patience.

3. All cruise control units have a connection to brake pedal, so that the unit is switched off the instant the driver touches the brakes.

4. These strange clips on cowl are to ground the hood when it closes, thereby cutting down radio static. Sometimes, similar ones are found on the rear deck lid.

5. If your horn sounds strange, remove the end bell and try adjusting the little nut. You'll also find a set of points that may need filing.

tery current to the solenoid, causing it to engage the pawl.

There is also a "kickdown" switch operated by the gas pedal that disengages the overdrive for faster acceleration. The kickdown switch not only breaks the circuit between the governor and the overdrive relay—causing it to shut off current to the solenoid—but also grounds the ignition system momentarily. The grounding of the ignition causes the engine to "cut out" for an instant to allow the overdrive pawl to retract.

The overdrive solenoid has two coils—one to move the plunger and a smaller one that holds the plunger once it is engaged. This prevents the solenoid unit from drawing excessive current while the overdrive is in operation.

Electric clocks were also all solenoid-operated accessories, until recently. The type of electric clock found on your kitchen wall is driven by a synchronous motor that depends on 60-cycle house current to keep it on time. If you were to wire it to 50-cycle current, it would take 72 sec-

onds to record one minute. Since automobile electrical systems work on direct current, this type of clock motor would not run at all on the dashboard of your car. Car clocks are therefore spring-driven, but utilize a solenoid to rewind the spring periodically. Every few minutes you can often hear the "Z-Z-Z-ZIP!" sound of their spring in the process of being re-tensioned. In recent models, the electronically controlled digital clock has become a popular accessory. These generate their own frequency-controlled alternating current for their synchronous motors, and are designed to be replaceable rather than repairable. They require a minimal amount of current draw.

Electric door locks are yet another accessory that makes use of solenoids. Custom car builders often use similar solenoids to provide automatic door opening or trunk unlocking. There is a double-action solenoid at each door which can be operated by the driver or by the passenger in the right-hand front seat. They are controlled by a single-pole, double-throw

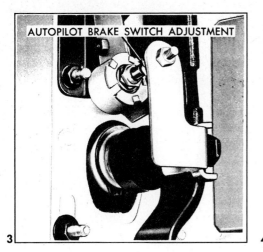

AUTOPILOT BRAKE SWITCH ADJUSTMENT

3

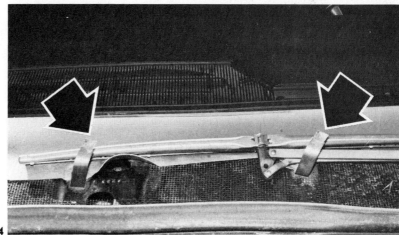

4

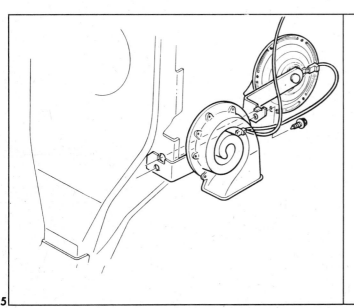

5

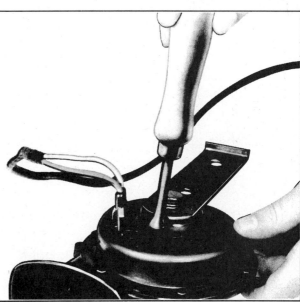

Accessories

switch that reverses the polarity of current to the solenoid with each change of direction. The reversing of the polarity changes the direction of current flow through the solenoid windings, causing the motion of the plunger to be in the opposite direction. All doors are locked or unlocked at once by this system.

Horns were motor-driven in the days of Henry's famous "Ah-OOO-gah!" type of horn—but all production models are now equipped with electromagnetic types. These usually require from 7 to 11 amperes apiece to operate—relatively heavy current for a simple accessory. Although some cars use the electrical contacts in the horn button to send current directly to the horns, most American cars have a horn relay. The horn button merely energizes the relay's field, thereby drawing two contacts together that send full battery current directly to the horns. This assures them of the volts they need even when many other accessories are in operation. On General Motors cars the horn relay is the main electrical path for all current flowing to and from the battery, with the exception of that used by the starter motor.

The voltage needed for proper horn functioning is within a very narrow permissible band. Each horn is therefore equipped with a current-adjusting nut to calibrate the instrument so that it will sound properly. This control is quite sensitive and only a small fraction of a turn is usually required to put the horn back in "full song" after age and wear have caused it to fall mute temporarily.

Radios are an item that could easily take an entire book to cover all by themselves. Such accessories as tape recorders, record players and televi-

sions are also available either as dealer options or from independent sources. These specialized pieces of equipment are not really automotive circuits and their service and repair is usually farmed out by service departments to shops specializing in this kind of work.

All present-day automotive audio equipment is transistorized, and there are several precautions that should be observed when installing or servicing either sound systems or their supplementary speakers. First, be very careful not to route current into them that is of the wrong polarity. Second,

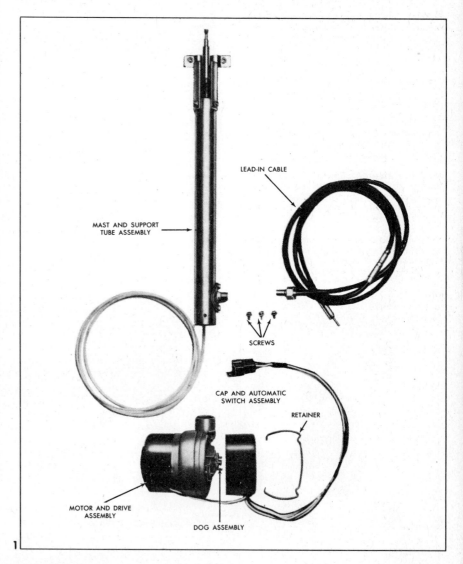

LEAD-IN CABLE

MAST AND SUPPORT TUBE ASSEMBLY

SCREWS

CAP AND AUTOMATIC SWITCH ASSEMBLY

RETAINER

MOTOR AND DRIVE ASSEMBLY

DOG ASSEMBLY

1

2

when installing extra speakers, be careful that the speaker or its mount does not come into contact with outside electrical sources such as bare electrical system wires or their terminals. Soldering irons and electric drills used in their installation should be properly grounded. Lastly, never operate a transistorized unit with its speaker(s) disconnected. Doing so will frequently damage or destroy the transistors.

Automatic headlight-dimmer systems rely on a photoelectric cell that triggers a relay controlling the high and low beams of the headlights. The photoelectric cell used in these units is often of the vacuum-tube type, since these react more quickly to changes in stimuli than solid-state types do.

Electrical anti-theft devices are widely available both as factory-installed options and as add-on accessories. The simplest are the off-on switches that can be placed in the main battery cables or are wired into the ignition system's primary lead.

Audible alarm systems are sold by many companies. Some sound the horn when the car is moved or when a door or other switch-protected compartment is opened. Others disa-

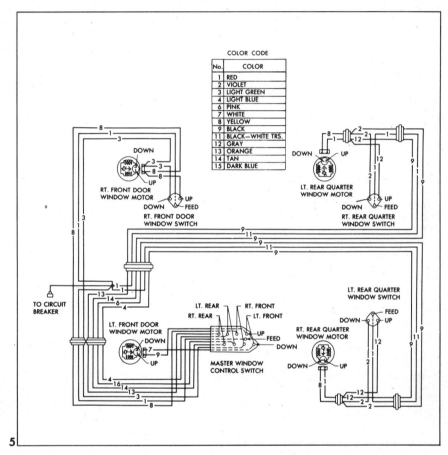

1. Electric radio antennas require a fairly hefty motor and clutch assembly to operate them. Control may be incorporated in the radio switch itself.

2. Electric sunroofs are becoming more and more popular. They are operated by a motor and cable system mounted above the windshield header.

3. Auto stereo systems draw power from the car's circuit for their amplifiers, and also to run their motor drive systems.

4. Electronically controlled digital clocks are replacing spring driven electrically wound types. Chrysler was the first manufacturer to offer them, now they appear on all makes.

5. Early electric window wiring diagram is lot like latest types. Recent ones have added a lock-out switch to allow only the driver to control the windows, and an interlock with the ignition switch so that windows cannot be operated if the ignition is not turned on.

ble the ignition or shut off the fuel supply in addition to activating the horn. Since many cars have their horns mounted where thieves can pull the connectors from them just by reaching through the grille opening with a long screwdriver, some of the audible systems come with an independent horn that can be mounted in a more inaccessible place.

Cigarette lighters and other minor gadgets are usually completely unsophisticated electrically. The lighter found on most cars is nothing more than a simple resistance-wire coil that heats up when the unit is pushed into contact with battery current. A temperature-sensitive spring clip keeps it there until the spring becomes hot enough to flex and release the lighter.

Automotive electrical systems have so many circuits and sub-circuits that it is difficult for even the dealers'

service departments to keep up with all of them. Their complexity far exceeds the wiring found in the average household, yet despite their involved layouts, only a few basic electrical principles are actually applied. Once you have grasped the workings of the ignition coil, the phenomenon of electromagnetism becomes understandable. This opens the way to learning about the operation of relays, solenoids, electric motors and generators.

There's no reason to be timid when faced with a job involving the electrical system. If you've never done much electrical work before, your progress may be slow at first. But after you've handled some of the more routine phases of troubleshooting and maintenance, you'll be surprised at the confidence you develop. Confidence and experience—these are the most important basic keys to becoming a real "pro."

Wiring Guide and Fusible Links

GUIDE TO FUSIBLE LINKS

MAKE	LOCATION	COLOR
AMC	Battery terminal of starter relay to main wire harness................	RED
	Battery terminal of horn relay to main wire harness................	PINK
	Accessory terminal of ignition switch to wire harness............	BROWN
	Battery terminal of starter relay to heated rear window relay....	RED
	B-3 terminal of ignition switch to circuit breaker	RED
	I-3 terminal of ignition* switch to circuit breaker................	YELLOW
	I-3 terminal of ignition* switch (single wire at the switch splits into two feed wires)................	YELLOW
	I-3 terminal of ignition* switch to throttle stop solenoid............	YELLOW
	*Only one of these links is used on any one vehicle.	
BUICK	Battery terminal of starter solenoid to lower end of main supply wires............................	BLACK
CADILLAC	Battery terminal of starter solenoid to main wire harness.	
CHEVROLET	Molded splice at solenoid battery terminal.........................	BROWN
	Molded splice at horn relay.......	BLACK
	Molded splice in voltage regulator # 3 terminal wire.............	ORANGE
	Molded splice in ammeter circuit (both sides of meter).............	ORANGE

MAKE	LOCATION	COLOR
CHRYSLER	On battery terminal of starter solenoid	DARK BLUE
	Above bulkhead connector.......	DARK BLUE
	Between battery and terminal block..................................	DARK GREEN
FORD LINCOLN MERCURY	Between starter solenoid battery terminal and alternator (Mustang and Cougar only). Looped outside wire harness between starter solenoid and alternator (T-Bird and Lincoln only), behind point at which harness is clipped to the right rocker cover (above starter). Twin links between starter solenoid and alternator (1) and starter solenoid to vehicle equipment harness.	
OLDSMOBILE	At horn relay jet block (All except Omega)..................	BLACK
	Twin links at horn relay jet block (Omega only)..................	BLACK/ORANGE
	At starter solenoid battery terminal (Omega only)..............	BROWN
PONTIAC	Positive battery cable pigtail lead (requires entire cable replacement)	BROWN
	At horn relay............................	BLACK
	Molded splice in circuit at jet block and horn relay (some single and some twin)........................	ORANGE

BELDEN AUTOMOTIVE PRIMARY WIRING SAFETY GUIDE

Total Approx. Circuit Amperes		Total Circuit Watts		Total Candle Power		Wire Gauge (For Length in Feet)											
6V	12V	6V	12V	6V	12V	3'	5'	7'	10'	15'	20'	25'	30'	40'	50'	75'	100'
0.5	1.0	3	12	3	6	18	18	18	18	18	18	18	18	18	18	18	18
0.75	1.5			5	10	18	18	18	18	18	18	18	18	18	18	18	18
1.0	2	6	24	8	16	18	18	18	18	18	18	18	18	18	18	16	16
1.5	3			12	24	18	18	18	18	18	18	18	18	18	18	14	14
2.0	4	12	48	15	30	18	18	18	18	18	18	18	18	16	16	12	12
2.5	5			20	40	18	18	18	18	18	18	18	18	16	14	12	12
3.0	6	18	72	25	50	18	18	18	18	18	18	16	16	16	14	12	10
3.5	7			30	60	18	18	18	18	18	16	16	16	14	14	10	10
4.0	8	24	96	35	70	18	18	18	18	18	16	16	16	14	12	10	10
5.0	10	30	120	40	80	18	18	18	18	16	16	16	14	12	12	10	10
5.5	11			45	90	18	18	18	18	16	16	14	14	12	12	10	8
6.0	12	36	144	50	100	18	18	18	18	16	16	14	14	12	12	10	8
7.5	15			60	120	18	18	18	18	14	14	12	12	12	10	8	8
9.0	18	54	216	70	140	18	18	16	16	14	14	12	12	10	10	8	8
10	20	60	240	80	160	18	18	16	16	14	12	10	10	10	10	8	6
11	22	66	264	90	180	18	18	16	16	12	12	10	10	10	8	6	6
12	24	72	288	100	200	*18	18	16	16	12	12	10	10	10	8	6	6
15	30					18	16	16	14	10	10	10	10	10	6	4	4
20	40					18	16	14	12	10	10	8	8	6	6	4	2
25	50					16	14	12	12	10	10	8	8	6	6	2	2
50	100					12	12	10	10	6	6	4	4	4	2	1	0
75	150					10	10	8	8	4	4	2	2	1	0	00	00
100	200					10	8	8	6	4	4	2	2	1	0	4/0	4/0

*18 AWG indicated above this line could be 20 AWG electrically—18 AWG is recommended for mechanical strength.